Important Information About Rails Versions

This book is written for Rails 3.

The Rails core team is continuing to work on Rails. From time to time, new releases may introduce incompatibilities for applications written for prior versions of Rails, including the code in this book.

To run the examples provided in this book, it is important that you install the correct version of Rails, as described in Chapter 1, *Installing Rails*, on page 3

To determine the version of Rails that you are running, you can issue rails -v at a command prompt.

Information on changes to Rails that affect this book can be found at http://www.pragprog.com/wikis/wiki/ChangesToRails.

▶ **Sam, Dave, and David**

When I started learning Ruby on Rails, I read the first edition of this book. Its holistic view of the Rails framework and community provides any new developer the kick start they need to a highly successful career. After reading through the latest edition cover to cover, I can happily say that it continues that trend and remains the first book I recommend to any new Rails developer.

▶ **Mikel Lindsaar**
Rails core commit team, creator of the Ruby Mail library, and director, RubyX

Agile Web Development with Rails does an excellent job of making the Rails environment accessible in an enjoyable and memorable way. In addition, this book is the first I've seen that provides a sensible and coherent explanation of the MVC pattern, and it does so in a natural progression using examples that completely remove any mystery.

▶ **Ken Coar**
Author, open software evangelist, and Apache developer

Agile Web Development with Rails successfully straddles a fine line between being a fun-to-read introduction to Rails (and Ruby) and a straightforward guide to some advanced features of the platform, nicely supplanting the ever-changing online documentation.

▶ **Glen Daniels**
Independent technologist and consultant

I've never read a programming book as successful as *Agile Web Development with Rails*. Sam made learning Ruby on Rails easy, comprehensive, and fun.

▶ **Keith Ballinger**
Chairman of WS-I's first Basic Profile working group; author; and key contributor to the .NET and Visual Studio .NET frameworks

Agile Web Development with Rails

Fourth Edition

Agile Web Development with Rails

Fourth Edition

Sam Ruby

Dave Thomas

David Heinemeier Hansson

with Leon Breedt
Mike Clark
James Duncan Davidson
Justin Gehtland
Andreas Schwarz

The Pragmatic Bookshelf
Raleigh, North Carolina   Dallas, Texas

Many of the designations used by manufacturers and sellers to distinguish their products are claimed as trademarks. Where those designations appear in this book, and The Pragmatic Programmers, LLC was aware of a trademark claim, the designations have been printed in initial capital letters or in all capitals. The Pragmatic Starter Kit, The Pragmatic Programmer, Pragmatic Programming, Pragmatic Bookshelf and the linking *g* device are trademarks of The Pragmatic Programmers, LLC.

Every precaution was taken in the preparation of this book. However, the publisher assumes no responsibility for errors or omissions, or for damages that may result from the use of information (including program listings) contained herein.

Our Pragmatic courses, workshops, and other products can help you and your team create better software and have more fun. For more information, as well as the latest Pragmatic titles, please visit us at http://www.pragprog.com.

ISBN-10: 1-934356-54-9
ISBN-13: 978-1-934356-54-8
Printed on acid-free paper.
P1.0 printing, March 2011
Version: 2011-3-11

Contents

Preface to the Fourth Edition

When Dave asked me to join as a coauthor of the third edition of this book, I was thrilled. After all, it was from the first printing of the first edition of this book that I had learned Rails. Dave and I also have much in common. Although he prefers Emacs and Mac OS X and my preferences tend toward Vim and Ubuntu, we both share a love for the command line and getting our fingers dirty with code—starting with tangible examples before diving into heavy theory.

Since the time the third edition was published (and, in fact, since the first, second, and third editions), much has changed. Rails is in the process of being significantly refactored, mostly internally. A number of features that were used in previous examples have been initially deprecated and subsequently removed. New features have been added, and much experience has been obtained as to what the best practices are for using Rails. Rails now also works on Ruby 1.9, and each of the examples has been tested with Ruby 1.8.7 and Ruby 1.9.2.

Additionally, Rails has exploded from being a popular framework to an active and vibrant ecosystem, complete with many popular plugins and deep integration into third-party tools. In the process, Rails has become mainstream, attracting a more diverse set of developers to the framework.

This has led to a reorganization of the book. Many newcomers to Rails have not had the pleasure of being introduced to Ruby, so this section has been promoted from an appendix to a chapter in Part I. We follow Part I with a step-by-step walk-through of building a real application, which has been updated and streamlined to focus on current best practices.

But the biggest change is in the final part: because it is no longer practical to cover the entire ecosystem of Rails given both its breadth and rate of change, this part is now focused on providing an overall perspective of the landscape, enabling you, the reader, to know what to look for and where to find plug-ins and related tools to address common needs that go far beyond what the framework itself contains.

In short, this book needed to adapt. Once again.

Sam Ruby
March 2011

Acknowledgments

You'd think that producing a new edition of a book would be easy. After all, you already have all the text. It's just a tweak to some code here and a minor wording change there, and you're done. You'd think....

It's difficult to tell exactly, but our impression is that creating each edition of *Agile Web Development with Rails* took about as much effort as the first edition. Rails is constantly evolving and, as it does, so has this book. Parts of the Depot application were rewritten several times, and all of the narrative was updated. The emphasis on REST and the avoidance of features as they become deprecated have repeatedly changed the structure of the book as what was once hot became just lukewarm.

So, this book would not exist without a massive amount of help from the Ruby and Rails communities. To start with, we had a number of incredibly helpful formal reviewers of drafts of this book:

> Jeremy Anderson, Ken Coar, Jeff Cohen, Joel Clermont, Geoff Drake,
> Pavan Gorakavi, Michael Jurewitz, Mikel Lindsaar, Paul Rayner,
> Martijn Reuvers, Doug Rhoten, Gary Sherman, Davanum Srinivas,
> Stefan Turalski, and José Valim

Additionally, each edition of this book has been released as a beta book: early versions were posted as PDFs, and people made comments online. And comment they did: more than 800 suggestions and bug reports were posted for this edition alone. The vast majority ended up being incorporated, making this book immeasurably more useful than it would have been. While thanks go out to all for supporting the beta book program and for contributing so much valuable feedback, a number of contributors went well beyond the call of duty:

> Manuel E. Vidaurre Arenas, Seth Arnold, Will Bowlin, Andy Brice,
> Jason Catena, Victor Marius Costan, David Hadley, Jason Holloway,
> David Kapp, Trung LE, Kristian Riiber Mandrup, mltsy,
> Steve Nicholson, Jim Puls, Johnathan Ritzi, Leonel S, Kim Shrier,
> Don Smith, Joe Straitiff, and Martin Zoller

Finally, the Rails core team has been incredibly helpful, answering questions, checking out code fragments, and fixing bugs. A big "thank you" to the following:

Scott Barron (htonl), Jamis Buck (minam), Thomas Fuchs (madrobby), Jeremy Kemper (bitsweat), Yehuda Katz (wycats), Michael Koziarski (nzkoz), Marcel Molina Jr, (noradio), Rick Olson (technoweenie), Nicholas Seckar (Ulysses), Sam Stephenson (sam), Tobias Lütke (xal), José Valim (josevalim), and Florian Weber (csshsh)

Sam Ruby
March 2011
rubys@intertwingly.net

Introduction

Ruby on Rails is a framework that makes it easier to develop, deploy, and maintain web applications. During the months that followed its initial release, Rails went from being an unknown toy to being a worldwide phenomenon, and more important, it has become the framework of choice for the implementation of a wide range of so-called Web 2.0 applications.

Why is that?

Rails Simply Feels Right

First, a large number of developers were frustrated with the technologies they were using to create web applications. It didn't seem to matter whether they were using Java, PHP, or .NET—there was a growing sense that their job was just too damn hard. And then, suddenly, along came Rails, and Rails was easier.

But easy on its own doesn't cut it. We're talking about professional developers writing real-world websites. They wanted to feel that the applications they were developing would stand the test of time—that they were designed and implemented using modern, professional techniques. So, these developers dug into Rails and discovered it wasn't just a tool for hacking out sites.

For example, *all* Rails applications are implemented using the Model-View-Controller (MVC) architecture. Java developers are used to frameworks such as Tapestry and Struts, which are based on MVC. But Rails takes MVC further: when you develop in Rails, you start with a working application, there's a place for each piece of code, and all the pieces of your application interact in a standard way.

Professional programmers write tests. And again, Rails delivers. All Rails applications have testing support baked right in. As you add functionality to the code, Rails automatically creates test stubs for that functionality. The framework makes it easy to test applications, and as a result, Rails applications tend to get tested.

Rails applications are written in Ruby, a modern, object-oriented scripting language. Ruby is concise without being unintelligibly terse—you can express ideas naturally and cleanly in Ruby code. This leads to programs that are easy to write and (just as important) are easy to read months later.

Rails takes Ruby to the limit, extending it in novel ways that make a programmer's life easier. This makes our programs shorter and more readable. It also allows us to perform tasks that would normally be done in external configuration files inside the codebase instead. This makes it far easier to see what's happening. The following code defines the model class for a project. Don't worry about the details for now. Instead, just think about how much information is being expressed in a few lines of code.

```ruby
class Project < ActiveRecord::Base
  belongs_to :portfolio
  has_one    :project_manager
  has_many   :milestones
  has_many   :deliverables, :through => :milestones

  validates  :name, :description, :presence => true
  validates  :non_disclosure_agreement, :acceptance => true
  validates  :short_name, :uniqueness => true
end
```

Two other philosophical underpinnings keep Rails code short and readable: DRY and convention over configuration. DRY stands for *don't repeat yourself*: every piece of knowledge in a system should be expressed in just one place. Rails uses the power of Ruby to bring that to life. You'll find very little duplication in a Rails application; you say what you need to say in one place—a place often suggested by the conventions of the MVC architecture—and then move on. For programmers used to other web frameworks, where a simple change to the schema could involve them in half a dozen or more code changes, this was a revelation.

Convention over configuration is crucial, too. It means that Rails has sensible defaults for just about every aspect of knitting together your application. Follow the conventions, and you can write a Rails application using less code than a typical Java web application uses in XML configuration. If you need to override the conventions, Rails makes that easy, too.

Developers coming to Rails found something else, too. Rails isn't playing catch-up with the new de facto web standards; it's helping define them. And Rails makes it easy for developers to integrate features such as Ajax and RESTful interfaces into their code, because support is built in. (And if you're not familiar with Ajax and REST interfaces, never fear—we'll explain them later in the book.)

Developers are worried about deployment too. They found that with Rails you can deploy successive releases of your application to any number of servers with a single command (and roll them back equally easily should the release prove to be somewhat less than perfect).

Rails was extracted from a real-world, commercial application. It turns out that the best way to create a framework is to find the central themes in a specific application and then bottle them up in a generic foundation of code. When you're developing your Rails application, you're starting with half of a really good application already in place.

But there's something else to Rails—something that's hard to describe. Somehow, it just feels right. Of course, you'll have to take our word for that until you write some Rails applications for yourself (which should be in the next forty-five minutes or so...). That's what this book is all about.

Rails Is Agile

The title of this book is *Agile Web Development with Rails*. You may be surprised to discover that we don't have explicit sections on applying agile practices X, Y, and Z to Rails coding.

The reason is both simple and subtle. Agility is part of the fabric of Rails.

Let's look at the values expressed in the Agile Manifesto as a set of four preferences:[1]

- Individuals and interactions over processes and tools
- Working software over comprehensive documentation
- Customer collaboration over contract negotiation
- Responding to change over following a plan

Rails is all about individuals and interactions. There are no heavy toolsets, no complex configurations, and no elaborate processes. There are just small groups of developers, their favorite editors, and chunks of Ruby code. This leads to transparency; what the developers do is reflected immediately in what the customer sees. It's an intrinsically interactive process.

Rails doesn't denounce documentation. Rails makes it trivially easy to create HTML documentation for your entire codebase. But the Rails development process isn't driven by documents. You won't find 500-page specifications at the heart of a Rails project. Instead, you'll find a group of users and developers jointly exploring their need and the possible ways of answering that need. You'll find solutions that change as both the developers and the users become more experienced with the problems they're trying to solve. You'll find

---

1. http://agilemanifesto.org/. Dave Thomas was one of the seventeen authors of this document.

a framework that delivers working software early in the development cycle. This software may be rough around the edges, but it lets the users start to get a glimpse of what you'll be delivering.

In this way, Rails encourages customer collaboration. When customers see just how quickly a Rails project can respond to change, they start to trust that the team can deliver what's required, not just what has been requested. Confrontations are replaced by "What if?" sessions.

That's all tied to the idea of being able to respond to change. The strong, almost obsessive, way that Rails honors the DRY principle means that changes to Rails applications impact a lot less code than the same changes would in other frameworks. And since Rails applications are written in Ruby, where concepts can be expressed accurately and concisely, changes tend to be localized and easy to write. The deep emphasis on both unit and functional testing, along with support for test fixtures and stubs during testing, gives developers the safety net they need when making those changes. With a good set of tests in place, changes are less nerve-racking.

Rather than constantly trying to tie Rails processes to the agile principles, we've decided to let the framework speak for itself. As you read through the tutorial chapters, try to imagine yourself developing web applications this way: working alongside your customers and jointly determining priorities and solutions to problems. Then, as you read the more advanced concepts that follow in Part III, see how the underlying structure of Rails can enable you to meet your customers' needs faster and with less ceremony.

One last point about agility and Rails: although it's probably unprofessional to mention this, think how much fun the coding will be.

Who This Book Is For

This book is for programmers looking to build and deploy web-based applications. This includes application programmers who are new to Rails (and perhaps even new to Ruby) and ones who are familiar with the basics but want a more in-depth understanding of Rails.

We presume some familiarity with HTML, Cascading Style Sheets (CSS), and JavaScript, in other words, the ability to view source on web pages. You do not need to be an expert on these subjects; the most you will ever be expected to do is to copy and paste material from the book, all of which can be downloaded.

How To Read This Book

The first part of this book makes sure you are ready. By the time you are done with it, you will have been introduced to Ruby (the language), you will have been exposed to an overview of Rails itself, you will have both Ruby and Rails installed, and you will have verified this installation with a simple example.

The next part takes you through the concepts behind Rails via an extended example; we build a simple online store. It doesn't take you one by one through each component of Rails ("here is a chapter on models, here is a chapter on views," and so forth). These components are designed to work together, and each chapter in this section tackles a specific set of related tasks that involve a number of these components working together.

Most folks seem to enjoy building the application along with the book. If you don't want to do all that typing, you can cheat and download the source code (a compressed tar archive or a zip file).[2]

The third part of the book, starting on page 251, surveys the entire Rails ecosystem. This starts with the functions and facilities of Rails that you will now be familiar with. It then covers a number of key dependencies that the Rails framework makes use of that contribute directly to the overall functionality that the Rails framework delivers. Finally, there is a survey of a number of popular plugins that augment the Rails framework and make Rails an open ecosystem rather than merely a framework.

Along the way, you'll see various conventions we've adopted.

Live Code

Most of the code snippets we show come from full-length, running examples that you can download. To help you find your way, if a code listing can be found in the download, there'll be a bar before the snippet (just like the one here).

work/demo1/app/controllers/say_controller.rb

```
class SayController < ApplicationController
  def hello
  end

  def goodbye
  end

end
```

This contains the path to the code within the download. If you're reading the ebook version of this book and your ebook viewer supports hyperlinks, you can click the bar, and the code should appear in a browser window. Some browsers (such as Safari) will mistakenly try to interpret some of the templates as HTML. If this happens, view the source of the page to see the real source code.

---

2. http://pragprog.com/titles/rails4/source_code has the links for the downloads.

And in some cases involving the modification of an existing file where the lines to be changed may not be immediately obvious, you will also see some helpful little triangles on the left of the lines that you will need to change. Two such lines are indicated in the previous code.

Ruby Tips

:name
↪ page 38

Although you need to know Ruby to write Rails applications, we realize that many folks reading this book will be learning both Ruby and Rails at the same time. You will find a (very) brief introduction to the Ruby language in Chapter 4, *Introduction to Ruby*, on page 37. When we use a Ruby-specific construct for the first time, we'll cross-reference it to that chapter. For example, this paragraph contains a gratuitous use of :name, a Ruby symbol. In the margin, you'll see an indication that symbols are explained on page 38.

David Says...

Every now and then you'll come across a *David Says...* sidebar. Here's where David Heinemeier Hansson gives you the real scoop on some particular aspect of Rails—rationales, tricks, recommendations, and more. Because he's the fellow who invented Rails, these are the sections to read if you want to become a Rails pro.

Joe Asks...

Joe, the mythical developer, sometimes pops up to ask questions about stuff we talk about in the text. We answer these questions as we go along.

This book isn't meant to be a reference manual for Rails. Our experience is that reference manuals are not the way most people learn. Instead, we show most of the modules and many of their methods, either by example or narratively in the text, in the context of how these components are used and how they fit together.

Nor do we have hundreds of pages of API listings. There's a good reason for this—you get that documentation whenever you install Rails, and it's guaranteed to be more up-to-date than the material in this book. If you install Rails using RubyGems (which we recommend), simply start the gem documentation server (using the command gem server), and you can access all the Rails APIs by pointing your browser at http://localhost:8808. You will find out on page 255 how to build even more documentation and guides.

In addition, you will see that Rails itself helps you by producing responses that clearly identify any error found, as well as traces that tell you not only what point the error was found but how you got there. You can see an example in Figure 10.3, on page 116. If you need additional information, peek ahead to Section 10.2, *Iteration E2: Handling Errors*, on page 116 to see how to insert logging statements.

Should you get really stuck, there are plenty of online resources to help. In addition to the code listings mentioned, there is a forum,[3] where you can ask questions and share experiences; an errata page,[4] where you can report bugs; and a wiki,[5] where you can discuss the exercises found throughout the book.

These resources are shared resources. Feel free to post not only questions and problems to the forum and wiki but also any suggestions and answers that you may have to questions others may have posted.

Let's get started! The first steps are to install Ruby and Rails and to verify the installation with a simple demonstration.

"Agile Web Development with Rails...I found it
in our local bookstore, and it seemed great!"
—*Dave's mum*

---

3. http://forums.pragprog.com/forums/148
4. http://www.pragprog.com/titles/rails4/errata
5. http://www.pragprog.com/wikis/wiki/RailsPlayTime

Part I

Getting Started

In this chapter, we'll see

- installing Ruby, RubyGems, SQLite3, and Rails; and
- development environments and tools.

Chapter 1

Installing Rails

In Part I of this book, we'll introduce you to both the Ruby language and the Rails framework. But we can't get anywhere until you've installed both and verified that they are operating correctly.

To get Rails running on your system, you'll need the following:

- A Ruby interpreter. Rails is written in Ruby, and you'll be writing your applications in Ruby too. Rails 3.0 requires Ruby version 1.8.7 or Ruby 1.9.2. It is known not to work on Ruby versions 1.8.6 and Ruby 1.9.1.

- The Ruby packaging system, namely, RubyGems. This edition is based on RubyGems version 1.3.7.

- Ruby on Rails. This beta book was written using Rails version 3 (specifically Rails 3.0.5 at the current time).

- Some libraries, depending on the operating system.

- A database. We're using SQLite 3 in this book.

For a development machine, that's about all you'll need (apart from an editor, and we'll talk about editors separately). However, if you are going to deploy your application, you will also need to install a production web server (as a minimum) along with some support code to let Rails run efficiently. We have a whole chapter devoted to this, starting on page 225, so we won't talk about it more here.

So, how do you get all this installed? It depends on your operating system....

1.1 Installing on Windows

On Windows, start by installing Ruby. The easiest way to do this on Windows is via the RubyInstaller[1] package. Be sure to download a version of Ruby that

---

1. http://rubyinstaller.org/

is 1.8.7 or newer. The examples in this book have been tested with Ruby 1.8.7 (2010-01-10 patchlevel 249).

Base installation is a snap. After you download, select Run → Next, click "I accept the License" (after reading it carefully of course), click Next, and check "Add Ruby executables to your PATH." Then select Install → Finish.

Now open a command prompt by selecting the Windows Start → Run..., enter cmd, and click OK.

RubyInstaller includes RubyGems, but it is important to verify that you are running with version 1.3.6 or newer. You can verify the version of RubyGems with the following command:

```
gem -v
```

Should this return 1.3.5 or earlier, you can upgrade to the latest version of RubyGems with the following commands:

```
gem update --system
gem uninstall rubygems-update
```

Next, install SQLite3.[2] Scroll down to Precompiled Binaries for Windows. Download and unzip the following files:

- Command-line shell for accessing and modifying SQLite databases
- DLL of the SQLite library

Copy the files inside these zips to your C:\Ruby\bin directory. The results should look something like this:

```
Directory of C:\Ruby\bin

02/11/2011  06:30 PM            3,744 sqlite3.def
02/11/2011  06:30 PM          511,383 sqlite3.dll
02/11/2011  06:31 PM          530,762 sqlite3.exe
               3 File(s)    1,045,889 bytes
```

Now install the Ruby bindings to SQLite3, as well as Rails itself:

```
gem install sqlite3
gem install rails
```

At this point, you're up and running. But, before continuing, you should know one important fact: the example sessions in this book are based on execution on a Mac. Although the ruby and rails commands are exactly the same, the Unix commands are different. This book uses only two Unix commands. The first is ls -a, for which the Windows equivalent is dir/w. The second is rm, for which the Windows equivalent is erase.

---

2. http://www.sqlite.org/download.html

We also will be optionally using the curl command on page 162. You can download this from curl.haxx.se.[7]

OK, you Windows users are done. You can skip forward to Section 1.4, *Choosing a Rails Version*, on page 7. See you there.

1.2 Installing on Mac OS X

Although versions of OS X since 10.4.6 (Tiger) have included a version of Ruby, and starting with of OS X 10.5 (Leopard) have included Rails itself, the versions that are included generally are older versions of these components, and you have some upgrading to do.

Tiger users will also need to upgrade SQLite 3. This can be done via compiling from source (which sounds scarier than it is). You can find the instructions to do so at http://www.sqlite.org/download.html.

An alternate way to install SQLite 3 is via the popular MacPorts package.[4] Although the instructions also look a bit daunting, the individual steps are pretty straightforward: run an installer, run another installer, add two lines to a file, run yet another installer, and then issue a single command. This may not turn out to be easier than compiling from source for yourself, but many find the investment to be worth it because it makes installing further packages as easy as a single command. So if you have MacPorts installed, let's use it to upgrade the version of SQLite 3 on your machine:

```
sudo port upgrade sqlite3
```

Next, users of OS X prior to Snow Leopard will need to upgrade their version of Ruby to 1.8.7. Again, this can be done with MacPorts:

```
sudo port install ruby
sudo port install rb-rubygems
```

All OS X users can use the following commands to update their system the rest of the way. If you just installed MacPorts, be sure to take heed of the important note to open a new shell and verify via the env command that your path and variable changes are in effect. If you haven't already done so, install Apple's Xcode Developer Tools (version 3.2 or newer for Leopard, 2.4.1 or newer for Tiger), found at the Apple Developer Connection site or on your Mac OS X installation CDs/DVD.

```
sudo gem update --system
sudo gem uninstall rubygems-update
sudo gem install rails
sudo gem install sqlite3
```

3. http://curl.haxx.se/download.html
4. http://www.macports.org/install.php

At this point, you are likely to have two versions of Ruby on your system, and it is important to verify that you are running the correct version of related tools. You can do that using the following command:

```
which ruby irb gem rake
```

All you need to do here is verify that each command is found in the same path, typically /opt/local/bin. If you are finding different tools at different paths, verify that your PATH environment variable is correct and/or reinstall the tool that doesn't match the desired version of Ruby.

You can reinstall RubyGems by using sudo port install rb-rubygems or by following the instructions on the RubyGems site[5] (steps 1 to 3 at the bottom of the page; you will likely need to prefix the ruby setup.rb command with sudo).

You can reinstall Rake with the following command:

```
sudo gem install rake
```

The following step is rarely necessary, but it can be helpful if things go wrong. You can verify which version of SQLite 3 your sqlite3 gem is bound to by running the following as a stand-alone Ruby program:

```
require 'rubygems'
require 'sqlite3'
tempname = "test.sqlite#{3+rand}"
db = SQLite3::Database.new(tempname)
puts db.execute('select sqlite_version()')
db.close
File.unlink(tempname)
```

OK, you OS X users are done. You can skip forward to join the Windows users in Section 1.4, *Choosing a Rails Version*, on the facing page. See you there.

1.3 Installing on Linux

Start with your platform's native package management system, be it apt-get, dpkg, portage, rpm, rug, synaptic, up2date, or yum.

The first step is to install the necessary dependencies. The following instructions are for Ubuntu 10.04, Lucid Lynx; you can adapt them as necessary for your installation:

```
sudo apt-get install build-essential libopenssl-ruby libfcgi-dev
sudo apt-get install ruby irb rubygems ruby1.8-dev
sudo apt-get install sqlite3 libsqlite3-dev
```

Before proceeding, it is important to verify that the version of RubyGems is at least 1.3.6. You can find out the version by issuing gem -v. How to upgrade your version of RubyGems is described in the sidebar on the next page.

---

5. http://rubygems.org/pages/download

Upgrading RubyGems on Linux

There are many different ways to upgrade RubyGems. Unfortunately, depending on which version of RubyGems you have installed and what distribution you are running, not all of the ways work. Be persistent. Try each of the following until you find one that works for you:

- Using the gem update system:

```
sudo gem update --system
```

- Using the gem designed to update troublesome systems:

```
sudo gem install rubygems-update
sudo update_rubygems
```

- Using setup.rb, which is provided with rubygems-update:

```
sudo gem install rubygems-update
cd /var/lib/gems/1.8/gems/rubygems-update-*
sudo ruby setup.rb
```

- Finally, installing from source:

```
wget http://rubyforge.org/frs/download.php/69365/rubygems-1.3.6.tgz
tar xzf rubygems-1.3.6.tgz
cd rubygems-1.3.6
sudo ruby setup.rb
```

Next we will install the Rails framework and the SQLite3 database:

```
sudo gem install rails
sudo gem install sqlite3
```

On the last command, you will be prompted to select which gem to install for your platform. Simply select the latest (topmost) gem that contains the word *ruby* in parentheses, and a native extension will be built for you.

At this time, try the command rails -v. If it can't find the rails command, you may need to add /var/lib/gems/1.8/bin to your PATH environment variable. You can do this by adding a line to your .bashrc file:

```
export PATH=/var/lib/gems/1.8/bin:$PATH
```

At this point, we've covered Windows, Mac OS X, and Linux. Instructions after this point are common to all three operating systems.

1.4 Choosing a Rails Version

The previous instructions helped you install the latest version of Rails. But occasionally you might not want to run the latest version. For example, you might want to run the version of Rails that matches this version used to develop this book so that you can be absolutely confident that the output and examples exactly match. Or perhaps you are developing on one machine but intending to deploy on another machine that contains a version of Rails that you don't have any control over.

If either of these situations applies to you, you need to be aware of a few things. For starters, you can find out all the versions of Rails you have installed using the gem command:

```
gem list --local rails
```

You can also verify what version of Rails you are running as the default by using the rails --version command. It should return 3.0.5 or newer.

Installing another version of Rails is also done via the gem command. Depending on your operating system, you might need to preface the command with sudo.

```
gem install rails --version 3.0.5
```

Now, having multiple versions of Rails wouldn't do anybody any good unless there were a way to pick one. As luck would have it, there is. On any rails command, you can control which version of Rails is used by inserting the full version number surrounded by underscores before the first parameter of the command:

```
rails _3.0.5_ --version
```

This is particularly handy when you create a new application, because once you create an application with a specific version of Rails, it will continue to use that version of Rails—even if newer versions are installed on the system—until *you* decide it is time to upgrade. To upgrade, simply update the version number in the Gemfile that is in the root directory of your application, and run bundle install. We will cover this command in greater depth on page 409.

1.5 Setting Up Your Development Environment

The day-to-day business of writing Rails programs is pretty straightforward. Everyone works differently; here's how we work.

The Command Line

We do a lot of work at the command line. Although there are an increasing number of GUI tools that help generate and manage a Rails application, we find the command line is still the most powerful place to be. It's worth spending a little while getting familiar with the command line on your operating system. Find out how to use it to edit commands that you're typing, how to search

---

Where's My IDE?

If you're coming to Ruby and Rails from languages such as C# and Java, you may be wondering about IDEs. After all, we all know that it's impossible to code modern applications without at least 100MB of IDE supporting our every keystroke. For you enlightened ones, here's the point in the book where we recommend you sit down—ideally propped up on each side by a pile of framework references and 1,000-page Made Easy books.

It may surprise you to know that most Rails developers don't use fully fledged IDEs for Ruby or Rails (although some of the environments come close). Indeed, many Rails developers use plain old editors. And it turns out that this isn't as much of a problem as you might think. With other, less expressive languages, programmers rely on IDEs to do much of the grunt work for them, because IDEs do code generation, assist with navigation, and compile incrementally to give early warning of errors.

With Ruby, however, much of this support just isn't necessary. Editors such as TextMate and BBEdit give you 90 percent of what you'd get from an IDE but are far lighter weight. Just about the only useful IDE facility that's missing is refactoring support.

---

for and edit previous commands, and how to complete the names of files and commands as you type.

So-called tab completion is standard on Unix shells such as Bash and zsh. It allows you to type the first few characters of a filename, hit Tab , and have the shell look for and complete the name based on matching files.

Version Control

We keep all our work in a version control system (currently Git). We make a point of checking a new Rails project into Git when we create it and committing changes once we have passed the tests. We normally commit to the repository many times an hour.

If you're working on a Rails project with other people, consider setting up a continuous integration (CI) system. When anyone checks in changes, the CI system will check out a fresh copy of the application and run all the tests. It's a simple way to ensure that accidental breakages get immediate attention. You can also set up your CI system so that your customers can use it to play with the bleeding-edge version of your application. This kind of transparency is a great way of ensuring that your project isn't going off the tracks.

Editors

We write our Rails programs using a programmer's editor. We've found over the years that different editors work best with different languages and environments. For example, Dave originally wrote this chapter using Emacs, because he thinks that its Filladapt mode is unsurpassed when it comes to neatly formatting XML as he types. Sam updated the chapter using Vim. But many think that neither Emacs nor Vim is ideal for Rails development and prefer to use TextMate. Although the choice of editor is a personal one, here are some suggestions of features to look for in a Rails editor:

- Support for syntax highlighting of Ruby and HTML. Ideally support for .erb files (a Rails file format that embeds Ruby snippets within HTML).

- Support of automatic indentation and reindentation of Ruby source. This is more than an aesthetic feature: having an editor indent your program as you type is the best way of spotting bad nesting in your code. Being able to reindent is important when you refactor your code and move stuff. (TextMate's ability to reindent when it pastes code from the clipboard is very convenient.)

- Support for insertion of common Ruby and Rails constructs. You'll be writing lots of short methods, and if the IDE creates method skeletons with a keystroke or two, you can concentrate on the interesting stuff inside.

- Good file navigation. As you'll see, Rails applications are spread across many files: a newly created Rails application enters the world containing forty-six files spread across thirty-four directories. That's before you've written a thing.

  You need an environment that helps you navigate quickly between these. You'll add a line to a controller to load a value, switch to the view to add a line to display it, and then switch to the test to verify you did it all right. Something like Notepad, where you traverse a File Open dialog box to select each file to edit, just won't cut it. We prefer a combination of a tree view of files in a sidebar, a small set of keystrokes that help us find a file (or files) in a directory tree by name, and some built-in smarts that know how to navigate (say) between a controller action and the corresponding view.

- Name completion. Names in Rails tend to be long. A nice editor will let you type the first few characters and then suggest possible completions to you at the touch of a key.

We hesitate to recommend specific editors because we've used only a few in earnest and we'll undoubtedly leave someone's favorite editor off the list. Nevertheless, to help you get started with something other than Notepad, here are some suggestions:

- The Ruby and Rails editor of choice on Mac OS X is TextMate (http://macromates.com/).

- Xcode 3.0 on Mac OS X has an Organizer that provides much of what you might need. A tutorial that will get you started with Rails on Leopard is available at http://developer.apple.com/tools/developonrailsleopard.html.

- For those who would otherwise like to use TextMate but happen to be using Windows, E-TextEditor (http://e-texteditor.com/) provides "the Power of TextMate on Windows."

- Aptana RadRails (http://www.aptana.com/products/radrails) is an integrated Rails development environment that runs in Aptana Studio and Eclipse. It runs on Windows, Mac OS X, and Linux. It won an award for being the best open source developer tool based on Eclipse in 2006, and Aptana became the home for the project in 2007.

- NetBeans IDE 6.5 (http://netbeans.org/features/ruby/index.html) supports Windows, Mac OS X, Solaris, and Linux. It's available in a download bundle with Ruby support or as a Ruby pack that can be downloaded later. In addition to specific support for Rails 2.0, Rake targets, and database migrations, it supports a Rails code generator graphical wizard and quick navigation from a Rails action to its corresponding view.

- jEdit (http://www.jedit.org/) is a fully featured editor with support for Ruby. It has extensive plugin support.

- Komodo (http://www.activestate.com/komodo-ide) is ActiveState's IDE for dynamic languages, including Ruby.

- RubyMine (http://www.jetbrains.com/ruby/features/index.html) is a commercial IDE for Ruby and is available for free to qualified educational and open source projects. It runs on Windows, Mac OS X, and Linux.

Ask experienced developers who use your kind of operating system which editor they use. Spend a week or so trying alternatives before settling in.

The Desktop

We're not going to tell you how to organize your desktop while working with Rails, but we will describe what we do.

Most of the time, we're writing code, running tests, and poking at an application in a browser. So, our main development desktop has an editor window and a browser window permanently open. We also want to keep an eye on the logging that's generated by the application, so we keep a terminal window open. In it, we use tail -f to scroll the contents of the log file as it's updated. We

> **Creating Your Own Rails API Documentation**
>
> You can create your own local version of the consolidated Rails API documentation. Just type the following commands at a command prompt:
>
> ```
> rails_apps> rails new dummy_app
> rails_apps> cd dummy_app
> dummy_app> rake doc:rails
> ```
>
> The last step takes a while. When it finishes, you'll have the Rails API documentation in a directory tree starting at doc/api. We suggest moving this folder to your desktop and then deleting the dummy_app tree.
>
> To view the Rails API documentation, open the location doc/api/index.html with your browser.

normally run this window with a very small font so it takes up less space—if we see something interesting flash by, we zoom it up to investigate.

We also need access to the Rails API documentation, which we view in a browser. In the introduction, we talked about using the gem server command to run a local web server containing the Rails documentation. This is convenient, but it unfortunately splits the Rails documentation across a number of separate documentation trees. If you're online, you can use http://api.rubyonrails.org/ to see a consolidated view of all the Rails documentation in one place.

1.6 Rails and Databases

The examples in this book were written using SQLite 3 (version 3.6.16 or thereabouts). If you want to follow along with our code, it's probably simplest if you use SQLite 3 too. If you decide to use something else, it won't be a major problem. You may have to make minor adjustments to any explicit SQL in our code, but Rails pretty much eliminates database-specific SQL from applications.

If you want to connect to a database other than SQLite 3, Rails also works with DB2, MySQL, Oracle, Postgres, Firebird, and SQL Server. For all but SQLite 3, you'll need to install a database driver, a library that Rails can use to connect to and use your database engine. This section contains links to instructions to get that done.

The database drivers are all written in C and are primarily distributed in source form. If you don't want to bother building a driver from source, take a careful look at the driver's website. Many times you'll find that the author also distributes binary versions.

If you can't find a binary version or if you'd rather build from source anyway, you'll need a development environment on your machine to build the library. Under Windows, this means having a copy of Visual C++. Under Linux, you'll need gcc and friends (but these will likely already be installed).

Under OS X, you'll need to install the developer tools (they come with the operating system but aren't installed by default). You'll also need to install your database driver into the correct version of Ruby. If you installed your own copy of Ruby, bypassing the built-in one, it is important to remember to have this version of Ruby first in your path when building and installing the database driver. You can use the command which ruby to make sure you're *not* running Ruby from /usr/bin.

The following are the available database adapters and the links to their respective home pages:

DB2	http://raa.ruby-lang.org/project/ruby-db2 or http://rubyforge.org/projects/rubyibm
Firebird	http://rubyforge.org/projects/fireruby/
MySQL	http://www.tmtm.org/en/mysql/ruby/
Oracle	http://rubyforge.org/projects/ruby-oci8
Postgres	http://rubyforge.org/projects/ruby-pg
SQL Server	https://github.com/rails-sqlserver
SQLite	http://rubyforge.org/projects/sqlite-ruby

A pure-Ruby version of the Postgres adapter is available. Download postgres-pr from the Ruby-DBI page at http://rubyforge.org/projects/postgres-pr.

MySQL and SQLite adapters are also available for download as RubyGems (mysql and sqlite3, respectively).

1.7 What We Just Did

- We installed (or upgraded) the Ruby language.

- We installed (or upgraded) the Rails framework.

- We installed (or upgraded) the SQLite3 database.

- We selected an editor.

Now that we have Rails installed, let's use it. It's time to move on to the next chapter where we create our first application.

In this chapter, we'll see

- creating a new application,
- starting the server,
- accessing the server from a browser,
- producing dynamic content,
- adding hypertext links, and
- passing data from the controller to the view.

Chapter 2

Instant Gratification

Let's write a simple application to verify we have Rails snugly installed on our machines. Along the way, we'll get a peek at the way Rails applications work.

2.1 Creating a New Application

When you install the Rails framework, you also get a new command-line tool, rails, that is used to construct each new Rails application you write.

Why do we need a tool to do this? Why can't we just hack away in our favorite editor and create the source for our application from scratch? Well, we could just hack. After all, a Rails application is just Ruby source code. But Rails also does a lot of magic behind the curtain to get our applications to work with a minimum of explicit configuration. To get this magic to work, Rails needs to find all the various components of your application. As we'll see later (in Section 18.1, *Where Things Go*, on page 251), this means we need to create a specific directory structure, slotting the code we write into the appropriate places. The rails command simply creates this directory structure for us and populates it with some standard Rails code.

To create your first Rails application, pop open a shell window, and navigate to a place in your filesystem where you want to create your application's directory structure. In our example, we'll be creating our projects in a directory called work. In that directory, use the rails command to create an application called demo. Be slightly careful here—if you have an existing directory called demo, you will be asked whether you want to overwrite any existing files. (Note: if you want to specify which Rails version to use, as described in Section 1.4, *Choosing a Rails Version*, on page 7, now would be the time to do so.)

```
rubys> cd work
work> rails new demo
create
create    README
create    .gitignore
```

```
create   Rakefile
  :        :       :
create   tmp/pids
create   vendor/plugins
create   vendor/plugins/.gitkeep
work>
```

The command has created a directory named demo. Pop down into that directory, and list its contents (using ls on a Unix box or dir under Windows). You should see a bunch of files and subdirectories:

```
work> cd demo
demo> ls -p
app/        config.ru  doc/      lib/  public/    README    test/   vendor/
config/     db/                  Gemfile  log/  Rakefile  script/   tmp/
```

All these directories (and the files they contain) can be intimidating to start with, but we can ignore most of them for now. In this chapter, we'll use only one of them directly: the app directory, where we'll write our application.

Included in these files is everything you need to start a stand-alone web server that can run our newly created Rails application. So, without further ado, let's start our demo application:

```
demo> rails server
=> Booting WEBrick
=> Rails 3.0.5 application starting on http://0.0.0.0:3000
=> Call with -d to detach
=> Ctrl-C to shutdown server
[2010-11-14 10:53:35] INFO  WEBrick 1.3.1
[2010-11-14 10:53:35] INFO  ruby 1.8.7 (2010-08-16) [i686-darwin9.8.0]
[2010-11-14 10:53:40] INFO  WEBrick::HTTPServer#start: pid=6044 port=3000
```

Which web server is run depends on what servers you have installed. WEBrick is a pure-Ruby web server that is distributed with Ruby 1.8.1 and newer and therefore is guaranteed to be available. However, if another web server is installed on your system (and Rails can find it), the rails server command may use it in preference to WEBrick. You can force Rails to use WEBrick by providing an option to the rails command:

```
demo> rails server webrick
```

As the last line of the startup tracing indicates, we just started a web server on port 3000. The 0.0.0.0 part of the address means that WEBrick will accept connections on all interfaces. On Dave's OS X system, that means both local interfaces (127.0.0.1 and ::1) and his LAN connection. We can access the application by pointing a browser at the URL http://localhost:3000. The result is shown in Figure 2.1.

If you look at the window where you started the server, you'll see tracing showing you started the application. We're going to leave the server running in this

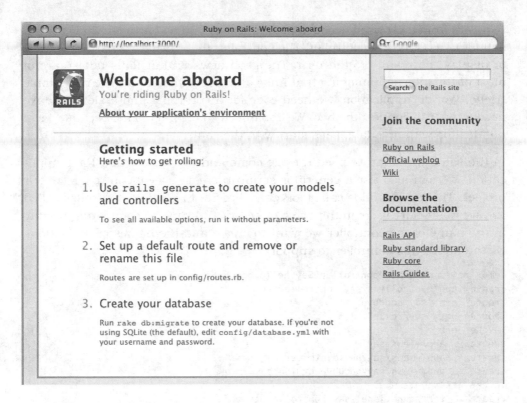

Figure 2.1: NEWLY CREATED RAILS APPLICATION

console window. Later, as we write application code and run it via our browser, we'll be able to use this console window to trace the incoming requests. When the time comes to shut down your application, you can press Ctrl-C in this window to stop WEBrick. (Don't do that yet—we'll be using this particular application in a minute.)

At this point, we have a new application running, but it has none of our code in it. Let's rectify this situation.

2.2 Hello, Rails!

We can't help it—we just have to write a "Hello, World!" program to try a new system. Let's start by creating a simple application that sends our cheery greeting to a browser. After we get that working, we will embellish it with the current time and links.

As we'll explore further in Chapter 3, *The Architecture of Rails Applications*, on page 29, Rails is a Model-View-Controller framework. Rails accepts incoming requests from a browser, decodes the request to find a controller, and calls an action method in that controller. The controller then invokes a particular view to display the results to the user. The good news is that Rails takes care of most of the internal plumbing that links all these actions. To write our simple "Hello, World!" application, we need code for a controller and a view, and we need a route to connect the two. We don't need code for a model, because we're not dealing with any data. Let's start with the controller.

In the same way that we used the rails command to create a new Rails application, we can also use a generator script to create a new controller for our project. This command is called rails generate. So, to create a controller called say, we make sure we're in the demo directory and run the command, passing in the name of the controller we want to create and the names of the actions we intend for this controller to support:

```
demo> rails generate controller Say hello goodbye
create  app/controllers/say_controller.rb
 route  get "say/goodbye"
 route  get "say/hello"
invoke  erb
create     app/views/say
create     app/views/say/hello.html.erb
create     app/views/say/goodbye.html.erb
invoke  test_unit
create     test/functional/say_controller_test.rb
invoke  helper
create     app/helpers/say_helper.rb
invoke     test_unit
create        test/unit/helpers/say_helper_test.rb
```

The rails generate command logs the files and directories it examines, noting when it adds new Ruby scripts or directories to your application. For now, we're interested in one of these scripts and (in a minute) the .html.erb files.

The first source file we'll be looking at is the controller. You'll find it in the file app/controllers/say_controller.rb. Let's take a look at it:

defining classes ↪ page 45

work/demo1/app/controllers/say_controller.rb

```
class SayController < ApplicationController
  def hello
  end

  def goodbye
  end

end
```

Pretty minimal, eh? SayController is a class that inherits from ApplicationController, so it automatically gets all the default controller behavior. What does this code have to do? For now, it does nothing—we simply have an empty

http://localhost:3000/say/hello
http://localhost:3000/say/hello · Q▾ Google »

Say#hello

Find me in app/views/say/hello.html.erb

Figure 2.2: TEMPLATE READY FOR US TO FILL IN

action method named hello. To understand why this method is named this way, we need to look at the way Rails handles requests.

Rails and Request URLs

Like any other web application, a Rails application appears to its users to be associated with a URL. When you point your browser at that URL, you are talking to the application code, which generates a response to you.

Let's try it now. Navigate to the URL http://localhost:3000/say/hello in a browser window. (Note that in the development environment we don't have any application string at the front of the path—we route directly to the controller.) You'll see something that looks like Figure 2.2.

Our First Action

At this point, we can see not only that have we connected the URL to our controller but also that Rails is pointing the way to our next step, namely, to tell Rails what to display. That's where views come in. Remember when we ran the script to create the new controller? That command added six files and a new directory to our application. That directory contains the template files for the controller's views. In our case, we created a controller named say, so the views will be in the directory app/views/say.

By default, Rails looks for templates in a file with the same name as the action it's handling. In our case, that means we need to replace a file called hello.html.erb in the directory app/views/say. (Why .html.erb? We'll explain in a minute.) For now, let's just put some basic HTML in there:

`work/demo1/app/views/say/hello.html.erb`

```
<h1>Hello from Rails!</h1>
```

```
demo/
  └app/
      ├ controllers/                    class SayController < ApplicationController
      │   └ say_controller.rb              def hello
      │                                     end
      ├ models/                          end
      │
      └ views/
          └ say/                        <h1>Hello from Rails!</h1>
              └ hello.html.erb
```

Figure 2.3: STANDARD LOCATIONS FOR CONTROLLERS AND VIEWS

Save the file hello.html.erb, and refresh your browser window. You should see it display our friendly greeting:

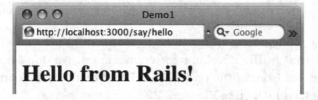

In total, we've looked at two files in our Rails application tree. We looked at the controller, and we modified a template to display a page in the browser. These files live in standard locations in the Rails hierarchy: controllers go into app/controllers, and views go into subdirectories of app/views. See Figure 2.3.

Making It Dynamic

So far, our Rails application is pretty boring—it just displays a static page. To make it more dynamic, let's have it show the current time each time it displays the page.

To do this, we need to make a change to the template file in the view—it now needs to include the time as a string. That raises two questions. First, how do we add dynamic content to a template? Second, where do we get the time from?

Dynamic Content

There are many ways of creating dynamic templates in Rails. The most common way, which we'll use here, is to embed Ruby code in the template itself.

That's why we named our template file hello.html.erb; the .html.erb suffix tells Rails to expand the content in the file using a system called ERb.

ERb is a filter that is installed as part of the Rails installation that takes an .erb file and outputs a transformed version. The output file is often HTML in Rails, but it can be anything. Normal content is passed through without being changed. However, content between <%= and %> is interpreted as Ruby code and executed. The result of that execution is converted into a string, and that value is substituted in the file in place of the <%=...%> sequence. For example, change hello.html.erb to display the current time:

work/demo2/app/views/say/hello.html.erb

```
<h1>Hello from Rails!</h1>
► <p>
►    It is now <%= Time.now %>
► </p>
```

When we refresh our browser window, we see the time displayed using Ruby's standard format:[1]

Notice that if you hit Refresh in your browser, the time updates each time the page is displayed. It looks as if we're really generating dynamic content.

Adding the Time

Our original problem was to display the time to users of our application. We now know how to make our application display dynamic data. The second issue we have to address is working out where to get the time from.

We've shown that the approach of embedding a call to Ruby's Time.now method in our hello.html.erb template works. Each time we access this page, the user will see the current time substituted into the body of the response. And for our

---

1. With Ruby 1.9, the standard format has changed, and times now look more like the following: 2011-02-11 14:33:14 -0500.

> ## Making Development Easier
>
> You might have noticed something about the development we've been doing so far. As we've been adding code to our application, we haven't had to restart the running application. It has been happily chugging away in the background. And yet each change we make is available whenever we access the application through a browser. What gives?
>
> It turns out that the Rails dispatcher is pretty clever. In development mode (as opposed to testing or production), it automatically reloads application source files when a new request comes along. That way, when we edit our application, the dispatcher makes sure it's running the most recent changes. This is great for development.
>
> However, this flexibility comes at a cost—it causes a short pause after you enter a URL before the application responds. That's caused by the dispatcher reloading stuff. For development it's a price worth paying, but in production it would be unacceptable. Because of this, this feature is disabled for production deployment (see Chapter 16, *Task K: Deployment and Production*, on page 225).

trivial application, that might be good enough. In general, though, we probably want to do something slightly different. We'll move the determination of the time to be displayed into the controller and leave the view with the simple job of displaying it. We'll change our action method in the controller to set the time value into an instance variable called @time:

instance variable
↪ page 45

```
work/demo3/app/controllers/say_controller.rb
```

```ruby
class SayController < ApplicationController
  def hello
▶   @time = Time.now
  end

  def goodbye
  end

end
```

In the .html.erb template, we'll use this instance variable to substitute the time into the output:

```
work/demo3/app/views/say/hello.html.erb
```

```erb
<h1>Hello from Rails!</h1>
<p>
▶  It is now <%= @time %>
</p>
```

When we refresh our browser window, we will again see the current time, showing that the communication between the controller and the view was successful.

Why did we go to the extra trouble of setting the time to be displayed in the controller and then using it in the view? Good question. In this application, it doesn't make much difference, but by putting the logic in the controller instead, we buy ourselves some benefits. For example, we may want to extend our application in the future to support users in many countries. In that case, we'd want to localize the display of the time, choosing a time appropriate to their time zone. That would be a fair amount of application-level code, and it would probably not be appropriate to embed it at the view level. By setting the time to display in the controller, we make our application more flexible—we can change the time zone in the controller without having to update any view that uses that time object. The time is *data*, and it should be supplied to the view by the controller. We'll see a lot more of this when we introduce models into the equation.

The Story So Far

Let's briefly review how our current application works:

1. The user navigates to our application. In our case, we do that using a local URL such as http://localhost:3000/say/hello.

2. Rails then matches the route pattern, which it previously split into two parts and analyzed.

   The say part is taken to be the name of a controller, so Rails creates a new instance of the Ruby class SayController (which it finds in app/controllers/say_controller.rb).

3. The next part of the pattern, hello, identifies an action. Rails invokes a method of that name in the controller. This action method creates a new Time object holding the current time and tucks it away in the @time instance variable.

4. Rails looks for a template to display the result. It searches the directory app/views for a subdirectory with the same name as the controller (say) and in that subdirectory for a file named after the action (hello.html.erb).

5. Rails processes this file through the ERb templating system, executing any embedded Ruby and substituting in values set up by the controller.

6. The result is returned to the browser, and Rails finishes processing this request.

This isn't the whole story—Rails gives you lots of opportunities to override this basic workflow (and we'll be taking advantage of them shortly). As it stands, our story illustrates convention over configuration, one of the fundamental parts of the philosophy of Rails. By providing convenient defaults and by applying certain conventions on how a URL is constructed or in what file a controller definition is placed and what class name and method names are used, Rails applications are typically written using little or no external configuration—things just knit themselves together in a natural way.

2.3 Linking Pages Together

It's a rare web application that has just one page. Let's see how we can add another stunning example of web design to our "Hello, World!" application.

Normally, each page in your application will correspond to a separate view. In our case, we'll also use a new action method to handle the page (although that isn't always the case, as we'll see later in the book). We'll use the same controller for both actions. Again, this needn't be the case, but we have no compelling reason to use a new controller right now.

We already defined a goodbye action for this controller, so all that remains is to create a new template in the directory app/views/say. This time it's called goodbye.html.erb, because by default templates are named after their associated actions.

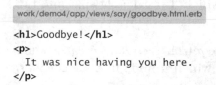

```
<h1>Goodbye!</h1>
<p>
  It was nice having you here.
</p>
```

Fire up our trusty browser again, but this time point to our new view using the URL http://localhost:3000/say/goodbye. You should see something like this:

Now we need to link the two screens. We'll put a link on the hello screen that takes us to the goodbye screen, and vice versa. In a real application, we might want to make these proper buttons, but for now we'll just use hyperlinks.

We already know that Rails uses a convention to parse the URL into a target controller and an action within that controller. So, a simple approach would be to adopt this URL convention for our links.

The file hello.html.erb would contain the following:

```
...
<p>
  Say <a href="/say/goodbye">Goodbye</a>!
</p>
...
```

And the file goodbye.html.erb would point the other way:

```
...
<p>
  Say <a href="/say/hello">Hello</a>!
</p>
...
```

This approach would certainly work, but it's a bit fragile. If we were to move our application to a different place on the web server, the URLs would no longer be valid. It also encodes assumptions about the Rails URL format into our code; it's possible a future version of Rails might change this.

Fortunately, these aren't risks we have to take. Rails comes with a bunch of *helper methods* that can be used in view templates. Here, we'll use the helper method link_to, which creates a hyperlink to an action. (The link_to method can do a lot more than this, but let's take it gently for now.) Using link_to, hello.html.erb becomes the following:

```
work/demo5/app/views/say/hello.html.erb
<h1>Hello from Rails!</h1>
<p>
  It is now <%= @time %>
</p>
► <p>
►   Time to say
►   <%= link_to "Goodbye", say_goodbye_path %>!
► </p>
```

There's a link_to call within an ERb <%=...%> sequence. This creates a link to a URL that will invoke the goodbye action. The first parameter in the call to link_to is the text to be displayed in the hyperlink, and the next parameter tells Rails to generate the link to the goodbye action.

Let's stop for a minute to consider how we generated the link. We wrote this:

```
link_to "Goodbye!", say_goodbye_path
```

First, link_to is a method call. (In Rails, we call methods that make it easier to write templates *helpers*.) If you come from a language such as Java, you might be surprised that Ruby doesn't insist on parentheses around method parameters. You can always add them if you like.

The say_goodbye_path is a precomputed value that Rails makes available to application views. It evaluates to the /say/goodbye path. Over time you will see that Rails provides the ability to name all the routes that you will be using in your application.

OK, back to the application. If we point our browser at our hello page, it will now contain the link to the goodbye page, as shown here:

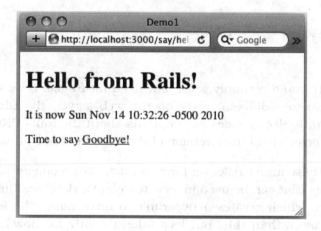

We can make the corresponding change in goodbye.html.erb, linking it back to the initial hello page:

> work/demo5/app/views/say/goodbye.html.erb

```
<h1>Goodbye!</h1>
<p>
   It was nice having you here.
</p>
► <p>
►    Say <%= link_to "Hello", say_hello_path %> again.
► </p>
```

At this point, we've completed our toy application and in the process verified that our installation of Rails is functioning properly. After a brief recap, it is now time to move on to building a real application.

2.4 What We Just Did

We constructed a toy application that showed us the following:

- How to create a new Rails application and how to create a new controller in that application
- How to create dynamic content in the controller and display it via the view template
- How to link pages together

This is a great foundation, and it didn't really take much time or effort. This experience will continue as we move on to the next chapter and build a much bigger application.

Playtime

Here's some stuff to try on your own:

- Experiment with the following expressions:
  - Addition: <%= 1+2 %>
  - Concatenation: <%= "cow" + "boy" %>
  - Time in one hour: <%= 1.hour.from_now %>
- A call to the following Ruby method returns a list of all the files in the current directory:
  ```
  @files = Dir.glob('*')
  ```
  Use it to set an instance variable in a controller action, and then write the corresponding template that displays the filenames in a list on the browser.

  Hint: you can iterate over a collection using something like this:
  ```
  <% for file in @files %>
    file name is: <%= file %>
  <% end %>
  ```
  You might want to use a *<ul>* for the list.

(You'll find hints at http://www.pragprog.com/wikis/wiki/RailsPlayTime.)

Cleaning Up

Maybe you've been following along and writing the code in this chapter. If so, chances are that the application is still running on your computer. When we start coding our next application in ten pages or so, we'll get a conflict the first time we run it, because it will also try to use the computer's port 3000 to talk with the browser. Now would be a good time to stop the current application by pressing Ctrl-C in the window you used to start it.

Now let's move on to an overview of Rails.

In this chapter, we'll see

- models,
- views, and
- controllers.

Chapter 3

The Architecture of Rails Applications

One of the interesting features of Rails is that it imposes some fairly serious constraints on how you structure your web applications. Surprisingly, these constraints make it easier to create applications—a lot easier. Let's see why.

3.1 Models, Views, and Controllers

Back in 1979, Trygve Reenskaug came up with a new architecture for developing interactive applications. In his design, applications were broken into three types of components: models, views, and controllers.

The *model* is responsible for maintaining the state of the application. Sometimes this state is transient, lasting for just a couple of interactions with the user. Sometimes the state is permanent and will be stored outside the application, often in a database.

A model is more than just data; it enforces all the business rules that apply to that data. For example, if a discount shouldn't be applied to orders of less than $20, the model will enforce the constraint. This makes sense; by putting the implementation of these business rules in the model, we make sure that nothing else in the application can make our data invalid. The model acts as both a gatekeeper and a data store.

The *view* is responsible for generating a user interface, normally based on data in the model. For example, an online store will have a list of products to be displayed on a catalog screen. This list will be accessible via the model, but it will be a view that accesses the list from the model and formats it for the end user. Although the view may present the user with various ways of inputting data, the view itself never handles incoming data. The view's work is done once the data is displayed. There may well be many views that access the same model data, often for different purposes. In the online store, there'll

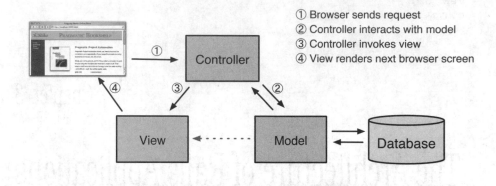

① Browser sends request
② Controller interacts with model
③ Controller invokes view
④ View renders next browser screen

Figure 3.1: THE MODEL-VIEW-CONTROLLER ARCHITECTURE

be a view that displays product information on a catalog page and another set of views used by administrators to add and edit products.

Controllers orchestrate the application. Controllers receive events from the outside world (normally user input), interact with the model, and display an appropriate view to the user.

This triumvirate—the model, view, and controller—together form an architecture known as MVC. To learn how the three concepts fit together, see Figure 3.1.

The MVC architecture was originally intended for conventional GUI applications, where developers found the separation of concerns led to far less coupling, which in turn made the code easier to write and maintain. Each concept or action was expressed in just one well-known place. Using MVC was like constructing a skyscraper with the girders already in place—it was a lot easier to hang the rest of the pieces with a structure already there. During the development of our application, we will be making heavy use of Rails' ability to generate *scaffolding* for our application.

Ruby on Rails is an MVC framework, too. Rails enforces a structure for your application—you develop models, views, and controllers as separate chunks of functionality, and it knits them all together as your program executes. One of the joys of Rails is that this knitting process is based on the use of intelligent defaults so that you typically don't need to write any external configuration

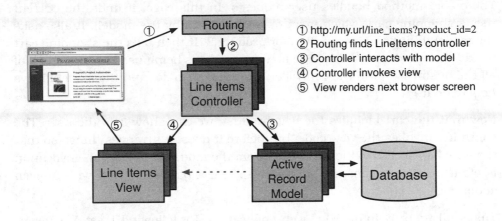

① http://my.url/line_items?product_id=2
② Routing finds LineItems controller
③ Controller interacts with model
④ Controller invokes view
⑤ View renders next browser screen

Figure 3.2: RAILS AND MVC

metadata to make it all work. This is an example of the Rails philosophy of favoring convention over configuration.

In a Rails application, an incoming request is first sent to a router, which works out where in the application the request should be sent and how the request itself should be parsed. Ultimately, this phase identifies a particular method (called an *action* in Rails parlance) somewhere in the controller code. The action might look at data in the request, it might interact with the model, and it might cause other actions to be invoked. Eventually the action prepares information for the view, which renders something to the user.

Rails handles an incoming request as shown in Figure 3.2. In this example, the application has previously displayed a product catalog page, and the user has just clicked the [Add to Cart] button next to one of the products. This button posts to http://localhost:3000/line_items?product_id=2, where line_items is a resource in our application and 2 is our internal id for the selected product.

The routing component receives the incoming request and immediately picks it apart. The request contains a path (/line_items?product_id=2) and a method (this button does a POST operation; other common methods are GET, PUT, and DELETE). In this simple case, Rails takes the first part of the path, line_items, as the name of the controller and the product_id as the id of a product. By convention, POST methods are associated with create actions. As a result of all this analysis, the router knows it has to invoke the create method in the controller class LineItemsController (we'll talk about naming conventions on page 260).

The create method handles user requests. In this case, it finds the current user's shopping cart (which is an object managed by the model). It also asks the model to find the information for product 2. It then tells the shopping cart to add that product to itself. (See how the model is being used to keep track of all the business data? The controller tells it *what* to do, and the model knows *how* to do it.)

Now that the cart includes the new product, we can show it to the user. The controller invokes the view code, but before it does, it arranges things so that the view has access to the cart object from the model. In Rails, this invocation is often implicit; again, conventions help link a particular view with a given action.

That's all there is to an MVC web application. By following a set of conventions and partitioning your functionality appropriately, you'll discover that your code becomes easier to work with and your application becomes easier to extend and maintain. Seems like a good trade.

If MVC is simply a question of partitioning your code a particular way, you might be wondering why you need a framework such as Ruby on Rails. The answer is straightforward: Rails handles all of the low-level housekeeping for you—all those messy details that take so long to handle by yourself—and lets you concentrate on your application's core functionality. Let's see how.

3.2 Rails Model Support

In general, we'll want our web applications to keep their information in a relational database. Order-entry systems will store orders, line items, and customer details in database tables. Even applications that normally use unstructured text, such as weblogs and news sites, often use databases as their back-end data store.

Although it might not be immediately apparent from the SQL[1] you use to access them, relational databases are actually designed around mathematical set theory. Although this is good from a conceptual point of view, it makes it difficult to combine relational databases with object-oriented (OO) programming languages. Objects are all about data and operations, and databases are all about sets of values. Operations that are easy to express in relational terms are sometimes difficult to code in an OO system. The reverse is also true.

Over time, folks have worked out ways of reconciling the relational and OO views of their corporate data. Let's look at the way that Rails chooses to map relational data onto objects.

---

1. SQL, referred to by some as *Structured Query Language*, is the language used to query and update relational databases.

Object-Relational Mapping

ORM libraries map database tables to classes. If a database has a table called orders, our program will have a class named Order. Rows in this table correspond to objects of the class—a particular order is represented as an object of class Order. Within that object, attributes are used to get and set the individual columns. Our Order object has methods to get and set the amount, the sales tax, and so on.

In addition, the Rails classes that wrap our database tables provide a set of class-level methods that perform table-level operations. For example, we might need to find the order with a particular id. This is implemented as a class method that returns the corresponding Order object. In Ruby code, this might look like this:

class method
↪ page 45
puts
↪ page 39

```
order = Order.find(1)
puts "Customer #{order.customer_id}, amount=$#{order.amount}"
```

Sometimes these class-level methods return collections of objects:

iterating
↪ page 43

```
Order.where(:name => 'dave').each do |order|
  puts order.amount
end
```

Finally, the objects corresponding to individual rows in a table have methods that operate on that row. Probably the most widely used is save, the operation that saves the row to the database:

```
Order.where(:name => 'dave').each do |order|
  order.pay_type = "Purchase order"
  order.save
end
```

So, an ORM layer maps tables to classes, rows to objects, and columns to attributes of those objects. Class methods are used to perform table-level operations, and instance methods perform operations on the individual rows.

In a typical ORM library, you supply configuration data to specify the mappings between entities in the database and entities in the program. Programmers using these ORM tools often find themselves creating and maintaining a boatload of XML configuration files.

Active Record

Active Record is the ORM layer supplied with Rails. It closely follows the standard ORM model: tables map to classes, rows to objects, and columns to object attributes. It differs from most other ORM libraries in the way it is configured. By relying on convention and starting with sensible defaults, Active Record minimizes the amount of configuration that developers perform.

To illustrate this, here's a program that uses Active Record to wrap our orders table:

```
require 'active_record'

class Order < ActiveRecord::Base
end

order = Order.find(1)
order.pay_type = "Purchase order"
order.save
```

This code uses the new Order class to fetch the order with an id of 1 and modify the pay_type. (We've omitted the code that creates a database connection for now.) Active Record relieves us of the hassles of dealing with the underlying database, leaving us free to work on business logic.

But Active Record does more than that. As you'll see when we develop our shopping cart application, starting on page 55, Active Record integrates seamlessly with the rest of the Rails framework. If a web form sends the application data related to a business object, Active Record can extract it into our model. Active Record supports sophisticated validation of model data, and if the form data fails validations, the Rails views can extract and format errors.

Active Record is the solid model foundation of the Rails MVC architecture.

3.3 Action Pack: The View and Controller

When you think about it, the view and controller parts of MVC are pretty intimate. The controller supplies data to the view, and the controller receives events from the pages generated by the views. Because of these interactions, support for views and controllers in Rails is bundled into a single component, *Action Pack*.

Don't be fooled into thinking that your application's view code and controller code will be jumbled up just because Action Pack is a single component. Quite the contrary; Rails gives you the separation you need to write web applications with clearly demarcated code for control and presentation logic.

View Support

In Rails, the view is responsible for creating either all or part of a response to be displayed in a browser, processed by an application or sent as an email. At its simplest, a view is a chunk of HTML code that displays some fixed text. More typically you'll want to include dynamic content created by the action method in the controller.

In Rails, dynamic content is generated by templates, which come in three flavors. The most common templating scheme, called Embedded Ruby (ERb), embeds snippets of Ruby code within a view document, in many ways similar to the way it is done in other web frameworks, such as PHP or JSP. Although this approach is very flexible, some are concerned that it violates the spirit of MVC. By embedding code in the view, we risk adding logic that should be in the model or the controller. As with everything, while judicious use in moderation is healthy, overuse can become a problem. Maintaining a clean separation of concerns is part of the job of the developer. (We look at HTML templates in Section 25.2, *Generating HTML with ERb*, on page 407.)

XML Builder can also be used to construct XML documents using Ruby code— the structure of the generated XML will automatically follow the structure of the code. We discuss xml.builder templates starting on page 405.

Rails also provides *RJS* views. These allow you to create JavaScript fragments on the server that are then executed on the browser. This is great for creating dynamic Ajax interfaces. We talk about these starting on page 131.

And the Controller!

The Rails controller is the logical center of your application. It coordinates the interaction between the user, the views, and the model. However, Rails handles most of this interaction behind the scenes; the code you write concentrates on application-level functionality. This makes Rails controller code remarkably easy to develop and maintain.

The controller is also home to a number of important ancillary services:

- It is responsible for routing external requests to internal actions. It handles people-friendly URLs extremely well.

- It manages caching, which can give applications orders-of-magnitude performance boosts.

- It manages helper modules, which extend the capabilities of the view templates without bulking up their code.

- It manages sessions, giving users the impression of ongoing interaction with our applications.

We've already seen and modified a controller in Section 2.2, *Hello, Rails!*, on page 17, and will be seeing and modifying a number of controllers in the development of a sample application, starting with the products controller in Section 8.1, *Iteration C1: Creating the Catalog Listing*, on page 89.

There's a lot to Rails. But before going any further, let's have a brief refresher— and for some of you, a brief introduction—to the Ruby language.

In this chapter, we'll see

- objects: names and methods;
- data: strings, arrays, hashes, and regular expressions;
- control: if, while, blocks, iterators, and exceptions;
- building blocks: classes and modules;
- YAML and marshalling; and
- common idioms that you will see used in this book.

Chapter 4

Introduction to Ruby

Many people who are new to Rails are also new to Ruby. If you are familiar with a language such as Java, JavaScript, PHP, Perl, or Python, you will find Ruby pretty easy to pick up.

This chapter is not a complete introduction to Ruby. It will not cover topics such as precedence rules (like most other programming languages, 1+2*3==7 in Ruby). It is only meant to explain enough Ruby that the examples in the book make sense.

This chapter draws heavily from material in Chapter 2 of *Programming Ruby* [TFH08]. If you think you need more background on the Ruby language, and at the risk of being grossly self-serving, we'd like to suggest that the best way to learn Ruby, and the best reference for Ruby's classes, modules, and libraries, is *Programming Ruby* [TFH08] (also known as the PickAxe book). Welcome to the Ruby community!

4.1 Ruby Is an Object-Oriented Language

Everything you manipulate in Ruby is an object, and the results of those manipulations are themselves objects.

When you write object-oriented code, you're normally looking to model concepts from the real world. Typically during this modeling process you'll discover categories of things that need to be represented. In an online store, the concept of a line item could be such a category. In Ruby, you'd define a *class* to represent each of these categories. You then use this class as a kind of factory that generates *objects*—instances of that class. An object is a combination of state (for example, the quantity and the product id) and methods that use that state (perhaps a method to calculate the line item's total cost). We'll show how to create classes on page 45.

Objects are created by calling a *constructor*, a special method associated with a class. The standard constructor is called new.

Given a class called LineItem, you could create line item objects as follows:

```
line_item_one = LineItem.new
line_item_one.quantity = 1
line_item_one.sku      = "AUTO_B_00"
```

Methods are invoked by sending a message to an object. The message contains the method's name, along with any parameters the method may need. When an object receives a message, it looks into its own class for a corresponding method. Let's look at some method calls:

```
"dave".length
line_item_one.quantity()
cart.add_line_item(next_purchase)
submit_tag "Add to Cart"
```

Parentheses are generally optional in method calls. In Rails applications, you'll find that most method calls involved in larger expressions will have parentheses, while those that look more like commands or declarations tend not to have them.

Methods have names, as do many other constructs in Ruby. Names in Ruby have special rules, rules that you may not have seen if you come to Ruby from another language.

Ruby Names

Local variables, method parameters, and method names should all start with a lowercase letter or with an underscore: order, line_item, and xr2000 are all valid. Instance variables (which we talk about on page 45) begin with an "at" (@) sign, such as @quantity and @product_id. The Ruby convention is to use underscores to separate words in a multiword method or variable name (so line_item is preferable to lineItem).

Class names, module names, and constants must start with an uppercase letter. By convention they use capitalization, rather than underscores, to distinguish the start of words within the name. Class names look like Object, PurchaseOrder, and LineItem.

Rails uses *symbols* to identify things. In particular, it uses them as keys when naming method parameters and looking things up in hashes. Here is an example:

```
redirect_to :action => "edit", :id => params[:id]
```

As you can see, a symbol looks like a variable name, but it's prefixed with a colon. Examples of symbols include :action, :line_items, and :id. You can think of symbols as string literals that are magically made into constants. Alternatively, you can consider the colon to mean "thing named," so :id is "the thing named *id*."

Now that we have used a few methods, let's move on to how they are defined.

Methods

Let's write a *method* that returns a cheery, personalized greeting. We'll invoke that method a couple of times:

```
def say_goodnight(name)
  result = 'Good night, ' + name
  return result
end

# Time for bed...
puts say_goodnight('Mary-Ellen')
puts say_goodnight('John-Boy')
```

Having defined the method, we call it twice. In both cases, we pass the result to the method puts, which outputs to the console its argument followed by a newline (moving on to the next line of output).

You don't need a semicolon at the end of a statement as long as you put each statement on a separate line. Ruby comments start with a # character and run to the end of the line. Indentation is not significant (but two-character indentation is the de facto Ruby standard).

Ruby doesn't use braces to delimit the bodies of compound statements and definitions (such as methods and classes). Instead, you simply finish the body with the keyword end. The keyword return is optional, and if not present, the results of the last expression evaluated will be returned.

4.2 Data Types

While everything in Ruby is an object, some of the data types in Ruby have special syntax support, in particular for defining literal values. In these examples, we've used some simple strings and even string concatenation.

Strings

This previous example also showed some Ruby string objects. One way to create a string object is to use *string literals*, which are sequences of characters between single or double quotation marks. The difference between the two forms is the amount of processing Ruby does on the string while constructing the literal. In the single-quoted case, Ruby does very little. With a few exceptions, what you type into the single-quoted string literal becomes the string's value.

In the double-quoted case, Ruby does more work. First, it looks for *substitutions*—sequences that start with a backslash character—and replaces them with some binary value. The most common of these is \n, which is replaced with a newline character. When you write a string containing a newline to the console, the \n forces a line break.

Second, Ruby performs *expression interpolation* in double-quoted strings. In the string, the sequence #{*expression*} is replaced by the value of *expression*. We could use this to rewrite our previous method:

```ruby
def say_goodnight(name)
  "Good night, #{name.capitalize}"
end
puts say_goodnight('pa')
```

When Ruby constructs this string object, it looks at the current value of name and substitutes it into the string. Arbitrarily complex expressions are allowed in the #{...} construct. Here we invoked the capitalize method, defined for all strings, to output our parameter with a leading uppercase letter.

Strings are a fairly primitive data type that contain an ordered collection of bytes or characters. Ruby also provides means for defining collections of arbitrary objects via arrays and hashes.

Arrays and Hashes

Ruby's arrays and hashes are indexed collections. Both store collections of objects, accessible using a key. With arrays, the key is an integer, whereas hashes support any object as a key. Both arrays and hashes grow as needed to hold new elements. It's more efficient to access array elements, but hashes provide more flexibility. Any particular array or hash can hold objects of differing types; you can have an array containing an integer, a string, and a floating-point number, for example.

You can create and initialize a new array object using an *array literal*—a set of elements between square brackets. Given an array object, you can access individual elements by supplying an index between square brackets, as the next example shows. Ruby array indices start at zero.

```ruby
a = [ 1, 'cat', 3.14 ]    # array with three elements
a[0]                      # access the first element (1)
a[2] = nil                # set the third element
                          # array now [ 1, 'cat', nil ]
```

You may have noticed that we used the special value nil in this example. In many languages, the concept of *nil* (or *null*) means "no object." In Ruby, that's not the case; nil is an object, just like any other, that happens to represent nothing.

The method << is commonly used with arrays. It appends a value to its receiver.

```
ages = []
for person in @people
  ages << person.age
end
```

Ruby has a shortcut for creating an array of words:

```
a = [ 'ant', 'bee', 'cat', 'dog', 'elk' ]
# this is the same:
a = %w{ ant bee cat dog elk }
```

Ruby hashes are similar to arrays. A hash literal uses braces rather than square brackets. The literal must supply two objects for every entry: one for the key, the other for the value. For example, you may want to map musical instruments to their orchestral sections:

```
inst_section = {
  :cello    => 'string',
  :clarinet => 'woodwind',
  :drum     => 'percussion',
  :oboe     => 'woodwind',
  :trumpet  => 'brass',
  :violin   => 'string'
}
```

The thing to the left of the => is the key, and that on the right is the corresponding value. Keys in a particular hash must be unique—you can't have two entries for :drum. The keys and values in a hash can be arbitrary objects—you can have hashes where the values are arrays, other hashes, and so on. In Rails, hashes typically use symbols as keys. Many Rails hashes have been subtly modified so that you can use either a string or a symbol interchangeably as a key when inserting and looking up values.

Hashes are indexed using the same square bracket notation as arrays:

```
inst_section[:oboe]     #=> 'woodwind'
inst_section[:cello]    #=> 'string'
inst_section[:bassoon]  #=> nil
```

As the previous example shows, a hash returns nil when indexed by a key it doesn't contain. Normally this is convenient, because nil means false when used in conditional expressions.

You can pass hashes as parameters on method calls. Ruby allows you to omit the braces, but only if the hash is the last parameter of the call. Rails makes extensive use of this feature. The following code fragment shows a two-element hash being passed to the redirect_to method. In effect, though, you can ignore that it's a hash and pretend that Ruby has keyword arguments.

```
redirect_to :action => 'show', :id => product.id
```

There is one more data type worth mentioning—the regular expression.

Regular Expressions

A regular expression lets you specify a *pattern* of characters to be matched in a string. In Ruby, you typically create a regular expression by writing /*pattern*/ or %r{*pattern*}.

For example, you could write a pattern that matches a string containing the text *Perl* or the text *Python* using the regular expression /Perl|Python/.

The forward slashes delimit the pattern, which consists of the two things we're matching, separated by a vertical bar (|). This bar character means "either the thing on the left or the thing on the right," in this case either *Perl* or *Python*. You can use parentheses within patterns, just as you can in arithmetic expressions, so you could also have written this pattern as /P(erl|ython)/. Programs typically test strings against regular expressions using the =~ match operator:

```
if line =~ /P(erl|ython)/
  puts "There seems to be another scripting language here"
end
```

You can specify *repetition* within patterns. /ab+c/ matches a string containing an *a* followed by one or more *b*'s, followed by a *c*. Change the plus to an asterisk, and /ab*c/ creates a regular expression that matches one *a*, zero or more *b*'s, and one *c*.

Backward slashes start special sequences; most notably, \d matches any digit, \s matches any whitespace character, and \w matches any alphanumeric ("word") character.

Ruby's regular expressions are a deep and complex subject; this section barely skims the surface. See the PickAxe book for a full discussion.

This book will only make light use of regular expressions.

With that brief introduction to data, let's move on to logic.

4.3 Logic

Method calls are statements. Ruby also provides a number of ways to make decisions that affect the repetition and order in which methods are invoked.

Control Structures

Ruby has all the usual control structures, such as if statements and while loops. Java, C, and Perl programmers may well get caught by the lack of braces around the bodies of these statements. Instead, Ruby uses the keyword end to signify the end of a body:

```
if count > 10
  puts "Try again"
elsif tries == 3
```

```
  puts "You lose"
else
  puts "Enter a number"
end
```

Similarly, while statements are terminated with end:

```
while weight < 100 and num_pallets <= 30
  pallet = next_pallet()
  weight += pallet.weight
  num_pallets += 1
end
```

Ruby also contains variants of these statements: unless is like if except that it checks for the condition to *not* be true. Similarly, until is like while except that the loop continues until the condition evaluates to be true.

Ruby *statement* modifiers are a useful shortcut if the body of an if, unless, while, or until statement is just a single expression. Simply write the expression, followed by the modifier keyword and the condition:

```
puts "Danger, Will Robinson" if radiation > 3000
```

```
distance = distance * 1.2 while distance < 100
```

Although if statements are fairly common in Ruby applications, newcomers to the Ruby language are often surprised to find that looping constructs are rarely used. Blocks and iterators often take their place.

Blocks and Iterators

Code blocks are just chunks of code between braces or between do...end. A common convention is that people use braces for single-line blocks and do/end for multiline blocks:

```
{ puts "Hello" }        # this is a block

do                      ###
  club.enroll(person)   # and so is this
  person.socialize      #
end                     ###
```

To pass a block to a method, place the block after the parameters (if any) to the method. In other words, put the start of the block at the end of the source line containing the method call. For example, in the following code, the block containing puts "Hi" is associated with the call to the method greet:

```
greet  { puts "Hi" }
```

If a method call has parameters, they appear before the block:

```
verbose_greet("Dave", "loyal customer")  { puts "Hi" }
```

A method can invoke an associated block one or more times using the Ruby yield statement. You can think of yield as being something like a method call that calls out to the block associated with the method containing the yield. You can pass values to the block by giving parameters to yield. Within the block, you list the names of the arguments to receive these parameters between vertical bars (|).

Code blocks appear throughout Ruby applications. Often they are used in conjunction with iterators: methods that return successive elements from some kind of collection, such as an array:

```
animals = %w( ant bee cat dog elk )    # create an array
animals.each {|animal| puts animal }   # iterate over the contents
```

Each integer *N* implements a times method, which invokes an associated block *N* times:

```
3.times { print "Ho! " }    #=>  Ho! Ho! Ho!
```

The & prefix operator will allow a method to capture a passed block as a named parameter.

```
def wrap &b
  print "Santa says: "
  3.times(&b)
  print "\n"
end
wrap { print "Ho! " }
```

Within a block, or a method, control is sequential except when there is an exception.

Exceptions

Exceptions are objects (of class Exception or its subclasses). The raise method causes an exception to be raised. This interrupts the normal flow through the code. Instead, Ruby searches back through the call stack for code that says it can handle this exception.

Both methods and blocks of code wrapped between begin and end keywords intercept certain classes of exceptions using rescue clauses.

```
begin
  content = load_blog_data(file_name)
rescue BlogDataNotFound
  STDERR.puts "File #{file_name} not found"
rescue BlogDataFormatError
  STDERR.puts "Invalid blog data in #{file_name}"
rescue Exception => exc
  STDERR.puts "General error loading #{file_name}: #{exc.message}"
end
```

rescue clauses can be directly placed on the outermost level of a method definition without needing to enclose the contents in a begin/end block.

That concludes our brief introduction to control flow, and at this point we have our basic building blocks upon which we can build larger structures.

4.4 Organizing Structures

There are two basic concepts in Ruby for organizing methods, namely, classes and modules. We cover each in turn.

Classes

Here's a Ruby class definition:

```
Line 1   class Order < ActiveRecord::Base

           has_many :line_items

     5     def self.find_all_unpaid
             self.where('paid = 0')
           end

           def total
    10       sum = 0
             line_items.each {|li| sum += li.total}
           end
         end
```

Class definitions start with the keyword class followed by the class name (which must start with an uppercase letter). This Order class is defined to be a subclass of the class Base within the ActiveRecord module.

Rails makes heavy use of class-level declarations. Here has_many is a method that's defined by Active Record. It's called as the Order class is being defined. Normally these kinds of methods make assertions about the class, so in this book we call them *declarations*.

Within a class body you can define class methods and instance methods. Prefixing a method name with self. (as we do on line 5) makes it a class method; it can be called on the class generally. In this case, we can make the following call anywhere in our application:

```
to_collect = Order.find_all_unpaid
```

Objects of a class hold their state in *instance variables*. These variables, whose names all start with @, are available to all the instance methods of a class. Each object gets its own set of instance variables.

Instance variables are not directly accessible outside the class. To make them available, write methods that return their values:

```
class Greeter
  def initialize(name)
    @name = name
  end

  def name
    @name
  end

  def name=(new_name)
    @name = new_name
  end
end

g = Greeter.new("Barney")
puts g.name    #=> Barney
g.name = "Betty"
puts g.name    #=> Betty
```

Ruby provides convenience methods that write these accessor methods for you (which is great news for folks tired of writing all those getters and setters):

```
class Greeter
  attr_accessor  :name      # create reader and writer methods
  attr_reader    :greeting   # create reader only
  attr_writer    :age        # create writer only
```

A class's instance methods are public by default; anyone can call them. You'll probably want to override this for methods that are intended to be used only by other class instance methods:

```
class MyClass
  def m1      # this method is public
  end

  protected

  def m2      # this method is protected
  end

  private

  def m3      # this method is private
  end
end
```

The private directive is the strictest; private methods can be called only from within the same instance. Protected methods can be called both in the same instance and by other instances of the same class and its subclasses.

Classes are not the only organizing structure in Ruby. The other organizing structure is a module.

Modules

Modules are similar to classes in that they hold a collection of methods, constants, and other module and class definitions. Unlike classes, you cannot create objects based on modules.

Modules serve two purposes. First, they act as a namespace, letting you define methods whose names will not clash with those defined elsewhere. Second, they allow you to share functionality between classes—if a class *mixes in* a module, that module's instance methods become available as if they had been defined in the class. Multiple classes can mix in the same module, sharing the module's functionality without using inheritance. You can also mix multiple modules into a single class.

Helper methods are an example of where Rails uses modules. Rails automatically mixes these helper modules into the appropriate view templates. For example, if you wanted to write a helper method that would be callable from views invoked by the store controller, you could define the following module in the file store_helper.rb in the app/helpers directory:

```
module StoreHelper
  def capitalize_words(string)
    string.split(' ').map {|word| word.capitalize}.join(' ')
  end
end
```

There is one module that is part of the standard library of Ruby that deserves special mention given its usage in Rails, namely, YAML.

YAML

YAML[1] is a recursive acronym that stands for YAML Ain't Markup Language. In the context of Rails, YAML is used as a convenient way to define configuration of things such as databases, test data, and translations. Here is an example:

```
development:
  adapter: sqlite3
  database: db/development.sqlite3
  pool: 5
  timeout: 5000
```

In YAML, indentation is important, so this defines development as having a set of four key/value pairs, separated by colons.

---

1. http://www.yaml.org/

While YAML is one way to represent data, particularly when interacting with humans, Ruby provides a more general way for representing data for use by applications.

4.5 Marshaling Objects

Ruby can take an object and convert it into a stream of bytes that can be stored outside the application. This process is called *marshaling*. This saved object can later be read by another instance of the application (or by a totally separate application), and a copy of the originally saved object can be reconstituted.

There are two potential issues when you use marshaling. First, some objects cannot be dumped. If the objects to be dumped include bindings, procedure or method objects, instances of class IO, or singleton objects, or if you try to dump anonymous classes or modules, a TypeError will be raised.

Second, when you load a marshaled object, Ruby needs to know the definition of the class of that object (and of all the objects it contains).

Rails uses marshaling to store session data. If you rely on Rails to dynamically load classes, it is possible that a particular class may not have been defined at the point it reconstitutes session data. For that reason, you'll use the model declaration in your controller to list all models that are marshaled. This preemptively loads the necessary classes to make marshaling work.

Now that you have the Ruby basics down, let's give what we learned a whirl with a slightly larger, annotated example that pulls together a number of concepts. We'll follow that with a walk-through of special features that will help you with your Rails coding.

4.6 Pulling It All Together

Let's look at an example of how Rails applies a number of Ruby features together to make the code you need to maintain more declarative. You will see this example again in Section 6.1, *Generating the Scaffold*, on page 62. For now, we will focus on the Ruby-language aspects of the example.

```ruby
class CreateProducts < ActiveRecord::Migration
  def self.up
    create_table :products do |t|
      t.string :title
      t.text :description
      t.string :image_url
      t.decimal :price, :precision => 8, :scale => 2

      t.timestamps
    end
  end
```

```
    def self.down
      drop_table :products
    end
end
```

Even if you didn't know any Ruby, you would probably be able to decipher that up creates a table named products and down drops that table. The fields defined when creating this table include title, description, image_url, and price as well as a few timestamps (we'll describe these on page 375).

Now let's look at the same example from a Ruby perspective. A class named CreateProducts is defined, which inherits from the Migration class from the ActiveRecord module. Two class methods are defined—one named up and the other named down. Each calls a single class method (defined in ActiveRecord::Migration), passing it the name of the table in the form of a symbol.

The call to up also passes a block that is to be evaluated before the table is created. This block, when called, is passed an object named t, which is used to accumulate a list of fields. Rails defines a number of methods on this object—methods with names that are named after common data types. These methods, when called, simply add a field definition to the ever-accumulating set of names.

The definition of decimal also accepts a number of optional parameters, expressed as a hash.

To someone new to Ruby, this is a lot of heavy machinery thrown at solving such a simple problem. To someone familiar with Ruby, none of this machinery is particularly heavy. In any case, Rails makes extensive use of the facilities provided by Ruby to make defining operations (for example, migration tasks) as simple and as declarative as possible. Even small features of the language, such as optional parentheses and braces, contribute to the overall readability and ease of authoring.

Finally, there are a number of small features, or rather idiomatic combinations of features, that are often not immediately obvious to people new to the Ruby language. We close this chapter with them.

4.7 Ruby Idioms

A number of individual Ruby features can be combined in interesting ways, and the meaning of such idiomatic usage is often not immediately obvious to people new to the language. We use these common Ruby idioms in this book:

Methods such as empty! and empty?
> Ruby method names can end with an exclamation mark (a bang method) or a question mark (a predicate method). Bang methods normally do

something destructive to the receiver. Predicate methods return true or false depending on some condition.

a || b

The expression a || b evaluates a. If it isn't false or nil, then evaluation stops, and the expression returns a. Otherwise, the statement returns b. This is a common way of returning a default value if the first value hasn't been set.

a ||= b

The assignment statement supports a set of shortcuts: a *op=* b is the same as a = a *op* b. This works for most operators.

```
count += 1         # same as count = count + 1
price *= discount  #         price = price * discount
count ||= 0        #         count = count || 0
```

So, count ||= 0 gives count the value 0 if count doesn't already have a value.

obj = self.new

Sometimes a class method needs to create an instance of that class.

```
class Person < ActiveRecord::Base
  def self.for_dave
    Person.new(:name => 'Dave')
  end
end
```

This works fine, returning a new Person object. But later, someone might subclass our class:

```
class Employee < Person
  # ..
end
```

```
dave = Employee.for_dave  # returns a Person
```

The for_dave method was hardwired to return a Person object, so that's what is returned by Employee.for_dave. Using self.new instead returns a new object of the receiver's class, Employee.

lambda

The lambda operator converts a block into an object of type Proc. We will see this used on page 283.

require File.dirname(__FILE__) + '/../test_helper'

Ruby's require method loads an external source file into our application. This is used to include library code and classes that our application relies on. In normal use, Ruby finds these files by searching in a list of directories, the LOAD_PATH.

Sometimes we need to be specific about what file to include. We can do that by giving require a full filesystem path. The problem is, we don't know what that path will be—our users could install our code anywhere.

Wherever our application ends up getting installed, the relative path between the file doing the requiring and the target file will be the same. Knowing this, we can construct the absolute path to the target by taking the absolute path to the file doing the requiring (available in the special variable __FILE__), stripping out all but the directory name, and then appending the relative path to the target file.

In addition, there are many good resources on the Web showing Ruby idioms and Ruby gotchas. Here are just a few:

- http://www.ruby-lang.org/en/documentation/ruby-from-other-languages/
- http://en.wikipedia.org/wiki/Ruby_programming_language
- http://www.zenspider.com/Languages/Ruby/QuickRef.html

By this point, we have a firm foundation upon which to build: we've installed Rails, verified that we have things working with a simple application, covered a brief description of what Rails is, and reviewed (or for some of you, learned for the first time) the basics of the Ruby language. Now it is time to put this knowledge in place to build a larger application.

Part II

Building an Application

In this chapter, we'll see

- incremental development;
- use cases, page flow, data; and
- priorities.

Chapter 5

The Depot Application

We could mess around all day hacking together simple test applications, but that won't help us pay the bills. So, let's get our teeth into something meatier. Let's create a web-based shopping cart application called Depot.

Does the world need another shopping cart application? Nope, but that hasn't stopped hundreds of developers from writing one. Why should we be different?

More seriously, it turns out that our shopping cart will illustrate many of the features of Rails development. We'll see how to create simple maintenance pages, link database tables, handle sessions, and create forms. Over the next twelve chapters, we'll also touch on peripheral topics such as unit testing, security, and page layout.

5.1 Incremental Development

We'll be developing this application incrementally. We won't attempt to specify everything before we start coding. Instead, we'll work out enough of a specification to let us start and then immediately create some functionality. We'll try ideas, gather feedback, and continue with another cycle of mini-design and development.

This style of coding isn't always applicable. It requires close cooperation with the application's users, because we want to gather feedback as we go along. We might make mistakes, or the client might discover they asked for one thing but really wanted something different. It doesn't matter what the reason—the earlier we discover we've made a mistake, the less expensive it will be to fix that mistake. All in all, with this style of development, there's a lot of change as we go along.

Because of this, we need to use a toolset that doesn't penalize us for changing our minds. If we decide we need to add a new column to a database table or change the navigation between pages, we need to be able to get in there and do it without a bunch of coding or configuration hassle. As you'll see, Ruby on Rails shines when it comes to dealing with change—it's an ideal agile programming environment.

Along the way, we will be building and maintaining a corpus of tests. These tests will ensure that the application is always doing what we intend to do. Not only does Rails enable the creation of such tests, but it actually provides you with an initial set of tests each time you define a new controller.

On with the application.

5.2 What Depot Does

Let's start by jotting down an outline specification for the Depot application. We'll look at the high-level use cases and sketch out the flow through the web pages. We'll also try working out what data the application needs (acknowledging that our initial guesses will likely be wrong).

Use Cases

A *use case* is simply a statement about how some entity uses a system. Consultants invent these kinds of phrases to label things we've all known all along—it's a perversion of business life that fancy words always cost more than plain ones, even though the plain ones are more valuable.

Depot's use cases are simple (some would say tragically so). We start off by identifying two different roles or actors: the *buyer* and the *seller*.

The buyer uses Depot to browse the products we have to sell, select some to purchase, and supply the information needed to create an order.

The seller uses Depot to maintain a list of products to sell, to determine the orders that are awaiting shipping, and to mark orders as shipped. (The seller also uses Depot to make scads of money and retire to a tropical island, but that's the subject of another book.)

For now, that's all the detail we need. We *could* go into excruciating detail about what it means to maintain products and what constitutes an order ready to ship, but why bother? If there are details that aren't obvious, we'll discover them soon enough as we reveal successive iterations of our work to the customer.

Talking of getting feedback, let's not forget to get some right now—let's make sure our initial (admittedly sketchy) use cases are on the mark by asking our user. Assuming the use cases pass muster, let's work out how the application will work from the perspectives of its various users.

Page Flow

We always like to have an idea of the main pages in our applications and to understand roughly how users navigate between them. This early in the development, these page flows are likely to be incomplete, but they still help us focus on what needs doing and know how actions are sequenced.

Some folks like to mock up web application page flows using Photoshop, Word, or (shudder) HTML. We like using a pencil and paper. It's quicker, and the customer gets to play too, grabbing the pencil and scribbling alterations right on the paper.

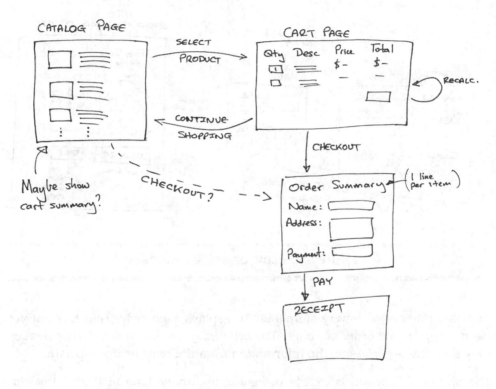

Figure 5.1: FLOW OF BUYER PAGES

The first sketch of the buyer flow is shown in Figure 5.1. It's pretty traditional. The buyer sees a catalog page, from which he selects one product at a time. Each product selected gets added to the cart, and the cart is displayed after each selection. The buyer can continue shopping using the catalog pages or check out and buy the contents of the cart. During checkout, we capture contact and payment details and then display a receipt page. We don't yet know how we're going to handle payment, so those details are fairly vague in the flow.

The seller flow, shown in Figure 5.2, is also fairly simple. After logging in, the seller sees a menu letting her create or view a product or ship existing orders. Once viewing a product, the seller may optionally edit the product information or delete the product entirely.

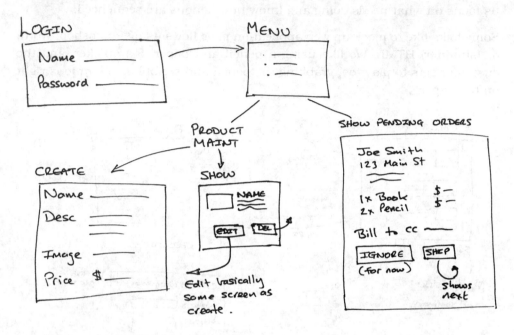

Figure 5.2: Flow of seller pages

The shipping option is very simplistic. It displays each order that has not yet been shipped, one order per page. The seller may choose to skip to the next or may ship the order, using the information from the page as appropriate.

The shipping function is clearly not going to survive long in the real world, but shipping is also one of those areas where reality is often stranger than you might think. Overspecify it up front, and we're likely to get it wrong. For now let's leave it as it is, confident that we can change it as the user gains experience using our application.

Data

Finally, we need to think about the data we're going to be working with.

Notice that we're not using words such as *schema* or *classes* here. We're also not talking about databases, tables, keys, and the like. We're simply talking about data. At this stage in the development, we don't know whether we'll even be using a database.

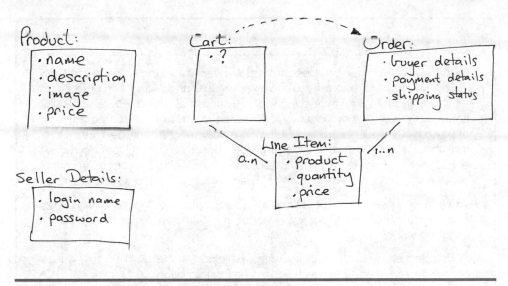

Figure 5.3: INITIAL GUESS AT APPLICATION DATA

Based on the use cases and the flows, it seems likely that we'll be working with the data shown in Figure 5.3. Again, using pencil and paper seems a whole lot easier than some fancy tool, but use whatever works for you.

Working on the data diagram raised a couple of questions. As the user buys items, we'll need somewhere to keep the list of products they bought, so we added a cart. But apart from its use as a transient place to keep this product list, the cart seems to be something of a ghost—we couldn't find anything meaningful to store in it. To reflect this uncertainty, we put a question mark inside the cart's box in the diagram. We're assuming this uncertainty will get resolved as we implement Depot.

Coming up with the high-level data also raised the question of what information should go into an order. Again, we chose to leave this fairly open for now—we'll refine this further as we start showing the customer our early iterations.

Finally, you might have noticed that we've duplicated the product's price in the line item data. Here we're breaking the "initially, keep it simple" rule slightly, but it's a transgression based on experience. If the price of a product changes, that price change should not be reflected in the line item price of currently open orders, so each line item needs to reflect the price of the product at the time the order was made.

> **General Recovery Advice**
>
> Everything in this book has been tested. If you follow along with this scenario precisely, using the recommended version of Rails and SQLite3 on Linux, Mac OS X, or Windows, then everything should work as described. However, deviations from this path may occur. Typos happen to the best of us, and not only are side explorations possible, but they are positively encouraged. Be aware that this might lead you to strange places. Don't be afraid: specific recovery actions for common problems appear in the specific sections where such problems often occur. A few additional general suggestions are included here.
>
> You should only ever need to restart the server in the few places where doing so is noted in the book. But if you ever get truly stumped, restarting the server might be worth trying.
>
> A "magic" command worth knowing, explained in detail in Part III, is rake db:migrate:redo. It will undo and reapply the last migration.
>
> If your server won't accept some input on a form, refresh the form on your browser, and resubmit it.

Again, at this point we'll double-check with the customer that we're still on the right track. (The customer was most likely sitting in the room with us while we drew these three diagrams.)

5.3 Let's Code

So, after sitting down with the customer and doing some preliminary analysis, we're ready to start using a computer for development! We'll be working from our original three diagrams, but the chances are pretty good that we'll be throwing them away fairly quickly—they'll become outdated as we gather feedback. Interestingly, that's why we didn't spend too long on them; it's easier to throw something away if you didn't spend a long time creating it.

In the chapters that follow, we'll start developing the application based on our current understanding. However, before we turn that page, we have to answer just one more question: what should we do first?

We like to work with the customer so we can jointly agree on priorities. In this case, we'd point out to her that it's hard to develop anything else until we have some basic products defined in the system, so we suggest spending a couple of hours getting the initial version of the product maintenance functionality up and running. And, of course, the client would agree.

In this chapter, we'll see
- creating a new application,
- configuring the database
- creating models and controllers, and
- updating a layout and a view.

Chapter 6

Task A: Creating the Application

Our first development task is to create the web interface that lets us maintain our product information—create new products, edit existing products, delete unwanted ones, and so on. We'll develop this application in small iterations, where *small* means "measured in minutes." Let's get started.

Typically, our iterations will involve multiple steps, as in iteration C, which will have steps C1, C2, C3, and so on. In this case, the iteration will have two steps.

6.1 Iteration A1: Creating the Products Maintenance Application

At the heart of the Depot application is a database. Getting this installed and configured and tested before proceeding further will prevent a lot of headaches. If you aren't sure of what you want, go with the defaults, and it will go easy. If you already know what you want, Rails makes it easy for you to describe your configuration.

Creating a Rails Application

Back on page 15, we saw how to create a new Rails application. We'll do the same thing here. Go to a command prompt, and type rails new followed by the name of our project. In this case, our project is called depot, so make sure you are not inside an existing application directory and type this:

```
work> rails new depot
```

We see a bunch of output scroll by. When it has finished, we find that a new directory, depot, has been created. That's where we'll be doing our work.

```
work> cd depot
depot> ls -p
app/       config.ru  doc/      lib/   public/   README    test/   vendor/
config/    db/        Gemfile   log/   Rakefile  script/   tmp/
```

Creating the Database

For this application, we'll use the open source SQLite database (which you'll need if you're following along with the code). We're using SQLite version 3 here.

SQLite 3 is the default database for Rails development and was installed along with Rails in Chapter 1, *Installing Rails*, on page 3. With SQLite 3 there are no steps required to create a database, and there are no special user accounts or passwords to deal with. So, now you get to experience one of the benefits of going with the flow (or, convention over configuration, as Rails folks say...ad nauseam).

If it's important to you to use a database server other than SQLite 3, the commands you'll need to create the database and grant permissions will be different. You will find some helpful hints in the Getting Started Rails Guide.[1]

Generating the Scaffold

Back in Figure 5.3, on page 59, we sketched out the basic content of the products table. Now let's turn that into reality. We need to create a database table and a Rails *model* that lets our application use that table, a number of *views* to make up the user interface, and a *controller* to orchestrate the application.

So, let's go ahead and create the model, views, controller, and migration for our products table. With Rails, you can do all that with one command by asking Rails to generate what is known as a *scaffold* for a given model. Note that on name mapping
↪ page 260 the command line[2] that follows, we use the singular form, Product. In Rails, a model is automatically mapped to a database tablewhose name is the plural form of the model's class. In our case, we asked for a model called Product, so Rails associated it with the table called products. (And how will it find that table? The development entry in config/database.yml tells Rails where to look for it. For SQLite 3 users, this will be a file in the db directory.)

```
depot> rails generate scaffold Product \
         title:string description:text image_url:string price:decimal
   invoke  active_record
   create    db/migrate/20110211000001_create_products.rb
   create    app/models/product.rb
   invoke    test_unit
   create      test/unit/product_test.rb
   create      test/fixtures/products.yml
    route   resources :products
   invoke  scaffold_controller
   create    app/controllers/products_controller.rb
   invoke    erb
```

---

1. http://guides.rubyonrails.org/getting_started.html#configuring-a-database
2. This command is too wide to fit comfortably on the page. To enter a command on multiple lines, simply put a backslash as the last character on all but the last line, and you will be prompted for more input. Windows users will need to substitute a caret (^) for the backslash.

```
create      app/views/products
create      app/views/products/index.html.erb
create      app/views/products/edit.html.erb
create      app/views/products/show.html.erb
create      app/views/products/new.html.erb
create      app/views/products/_form.html.erb
invoke   test_unit
create      test/functional/products_controller_test.rb
invoke   helper
create      app/helpers/products_helper.rb
invoke   test_unit
create       test/unit/helpers/products_helper_test.rb
invoke   stylesheets
create      public/stylesheets/scaffold.css
```

The generator creates a bunch of files. The one we're interested in first is the *migration* one, namely, 20110211000001_create_products.rb.

A migration represents a change we want to make to the data, expressed in a source file in database-independent terms. These changes can update both the database schema and the data in the database tables. We apply these migrations to update our database, and we can unapply them to roll our database back. We have a whole section on migrations starting on page 375. For now, we'll just use them without too much more comment.

The migration has a UTC-based timestamp prefix (20110211000001), a name (create_products), and a file extension (.rb, because it's a Ruby program).

The timestamp prefix you will see will be different. In fact, the timestamps used in this book are clearly fictitious. Typically your timestamps will not be consecutive; instead, they will reflect the time the migration was created.

Applying the Migration

Although we have already told Rails about the basic data types of each property, let's go ahead and refine the definition of the price to have eight digits of significance and two digits after the decimal point.

`depot_a/db/migrate/20110211000001_create_products.rb`

```ruby
class CreateProducts < ActiveRecord::Migration
  def self.up
    create_table :products do |t|
      t.string :title
      t.text :description
      t.string :image_url
►     t.decimal :price, :precision => 8, :scale => 2

      t.timestamps
    end
  end
end
```

```
  def self.down
    drop_table :products
  end
end
```

Now that we are done with our changes, we need to get Rails to apply this migration to our development database. We do this using the rake command. Rake is like having a reliable assistant on hand all the time: you tell it to do some task, and that task gets done. In this case, we'll tell Rake to apply any unapplied migrations to our database:

```
depot> rake db:migrate
(in /Users/rubys/work/depot)
==  CreateProducts: migrating ================================================
-- create_table(:products)
   -> 0.0027s
==  CreateProducts: migrated (0.0023s) =======================================
```

And that's it. Rake looks for all the migrations not yet applied to the database and applies them. In our case, the products table is added to the database defined by the development section of the database.yml file.

OK, all the groundwork has been done. We set up our Depot application as a Rails project. We created the development database and configured our application to be able to connect to it. We created a products controller and a Product model and used a migration to create the corresponding products table. And a number of views have been created for us. It's time to see all this in action.

Seeing the List of Products

With three commands we have created an application and a database (or a table inside an existing database, if you chose something other than SQLite 3). Before we worry too much about just what happened behind the scenes here, let's try our shiny new application.

First, we'll start a local server, supplied with Rails:

```
depot> rails server
=> Booting WEBrick
=> Rails 3.0.5 application starting in development on http://0.0.0.0:3000
=> Call with -d to detach
=> Ctrl-C to shutdown server
[2010-05-05 17:45:38] INFO  WEBrick 1.3.1
[2010-05-05 17:45:38] INFO  ruby 1.8.7 (2010-01-10) [x86_64-linux]
[2010-05-05 17:45:43] INFO  WEBrick::HTTPServer#start: pid=24649 port=3000
```

Just as it did with our demo application in Chapter 2, *Instant Gratification*, this command starts a web server on our local host, port 3000. If you get an error saying Address already in use when you try to run the server, that simply means you already have a Rails server running on your machine. If you've been following along with the examples in the book, that might well be the "Hello,

World!" application from Chapter 4. Find its console, and kill the server using Ctrl-C. If you are running on Windows, you may see the prompt Terminate batch job (Y/N)?. If so, respond with y.

Let's connect to it. Remember, the URL we give to our browser contains both the port number (3000) and the name of the controller in lowercase (products).

That's pretty boring. It's showing us an empty list of products. Let's add some. Click the New product link, and a form should appear.

These forms are simply HTML templates, just like the ones you created in Section 2.2, *Hello, Rails!*, on page 17. In fact, we can modify them. Let's change the number of lines in the description field:

depot_a/app/views/products/_form.html.erb

```
<%= form_for(@product) do |f| %>
  <% if @product.errors.any? %>
    <div id="error_explanation">
      <h2><%= pluralize(@product.errors.count, "error") %>
      prohibited this product from being saved:</h2>
```

```
    <ul>
    <% @product.errors.full_messages.each do |msg| %>
      <li><%= msg %></li>
    <% end %>
    </ul>
  </div>
<% end %>


<div class="field">
  <%= f.label :title %><br />
  <%= f.text_field :title %>
</div>
<div class="field">
  <%= f.label :description %><br />
  <%= f.text_area :description, :rows => 6 %>
</div>
<div class="field">
  <%= f.label :image_url %><br />
  <%= f.text_field :image_url %>
</div>
<div class="field">
  <%= f.label :price %><br />
  <%= f.text_field :price %>
</div>
<div class="actions">
  <%= f.submit %>
</div>
<% end %>
```

We will explore this more in Chapter 8, *Task C: Catalog Display*, on page 89.
But for now, we've adjusted one field to taste, so let's go ahead and fill it in:

Click the Create button, and you should see the new product was successfully created. If you now click the Back link, you should see the new product in the list:

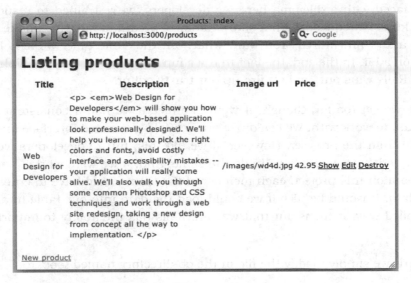

Perhaps it isn't the prettiest interface, but it works, and we can show it to our client for approval. She can play with the other links (showing details, editing existing products, and so on). We explain to her that this is only a first step—we know it's rough, but we wanted to get her feedback early. (And four commands probably count as early in anyone's book.)

At this point, you've accomplished a lot with only four commands. Before we move on, let's try one more command:

```
rake test
```

Included in the output should be two lines that each say 0 failures, 0 errors. This is for the unit, functional, and integration tests that Rails generates along with the scaffolding. They are minimal at this point, but simply knowing that they are there and that they pass should give you confidence. As you proceed through these chapters in Part II, you are encouraged to run this command frequently because it will help you spot and track down errors. We will cover this more in Section 7.2, *Iteration B2: Unit Testing of Models*, on page 80.

Note that if you've used a database other than SQLite3, this step may have failed. Check your database.yml file, and see the notes on page 393.

6.2 Iteration A2: Making Prettier Listings

Our customer has one more request (customers always seem to have one more request, don't they?). The listing of all the products is ugly. Can we "pretty it up" a bit? And, while we're in there, can we also display the product image along with the image URL?

We're faced with a dilemma here. As developers, we're trained to respond to these kinds of requests with a sharp intake of breath, a knowing shake of the head, and a murmured "You want what?" At the same time, we also like to show off a bit. In the end, the fact that it's fun to make these kinds of changes using Rails wins out, and we fire up our trusty editor.

Before we get too far, though, it would be nice if we had a consistent set of test data to work with. We *could* use our scaffold-generated interface and type data in from the browser. However, if we did this, future developers working on our codebase would have to do the same. And, if we were working as part of a team on this project, each member of the team would have to enter their own data. It would be nice if we could load the data into our table in a more controlled way. It turns out that we can. Rails has the ability to import seed data.

To start, we simply modify the file in the db directory named seeds.rb.

download
↪ page xxi

We then add the code to populate the products table. This uses the create method of the Product model. The following is an extract from that file. Rather than type the file by hand, you might want to download the file from the sample code available online.[3]

While you're there, copy the images[4] and the depot.css file[5] into corresponding places (public/images and public/stylesheets in your application). Be warned: this seeds.rb script removes existing data from the products table before loading in the new data. You might not want to run it if you've just spent several hours typing your own data into your application!

`depot_b/db/seeds.rb`

```
Product.delete_all
# . . .
Product.create(:title => 'Programming Ruby 1.9',
  :description =>
    %{<p>
        Ruby is the fastest growing and most exciting dynamic language
        out there. If you need to get working programs delivered fast,
        you should add Ruby to your toolbox.
      </p>},
  :image_url => '/images/ruby.jpg',
  :price => 49.50)
# . . .
```

---

3. http://media.pragprog.com/titles/rails4/code/depot_b/db/seeds.rb
4. http://media.pragprog.com/titles/rails4/code/depot_b/public/images/
5. http://media.pragprog.com/titles/rails4/code/depot_b/public/stylesheets/depot.css

(Note that this code uses %{...}. This is an alternative syntax for double-quoted string literals, convenient for use with long strings. Note also that because it uses Rails' create method, it will fail silently if records cannot be inserted because of validation errors.)

To populate your products table with test data, simply run the following command:

```
depot> rake db:seed
```

Now let's get the product listing tidied up. There are two pieces to this. Eventually we'll be writing some HTML that uses CSS to style the presentation. But for this to work, we'll need to tell the browser to fetch the stylesheet.

We need somewhere to put our CSS style definitions. All scaffold-generated applications use the stylesheet scaffold.css in the directory public/stylesheets. Rather than alter this file, we created a new application stylesheet, depot.css, and put it in the same directory.[6]

Finally, we need to link these stylesheets into our HTML page. If you look at the .html.erb files we've created so far, you won't find any reference to stylesheets. You won't even find the HTML <head> section where such references would normally live. Instead, Rails keeps a separate file that is used to create a standard page environment for the entire application. This file, called application.html.erb, is a Rails layout and lives in the layouts directory:

> depot_b/app/views/layouts/application.html.erb

```
<!DOCTYPE html>
<html>
<head>
  <title>Depot</title>
  <%= stylesheet_link_tag :all %>
  <%= javascript_include_tag :defaults %>
  <%= csrf_meta_tag %>
</head>
<body>

<%= yield %>

</body>
</html>
```

The stylesheet_link_tag creates an HTML <link> tag, which loads stylesheets from the public/stylesheets directory. We could list the name of the stylesheets we want to be linked here, but because it is currently set up to load all stylesheets, we'll leave it alone for now. We'll look at the rest of the file in more detail in Section 8.2, *Iteration C2: Adding a Page Layout*, on page 92.

---

6. If you haven't already done so, you can download this stylesheet from http://media.pragprog. com/titles/rails4/code/depot_b/public/stylesheets/depot.css.

Now that we have the stylesheet all in place, we will use a simple table-based template, editing the file index.html.erb in app/views/products, replacing the scaffold-generated view:

`depot_b/app/views/products/index.html.erb`

```erb
<div id="product_list">
  <h1>Listing products</h1>

  <table>
  <% @products.each do |product| %>
    <tr class="<%= cycle('list_line_odd', 'list_line_even') %>">

      <td>
        <%= image_tag(product.image_url, :class => 'list_image') %>
      </td>

      <td class="list_description">
        <dl>
          <dt><%= product.title %></dt>
          <dd><%= truncate(strip_tags(product.description),
                    :length => 80) %></dd>
        </dl>
      </td>

      <td class="list_actions">
        <%= link_to 'Show', product %><br/>
        <%= link_to 'Edit', edit_product_path(product) %><br/>
        <%= link_to 'Destroy', product,
                    :confirm => 'Are you sure?',
                    :method => :delete %>
      </td>
    </tr>
  <% end %>
  </table>
</div>

<br />

<%= link_to 'New product', new_product_path %>
```

Even this simple template uses a number of built-in Rails features:

- The rows in the listing have alternating background colors. The Rails helper method called cycle does this by setting the CSS class of each row to either list_line_even or list_line_odd, automatically toggling between the two style names on successive lines.

- The truncate helper is used to display just the first eighty characters of the description. But before we call truncate, we called strip_tags in order to remove the HTML tags from the description.

- Look at the link_to 'Destroy' line. See how it has the parameter :confirm => 'Are you sure?'. If you click this link, Rails arranges for your browser to pop up a dialog box asking for confirmation before following the link and

What's with :method => :delete?

You may have noticed that the scaffold-generated Destroy link includes the parameter :method => :delete. This determines which method is called in the ProductsController class and also affects which HTTP method is used.

Browsers use HTTP to talk with servers. HTTP defines a set of verbs that browsers can employ and defines when each can be used. A regular hyperlink, for example, uses an HTTP GET request. A GET request is defined by HTTP to be used to retrieve data; it isn't supposed to have any side effects. Using this parameter in this way indicates that an HTTP DELETE method should be used for this hyperlink. Rails uses this information to determine which action in the controller to route this request to.

Note that when used within a browser, Rails will substitute the POST HTTP method for PUT and DELETE methods and in the process tack on an additional parameter so that the router can determine the original intent. Either way, the request will not be cached or triggered by web crawlers.

deleting the product. (Also, see the sidebar on the current page for some inside scoop on this action.)

We loaded some test data into the database, we rewrote the index.html.erb file that displays the listing of products, we added a depot.css stylesheet, and that stylesheet was loaded into our page by the layout file application.html.erb. Now, let's bring up a browser and point to http://localhost:3000/products; the resulting product listing might look something like the following:

So, we proudly show our customer her new product listing, and she's pleased. Now it is time to create the storefront.

What We Just Did

In this chapter, we laid the groundwork for our store application:

- We created a development database.
- We used migration to create and modify the schema in our development database.
- We created the products table and used the scaffold generator to write an application to maintain it.
- We updated an application-wide layout as well as a controller-specific view in order to show a list of products.

What we've done did not require much effort, and it got us up and running quickly. Databases are vital to this application but need not be scary—in fact, in many cases we can defer the selection of the database to later and simply get started using the default that Rails provides.

Getting the model right is more important at this stage. As we will soon see, simple selection of data types doesn't always fully capture the *essence* of all the properties of the model, even in this small application, so that's what we will tackle next.

Playtime

Here's some stuff to try on your own:

- If you're feeling frisky, you can experiment with rolling back the migration. Just type the following:

```
depot> rake db:rollback
```

Your schema will be transported back in time, and the products table will be gone. Calling rake db:migrate again will re-create it. You will also want to reload the seed data. More information can be found in Chapter 23, *Migrations*, on page 375.

- We mentioned version control in Section 1.5, *Version Control*, on page 9, and now would be a great point at which to save your work. Should you happen to choose Git (highly recommended, by the way), there is a tiny bit of configuration you need to do first; basically, all you need to do is provide your name and email address. This typically goes into your home directory, with a filename of .gitconfig. Ours looks like this:

```
[user]
name = Sam Ruby
email = rubys@intertwingly.net
```

You can verify the configuration with the following command:

```
depot> git repo-config --get-regexp user.*
```

Rails also provides a file named .gitignore, which tells Git which files are not to be version controlled:

`depot_b/.gitignore`

```
.bundle
db/*.sqlite3
log/*.log
tmp/
```

Note that because this filename begins with a dot, Unix-based operating systems won't show it by default in directory listings. Use ls -a to see it.

At this point, you are fully configured. The only tasks that remain are to initialize a repository, add all the files, and commit them with a commit message:

```
depot> git init
depot> git add .
depot> git commit -m "Depot Scaffold"
```

This may not seem very exciting at this point, but it does mean you are more free to experiment. Should you overwrite or delete a file that you didn't mean to, you can get back to this point by issuing a single command:

```
depot> git checkout .
```

Chapter 7

Task B: Validation and Unit Testing

At this point, we have an initial model for a product, as well as a complete maintenance application for this data provided for us by Rails scaffolding. In this chapter, we are going to focus on making the model more bulletproof—as in, making sure that errors in the data provided never get committed to the database—before we proceed to other aspects of the Depot application in subsequent chapters.

7.1 Iteration B1: Validating!

While playing with the results of iteration A1, our client noticed something. If she entered an invalid price or forgot to set up a product description, the application happily accepted the form and added a line to the database. Although a missing description is embarrassing, a price of $0.00 actually costs her money, so she asked that we add validation to the application. No product should be allowed in the database if it has an empty title or description field, an invalid URL for the image, or an invalid price.

So, where do we put the validation? The model layer is the gatekeeper between the world of code and the database. Nothing to do with our application comes out of the database or gets stored into the database that doesn't first go through the model. This makes models an ideal place to put validations; it doesn't matter whether the data comes from a form or from some programmatic manipulation in our application. If a model checks it before writing to the database, then the database will be protected from bad data.

Let's look again at the source code of the model class (in app/models/product.rb):

```
class Product < ActiveRecord::Base
end
```

Adding our validation should be fairly clean. Let's start by validating that the text fields all contain something before a row is written to the database. We do this by adding some code to the existing model:

```
validates :title, :description, :image_url, :presence => true
```

The validates method is the standard Rails validator. It will check one or more model fields against one or more conditions.

:presence => true tells the validator to check that each of the named fields is present and its contents are not empty. In Figure 7.1, on the facing page, we can see what happens if we try to submit a new product with none of the fields filled in. It's pretty impressive: the fields with errors are highlighted, and the errors are summarized in a nice list at the top of the form. That's not bad for one line of code. You might also have noticed that after editing and saving the product.rb file you didn't have to restart the application to test your changes—the same reloading that caused Rails to notice the earlier change to our schema also means it will always use the latest version of our code.

We'd also like to validate that the price is a valid, positive number. We'll use the delightfully named numericality option to verify that the price is a valid number. We also pass the rather verbosely named :greater_than_or_equal_to option a value of 0.01:

```
validates :price, :numericality => {:greater_than_or_equal_to => 0.01}
```

Now, if we add a product with an invalid price, the appropriate message will appear, as shown in Figure 7.2, on page 78.

Why test against 1 cent, rather than zero? Well, it's possible to enter a number such as 0.001 into this field. Because the database stores just two digits after the decimal point, this would end up being zero in the database, even though it would pass the validation if we compared against zero. Checking that the number is at least 1 cent ensures only correct values end up being stored.

We have two more items to validate. First, we want to make sure each product has a unique title. One more line in the Product model will do this. The uniqueness validation will perform a simple check to ensure that no other row in the products table has the same title as the row we're about to save:

```
validates :title, :uniqueness => true
```

regular expression
↪ page 42
Lastly, we need to validate that the URL entered for the image is valid. We'll do this using the format option, which matches a field against a regular expression. For now we'll just check that the URL ends with one of .gif, .jpg, or .png.

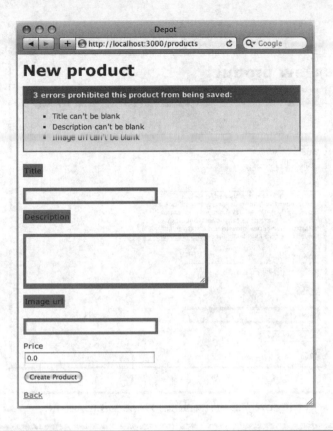

Figure 7.1: VALIDATING THAT FIELDS ARE PRESENT

```
validates :image_url, :format => {
  :with    => %r{\.(gif|jpg|png)$}i,
  :message => 'must be a URL for GIF, JPG or PNG image.'
}
```

Later, we'd probably want to change this form to let the user select from a list of available images, but we'd still want to keep the validation to prevent malicious folks from submitting bad data directly.

So, in a couple of minutes we've added validations that check the following:

- The field's title, description, and image URL are not empty.

- The price is a valid number not less than $0.01.

- The title is unique among all products.

- The image URL looks reasonable.

Figure 7.2: THE PRICE FAILS VALIDATION.

Your updated Product model should look like this:

depot_b/app/models/product.rb

```ruby
class Product < ActiveRecord::Base
  validates :title, :description, :image_url, :presence => true
  validates :price, :numericality => {:greater_than_or_equal_to => 0.01}
  validates :title, :uniqueness => true
  validates :image_url, :format => {
    :with    => %r{\.(gif|jpg|png)$}i,
    :message => 'must be a URL for GIF, JPG or PNG image.'
  }
end
```

Nearing the end of this cycle, we ask our customer to play with the application, and she's a lot happier. It took only a few minutes, but the simple act of adding validation has made the product maintenance pages seem a lot more solid.

Before we move on, we once again try our tests:

```
rake test
```

Uh-oh. This time we see failures. Two, actually—one in test_should_create_
product and one in test_should_update_product. Clearly something we did caused
something to do with the creation and updating of products to fail. This isn't
all that surprising. After all, when you think about it, isn't that the whole point
of validation?

The solution is to give valid test data in test/functional/products_controller_test.rb:

depot_c/test/functional/products_controller_test.rb

```ruby
require 'test_helper'

class ProductsControllerTest < ActionController::TestCase
  setup do
    @product = products(:one)
    @update = {
      :title       => 'Lorem Ipsum',
      :description => 'Wibbles are fun!',
      :image_url   => 'lorem.jpg',
      :price       => 19.95
    }
  end

  test "should get index" do
    get :index
    assert_response :success
    assert_not_nil assigns(:products)
  end

  test "should get new" do
    get :new
    assert_response :success
  end

  test "should create product" do
    assert_difference('Product.count') do
      post :create, :product => @update
    end

    assert_redirected_to product_path(assigns(:product))
  end

  # ...
  test "should update product" do
    put :update, :id => @product.to_param, :product => @update
    assert_redirected_to product_path(assigns(:product))
  end

  # ...
end
```

After making this change, we rerun the tests, and they report that all is well. But all that means is that we didn't break anything. We need to do more than that. We need to make sure the validation code that we just added not only works now but will continue to work as we make further changes. We'll cover functional tests in more detail in Section 8.4, *Iteration C4: Functional Testing of Controllers*, on page 97. As for now, it is time for us to write some unit tests.

7.2 Iteration B2: Unit Testing of Models

One of the real joys of the Rails framework is that it has support for testing baked right in from the start of every project. As we have seen, from the moment you create a new application using the rails command, Rails starts generating a test infrastructure for you.

Let's take a peek inside the unit subdirectory to see what's already there:

```
depot> ls test/unit
helpers product_test.rb
```

product_test.rb is the file that Rails created to hold the unit tests for the model we created earlier with the generate script. This is a good start, but Rails can help us only so much.

Let's see what kind of test goodies Rails generated inside test/unit/product_test.rb when we generated that model:

`depot_b/test/unit/product_test.rb`

```
require 'test_helper'

class ProductTest < ActiveSupport::TestCase
  # Replace this with your real tests.
  test "the truth" do
    assert true
  end
end
```

The generated ProductTest is a subclass of ActiveSupport::TestCase. The fact that ActiveSupport::TestCase is a subclass of the Test::Unit::TestCase class tells us that Rails generates tests based on the Test::Unit framework that comes preinstalled with Ruby. This is good news because it means if we've already been testing our Ruby programs with Test::Unit tests (and why wouldn't we be?), then we can build on that knowledge to test Rails applications. If you're new to Test::Unit, don't worry. We'll take it slow.

Inside this test case, Rails generated a single test called "the truth". The test...do syntax may seem surprising at first, but here Active Support is combining a class method, optional parentheses, and a block to make defining a test method just the tiniest bit simpler for you. Sometimes it is the little things that make all the difference.

The assert line in this method is an actual test. It isn't much of one, though—all it does is test that true is true. Clearly, this is a placeholder, but it's an important one, because it lets us see that all the testing infrastructure is in place.

A Real Unit Test

Let's get onto the business of testing validation. First, if we create a product with no attributes set, we'll expect it to be invalid and for there to be an error associated with each field. We can use the model's errors and invalid? methods to see whether it validates, and we can use the any? method of the error list to see whether there is an error associated with a particular attribute.

Now that we know *what* to test, we need to know *how* to tell the test framework whether our code passes or fails. We do that using *assertions*. An assertion is simply a method call that tells the framework what we expect to be true. The simplest assertion is the method assert, which expects its argument to be true. If it is, nothing special happens. However, if the argument to assert is false, the assertion fails. The framework will output a message and will stop executing the test method containing the failure. In our case, we expect that an empty Product model will not pass validation, so we can express that expectation by asserting that it isn't valid.

```
assert product.invalid?
```

Replace the the truth test with the following code:

depot_c/test/unit/product_test.rb

```
test "product attributes must not be empty" do
  product = Product.new
  assert product.invalid?
  assert product.errors[:title].any?
  assert product.errors[:description].any?
  assert product.errors[:price].any?
  assert product.errors[:image_url].any?
end
```

We can rerun just the unit tests by issuing the command rake test:units. When we do so, we now see the test executed successfully:

```
depot> rake test:units
Loaded suite lib/rake/rake_test_loader
Started
..
Finished in 0.092314 seconds.
1 tests, 5 assertions, 0 failures, 0 errors
```

Sure enough, the validation kicked in, and all our assertions passed.

Clearly at this point we can dig deeper and exercise individual validations. Let's look at just three of the many possible tests.

First, we'll check that the validation of the price works the way we expect:

depot_c/test/unit/product_test.rb

```ruby
test "product price must be positive" do
  product = Product.new(:title       => "My Book Title",
                        :description => "yyy",
                        :image_url   => "zzz.jpg")
  product.price = -1
  assert product.invalid?
  assert_equal "must be greater than or equal to 0.01",
    product.errors[:price].join('; ')

  product.price = 0
  assert product.invalid?
  assert_equal "must be greater than or equal to 0.01",
    product.errors[:price].join('; ')

  product.price = 1
  assert product.valid?
end
```

In this code we create a new product and then try setting its price to -1, 0, and +1, validating the product each time. If our model is working, the first two should be invalid, and we verify the error message associated with the price attribute is what we expect. Because the list of error messages is an array, we use the handy join[1] method to concatenate each message, and we express the assertion based on the assumption that there is only one such message.

The last price is acceptable, so we assert that the model is now valid. (Some folks would put these three tests into three separate test methods—that's perfectly reasonable.)

Next, we'll test that we're validating that the image URL ends with one of .gif, .jpg, or .png:

depot_c/test/unit/product_test.rb

```ruby
def new_product(image_url)
  Product.new(:title       => "My Book Title",
              :description => "yyy",
              :price       => 1,
              :image_url   => image_url)
end

test "image url" do
  ok = %w{ fred.gif fred.jpg fred.png FRED.JPG FRED.Jpg
           http://a.b.c/x/y/z/fred.gif }
  bad = %w{ fred.doc fred.gif/more fred.gif.more }
```

---

1. http://ruby-doc.org/core/classes/Array.html#M002182

```
ok.each do |name|
  assert new_product(name).valid?, "#{name} shouldn't be invalid"
end

bad.each do |name|
  assert new_product(name).invalid?, "#{name} shouldn't be valid"
end
end
```

Here we've mixed things up a bit. Rather than write out the nine separate tests, we've used a couple of loops—one to check the cases we expect to pass validation and the second to try cases we expect to fail. At the same time, we factored out the common code between the two loops.

You'll notice that we've also added an extra parameter to our assert method calls. All of the testing assertions accept an optional trailing parameter containing a string. This will be written along with the error message if the assertion fails and can be useful for diagnosing what went wrong.

Finally, our model contains a validation that checks that all the product titles in the database are unique. To test this one, we're going to need to store product data in the database.

One way to do this would be to have a test create a product, save it, then create another product with the same title, and try to save it too. This would clearly work. But there's a much simpler way—we can use Rails *fixtures*.

Test Fixtures

In the world of testing, a *fixture* is an environment in which you can run a test. If you're testing a circuit board, for example, you might mount it in a test fixture that provides it with the power and inputs needed to drive the function to be tested.

In the world of Rails, a test fixture is simply a specification of the initial contents of a model (or models) under test. If, for example, we want to ensure that our products table starts off with known data at the start of every unit test, we can specify those contents in a fixture, and Rails will take care of the rest.

You specify fixture data in files in the test/fixtures directory. These files contain test data in either comma-separated value (CSV) or YAML format. For our tests, we'll use YAML, the preferred format. Each fixture file contains the data for a single model. The name of the fixture file is significant; the base name of the file must match the name of a database table. Because we need some data for a Product model, which is stored in the products table, we'll add it to the file called products.yml.

YAML
↪ page 47

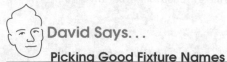

David Says. . .

Picking Good Fixture Names

Just like the names of variables in general, you want to keep the names of fixtures as self-explanatory as possible. This increases the readability of the tests when you're asserting that product(:valid_order_for_fred) is indeed Fred's valid order. It also makes it a lot easier to remember which fixture you're supposed to test against without having to look up p1 or order4. The more fixtures you get, the more important it is to pick good fixture names. So, starting early keeps you happy later.

But what do we do with fixtures that can't easily get a self-explanatory name like valid_order_for_fred? Pick natural names that you have an easier time associating to a role. For example, instead of using order1, use christmas_order. Instead of customer1, use fred. Once you get into the habit of natural names, you'll soon be weaving a nice little story about how fred is paying for his christmas_order with his invalid_credit_card first, then paying with his valid_credit_card, and finally choosing to ship it all off to aunt_mary.

Association-based stories are key to remembering large worlds of fixtures with ease.

Rails already created this fixture file when we first created the model:

`depot_b/test/fixtures/products.yml`

```
# Read about fixtures at http://ar.rubyonrails.org/classes/Fixtures.html

one:
  title: MyString
  description: MyText
  image_url: MyString
  price: 9.99

two:
  title: MyString
  description: MyText
  image_url: MyString
  price: 9.99
```

The fixture file contains an entry for each row that we want to insert into the database. Each row is given a name. In the case of the Rails-generated fixture, the rows are named *one* and *two*. This name has no significance as far as the database is concerned—it is not inserted into the row data. Instead, as we'll see shortly, the name gives us a convenient way to reference test data inside our test code. They also are the names used in the generated integration tests, so for now, we'll leave them alone.

Inside each entry you'll see an indented list of name/value pairs. Just like in your config/database.yml, you must use spaces, not tabs, at the start of each of the data lines, and all the lines for a row must have the same indentation. Be careful as you make changes because you will need to make sure the names of the columns are correct in each entry; a mismatch with the database column names may cause a hard-to-track-down exception.

Let's add some more data to the fixture file with something we can use to test our Product model:

`depot_c/test/fixtures/products.yml`

```
ruby:
  title:        Programming Ruby 1.9
  description:
    Ruby is the fastest growing and most exciting dynamic
    language out there.  If you need to get working programs
    delivered fast, you should add Ruby to your toolbox.
  price:        49.50
  image_url:    ruby.png
```

Now that we have a fixture file, we want Rails to load the test data into the products table when we run the unit test. And, in fact, Rails is already doing this (convention over configuration for the win!), but you can control which fixtures to load by specifying the following line in test/unit/product_test.rb:

```
class ProductTest < ActiveSupport::TestCase
►  fixtures :products
  #...
end
```

The fixtures directive loads the fixture data corresponding to the given model name into the corresponding database table before each test method in the test case is run. The name of the fixture file determines the table that is loaded, so using :products will cause the products.yml fixture file to be used.

Let's say that again another way. In the case of our ProductTest class, adding the fixtures directive means that the products table will be emptied out and then populated with the three rows defined in the fixture before each test method is run.

Note that most of the scaffolding that Rails generates doesn't contain calls to the fixtures method. That's because the default for tests is to load all fixtures before running the test. Because that default is generally the one you want, there usually isn't any need to change it. Once again, conventions are used to eliminate the need for unnecessary configuration.

The products method indexes into the table created by loading the fixture. We need to change the index used to match the name we gave in the fixture itself.

So far, we've been doing all our work in the development database. Now that we're running tests, though, Rails needs to use a test database. If you look in the database.yml file in the config directory, you'll notice Rails actually created a configuration for three separate databases:

- db/development.sqlite3 will be our development database. All of our programming work will be done here.

- db/test.sqlite3 is a test database.

- db/production.sqlite3 is the production database. Our application will use this when we put it online.

Each test method gets a freshly initialized table in the test database, loaded from the fixtures we provide. This is automatically done by the rake test command but can be done separately by running rake db:test:prepare.

Using Fixture Data

Now that we know how to get fixture data into the database, we need to find ways of using it in our tests.

Clearly, one way would be to use the finder methods in the model to read the data. However, Rails makes it easier than that. For each fixture it loads into a test, Rails defines a method with the same name as the fixture. You can use this method to access preloaded model objects containing the fixture data: simply pass it the name of the row as defined in the YAML fixture file, and it'll return a model object containing that row's data. In the case of our product data, calling products(:ruby) returns a Product model containing the data we defined in the fixture. Let's use that to test the validation of unique product titles:

`depot_c/test/unit/product_test.rb`

```ruby
test "product is not valid without a unique title" do
  product = Product.new(:title       => products(:ruby).title,
                        :description => "yyy",
                        :price       => 1,
                        :image_url   => "fred.gif")

  assert !product.save
  assert_equal "has already been taken", product.errors[:title].join('; ')
end
```

The test assumes that the database already includes a row for the Ruby book. It gets the title of that existing row using this:

```ruby
products(:ruby).title
```

It then creates a new Product model, setting its title to that existing title. It asserts that attempting to save this model fails and that the title attribute has the correct error associated with it.

If you want to avoid using a hard-coded string for the Active Record error, you can compare the response against its built-in error message table:

```
depot_o/test/unit/product_test.rb

test "product is not valid without a unique title - i18n" do
  product = Product.new(:title       => products(:ruby).title,
                        :description => "yyy",
                        :price       => 1,
                        :image_url   => "fred.gif")

  assert !product.save
  assert_equal I18n.translate('activerecord.errors.messages.taken'),
          product.errors[:title].join('; ')
end
```

We will cover the I18n functions in Chapter 15, *Task J: Internationalization*, on page 205.

Now we can feel confident that our validation code not only works but will continue to work. Our product now has a model, a set of views, a controller, and a set of unit tests. It will serve as a good foundation upon which to build the rest of the application.

What We Just Did

In just about a dozen lines of code, we augmented that generated code with validation:

- We ensured that required fields were present.

- We ensured that price fields were numeric and at least one cent.

- We ensured that titles were unique.

- We ensured that images matched a given format.

- We updated the unit tests that Rails provided, both to conform to the constraints we have imposed on the model and to verify the new code that we added.

We show this to our customer, and although she agrees that this is something an administrator could use, she says that it certainly isn't anything that she would feel comfortable turning loose on her customers. Clearly, in the next iteration we are going to have to focus a bit on the user interface.

Playtime

Here's some stuff to try on your own:

- If you are using Git, now might be a good time to commit our work. You can first see what files we changed by using the git status command:

```
depot> git status
# On branch master
# Changed but not updated:
#   (use "git add <file>..." to update what will be committed)
#
# modified:   app/models/product.rb
# modified:   test/fixtures/products.yml
# modified:   test/functional/products_controller_test.rb
# modified:   test/unit/product_test.rb
# no changes added to commit (use "git add" and/or "git commit -a")
```

Since we only modified some existing files and didn't add any new ones, we can combine the git add and git commit commands and simply issue a single git commit command with the -a option:

```
depot> git commit -a -m 'Validation!'
```

With this done, we can play with abandon, secure in the knowledge that we can return to this state at any time using a single git checkout . command.

- The validation option :length checks the length of a model attribute. Add validation to the Product model to check that the title is at least ten characters long.

- Change the error message associated with one of your validations.

(You'll find hints at http://www.pragprog.com/wikis/wiki/RailsPlayTime.)

In this chapter, we'll see

- writing our own views,
- using layouts to decorate pages,
- integrating CCC,
- using helpers, and
- writing functional tests.

Chapter 8

Task C: Catalog Display

All in all, it's been a successful set of iterations. We gathered the initial requirements from our customer, documented a basic flow, worked out a first pass at the data we'll need, and put together the maintenance page for the Depot application's products. It hasn't even taken many lines of code. We even have a small but growing test suite.

Thus emboldened, it's on to our next task. We chatted about priorities with our customer, and she said she'd like to start seeing what the application looks like from the buyer's point of view. Our next task is to create a simple catalog display.

This also makes a lot of sense from our point of view. Once we have the products safely tucked into the database, it should be fairly simple to display them. It also gives us a basis from which to develop the shopping cart portion of the code later.

We should also be able to draw on the work we just did in the product maintenance task—the catalog display is really just a glorified product listing.

Finally, we will also need to complement our unit tests for the model with some functional tests for the controller.

8.1 Iteration C1: Creating the Catalog Listing

We've already created the products controller, used by the seller to administer the Depot application. Now it's time to create a second controller, one that interacts with the paying customers. Let's call it Store.

```
depot> rails generate controller store index
    create    app/controllers/store_controller.rb
     route    get "store/index"
    invoke    erb
    create      app/views/store
    create      app/views/store/index.html.erb
```

◄ 89 ►

```
invoke   test_unit
create     test/functional/store_controller_test.rb
invoke   helper
create     app/helpers/store_helper.rb
invoke   test_unit
create       test/unit/helpers/store_helper_test.rb
```

Just as in the previous chapter, where we used the generate utility to create a controller and associated scaffolding to administer the products, here we've asked it to create a controller (class StoreController in the file store_controller.rb) containing a single action method, index.

While everything is already set up for this action to be accessed via http://localhost:3000/store/index (feel free to try it!), we can do better. Let's simplify things for the user and make this the root URL for the website. We do this by editing config/routes.rb:

`depot_d/config/routes.rb`

```
Depot::Application.routes.draw do
  get "store/index"

  resources :products

  # ...

  # You can have the root of your site routed with "root"
  # just remember to delete public/index.html.
  # root :to => "welcome#index"
► root :to => 'store#index', :as => 'store'

  # ...
end
```

At the top of the file, you can see the lines added to support the store and products controllers. We'll leave those lines alone. Further along in the file you will see a commented-out line that defines a *root* for the website. Either uncomment out that line or add a new line immediately after that one. All we are changing on that line is the name of the controller (from welcome to store) and adding :as => store. The latter tells Rails to create a store_path variable, just like the say_goodbye_path that we saw on page 26.

Note that the comments also instruct you to delete public/index.html. Let's do that now:[1]

```
depot> rm public/index.html
```

---

1. Windows users will want to execute erase public\index.html; if you are managing your source code using Git, you will want to use git rm public/index.html.

Let's try it. Point a browser at http://localhost:3000/, and up pops our web page:

It might not make us rich, but at least we know everything is wired together correctly. The page even tells us where to find the template file that draws this page.

Let's start by displaying a simple list of all the products in our database. We know that eventually we'll have to be more sophisticated, breaking them into categories, but this will get us going.

We need to get the list of products out of the database and make it available to the code in the view that will display the table. This means we have to change the index method in store_controller.rb. We want to program at a decent level of abstraction, so let's just assume we can ask the model for a list of the products we can sell:

depot_d/app/controllers/store_controller.rb

```
class StoreController < ApplicationController
  def index
    @products = Product.all
  end

end
```

We ask our customer whether she had a preference regarding the order things should be listed in, and we jointly decided to see what happened if we displayed the products in alphabetical order. We do this by adding a default_scope call to the Product model. Default scopes apply to all queries that start with this model.

depot_d/app/models/product.rb

```
class Product < ActiveRecord::Base
  default_scope :order => 'title'

  # validation stuff...
end
```

Now we need to write our view template. To do this, edit the file index.html.erb in app/views/store. (Remember that the path name to the view is built from the name of the controller [store] and the name of the action [index]. The .html.erb part signifies an ERb template that produces an HTML result.)

depot_d/app/views/store/index.html.erb

```
<% if notice %>
<p id="notice"><%= notice %></p>
<% end %>

<h1>Your Pragmatic Catalog</h1>

<% @products.each do |product| %>
  <div class="entry">
    <%= image_tag(product.image_url) %>
    <h3><%= product.title %></h3>
    <%= sanitize(product.description) %>
    <div class="price_line">
      <span class="price"><%= product.price %></span>
    </div>
  </div>
<% end %>
```

Note the use of the sanitize method for the description. This allows us to safely add HTML stylings to make the descriptions more interesting for our customers. (Note that this decision opens a potential security hole, but because product descriptions are created by people who work for our company, we think that the risk is minimal. See the discussion on page 408 for details.)

We've also used the image_tag helper method. This generates an HTML <img> tag using its argument as the image source.

Hitting Refresh brings up the display shown on Figure 8.1, on the facing page. It's pretty ugly, because we haven't yet included the CSS stylesheet. The customer happens to be walking by as we ponder this, and she points out that she'd also like to see a decent-looking title and sidebar on public-facing pages.

At this point in the real world, we'd probably want to call in the design folks—we've all seen too many programmer-designed websites to feel comfortable inflicting another on the world. But Pragmatic Web Designer is off getting inspiration on a beach somewhere and won't be back until later in the year, so let's put a placeholder in for now. It's time for another iteration.

8.2 Iteration C2: Adding a Page Layout

The pages in a typical website often share a similar layout—the designer will have created a standard template that is used when placing content. Our job is to add this page decoration to each of the store pages.

Figure 8.1: OUR FIRST (UGLY) CATALOG PAGE

By naming the layout application.html.erb, it will be the layout used for all views for all controllers that don't otherwise provide a layout. By using only one layout, we can change the look and feel of the entire site by editing just one file. This makes us feel better about putting a placeholder page layout in for now; we can update it when the designer eventually returns from the islands.

We place this file in the app/views/layouts directory:

depot_e/app/views/layouts/application.html.erb

```
Line 1   <!DOCTYPE html>
   -     <html>
   -     <head>
   -       <title>Pragprog Books Online Store</title>
   5       <%= stylesheet_link_tag "scaffold" %>
   -       <%= stylesheet_link_tag "depot", :media => "all" %>
   -       <%= javascript_include_tag :defaults %>
   -       <%= csrf_meta_tag %>
   -     </head>
```

```
10   <body id="store">
 -     <div id="banner">
 -       <%= image_tag("logo.png") %>
 -       <%= @page_title || "Pragmatic Bookshelf" %>
 -     </div>
15     <div id="columns">
 -       <div id="side">
 -         <a href="http://www....">Home</a><br />
 -         <a href="http://www..../faq">Questions</a><br />
 -         <a href="http://www..../news">News</a><br />
20         <a href="http://www..../contact">Contact</a><br />
 -       </div>
 -       <div id="main">
 -         <%= yield %>
 -       </div>
25     </div>
 -   </body>
 - </html>
```

Apart from the usual HTML gubbins, this layout has four Rails-specific items. Line 6 uses a Rails helper method to generate a *<link>* tag to our depot.css stylesheet. Line 8 sets up all the behind-the-scenes data needed to prevent cross-site request forgery attacks, which will be important once we add forms in Chapter 12, *Task G: Check Out!*, on page 145. On line 13, we set the page heading to the value in the instance variable @page_title. The real magic, however, takes place on line 23. When we invoke yield, Rails automatically substitutes in the page-specific content—the stuff generated by the view invoked by this request. Here, this will be the catalog page generated by index.html.erb.

yield
↪ page 44

To make this all work, we need to add the following to our depot.css stylesheet:

depot_e/public/stylesheets/depot.css

```css
/* Styles for main page */

#banner {
  background: #9c9;
  padding-top: 10px;
  padding-bottom: 10px;
  border-bottom: 2px solid;
  font: small-caps 40px/40px "Times New Roman", serif;
  color: #282;
  text-align: center;
}

#banner img {
  float: left;
}

#columns {
  background: #141;
}
```

Figure 8.2: CATALOG WITH LAYOUT ADDED

```
#main {
  margin-left: 17em;
  padding-top: 4ex;
  padding-left: 2em;
  background: white;
}

#side {
  float: left;
  padding-top: 1em;
  padding-left: 1em;
  padding-bottom: 1em;
  width: 16em;
  background: #141;
}

#side a {
  color: #bfb;
  font-size: small;
}
```

Hit Refresh, and the browser window looks something like Figure 8.2. It won't win any design awards, but it'll show our customer roughly what the final page will look like.

Looking at this page, we spot a minor problem with how prices are displayed. The database stores the price as a number, but we'd like to show it as dollars and cents. A price of 12.34 should be shown as $12.34, and 13 should display as $13.00. We'll tackle that next.

8.3 Iteration C3: Using a Helper to Format the Price

Ruby provides a sprintf function that can be used to format prices. We could place logic that makes use of this function directly in the view. For example, we could say this:

```
<span class="price"><%= sprintf("$%0.02f", product.price) %></span>
```

This would work, but it embeds knowledge of currency formatting into the view. Should we want to internationalize the application later, this would be a maintenance problem.

Instead, let's use a helper method to format the price as a currency. Rails has an appropriate one built in—it's called number_to_currency.

Using our helper in the view is simple; in the index template, we change this:

```
<span class="price"><%= product.price %></span>
```

to the following:

depot_e/app/views/store/index.html.erb

```
<span class="price"><%= number_to_currency(product.price) %></span>
```

Sure enough, when we hit Refresh, we see a nicely formatted price:

Although it looks nice enough, we are starting to get a nagging feeling that we really should be running and writing tests for all this new functionality, particularly after our experience of adding logic to our model.

8.4 Iteration C4: Functional Testing of Controllers

Now for the moment of truth. Before we focus on writing new tests, we need to determine whether we have actually broken anything. Remembering our experience after we added validation logic to our model, with some trepidation we run our tests again:

```
depot> rake test
```

This time, all is well. We added a lot, but we didn't break anything. That's a relief, but our work is not yet done; we still need tests for what we just added.

The unit testing of models that we did previously seemed straightforward enough. We called a method and compared what it returned against what we expected it to return. But now we are dealing with a server that processes requests and a user viewing responses in a browser. What we will need is *functional* tests that verify that the model, view, and controller work well together. Never fear, Rails makes this easy too.

First, let's take a look at what Rails generated for us:

depot_d/test/functional/store_controller_test.rb

```ruby
require 'test_helper'

class StoreControllerTest < ActionController::TestCase
  test "should get index" do
    get :index
    assert_response :success
  end

end
```

The *should get index* test gets the index and asserts that a successful response is expected. That certainly seems straightforward enough. That's a reasonable beginning, but we also want to verify that the response contains our layout, our product information, and our number formatting. Let's see what that looks like in code:

depot_e/test/functional/store_controller_test.rb

```ruby
require 'test_helper'

class StoreControllerTest < ActionController::TestCase
  test "should get index" do
    get :index
    assert_response :success
▶   assert_select '#columns #side a', :minimum => 4
▶   assert_select '#main .entry', 3
▶   assert_select 'h3', 'Programming Ruby 1.9'
▶   assert_select '.price', /\$[,\d]+\.\d\d/
  end

end
```

The four lines we added take a look *into* the HTML that is returned, using CSS selector notation. As a refresher, selectors that start with a number sign (#) match on id attributes, selectors that start with a dot (.) match on class attributes, and selectors that contain no prefix at all match on element names.

So, the first select test looks for an element named a that is contained in an element with an id with a value of side, which is contained within an element with an id with a value of columns. This test verifies that there are a minimum of four such elements. Pretty powerful stuff, assert_select, eh?

The next three lines verify that all of our products are displayed. The first verifies that there are three elements with a class name of entry inside the main portion of the page. The next line verifies that there is an h3 element with the title of the Ruby book that we had entered previously. The third line verifies that the price is formatted correctly. These assertions are based on the test data that we had put inside our fixtures:

depot_e/test/fixtures/products.yml

```
# Read about fixtures at http://ar.rubyonrails.org/classes/Fixtures.html

one:
  title: MyString
  description: MyText
  image_url: MyString
  price: 9.99

two:
  title: MyString
  description: MyText
  image_url: MyString
  price: 9.99

ruby:
  title:        Programming Ruby 1.9
  description:
    Ruby is the fastest growing and most exciting dynamic
    language out there.  If you need to get working programs
    delivered fast, you should add Ruby to your toolbox.
  price:        49.50
  image_url:    ruby.png
```

If you noticed, the type of test that assert_select performs varies based on the type of the second parameter. If it is a number, it will be treated as a quantity. If it is a string, it will be treated as an expected result. Another useful type of test is a regular expression, which is what we use in our final assertion. We verify that there is a price that has a value that contains a dollar sign followed by any number (but at least one), commas, or digits; followed by a decimal point; followed by two digits.

regular expression
↪ page 42

One final point before we move on: both validation and functional tests will test the behavior of controllers only; they will not retroactively affect any objects that already exist in the database or in fixtures. In the previous example, two products contain the same title. Such data will cause no problems and will go undetected up to the point where such records are modified and saved.

We've touched on only a few things that assert_select can do. More information can be found in the online documentation.[2]

That's a lot of verification in just a few lines of code. We can see that it works by rerunning just the functional tests (after all, that's all we changed):

```
depot> rake test:functionals
```

Now we not only have something recognizable as a storefront, we have tests that ensure that all of the pieces—the model, view, and controller—are all working together to produce the desired result. Although this sounds like a lot, with Rails it was easy. In fact, it was mostly HTML and CSS and not much in the way of code or tests.

What We Just Did

We've put together the basis of the store's catalog display. The steps were as follows:

1. Create a new controller to handle customer-centric interactions.

2. Implement the default index action.

3. Add a default_scope to the Product model to specify the order to list the items on the website.

4. Implement a view (an .html.erb file) and a layout to contain it (another .html.erb file).

5. Use a helper to format prices the way we want.

6. Make use of a CSS stylesheet.

7. Write functional tests for our controller.

It's time to check it all in and move on to the next task, namely, making a shopping cart!

Playtime

Here's some stuff to try on your own:

- Add a date and time to the sidebar. It doesn't have to update; just show the value at the time the page was displayed.

---

2. http://api.rubyonrails.org/classes/ActionDispatch/Assertions/SelectorAssertions.html

- Experiment with setting various number_to_currency helper method options, and see the effect on your catalog listing.

- Write some functional tests for the product maintenance application using assert_select. The tests will need to be placed into the test/functional/ products_controller_test.rb file.

- Just a reminder—the end of an iteration is a good time to save your work using Git. If you have been following along, you have the basics you need at this point. We will pick things back up, in terms of exploring more Git functionality, in Section 16.2, *Prepping Your Deployment Server*, on page 233.

(You'll find hints at http://www.pragprog.com/wikis/wiki/RailsPlayTime.)

In this chapter, we'll see

- sessions and session management,
- adding relationships between models, and
- adding a button to add a product to a cart.

Chapter 9

Task D: Cart Creation

Now that we have the ability to display a catalog containing all our wonderful products, it would be nice to be able to sell them. Our customer agrees, so we've jointly decided to implement the shopping cart functionality next. This is going to involve a number of new concepts, including sessions, relationships between models, and adding a button to the view, so let's get started.

9.1 Iteration D1: Finding a Cart

As users browse our online catalog, they will (we hope) select products to buy. The convention is that each item selected will be added to a virtual shopping cart, held in our store. At some point, our buyers will have everything they need and will proceed to our site's checkout, where they'll pay for the stuff in the carts.

This means that our application will need to keep track of all the items added to the cart by the buyer. To do that, we'll keep a cart in the database and store its unique identifier, cart.id, in the session. Every time a request comes in, we can recover the identity from the session and use it to find the cart in the database.

Let's go ahead and create a cart:

```
depot> rails generate scaffold cart
  ...
depot> rake db:migrate
==  CreateCarts: migrating ========================================================
-- create_table(:carts)
   -> 0.0012s
==  CreateCarts: migrated (0.0014s) ===============================================
```

Rails makes the current session look like a hash to the controller, so we'll store the id of the cart in the session by indexing it with the symbol :cart_id.

```
depot_f/app/controllers/application_controller.rb
```

```ruby
class ApplicationController < ActionController::Base
  protect_from_forgery

  private

    def current_cart
      Cart.find(session[:cart_id])
    rescue ActiveRecord::RecordNotFound
      cart = Cart.create
      session[:cart_id] = cart.id
      cart
    end
end
```

The current_cart starts by getting the :cart_id from the session object and then attempts to find a cart corresponding to this id. If such a cart record is not found (which will happen if the id is nil or invalid for any reason), then this method will proceed to create a new Cart, store the id of the created cart into the session, and then return the new cart.

Note that we place the current_cart method in the ApplicationController and mark it as private. This makes this method available only to controllers and furthermore prevents Rails from ever making it available as an action on the controller.

private
↪ page 46

9.2 Iteration D2: Connecting Products to Carts

We're looking at sessions because we need somewhere to keep our shopping cart. We'll cover sessions in more depth in Section 20.3, *Rails Sessions*, on page 323, but for now let's move on to implement the cart.

Let's keep things simple. A cart contains a set of products. Based on the diagram on page 59, combined with a brief chat with our customer, we can now generate the Rails models and populate the migrations to create the corresponding tables:

```
depot> rails generate scaffold line_item product_id:integer  cart_id:integer
  . . .
depot> rake db:migrate
==  CreateLineItems: migrating ================================================
-- create_table(:line_items)
   -> 0.0013s
==  CreateLineItems: migrated (0.0014s) =======================================
```

The database now has a place to store the relationships between line items, carts, and products. However, the Rails application does not. We need to add some declarations to our model files that specify their interrelationships.

Open the newly created cart.rb file in app/models, and add a call to has_many:

```
class Cart < ActiveRecord::Base
▶   has_many :line_items, :dependent => :destroy
end
```

That has_many :line_items part of the directive is fairly self-explanatory: a cart (potentially) has many associated line items. These are linked to the cart because each line item contains a reference to its cart's id. The :dependent => :destroy part indicates that the existence of line items is dependent on the existence of the cart. If we destroy a cart, deleting it from the database, we'll want Rails also to destroy any line items that are associated with that cart.

Next, we'll specify links in the opposite direction, from the line item to the carts and products tables. To do this, we use the belongs_to declaration twice in the line_item.rb file:

depot_f/app/models/line_item.rb

```
class LineItem < ActiveRecord::Base
▶   belongs_to :product
▶   belongs_to :cart
end
```

belongs_to tells Rails that rows in the line_items table are children of rows in the carts and products tables. No line item can exist unless the corresponding cart and product rows exist. There's an easy way to remember where to put belongs_to declarations: if a table has foreign keys, the corresponding model should have a belongs_to for each.

Just what do these various declarations do? Basically, they add navigation capabilities to the model objects. Because we added the belongs_to declaration to LineItem, we can now retrieve its Product and display the book's title:

```
li = LineItem.find(...)
puts "This line item is for #{li.product.title}"
```

And because Cart is declared to have many line items, we can reference them (as a collection) from a cart object:

```
cart = Cart.find(...)
puts "This cart has #{cart.line_items.count} line items"
```

Now, for completeness, we should add a has_many directive to our Product model. After all, if we have lots of carts, each product might have many line items referencing it. This time, we will make use of validation code to prevent removal of products that are referenced by line items.

depot_f/app/models/product.rb

```
class Product < ActiveRecord::Base
  default_scope :order => 'title'
▶   has_many :line_items
```

```
▶       before_destroy :ensure_not_referenced_by_any_line_item

        #...

▶       private

▶         # ensure that there are no line items referencing this product
▶         def ensure_not_referenced_by_any_line_item
▶           if line_items.empty?
▶             return true
▶           else
▶             errors.add(:base, 'Line Items present')
▶             return false
▶           end
▶         end
      end
```

Here we declare that a product has many line items and define a *hook* method named ensure_not_referenced_by_any_line_item. A hook method is a method that Rails calls automatically at a given point in an object's life. In this case, the method will be called before Rails attempts to destroy a row in the database. If the hook method returns false, the row will not be destroyed.

Note that we have direct access to the errors object. This is the same place that the validates stores error messages. Errors can be associated with individual attributes, but in this case we associate the error with the base object itself.

We'll have more to say about intermodel relationships starting on page 272.

9.3 Iteration D3: Adding a Button

Now that that's done, it is time to add an Add to Cart button for each product.

There is no need to create a new controller or even a new action. Taking a look at the actions provided by the scaffold generator, you find index, show, new, edit, create, update, and destroy. The one that matches this operation is create. (new may sound similar, but its use is to get a form that is used to solicit input for a subsequent create action.)

Once this decision is made, the rest follows. What are we creating? Certainly not a Cart or even a Product. What we are creating is a LineItem. Looking at the comment associated with the create method in app/controllers/line_items_controller.rb, you see that this choice also determines the URL to use (/line_items) and the HTTP method (POST).

This choice even suggests the proper UI control to use. When we added links before, we used link_to, but links default to using HTTP GET. We want to use POST, so we will add a button this time; this means we will be using the button_to method.

We could connect the button to the line item by specifying the URL, but again we can let Rails take care of this for us by simply appending _path to the controller's name. In this case, we will use line_items_path.

However, there's a problem with this: how will the line_items_path method know *which* product to add to our cart? We'll need to pass it the id of the product corresponding to the button. That's easy enough—all we need to do is add the :product_id option to the line_items_path call. We can even pass in the product instance itself—Rails knows to extract the id from the record in circumstances such as these.

In all, the *one* line that we need to add to our index.html.erb looks like this:

`depot_f/app/views/store/index.html.erb`

```
<% if notice %>
<p id="notice"><%= notice %></p>
<% end %>

<h1>Your Pragmatic Catalog</h1>

<% @products.each do |product| %>
  <div class="entry">
    <%= image_tag(product.image_url) %>
    <h3><%= product.title %></h3>
    <%= sanitize(product.description) %>
    <div class="price_line">
      <span class="price"><%= number_to_currency(product.price) %></span>
      <%= button_to 'Add to Cart', line_items_path(:product_id => product) %>
    </div>
  </div>
<% end %>
```

There's one more formatting issue. button_to creates an HTML *<form>*, and that form contains an HTML *<div>*. Both of these are normally block elements, which will appear on the next line. We'd like to place them next to the price, so we need a little CSS magic to make them inline:

`depot_f/public/stylesheets/depot.css`

```
#store .entry form, #store .entry form div {
  display: inline;
}
```

Now our index page looks like Figure 9.1, on the next page. But before we push the button, we need to modify the create method in the line items controller to expect a product id as a form parameter. Here's where we start to see how important the id field is in our models. Rails identifies model objects (and the corresponding database rows) by their id fields. If we pass an id to create, we're uniquely identifying the product to add.

Figure 9.1: NOW THERE'S AN *Add to Cart* BUTTON.

Why the create method? The default HTTP method for a link is a get, the default HTTP method for a button is a post, and Rails uses these conventions to determine which method to call. See the comments inside the app/controllers/ line_items_controller.rb file to see other conventions. We'll be making extensive use of these conventions inside the Depot application.

Now let's modify the LineItemsController to find the shopping cart for the current session (creating one if there isn't one there already), add the selected product to that cart, and display the cart contents. All we need to modify is a few lines of code in the create method in app/controllers/line_items_controller.rb:[1]

depot_f/app/controllers/line_items_controller.rb

```
def create
▶   @cart = current_cart
▶   product = Product.find(params[:product_id])
▶   @line_item = @cart.line_items.build(:product => product)

    respond_to do |format|
      if @line_item.save
▶       format.html { redirect_to(@line_item.cart,
          :notice => 'Line item was successfully created.') }
        format.xml  { render :xml => @line_item,
          :status => :created, :location => @line_item }
      else
        format.html { render :action => "new" }
        format.xml  { render :xml => @line_item.errors,
          :status => :unprocessable_entity }
      end
    end
end
```

---

1. Some lines have been wrapped to fit on the page.

We use the current_cart method we implemented on page 102 to find (or create) a cart in the session. Next, we use the params object to get the :product_id parameter from the request. The params object is important inside Rails applications. It holds all of the parameters passed in a browser request. We store the result in a local variable because there is no need to make this available to the view.

We then pass that product we found into @cart.line_items.build. This causes a new line item relationship to be built between the @cart object and the product. You can build the relationship from either end, and Rails will take care of establishing the connections on both sides.

We save the resulting line item into an instance variable named @line_item.

The remainder of this method takes care of XML requests, which we will cover on page 405, and handling errors, which we will cover in more detail on page 116. But for now, we only want to modify one more thing: once the line item is created, we want to redirect you to the cart instead of back to the line item itself. Since the line item object knows how to find the cart object, all we need to do is add .cart to the method call.

As we changed the function of our controller, we know that we will need to update the corresponding functional test. We need to pass a product id on the call to create and change what we expect for the target of the redirect. We do this by updating test/functional/line_items_controller_test.rb.

depot_g/test/functional/line_items_controller_test.rb

```
test "should create line_item" do
  assert_difference('LineItem.count') do
►   post :create, :product_id => products(:ruby).id
  end

► assert_redirected_to cart_path(assigns(:line_item).cart)
end
```

While we haven't talked about the assigns method to date, that's because it has been in generated scaffolding. This method gives us access to the variables that have been (or can be) assigned by views.

We now rerun the functional tests:

```
depot> rake test:functionals
```

Confident that the code works as intended, we try the `Add to Cart` buttons in our browser.

And here is what we see:

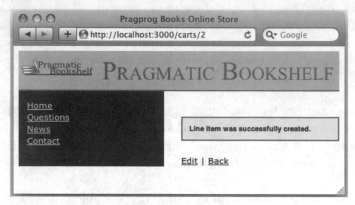

This is a bit underwhelming. Although we have scaffolding for the cart, when we created it, we didn't provide any attributes, so the view doesn't have anything to show. For now, let's write a trivial template (we'll tart it up in a minute):

depot_f/app/views/carts/show.html.erb

```
<h2>Your Pragmatic Cart</h2>
<ul>
  <% @cart.line_items.each do |item| %>
    <li><%= item.product.title %></li>
  <% end %>
</ul>
```

So, with everything plumbed together, let's hit Refresh in our browser and see our simple view displayed:

Go back to http://localhost:3000/, the main catalog page, and add a different product to the cart. You'll see the original two entries plus our new item in your cart. It looks like we have sessions working. It's time to show our customer, so we call her over and proudly display our handsome new cart. Somewhat to our dismay, she makes that *tsk-tsk* sound that customers make just before telling you that you clearly don't get something.

Real shopping carts, she explains, don't show separate lines for two of the same product. Instead, they show the product line once with a quantity of 2. Looks like we're lined up for our next iteration.

What We Just Did

It has been a busy, productive day so far. We've added a shopping cart to our store, and along the way we've dipped our toes into some neat Rails features:

- We created a Cart object in one request and were able to successfully locate the same cart in subsequent requests using a session object,
- We added a private method in the base class for all of our controllers, making it accessible to all of our controllers,
- We created relationships between carts and line items and relationships between line items and products, and we were able to navigate using these relationships.
- We added a button that caused a product to be posted to a cart, causing a new line item to be created.

Playtime

Here's some stuff to try on your own:

- Change the application so that clicking a book's image will also invoke the create action. Hint: the first parameter to link_to is placed in the generated <a> tag, and the Rails helper image_tag constructs an HTML <*img*> tag. Include a call to it as the first parameter to a link_to call. Be sure to include :method => :post in your html_options on your call to link_to.
- Add a new variable to the session to record how many times the user has accessed the store controller's index action. Note that the first time this page is accessed, your count won't be in the session. You can test for this with code like this:

```
if session[:counter].nil?
   ...
```

If the session variable isn't there, you'll need to initialize it. Then you'll be able to increment it.

- Pass this counter to your template, and display it at the top of the catalog page. Hint: the pluralize helper (described on page 346) might be useful when forming the message you display.
- Reset the counter to zero whenever the user adds something to the cart.
- Change the template to display the counter only if it is greater than five.

(You'll find hints at http://pragprog.com/wikis/wiki/RailsPlayTime.)

In this chapter, we'll see

- modifying the schema and existing data,
- error diagnosis and handling,
- the flash, and
- logging.

Chapter 10

Task E: A Smarter Cart

Although we have rudimentary cart functionality implemented, we have much to do. To start with, we will need to recognize when customers add multiples of the same item to the cart. Once that's done, we will also have to make sure that the cart itself can handle error cases and communicate problems encountered along the way to the customer or the system administrator, as appropriate.

10.1   Iteration E1: Creating a Smarter Cart

Associating a count with each product in our cart is going to require us to modify the line_items table. We've used migration before in Section 6.1, *Applying the Migration*, on page 63 to update the schema of the database. While that was as part of creating the initial scaffolding for a model, the basic approach is the same.

```
depot> rails generate migration add_quantity_to_line_items quantity:integer
```

Rails can tell from the name of the migration that you are adding one or more columns to the line_items table and can pick up the names and data types for each column from the last argument. The two patterns that Rails matches on is add_XXX_to_TABLE and remove_XXX_from_TABLE where the value of XXX is ignored; what matters is the list of column names and types that appear after the migration name.

The only thing Rails can't tell is what a reasonable default is for this column. In many cases, a null value would do, but let's make it the value 1 for existing carts by modifying the migration before we apply it:

depot_g/db/migrate/20110211000004_add_quantity_to_line_items.rb

```
class AddQuantityToLineItems < ActiveRecord::Migration
  def self.up
    add_column :line_items, :quantity, :integer, :default => 1
  end
```

```
    def self.down
      remove_column :line_items, :quantity
    end
  end
```

Once complete, we run the migration:

```
depot> rake db:migrate
```

Now we need a smart add_product method in our Cart, one that checks whether our list of items already includes the product we're adding; if it does, it bumps the quantity, and if it doesn't, it builds a new LineItem:

depot_g/app/models/cart.rb

```
def add_product(product_id)
  current_item = line_items.find_by_product_id(product_id)
  if current_item
    current_item.quantity += 1
  else
    current_item = line_items.build(:product_id => product_id)
  end
  current_item
end
```

This code uses a clever little Active Record trick. You see that the first line of the method calls find_by_product_id. But we don't define a method with that name. However, Active Record notices the call to an undefined method and spots that it starts with the string find_by and ends with the name of a column. It then dynamically constructs a finder method for us, adding it to our class. We talk more about these dynamic finders starting on page 277.

We also need to modify the line item controller to make use of this method:

depot_g/app/controllers/line_items_controller.rb

```
def create
  @cart = current_cart
  product = Product.find(params[:product_id])
► @line_item = @cart.add_product(product.id)

  respond_to do |format|
    if @line_item.save
      format.html { redirect_to(@line_item.cart,
        :notice => 'Line item was successfully created.') }
      format.xml  { render :xml => @line_item,
        :status => :created, :location => @line_item }
    else
      format.html { render :action => "new" }
      format.xml  { render :xml => @line_item.errors,
        :status => :unprocessable_entity }
    end
  end
end
```

There's one last quick change to the show view to use this new information:

depot_g/app/views/carts/show.html.erb

```erb
<h2>Your Pragmatic Cart</h2>
<ul>
  <% @cart.line_items.each do |item| %>
    <li><%= item.quantity %> &times; <%= item.product.title %></li>
  <% end %>
</ul>
```

Now that all the pieces are in place, we can go back to the store page and hit the `Add to Cart` button for a product that is already in the cart. What we are likely to see is a mixture of individual products listed separately and a single product listed with a quantity of two. This is because we added a quantity of 1 to existing columns instead of collapsing multiple rows when possible. What we need to do next is migrate the data.

We start by creating a migration:

```
depot> rails generate migration combine_items_in_cart
```

This time, Rails can't infer what we are trying to do, so it is entirely up to us to fill in the self.up method:

depot_g/db/migrate/20110211000005_combine_items_in_cart.rb

```ruby
def self.up
  # replace multiple items for a single product in a cart with a single item
  Cart.all.each do |cart|
    # count the number of each product in the cart
    sums = cart.line_items.group(:product_id).sum(:quantity)

    sums.each do |product_id, quantity|
      if quantity > 1
        # remove individual items
        cart.line_items.where(:product_id=>product_id).delete_all

        # replace with a single item
        cart.line_items.create(:product_id=>product_id, :quantity=>quantity)
      end
    end
  end
end
```

This is easily the most extensive code we've seen so far. Let's look at it in small pieces:

- We start by iterating over each cart.

iterating
↪ page 43

- For each cart, we get a sum of the quantity fields for each of the line items associated with this cart, grouped by product_id. The resulting sums will be a list of ordered pairs of product_ids and quantity.

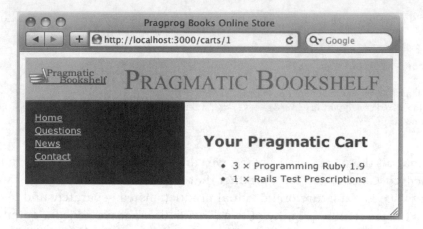

Figure 10.1: A CART WITH QUANTITIES

- We iterate over these sums, extracting the product_id and quantity from each.

- In cases where the quantity is greater than 1, we will delete all of the individual line items associated with this cart and this product and replace them with a single line item with the correct quantity.

Note how easily and elegantly Rails enables you to express this algorithm.

With this code in place, we apply this migration just like any other migration:

```
depot> rake db:migrate
```

We can immediately see the results by looking at the cart, as shown in Figure 10.1. Although we have reason to be pleased with ourselves, we are not done yet. An important principle of migrations is that each step needs to be reversible, so we implement a self.down too. This method finds line items with a quantity of greater than 1; adds new line items for this cart and product, each with a quantity of 1; and finally deletes the line item. The following code accomplishes that:

```
depot_g/db/migrate/20110211000005_combine_items_in_cart.rb
def self.down
  # split items with quantity>1 into multiple items
  LineItem.where("quantity>1").each do |line_item|
    # add individual items
    line_item.quantity.times do
      LineItem.create :cart_id=>line_item.cart_id,
        :product_id=>line_item.product_id, :quantity=>1
    end
```

Figure 10.2: A CART AFTER THE MIGRATION HAS BEEN ROLLED BACK

```
    # remove original item
    line_item.destroy
  end
end
```

At this point, we can just as easily roll back our migration with a single command:

depot> `rake db:rollback`

Once again, we can immediately inspect the results by looking at the cart, as shown in Figure 10.2. Once we reapply the migration (with the rake db:migrate command), we have a cart that maintains a count for each of the products it holds, and we have a view that displays that count.

Happy that we have something presentable, we call our customer over and show her the result of our morning's work. She's pleased—she can see the site starting to come together. However, she's also troubled, having just read an article in the trade press on the way ecommerce sites are being attacked and compromised daily. She read that one kind of attack involves feeding requests with bad parameters into web applications, hoping to expose bugs and security flaws. She noticed that the link to the cart looks like carts/*nnn*, where *nnn* is our internal cart id. Feeling malicious, she manually types this request into a browser, giving it a cart id of *wibble*. She's not impressed when our application displays the page in Figure 10.3, on the following page. This reveals way too much information about our application. It also seems fairly unprofessional. So, our next iteration will be spent making the application more resilient.

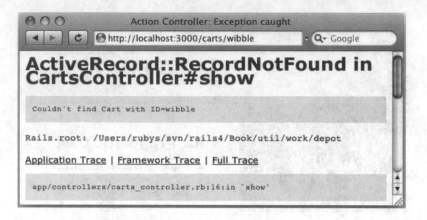

Figure 10.3: OUR APPLICATION SPILLS ITS GUTS.

10.2 Iteration E2: Handling Errors

Looking at the page displayed in Figure 10.3, it's apparent that our application raised an exception at line 16 of the carts controller.[1] That turns out to be this line:

```
@cart = Cart.find(params[:id])
```

If the cart cannot be found, Active Record raises a RecordNotFound exception, which we clearly need to handle. The question arises—how?

We could just silently ignore it. From a security standpoint, this is probably the best move, because it gives no information to a potential attacker. However, it also means that should we ever have a bug in our code that generates bad cart ids, our application will appear to the outside world to be unresponsive—no one will know there has been an error.

Instead, we'll take two actions when an exception is raised. First, we'll log the fact to an internal log file using Rails' logger facility.[2] Second, we'll redisplay the catalog page, along with a short message to the user (something along the lines of "Invalid cart") so they can continue to use our site.

Rails has a convenient way of dealing with errors and error reporting. It defines a structure called a *flash*. A flash is a bucket (actually closer to a Hash) in which you can store stuff as you process a request. The contents of the flash are available to the next request in this session before being deleted automatically.

---

1. Your line number might be different. We have some book-related formatting stuff in our source files.
2. http://guides.rubyonrails.org/debugging_rails_applications.html#the-logger

Typically the flash is used to collect error messages. For example, when our show method detects that it was passed an invalid cart id, it can store that error message in the flash area and redirect to the index action to redisplay the catalog. The view for the index action can extract the error and display it at the top of the catalog page. The flash information is accessible within the views by using the flash accessor method.

Why couldn't we just store the error in any old instance variable? Remember that after a redirect is sent by our application to the browser, the browser sends a new request back to our application. By the time we receive that request, our application has moved on—all the instance variables from previous requests are long gone. The flash data is stored in the session in order to make it available between requests.

Armed with all this background about flash data, we can now change our show method to intercept bad product ids and report on the problem:

depot_h/app/controllers/carts_controller.rb

```
# GET /carts/1
# GET /carts/1.xml
def show
►   begin
      @cart = Cart.find(params[:id])
►   rescue ActiveRecord::RecordNotFound
►     logger.error "Attempt to access invalid cart #{params[:id]}"
►     redirect_to store_url, :notice => 'Invalid cart'
►   else
      respond_to do |format|
        format.html # show.html.erb
        format.xml  { render :xml => @cart }
      end
►   end
end
```

The rescue clause intercepts the exception raised by Cart.find. In the handler, we do the following:

- Use the Rails logger to record the error. Every controller has a logger attribute. Here we use it to record a message at the error logging level.

- Redirect to the catalog display using the redirect_to method. The :notice parameter specifies a message to be stored in the flash as a notice. Why redirect, rather than just display the catalog, here? If we redirect, the user's browser will end up displaying the store URL, rather than http://.../cart/wibble. We expose less of the application this way. We also prevent the user from retriggering the error by hitting the Reload button.

With this code in place, we can rerun our customer's problematic query. This time, when we enter the following URL:

```
http://localhost:3000/carts/wibble
```

Figure 10.4: MUCH MORE USER-ORIENTED ERROR MESSAGE

we don't see a bunch of errors in the browser. Instead, the catalog page is displayed. If we look at the end of the log file (development.log in the log directory), we'll see our message:

```
Processing CartsController#show to */*
  sql (0.0ms)   SELECT * FROM "products" WHERE (("products"."id" = 2))
Completed in 38ms (View: 28, DB: 0) | 200 [unknown]
  Parameters: {"id"=>"1"}
  sql (0.0ms)   SELECT * FROM "carts" WHERE (("carts"."id" = 0))

ActiveRecord::RecordNotFound (Couldn't find Cart with ID=wibble):
  app/controllers/carts_controller.rb:22:in 'show'
  :   :
```

▶ Attempt to access invalid cart wibble
```
  sql (0.0ms)   SELECT * FROM "carts" WHERE (("carts"."id" = 0))
Redirected to http://127.0.0.1:3000/store
  :   :
Rendering app/views/store/index.html.erb
Rendering template within app/views/layouts/application.html.erb
```

For a much more user-friendly result, see Figure 10.4.

On Unix machines, we'd probably use a command such as tail or less to view this file. On Windows, you could use your favorite editor. It's often a good idea to keep a window open showing new lines as they are added to this file. In Unix you'd use tail -f. You can download a tail command for Windows from http://gnuwin32.sourceforge.net/packages/coreutils.htm or get a GUI-based tool from http://tailforwin32.sourceforge.net/. Finally, some OS X users use Console.app to track log files. Just say open *name.log* at the command line.

Sensing the end of an iteration, we call our customer over and show her that the error is now properly handled. She's delighted and continues to play with the application. She notices a minor problem on our new cart display—there's no way to empty items out of a cart. This minor change will be our next iteration. We should make it before heading home.

10.3 Iteration E3: Finishing the Cart

We know by now that in order to implement the "empty cart" function, we have to add a link to the cart and modify the destroy method in the carts controller to clean up the session. Let's start with the template and again use the button_to method to put a button on the page:

```
depot_h/app/views/carts/show.html.erb
```

```erb
<h2>Your Pragmatic Cart</h2>
<ul>
  <% @cart.line_items.each do |item| %>
    <li><%= item.quantity %> &times; <%= item.product.title %></li>
  <% end %>
</ul>
```
► `<%= button_to 'Empty cart', @cart, :method => :delete,`
► `    :confirm => 'Are you sure?' %>`

In the controller, we'll modify the destroy method to ensure that the user is deleting their own cart (think about it!) and to remove the cart from the session before redirecting to the index page with a notification message:

```
depot_h/app/controllers/carts_controller.rb
```

```ruby
def destroy
```
► `  @cart = current_cart`
```ruby
  @cart.destroy
```
► `  session[:cart_id] = nil`

```ruby
  respond_to do |format|
```
► `    format.html { redirect_to(store_url,`
► `      :notice => 'Your cart is currently empty') }`
```ruby
    format.xml  { head :ok }
  end
end
```

And we update the corresponding test in test/functional/carts_controller_test.rb.

```
depot_i/test/functional/carts_controller_test.rb
```

```ruby
test "should destroy cart" do
  assert_difference('Cart.count', -1) do
```
► `    session[:cart_id] = @cart.id`
```ruby
    delete :destroy, :id => @cart.to_param
  end
```
► `  assert_redirected_to store_path`
```ruby
end
```

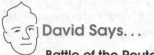

David Says...
Battle of the Routes: product_path vs. product_url

It can seem hard in the beginning to know when to use product_path and when to use product_url when you want to link or redirect to a given route. In reality, it's really quite simple.

When you use product_url, you'll get the full enchilada with protocol and domain name, like http://example.com/products/1. That's the thing to use when you're doing redirect_to because the HTTP spec requires a fully qualified URL when doing 302 Redirect and friends. You also need the full URL if you're redirecting from one domain to another, ala product_url(:domain => "example2.com", :product => product).

The rest of the time, you can happily use product_path. This will generate only the /products/1 part, and that's all you need when doing links or pointing forms, like link_to "My lovely product", product_path(product).

Now the confusing part is that oftentimes the two are interchangeable because of lenient browsers. You can do a redirect_to with a product_path and it'll probably work, but it won't be valid according to spec. And you can link_to a product_url, but then you're littering up your HTML with needless characters, which is a bad idea too.

Now when we view our cart and click the [Empty Cart] button, we get taken back to the catalog page, and a nice little message says this:

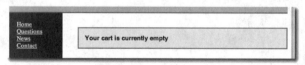

We can also remove the flash message that is automatically generated when a line item is added:

`depot_i/app/controllers/line_items_controller.rb`

```ruby
def create
  @cart = current_cart
  product = Product.find(params[:product_id])
  @line_item = @cart.add_product(product.id)

  respond_to do |format|
    if @line_item.save
      format.html { redirect_to(@line_item.cart) }
      format.xml  { render :xml => @line_item,
        :status => :created, :location => @line_item }
```

```
      else
        format.html { render :action => "new" }
        format.xml  { render :xml => @line_item.errors,
          :status => :unprocessable_entity }
      end
    end
end
```

And, finally, we'll get around to tidying up the cart display. Rather than use *<li>* elements for each item, let's use a table. Again, we'll rely on CSS to do the styling:

depot_i/app/views/carts/show.html.erb

```
<div class="cart_title">Your Cart</div>
<table>
  <% @cart.line_items.each do |item| %>
    <tr>
      <td><%= item.quantity %>&times;</td>
      <td><%= item.product.title %></td>
      <td class="item_price"><%= number_to_currency(item.total_price) %></td>
    </tr>
  <% end %>

  <tr class="total_line">
    <td colspan="2">Total</td>
    <td class="total_cell"><%= number_to_currency(@cart.total_price) %></td>
  </tr>

</table>

<%= button_to 'Empty cart', @cart, :method => :delete,
    :confirm => 'Are you sure?' %>
```

To make this work, we need to add a method to both the LineItem and Cart models that returns the total price for the individual line item and entire cart, respectively. First the line item, which involves only simple multiplication:

depot_i/app/models/line_item.rb

```
def total_price
  product.price * quantity
end
```

We implement the Cart method using Rails' nifty Array::sum method to sum the prices of each item in the collection:

depot_i/app/models/cart.rb

```
def total_price
  line_items.to_a.sum { |item| item.total_price }
end
```

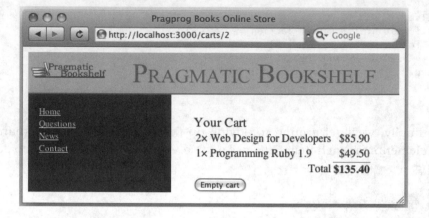

Figure 10.5: CART DISPLAY WITH A TOTAL

Then we need to add a small bit to our depot.css stylesheet:

`depot_i/public/stylesheets/depot.css`

```
/* Styles for the cart in the main page */

#store .cart_title {
  font: 120% bold;
}

#store .item_price, #store .total_line {
  text-align: right;
}

#store .total_line .total_cell {
  font-weight: bold;
  border-top: 1px solid #595;
}
```

For a nicer-looking cart, see Figure 10.5.

What We Just Did

Our shopping cart is now something the client is happy with. Along the way, we covered the following:

- Adding a column to an existing table, with a default value
- Migrating existing data into the new table format
- Providing a flash notice of an error that was detected
- Using the logger to log events
- Deleting a record
- Adjusting the way a table is rendered, using CSS

But, just as we think we've wrapped this functionality up, our customer wanders over with a copy of *Information Technology and Golf Weekly*. Apparently, there's an article about a new style of browser interface, where stuff gets updated on the fly. "Ajax," she says, proudly. Hmmm...let's look at that tomorrow.

Playtime

Here's some stuff to try on your own:

- Create a migration that copies the product price into the line item, and change the add_product method in the Cart model to capture the price whenever a new line item is created.

- Add unit tests that add unique products and duplicate products. Note that you will need to modify the fixture to refer to products and carts by name, for example product: ruby.

- Check products and line items for other places where a user-friendly error message would be in order.

- Add the ability to delete individual line items from the cart. This will require buttons on each line, and such buttons will need to be linked to the destroy action in the LineItemsController.

(You'll find hints at http://www.pragprog.com/wikis/wiki/RailsPlayTime.)

In this chapter, we'll see

- using partial templates,
- rendering into the page layout,
- updating pages dynamically with Ajax and RJS,
- highlighting changes with Script.aculo.us,
- hiding and revealing DOM elements, and
- testing the Ajax updates.

Chapter 11

Task F: Add a Dash of Ajax

Our customer wants us to add Ajax support to the store. But just what *is* Ajax?

In the old days (up until 2005 or so), browsers were treated as really dumb devices. When you wrote a browser-based application, you'd send stuff to the browser and then forget about that session. At some point, the user would fill in some form fields or click a hyperlink, and your application would get woken up by an incoming request. It would render a complete page back to the user, and the whole tedious process would start afresh. That's exactly how our Depot application behaves so far.

But it turns out that browsers aren't really that dumb (who knew?). They can run code. Almost all browsers can run JavaScript. And it turns out that the JavaScript in the browser can interact behind the scenes with the application on the server, updating the stuff the user sees as a result. Jesse James Garrett named this style of interaction *Ajax* (which once stood for Asynchronous JavaScript and XML but now just means "making browsers suck less").

So, let's Ajaxify our shopping cart. Rather than having a separate shopping cart page, let's put the current cart display into the catalog's sidebar. Then, we'll add the Ajax magic that updates the cart in the sidebar without redisplaying the whole page.

Whenever you work with Ajax, it's good to start with the non-Ajax version of the application and then gradually introduce Ajax features. That's what we'll do here. For starters, let's move the cart from its own page and put it in the sidebar.

◄ 125 ►

11.1 Iteration F1: Moving the Cart

Currently, our cart is rendered by the show action in the CartController and the corresponding .html.erb template. What we'd like to do is to move that rendering into the sidebar. This means it will no longer be in its own page. Instead, we'll render it in the layout that displays the overall catalog. And that's easy using *partial templates*.

Partial Templates

Programming languages let you define *methods*. A method is a chunk of code with a name: invoke the method by name, and the corresponding chunk of code gets run. And, of course, you can pass parameters to a method, which lets you write one piece of code that can be used in many different circumstances.

You can think of Rails partial templates (*partials* for short) as a kind of method for views. A partial is simply a chunk of a view in its own separate file. You can invoke (render) a partial from another template or from a controller, and the partial will render itself and return the results of that rendering. And, just as with methods, you can pass parameters to a partial, so the same partial can render different results.

We'll use partials twice in this iteration. First, let's look at the cart display itself:

`depot_i/app/views/carts/show.html.erb`

```
<div class="cart_title">Your Cart</div>
<table>
  <% @cart.line_items.each do |item| %>
    <tr>
      <td><%= item.quantity %>&times;</td>
      <td><%= item.product.title %></td>
      <td class="item_price"><%= number_to_currency(item.total_price) %></td>
    </tr>
  <% end %>

  <tr class="total_line">
    <td colspan="2">Total</td>
    <td class="total_cell"><%= number_to_currency(@cart.total_price) %></td>
  </tr>

</table>

<%= button_to 'Empty cart', @cart, :method => :delete,
    :confirm => 'Are you sure?' %>
```

It creates a list of table rows, one for each item in the cart. Whenever you find yourself iterating like this, you might want to stop and ask yourself, is this too much logic in a template? It turns out we can abstract away the loop using partials (and, as we'll see, this also sets the stage for some Ajax magic later). To do this, we'll make use of the fact that you can pass a collection to the method that renders partial templates, and that method will automatically invoke the partial once for each item in the collection. Let's rewrite our cart view to use this feature:

depot_j/app/views/carts/show.html.erb

```
<div class="cart_title">Your Cart</div>
<table>
▶    <%= render(@cart.line_items) %>

  <tr class="total_line">
    <td colspan="2">Total</td>
    <td class="total_cell"><%= number_to_currency(@cart.total_price) %></td>
  </tr>

</table>

<%= button_to 'Empty cart', @cart, :method => :delete,
    :confirm => 'Are you sure?' %>
```

That's a lot simpler. The render method will iterate over any collection that is passed to it. The partial template itself is simply another template file (by default in the same directory as the object being rendered and with the name of the table as the name). However, to keep the names of partials distinct from regular templates, Rails automatically prepends an underscore to the partial name when looking for the file. That means we need to name our partial _line_item.html.erb and place it in the app/views/line_items directory.

depot_j/app/views/line_items/_line_item.html.erb

```
<tr>
  <td><%= line_item.quantity %>&times;</td>
  <td><%= line_item.product.title %></td>
  <td class="item_price"><%= number_to_currency(line_item.total_price) %></td>
</tr>
```

There's something subtle going on here. Inside the partial template, we refer to the current object using the variable name that matches the name of the template. In this case, the partial is named line_item, so inside the partial we expect to have a variable called line_item.

So, now we've tidied up the cart display, but that hasn't moved it into the sidebar. To do that, let's revisit our layout. If we had a partial template that could display the cart, we could simply embed a call like this within the sidebar:

```
render("cart")
```

But how would the partial know where to find the cart object? One way would be for it to make an assumption. In the layout, we have access to the @cart instance variable that was set by the controller. It turns out that this is also available inside partials called from the layout. However, this is a bit like calling a method and passing it some value in a global variable. It works, but it's ugly coding, and it increases coupling (which in turn makes your programs brittle and hard to maintain).

Now that we have a partial for a line item, let's do the same for the cart. First, we'll create the _cart.html.erb template. This is basically our carts/show.html.erb template but using cart instead of @cart. (Note that it's OK for a partial to invoke other partials.)

depot_j/app/views/carts/_cart.html.erb

```erb
<div class="cart_title">Your Cart</div>
<table>
►   <%= render(cart.line_items) %>

    <tr class="total_line">
      <td colspan="2">Total</td>
►     <td class="total_cell"><%= number_to_currency(cart.total_price) %></td>
    </tr>

</table>

► <%= button_to 'Empty cart', cart, :method => :delete,
      :confirm => 'Are you sure?' %>
```

As the Rails mantra goes, Don't Repeat Yourselves (DRY), and we have just done that. At the moment the two files are in sync, so there may not seem to be much of a problem, but having one set of logic for the Ajax calls and another set of logic to handle the case where JavaScript is disabled invites problems. Let's avoid all of that and replace the original template with code that causes the partial to be rendered:

depot_k/app/views/carts/show.html.erb

```erb
► <%= render @cart %>
```

Now we will change the application layout to include this new partial in the sidebar:

depot_j/app/views/layouts/application.html.erb

```erb
<!DOCTYPE html>
<html>
<head>
  <title>Pragprog Books Online Store</title>
  <%= stylesheet_link_tag "scaffold" %>
  <%= stylesheet_link_tag "depot", :media => "all" %>
  <%= javascript_include_tag :defaults %>
  <%= csrf_meta_tag %>
</head>
```

```
<body id="store">
  <div id="banner">
    <%= image_tag("logo.png") %>
    <%= @page_title || "Pragmatic Bookshelf" %>
  </div>
  <div id="columns">
    <div id="side">
►     <div id="cart">
►       <%= render @cart %>
►     </div>

      <a href="http://www....">Home</a><br />
      <a href="http://www..../faq">Questions</a><br />
      <a href="http://www..../news">News</a><br />
      <a href="http://www..../contact">Contact</a><br />
    </div>
    <div id="main">
      <%= yield %>
    </div>
  </div>
</body>
</html>
```

Now we have to make a small change to the store controller. We're invoking the layout while looking at the store's index action, and that action doesn't currently set @cart. That's easy enough to remedy:

> depot_j/app/controllers/store_controller.rb

```
def index
  @products = Product.all
► @cart = current_cart
end
```

Now we add a bit of CSS:

> depot_j/public/stylesheets/depot.css

```css
/* Styles for the cart in the sidebar */

#cart, #cart table {
  font-size: smaller;
  color:     white;
}

#cart table {
  border-top:    1px dotted #595;
  border-bottom: 1px dotted #595;
  margin-bottom: 10px;
}
```

If you display the catalog after adding something to your cart, you should see something like Figure 11.1, on the next page. Let's just wait for the Webby Award nomination.

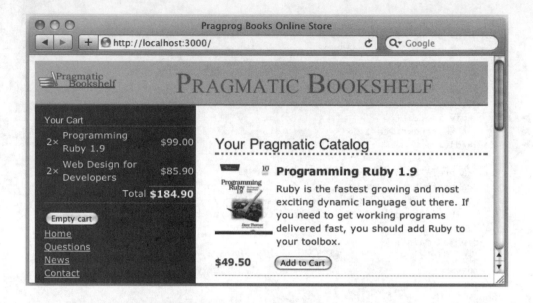

Figure 11.1: THE CART IS IN THE SIDEBAR.

Changing the Flow

Now that we're displaying the cart in the sidebar, we can change the way that the Add to Cart button works. Rather than displaying a separate cart page, all it has to do is refresh the main index page.

The change is pretty simple: at the end of the create action, we simply redirect the browser back to the index:

depot_k/app/controllers/line_items_controller.rb

```
def create
  @cart = current_cart
  product = Product.find(params[:product_id])
  @line_item = @cart.add_product(product.id)

  respond_to do |format|
    if @line_item.save
▶     format.html { redirect_to(store_url) }
      format.xml  { render :xml => @line_item,
        :status => :created, :location => @line_item }
    else
      format.html { render :action => "new" }
      format.xml  { render :xml => @line_item.errors,
        :status => :unprocessable_entity }
    end
  end
end
```

So, now we have a store with a cart in the sidebar. When we click to add an item to the cart, the page is redisplayed with an updated cart. However, if our catalog is large, that redisplay might take a while. It uses bandwidth, and it uses server resources. Fortunately, we can use Ajax to make this better.

11.2 Iteration F2: Creating an Ajax-Based Cart

Ajax lets us write code that runs in the browser that interacts with our server-based application. In our case, we'd like to make the $\boxed{\text{Add to Cart}}$ buttons invoke the server create action on the LineItems controller in the background. The server can then send down just the HTML for the cart, and we can replace the cart in the sidebar with the server's updates.

Now, normally we'd do this by writing JavaScript that runs in the browser and by writing server-side code that communicated with this JavaScript (possibly using a technology such as JavaScript Object Notation [JSON]). The good news is that, with Rails, all this is hidden from us. We can do everything we need to do using Ruby (and with a whole lot of support from some Rails helper methods).

The trick when adding Ajax to an application is to take small steps. So, let's start with the most basic one. Let's change the catalog page to send an Ajax request to our server application and have the application respond with the HTML fragment containing the updated cart.

On the index page, we're using button_to to create the link to the create action. We want to change this to send an Ajax request instead. To do this, we simply add a :remote => true parameter to the call.

```
depot_I/app/views/store/index.html.erb
<% if notice %>
<p id="notice"><%= notice %></p>
<% end %>

<h1>Your Pragmatic Catalog</h1>

<% @products.each do |product| %>
  <div class="entry">
    <%= image_tag(product.image_url) %>
    <h3><%= product.title %></h3>
    <%= sanitize(product.description) %>
    <div class="price_line">
      <span class="price"><%= number_to_currency(product.price) %></span>
►     <%= button_to 'Add to Cart', line_items_path(:product_id => product),
►        :remote => true %>
    </div>
  </div>
<% end %>
```

So far, we've arranged for the browser to send an Ajax request to our application. The next step is to have the application return a response. The plan is to create the updated HTML fragment that represents the cart and to have the browser stick that HTML into the browser's internal representation of the structure and content of the document being displayed, namely, the Document Object Model (DOM). By manipulating the DOM, we cause the display to change in front of the user's eyes.

The first change is to stop the create action from redirecting to the index display if the request is for JavaScript. We do this by adding a call to respond_to telling it that we want to respond with a format of .js.

This syntax may seem surprising at first, but it is simply a method call that is passing an optional block as an argument. Blocks are described in Section 4.3, *Blocks and Iterators*, on page 43. We will cover the respond_to method in greater detail on page 309.

`depot_I/app/controllers/line_items_controller.rb`

```ruby
def create
  @cart = current_cart
  product = Product.find(params[:product_id])
  @line_item = @cart.add_product(product.id)

  respond_to do |format|
    if @line_item.save
      format.html { redirect_to(store_url) }
      format.js
      format.xml  { render :xml => @line_item,
        :status => :created, :location => @line_item }
    else
      format.html { render :action => "new" }
      format.xml  { render :xml => @line_item.errors,
        :status => :unprocessable_entity }
    end
  end
end
```

Because of this change, when create finishes handling the Ajax request, Rails will look for a create template to render.

Rails supports RJS templates—the *JS* stands for JavaScript. A .js.rjs template is a way of getting JavaScript on the browser to do what you want, all by writing server-side Ruby code. Let's write our first: create.js.rjs. It goes in the app/views/line_items directory, just like any other view for line items:

`depot_I/app/views/line_items/create.js.rjs`

```ruby
page.replace_html('cart', render(@cart))
```

Let's analyze that template. The page variable is an instance of something called a JavaScript generator—a Rails class that knows how to create Java-

Script on the server and have it executed by the browser. Here, we tell it to replace the content of the element on the current page with the id cart with the rendered partial for a given cart. This simple RJS template then tells the browser to replace the content of the element whose id="cart" with that HTML.

Does it work? Well, it's hard to show in a book, but it sure does. Make sure you reload the index page in order to get the remote version of the form and the JavaScript libraries loaded into your browser. Then, click one of the `Add to Cart` buttons. You should see the cart in the sidebar update. And you *shouldn't* see your browser show any indication of reloading the page. You've just created an Ajax application.

Troubleshooting

Although Rails makes Ajax incredibly simple, it can't make it foolproof. And, because you're dealing with the loose integration of a number of technologies, it can be hard to work out why your Ajax doesn't work. That's one of the reasons you should always add Ajax functionality one step at a time.

Here are a few hints if your Depot application didn't show any Ajax magic:

- Does your browser have any special incantation to force it to reload everything on a page? Sometimes browsers hold local cached versions of page assets, and this can mess up testing. Now would be a good time to do a full reload.

- Did you have any errors reported? Look in development.log in the logs directory. Also look in the Rails server window because some errors are reported there.

- Still looking at the log file, do you see incoming requests to the action create? If not, it means your browser isn't making Ajax requests. If the JavaScript libraries have been loaded (using View → Source in your browser will show you the HTML), perhaps your browser has JavaScript execution disabled?

- Some readers have reported that they had to stop and start their application to get the Ajax-based cart to work.

- If you're using Internet Explorer, it might be running in what Microsoft calls *quirks mode*, which is backward compatible with old Internet Explorer releases but is also broken. Internet Explorer switches into *standards mode*, which works better with the Ajax stuff, if the first line of the downloaded page is an appropriate DOCTYPE header. Our layouts use this:

```
<!DOCTYPE html>
```

The Customer Is Never Satisfied

We're feeling pretty pleased with ourselves. We changed a handful of lines of code, and our boring old Web 1.0 application now sports Web 2.0 Ajax speed stripes. We breathlessly call the client over to come look. Without saying anything, we proudly press `Add to Cart` and look at her, eager for the praise we know will come. Instead, she looks surprised. "You called me over to show me a bug?" she asks. "You click that button, and nothing happens."

We patiently explain that, in fact, quite a lot happened. Just look at the cart in the sidebar. See? When we add something, the quantity changes from 4 to 5.

"Oh," she says, "I didn't notice that." And, if she didn't notice the page update, it's likely our customers won't either. It's time for some user-interface hacking.

11.3 Iteration F3: Highlighting Changes

Included with Rails is a number of JavaScript libraries. One of those libraries, effects.js, lets you decorate your web pages with a number of visually interesting effects.[1] One of these effects is the (now) infamous Yellow Fade Technique. This highlights an element in a browser: by default it flashes the background yellow and then gradually fades it back to white. We can see the Yellow Fade Technique being applied to our cart in Figure 11.2, on the facing page; the image at the back shows the original cart. The user clicks the `Add to Cart` button, and the count updates to 2 as the line flares brighter. It then fades back to the background color over a short period of time.

Let's add this kind of highlight to our cart. Whenever an item in the cart is updated (either when it is added or when we change the quantity), let's flash its background. That will make it clearer to our users that something has changed, even though the whole page hasn't been refreshed.

The first problem we have is identifying the most recently updated item in the cart. Right now, each item is simply a *<tr>* element. We need to find a way to flag the most recently changed one. The work starts in the LineItemsController. Let's pass the current line item down to the template by assigning it to an instance variable:

depot_m/app/controllers/line_items_controller.rb

```
def create
  @cart = current_cart
  product = Product.find(params[:product_id])
  @line_item = @cart.add_product(product.id)

  respond_to do |format|
    if @line_item.save
```

---

1. effects.js is part of the Script.aculo.us library. Take a look at the visual effects page at https://github.com/madrobby/scriptaculous/wikis to see the cool things you can do with it.

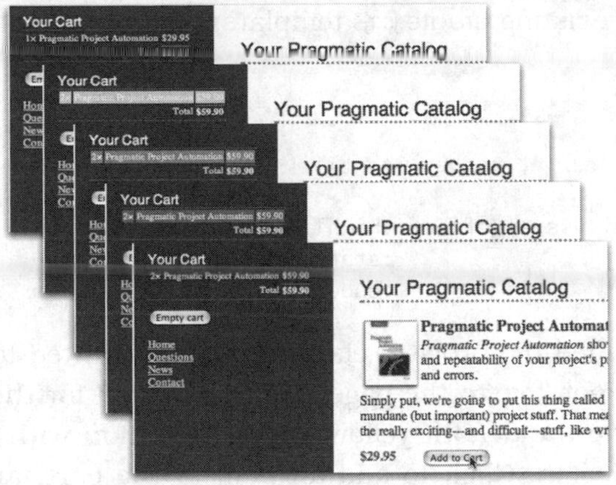

Figure 11.2: OUR CART WITH THE YELLOW FADE TECHNIQUE

```
        format.html { redirect_to(store_url) }
►       format.js   { @current_item = @line_item }
        format.xml  { render :xml => @line_item,
          :status => :created, :location => @line_item }
      else
        format.html { render :action => "new" }
        format.xml  { render :xml => @line_item.errors,
          :status => :unprocessable_entity }
      end
    end
  end
```

In the _line_item.html.erb partial, we then check to see whether the item we're rendering is the one that just changed. If so, we tag it with an id of current_item:

```
depot_m/app/views/line_items/_line_item.html.erb
```

```
►   <% if line_item == @current_item %>
►   <tr id="current_item">
►   <% else %>
►   <tr>
►   <% end %>
      <td><%= line_item.quantity %>&times;</td>
      <td><%= line_item.product.title %></td>
      <td class="item_price"><%= number_to_currency(line_item.total_price) %></td>
    </tr>
```

As a result of these two minor changes, the <tr> element of the most recently changed item in the cart will be tagged with id="current_item". Now we just need to tell the JavaScript to invoke the highlight effect on that item.

We do this in the existing create.js.rjs template, adding a call to the visual_effect method:

`depot_m/app/views/line_items/create.js.rjs`

```
page.replace_html('cart', render(@cart))
▶
▶ page[:current_item].visual_effect :highlight,
▶                                   :startcolor => "#88ff88",
▶                                   :endcolor => "#114411"
```

See how we identified the browser element that we wanted to apply the effect to by passing :current_item to the page? We then asked for the *highlight* visual effect and overrode the default yellow/white transition with colors that work better with our design. Click to add an item to the cart, and you'll see the changed item in the cart glows a light green before fading back to merge with the background.

11.4 Iteration F4: Hiding an Empty Cart

There's one last request from the customer. Right now, even carts with nothing in them are still displayed in the sidebar. Can we arrange for the cart to appear only when it has some content? But of course!

In fact, we have a number of options. The simplest is probably to include the HTML for the cart only if the cart has something in it. We could do this totally within the _cart partial:

```
▶ <% unless cart.line_items.empty? %>
<div class="cart_title">Your Cart</div>
<table>
  <%= render(cart.line_items) %>

  <tr class="total_line">
    <td colspan="2">Total</td>
    <td class="total_cell"><%= number_to_currency(cart.total_price) %></td>
  </tr>
</table>

<%= button_to 'Empty cart', cart, :method => :delete,
    :confirm => 'Are you sure?' %>
▶ <% end %>
```

Although this works, the user interface is somewhat brutal: the whole sidebar redraws on the transition between a cart that's empty and a cart with something in it. So, let's not use this code. Instead, let's smooth it out a little.

The Script.aculo.us effects library contains a number of nice transitions that make elements appear. Let's use blind_down, which will smoothly reveal the cart, sliding the rest of the sidebar down to make room.

Not surprisingly, we'll use our existing .js.rjs template to call the effect. Because the create template is invoked only when we add something to the cart, we know that we have to reveal the cart in the sidebar whenever there is exactly one item in the cart (because that means previously the cart was empty and hence hidden). And, because the cart should be visible before we start the highlight effect, we'll add the code to reveal the cart before the code that triggers the highlight.

The template now looks like this:

depot_n/app/views/line_items/create.js.rjs

```
page.replace_html('cart', render(@cart))

page[:cart].visual_effect :blind_down if @cart.total_items == 1

page[:current_item].visual_effect :highlight,
                                  :startcolor => "#88ff88",
                                  :endcolor => "#114411"
```

This won't yet work, because we don't have a total_items method in our cart model:

depot_n/app/models/cart.rb

```
def total_items
  line_items.sum(:quantity)
end
```

We have to arrange to hide the cart when it's empty. There are two basic ways of doing this. One, illustrated by the code at the start of this section, is not to generate any HTML at all. Unfortunately, if we do that, then when we add something to the cart and suddenly create the cart HTML, we see a flicker in the browser as the cart is first displayed and then hidden and slowly revealed by the blind_down effect.

A better way to handle the problem is to create the cart HTML but set the CSS style to display: none if the cart is empty. To do that, we need to change the application.html.erb layout in app/views/layouts. Our first attempt is something like this:

```
<div id="cart"
    <% if @cart.line_items.empty? %>
        style="display: none"
    <% end %>
  >
  <%= render(@cart) %>
</div>
```

This code adds the CSS style= attribute to the <div> tag, but only if the cart is empty. It works fine, but it's really, really ugly. That dangling > character looks misplaced (even though it isn't), and the way logic is interjected into the middle of a tag is the kind of thing that gives templating languages a bad name. Let's not let that kind of ugliness litter our code. Instead, let's create an abstraction that hides it—we'll write a helper method.

Helper Methods

Whenever we want to abstract some processing out of a view (any kind of view), we should write a helper method.

If you look in the app directory, you'll find five subdirectories:

```
depot> ls -p app
controllers/  helpers/  mailers/  models/  views/
```

Not surprisingly, our helper methods go in the helpers directory. If you look in that directory, you'll find it already contains some files:

```
depot> ls -p app/helpers
application_helper.rb  line_items_helper.rb  store_helper.rb
carts_helper.rb        products_helper.rb
```

The Rails generators automatically created a helper file for each of our controllers (products and store). The Rails command itself (the one that created the application initially) created the file application_helper.rb. If you like, you can organize your methods into controller-specific helpers, but because this method will be used in the application layout, let's put it in the application helper.

Let's write a helper method called hidden_div_if. It takes a condition, an optional set of attributes, and a block. It wraps the output generated by the block in a *<div>* tag, adding the display: none style if the condition is true. Use it in the store layout like this:

depot_n/app/views/layouts/application.html.erb

```erb
<%= hidden_div_if(@cart.line_items.empty?, :id => "cart") do %>
  <%= render @cart %>
<% end %>
```

We'll write our helper so that it is visible to the store controller by adding it to application_helper.rb in the app/helpers directory:

depot_n/app/helpers/application_helper.rb

```ruby
module ApplicationHelper
  def hidden_div_if(condition, attributes = {}, &block)
    if condition
      attributes["style"] = "display: none"
    end
    content_tag("div", attributes, &block)
  end
end
```

This code uses the Rails standard helper, content_tag, which can be used to wrap the output created by a block in a tag. By using the &block notation, we get Ruby to pass the block that was given to hidden_div_if down to content_tag. &block notation ↪ page 43

And, finally, we need to stop setting the message in the flash that we used to display when the user empties a cart. It really isn't needed anymore, because the cart clearly disappears from the sidebar when the catalog index page is redrawn. But there's another reason to remove it, too. Now that we're using Ajax to add products to the cart, the main page doesn't get redrawn between requests as people shop. That means we'll continue to display the flash message saying the cart is empty even as we display a cart in the sidebar.

`depot_n/app/controllers/carts_controller.rb`

```
def destroy
  @cart = current_cart
  @cart.destroy
  session[:cart_id] = nil

  respond_to do |format|
    format.html { redirect_to(store_url) }
    format.xml  { head :ok }
  end
end
```

Now that we have added all this Ajax goodness, go ahead and empty your cart and add an item.

Although this might seem like a lot of work, there really are only two essential steps to what we did. First, we make the cart hide and reveal itself by making the CSS display style conditional on the number of items in the cart. Second, we used an RJS template to invoke the blind_down effect when the cart went from being empty to having one item.

At this point, it occurs to us that we hadn't really done much with respect to testing, but it doesn't really feel like we've made much in the way of functional changes, so we should be fine. But just to be sure, we run our tests again:

```
depot> rake test
  Loaded suite
  Started
  ........
  Finished in 0.172988 seconds.
  8 tests, 29 assertions, 0 failures, 0 errors

  Loaded suite
  Started
  ...E...F.EEEE....EEEE..
  Finished in 0.640226 seconds.
  23 tests, 29 assertions, 1 failures, 9 errors
```

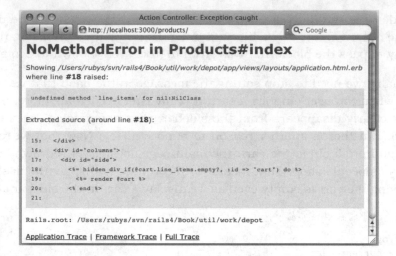

Figure 11.3: AN ERROR IN A LAYOUT CAN AFFECT THE ENTIRE APPLICATION.

Oh dear. Failures and errors. This is not good. Clearly, we need to revisit our approach to testing. In fact, we will do that next.

11.5 Testing Ajax Changes

We look at the test failures, and we see a number of errors that look like the following:

```
test_should_get_index(ProductsControllerTest):
ActionView::Template::Error: undefined method 'line_items' for nil:NilClass
```

Since this error represents the majority of the problems reported, let's address it first so that we can focus on the rest. According to the test, we will have a problem if we get the product index, and sure enough, when we point our browser to http://localhost:3000/products/, we see Figure 11.3.

This information is very helpful. The message identifies the template file was being processed at the point where the error occurs (app/views/layouts/application.html.erb), the line number where the error occurred, and an excerpt from the template of lines around the error. From this, we can see that the expression being evaluated at the point of error is @cart.line_items, and the message produced is undefined method 'line_items' for nil.

So, @cart is apparently nil when we display an index of our products. That makes sense, because it is set only in the store controller. This is easy enough to fix; all we need to do is avoid displaying the cart at all unless this value is set:

```
depot_o/app/views/layouts/application.html.erb
```

```
► <% if @cart %>
    <%= hidden_div_if(@cart.line_items.empty?, :id => "cart") do %>
      <%= render @cart %>
    <% end %>
► <% end %>
```

After this fix, we rerun the tests again and see that we are down to one error. The value of the redirect was not what was expected. This occurred on creating a line item. Sure enough, we did change that on Section 11.1, *Changing the Flow*, on page 130. Unlike the last change, which was entirely accidental, this change was intentional, so we update the corresponding functional test case:

```
depot_o/test/functional/line_items_controller_test.rb
```

```
test "should create line_item" do
  assert_difference('LineItem.count') do
    post :create, :product_id => products(:ruby).id
  end
► assert_redirected_to store_path
end
```

With this change in place, our tests now once again pass. Just imagine what could have happened. A change in one part of an application in order to support a new requirement breaks a function we previously implemented in another part of the application. If you are not careful, this can happen in a small application like Depot. Even if you are careful, this will happen in a large application.

But we are not done yet. We haven't tested any of our Ajax additions, such as what happens when we click the Add to Cart button. Rails makes that easy too.

We already have a test for *should create line item*, so let's add another one called *should create line item via ajax*:

```
depot_o/test/functional/line_items_controller_test.rb
```

```
test "should create line_item via ajax" do
  assert_difference('LineItem.count') do
    xhr :post, :create, :product_id => products(:ruby).id
  end

  assert_response :success
  assert_select_rjs :replace_html, 'cart' do
    assert_select 'tr#current_item td', /Programming Ruby 1.9/
  end
end
```

This test differs in the name of the test in the manner of invocation from the create line item test (xhr :post vs. simply post, where *xhr* stands for the XMLHttpRequest mouthful) and in the expected results. Instead of a redirect, we expect a successful response containing a call to replace the HTML for the cart, and in that HTML we expect to find a row with an id of current_item with a value matching Programming Ruby 1.9. This is achieved by applying the assert_select_rjs to extract the relevant HTML and then processing that HTML via whatever additional assertions you want to apply.

Keeping tests up-to-date is an important part of maintaining your application. Rails makes this easy to do. Agile programmers make testing an integral part of their development efforts. Many even go so far as to write their tests first, before the first line of code is written.

What We Just Did

In this iteration, we added Ajax support to our cart:

- We moved the shopping cart into the sidebar. We then arranged for the create action to redisplay the catalog page.
- We used :remote => true to invoke the LineItemsController.create action using Ajax.
- We then used an RJS template to update the page with just the cart's HTML.
- To help the user see changes to the cart, we added a highlight effect, again using the RJS template.
- We wrote a helper method that hides the cart when it is empty and used the RJS template to reveal it when an item is added.
- We wrote a test that verifies not only the creation of a line item but also the content of the response that is returned from such a request.

The key point to take away is the incremental style of Ajax development. Start with a conventional application, and then add Ajax features, one by one. Ajax can be hard to debug: by adding it slowly to an application, you make it easier to track down what changed if your application stops working. And, as we saw, starting with a conventional application makes it easier to support both Ajax and non-Ajax behavior in the same codebase.

Finally, we'll give you a couple of hints. First, if you plan to do a lot of Ajax development, you'll probably need to get familiar with your browser's JavaScript debugging facilities and with its DOM inspectors, such as Firefox's Firebug, Internet Explorer 8's Developer Tools, Google Chrome's Developer Tools, Safari's Web Inspector, or Opera's Dragonfly. And, second, the NoScript plug-in for Firefox makes checking JavaScript/no JavaScript a one-click breeze. Others find it useful to run two different browsers when they are developing—with JavaScript enabled in one and disabled in the other. Then, as new features are added, poking at it with both browsers will make sure your application works regardless of the state of JavaScript.

Playtime

Here's some stuff to try on your own:

- In Section 9.3, *Playtime*, on page 109, one of the activities was to make clicking the image add the item to the cart. Change this to use :remote => true and image_submit_tag.

- The cart is currently hidden when the user empties it by redrawing the entire catalog. Can you change the application to use the Script.aculo.us blind_up effect instead?

- Does the change you made work if the browser has JavaScript disabled?

- Experiment with other visual effects for new cart items. For example, can you set their initial state to hidden and then have them grow into place? Does this make it problematic to share the cart item partial between the Ajax code and the initial page display?

- Add a link next to each item in the cart. When clicked, it should invoke an action to decrement the quantity of the item, deleting it from the cart when the quantity reaches zero. Get it working without using Ajax first, and then add the Ajax goodness.

- Write a test for empty cart. Verify that the cart has been removed from the sidebar.

(You'll find hints at http://www.pragprog.com/wikis/wiki/RailsPlayTime.)

In this chapter, we'll see

- linking tables with foreign keys;
- using belongs_to, has_many, and :through;
- creating forms based on models (form_for);
- linking forms, models, and views;
- installing and using plugins; and
- generating a feed using atom_helper on model objects.

Chapter 12

Task G: Check Out!

Let's take stock. So far, we've put together a basic product administration system, we've implemented a catalog, and we have a pretty spiffy-looking shopping cart. So, now we need to let the buyer actually purchase the contents of that cart. Let's implement the checkout function.

We're not going to go overboard here. For now, all we'll do is capture the customer's contact details and payment option. Using these, we'll construct an order in the database. Along the way, we'll be looking a bit more at models, validation, and form handling.

12.1 Iteration G1: Capturing an Order

An order is a set of line items, along with details of the purchase transaction. Our cart already contains line_items, so all we need to do is add an order_id column to the line_items table and create an orders table based on the diagram on page 59, combined with a brief chat with our customer.

First we create the order model and update the line_items table:

```
depot> rails generate scaffold order name:string address:text \
  email:string pay_type:string
 . . .
depot> rails generate migration add_order_id_to_line_item \
  order_id:integer
```

Now that we've created the migrations, we can apply them:

```
depot> rake db:migrate
==  CreateOrders: migrating ======================================
-- create_table(:orders)
   -> 0.0014s
==  CreateOrders: migrated (0.0015s) ============================

==  AddOrderIdToLineItem: migrating =============================
-- add_column(:line_items, :order_id, :integer)
   -> 0.0008s
==  AddOrderIdToLineItem: migrated (0.0009s) ====================
```

> ### ⚡ Joe Asks...
> #### Where's the Credit-Card Processing?
>
> In the real world, we'd probably want our application to handle the commercial side of checkout. We might even want to integrate credit-card processing. However, integrating with back-end payment-processing systems requires a fair amount of paperwork and jumping through hoops. And this would distract from looking at Rails, so we're going to punt on this particular detail for the moment.
>
> We will come back to this in Section 26.1, *Credit Card Processing with Active Merchant*, on page 421, where we will explore a plugin that can help us with this function.

Because the database did not have entries for these two new migrations in the schema_migrations table, the db:migrate task applied both migrations to the database. We could, of course, have applied them separately by running the migration task after creating the individual migrations.

Creating the Order Capture Form

Now that we have our tables and our models as we need them, we can start the checkout process. First, we need to add a [Checkout] button to the shopping cart. Because it will create a new order, we'll link it back to a new action in our order controller:

`depot_p/app/views/carts/_cart.html.erb`

```erb
<div class="cart_title">Your Cart</div>
<table>
  <%= render(cart.line_items) %>

  <tr class="total_line">
    <td colspan="2">Total</td>
    <td class="total_cell"><%= number_to_currency(cart.total_price) %></td>
  </tr>

</table>
```
```erb
▶ <%= button_to "Checkout", new_order_path, :method => :get %>
  <%= button_to 'Empty cart', cart, :method => :delete,
      :confirm => 'Are you sure?' %>
```

The first thing we want to do is check to make sure that there's something in the cart. If there is nothing in the cart, we redirect the user back to the storefront, provide a notice of what we did, and return immediately. This prevents people from navigating directly to the checkout option and creating empty orders. The return statement is important here; without, it you will get a *double render error* because your controller will attempt to both redirect and render output.

```
depot_p/app/controllers/orders_controller.rb
def new
▶   @cart = current_cart
▶   if @cart.line_items.empty?
▶     redirect_to store_url, :notice => "Your cart is empty"
▶     return
▶   end
▶
    @order = Order.new

    respond_to do |format|
      format.html # new.html.erb
      format.xml  { render :xml => @order }
    end
end
```

And we add a test for *requires item in cart* and modify the existing test for *should get new* to ensure that there is an item in the cart:

```
depot_p/test/functional/orders_controller_test.rb
▶ test "requires item in cart" do
▶   get :new
▶   assert_redirected_to store_path
▶   assert_equal flash[:notice], 'Your cart is empty'
▶ end

  test "should get new" do
▶   cart = Cart.create
▶   session[:cart_id] = cart.id
▶   LineItem.create(:cart => cart, :product => products(:ruby))
▶
    get :new
    assert_response :success
  end
```

Now we want the new action to present our user with a form, prompting them to enter the information in the orders table: their name, address, email address, and payment type. This means we will need to display a Rails template containing a form. The input fields on this form will have to link to the corresponding attributes in a Rails model object, so we'll need to create an empty model object in the new action to give these fields something to work with.

As always with HTML forms, the trick is populating any initial values into the form fields and then extracting those values back out into our application when the user hits the submit button.

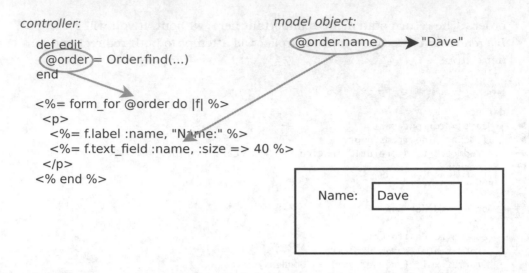

Figure 12.1: NAMES IN FORM_FOR MAP TO OBJECTS AND ATTRIBUTES

In the controller, the @order instance variable is set to reference a new Order model object. This is done because the view populates the form from the data in this object. As it stands, that's not particularly interesting. Because it's a new model object, all the fields will be empty. However, consider the general case. Maybe we want to edit an existing order. Or maybe the user has tried to enter an order but their data has failed validation. In these cases, we want any existing data in the model shown to the user when the form is displayed. Passing in the empty model object at this stage makes all these cases consistent—the view can always assume it has a model object available.

Then, when the user hits the submit button, we'd like the new data from the form to be extracted into a model object back in the controller.

Fortunately, Rails makes this relatively painless. It provides us with a bunch of *form helper* methods. These helpers interact with the controller and with the models to implement an integrated solution for form handling. Before we start on our final form, let's look at a simple example:

```
Line 1  <%= form_for @order do |f| %>
     2    <p>
     3      <%= f.label :name, "Name:" %>
     4      <%= f.text_field :name, :size => 40 %>
     5    </p>
     6  <% end %>
```

There are two interesting things in this code. First, the form_for helper on line 1 sets up a standard HTML form. But it does more. The first parameter, @order, tells the method the instance variable to use when naming fields and when arranging for the field values to be passed back to the controller.

You'll see that form_for sets up a Ruby block environment (this block ends on line 6). Within this block, you can put normal template stuff (such as the <p> tag). But you can also use the block's parameter (f in this case) to reference a form context. We use this context on line 4 to add a text field to the form. Because the text field is constructed in the context of the form_for, it is automatically associated with the data in the @order object.

All these relationships can be confusing. It's important to remember that Rails needs to know both the *names* and the *values* to use for the fields associated with a model. The combination of form_for and the various field-level helpers (such as text_field) give it this information. We can see this process in Figure 12.1, on the facing page.

Now we can update the template for the form that captures a customer's details for checkout. It's invoked from the new action in the order controller, so the template is called new.html.erb and can be found in the directory app/views/orders:

```
depot_p/app/views/orders/new.html.erb
<div class="depot_form">
  <fieldset>
    <legend>Please Enter Your Details</legend>
    <%= render 'form' %>
  </fieldset>
</div>
```

This template makes use of a partial named _form:

```
depot_p/app/views/orders/_form.html.erb
<%= form_for(@order) do |f| %>
  <% if @order.errors.any? %>
    <div id="error_explanation">
      <h2><%= pluralize(@order.errors.count, "error") %>
      prohibited this order from being saved:</h2>

      <ul>
      <% @order.errors.full_messages.each do |msg| %>
        <li><%= msg %></li>
      <% end %>
      </ul>
    </div>
  <% end %>

  <div class="field">
    <%= f.label :name %><br />
    <%= f.text_field :name, :size => 40 %>
  </div>
```

```
    <div class="field">
      <%= f.label :address %><br />
▶     <%= f.text_area :address, :rows => 3, :cols => 40 %>
    </div>
    <div class="field">
      <%= f.label :email %><br />
▶     <%= f.email_field :email, :size => 40 %>
    </div>
    <div class="field">
      <%= f.label :pay_type %><br />
▶     <%= f.select :pay_type, Order::PAYMENT_TYPES,
▶                   :prompt => 'Select a payment method' %>
    </div>
    <div class="actions">
▶     <%= f.submit 'Place Order' %>
    </div>
<% end %>
```

Rails has form helpers for all the different HTML-level form elements. In the
previous code, we use text_field, email_field, and text_area helpers to capture the
customer's name, email, and address. We cover form helpers in more depth in
Section 21.2, *Generating Forms*, on page 335.

The only tricky thing in there is the code associated with the selection list.
We've assumed that the list of available payment options is an attribute of the
Order model. We'd better define the option array in the model order.rb before we
forget:

`depot_p/app/models/order.rb`

```
class Order < ActiveRecord::Base
▶ PAYMENT_TYPES = [ "Check", "Credit card", "Purchase order" ]
end
```

In the template, we pass this array of payment type options to the select helper.
We also pass the :prompt parameter, which adds a dummy selection containing
the prompt text.

Add a little CSS magic:

`depot_p/public/stylesheets/depot.css`

```
/* Styles for order form */

.depot_form fieldset {
  background: #efe;
}

.depot_form legend {
  color: #dfd;
  background: #141;
  font-family: sans-serif;
  padding: 0.2em 1em;
}
```

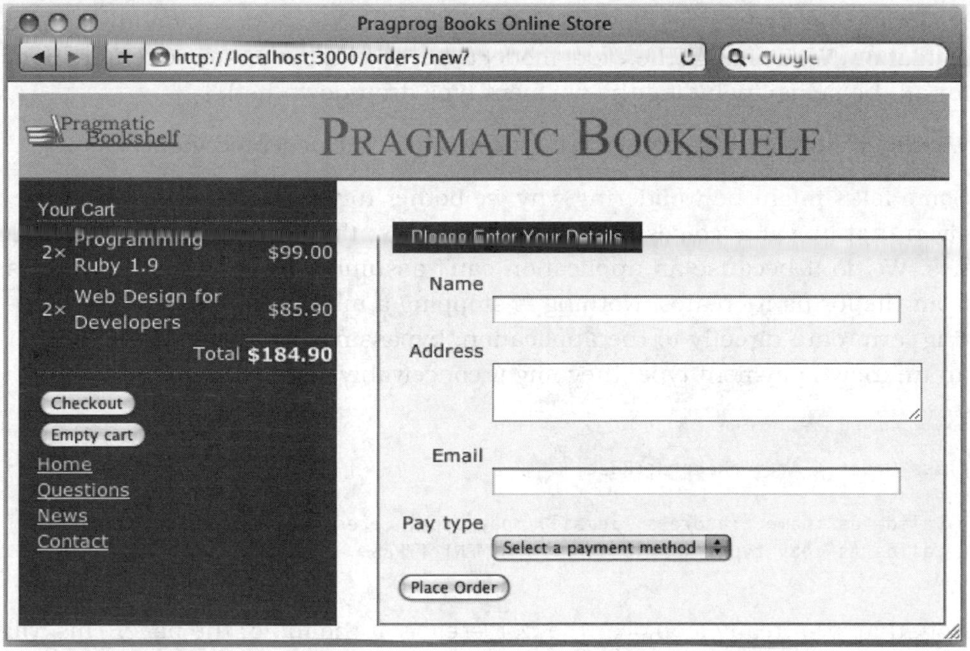

Figure 12.2: OUR CHECKOUT SCREEN

```
.depot_form label {
  width: 5em;
  float: left;
  text-align: right;
  padding-top: 0.2em;
  margin-right: 0.1em;
  display: block;
}

.depot_form select, .depot_form textarea, .depot_form input {
  margin-left: 0.5em;
}

.depot_form .submit {
  margin-left: 4em;
}

.depot_form div {
  margin: 0.5em 0;
}
```

We're ready to play with our form. Add some stuff to your cart, and then click the Checkout button. You should see something like Figure 12.2.

Looking good! Before we move on, let's finish the new action by adding some validation. We'll change the Order model to verify that the customer enters data for all the fields (including the payment type drop-down list).

We also validate that the payment type is one of the accepted values.

Some folks might be wondering why we bother to validate the payment type, given that its value comes from a drop-down list that contains only valid values. We do it because an application can't assume that it's being fed values from the forms it creates. Nothing is stopping a malicious user from submitting form data directly to the application, bypassing our form. If the user set an unknown payment type, they might conceivably get our products for free.

depot_p/app/models/order.rb

```
class Order < ActiveRecord::Base
  # ...
► validates :name, :address, :email, :pay_type, :presence => true
► validates :pay_type, :inclusion => PAYMENT_TYPES
end
```

Note that we already loop over the @order.errors at the top of the page. This will report validation failures.

Since we modified validation rules, we need to modify our test fixture to match:

depot_p/test/fixtures/orders.yml

```
# Read about fixtures at http://ar.rubyonrails.org/classes/Fixtures.html

one:
► name: Dave Thomas
  address: MyText
► email: dave@example.org
► pay_type: Check

two:
  name: MyString
  address: MyText
  email: MyString
  pay_type: MyString
```

Furthermore, for an order to be created, a line item needs to be in the cart, so we need to modify the line items test fixture too:

depot_o/test/fixtures/line_items.yml

```
# Read about fixtures at http://ar.rubyonrails.org/classes/Fixtures.html

one:
► product: ruby
► cart: one
```

```
two:
▶  product: ruby
▶  cart: one
```

Note that we removed the _id suffix from the attribute name. This tells Rails that the value provided is no longer an actual numeric id; instead, the id attributed should match the one in the record identified by the name provided.

Feel free to modify both orders, but only the first is currently used in the functional tests.

Capturing the Order Details

Let's implement the create action in the controller. This method has to do the following:

1. Capture the values from the form to populate a new Order model object.

2. Add the line items from our cart to that order.

3. Validate and save the order. If this fails, display the appropriate messages, and let the user correct any problems.

4. Once the order is successfully saved, delete the cart, redisplay the catalog page, and display a message confirming that the order has been placed.

First, we define the relationships themselves, first from the line item to the order:

`depot_p/app/models/line_item.rb`

```ruby
class LineItem < ActiveRecord::Base
▶  belongs_to :order
  belongs_to :product
  belongs_to :cart

  def total_price
    product.price * quantity
  end
end
```

then from the order to the line item, once again indicating that all line items that belong to an order are to be destroyed whenever the order is destroyed:

`depot_p/app/models/order.rb`

```ruby
class Order < ActiveRecord::Base
▶  has_many :line_items, :dependent => :destroy
  # ...
end
```

> ## Joe Asks...
> ### Aren't You Creating Duplicate Orders?
>
> Joe is concerned to see our controller creating Order model objects in two actions: new and create. He's wondering why this doesn't lead to duplicate orders in the database.
>
> The answer is simple: the checkout action creates an Order object *in memory* simply to give the template code something to work with. Once the response is sent to the browser, that particular object gets abandoned, and it will eventually be reaped by Ruby's garbage collector. It never gets close to the database.
>
> The create action also creates an Order object, populating it from the form fields. This object *does* get saved in the database. So, model objects perform two roles: they map data into and out of the database, but they are also just regular objects that hold business data. They affect the database only when you tell them to, typically by calling save.

The method itself ends up looking something like this:

`depot_p/app/controllers/orders_controller.rb`

```
def create
  @order = Order.new(params[:order])
► @order.add_line_items_from_cart(current_cart)

  respond_to do |format|
    if @order.save
►     Cart.destroy(session[:cart_id])
►     session[:cart_id] = nil
►     format.html { redirect_to(store_url, :notice =>
►       'Thank you for your order.') }
      format.xml  { render :xml => @order, :status => :created,
        :location => @order }
    else
      format.html { render :action => "new" }
      format.xml  { render :xml => @order.errors,
        :status => :unprocessable_entity }
    end
  end
end
```

We start by creating a new Order object and initialize it from the form data. In this case, we want all the form data related to order objects, so we select the :order hash from the parameters (this is the name we passed as the first parameter to form_for). The next line adds into this order the items that are already stored in the cart—we'll write the actual method to do this in a minute.

Next we tell the order object to save itself (and its children, the line items) to the database. Along the way, the order object will perform validation (but we'll get to that in a minute). If the save succeeds, we do two things. First, we ready ourselves for this customer's next order by deleting the cart from the session. Then, we redisplay the catalog using the redirect_to method to display a cheerful message. If, instead, the save fails, we redisplay the checkout form.

In the create action we assumed that the order object contains the method add_line_items_from_cart, so let's implement that method now:

depot_p/app/models/order.rb

```
class Order < ActiveRecord::Base
  # ...
► def add_line_items_from_cart(cart)
►   cart.line_items.each do |item|
►     item.cart_id = nil
►     line_items << item
►   end
► end
end
```

For each item that we transfer from the cart to the order, we need to do two things. First we set the cart_id to nil in order to prevent the item from going poof when we destroy the cart.

Then we add the item itself to the line_items collection for the order. Notice that we didn't have to do anything special with the various foreign key fields, such as setting the order_id column in the line item rows to reference the newly created order row. Rails does that knitting for us using the has_many and belongs_to declarations we added to the Order and LineItem models. Appending each new line item to the line_items collection hands the responsibility for key management over to Rails.

We will also need to modify the test to reflect the new redirect:

depot_p/test/functional/orders_controller_test.rb

```
require 'test_helper'

class OrdersControllerTest < ActionController::TestCase
  # ...
  test "should create order" do
    assert_difference('Order.count') do
      post :create, :order => @order.attributes
    end

►   assert_redirected_to store_path
  end
  # ...
end
```

And we modify the test fixture to make one product be in the first order (leaving one product in the first cart for use in the cart tests):

```
# Read about fixtures at http://ar.rubyonrails.org/classes/Fixtures.html

one:
  product: ruby
► order: one

two:
  product: ruby
  cart: one
```

So, as a first test of all of this, hit the Place Order button on the check-out page without filling in any of the form fields. You should see the check-out page redisplayed along with some error messages complaining about the empty fields, as shown in Figure 12.3, on the next page. (If you're following along at home and you get the message No action responded to create, it's possible that you added the create method after the private declaration in the controller. Private methods cannot be called as actions.)

If we fill in some data (as shown at the top of Figure 12.4, on page 158) and click Place Order, we should get taken back to the catalog, as shown at the bottom of the figure. But did it work? Let's look in the database.

```
depot> sqlite3 -line db/development.sqlite3
SQLite version 3.6.16
Enter ".help" for instructions
sqlite> select * from orders;
           id = 1
         name = Dave Thomas
      address = 123 Main St
        email = customer@example.com
     pay_type = Check
   created_at = 2010-06-09 13:40:40
   updated_at = 2010-06-09 13:40:40

sqlite> select * from line_items;
           id = 10
   product_id = 3
      cart_id =
   created_at = 2010-06-09 13:40:40
   updated_at = 2010-06-09 13:40:40
     quantity = 1
        price = 49.5
     order_id = 1

sqlite> .quit
```

Although what you see will differ on details such as version numbers and dates (and price will be present only if you completed the exercises defined in

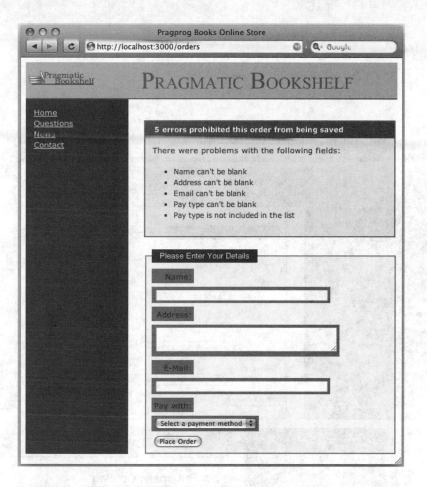

Figure 12.3: FULL HOUSE! EVERY FIELD FAILS VALIDATION.

Section 10.3, *Playtime*, on page 123), you should see a single order and one or more line items that match your selections.

One Last Ajax Change

After we accept an order, we redirect to the index page, displaying the cheery flash message "Thank you for your order." If the user continues to shop and they have JavaScript enabled in their browser, we'll fill the cart in their sidebar without redrawing the main page. This means the flash message will continue to be displayed. We'd rather it went away after we add the first item to the cart (as it does when JavaScript is disabled in the browser). Fortunately, the fix is simple: we just hide the *<div>* that contains the flash message when we add something to the cart. Except, nothing is really ever that simple.

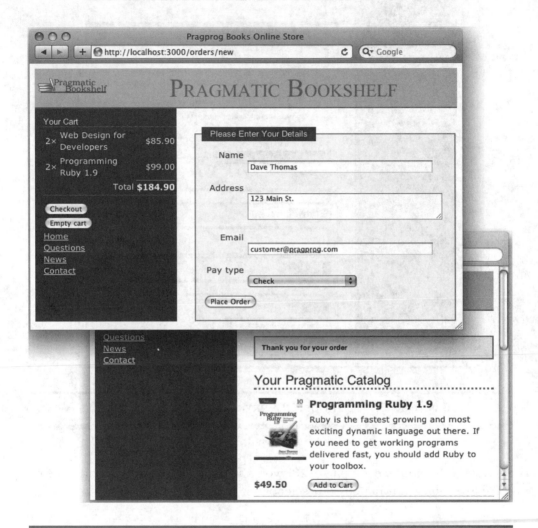

Figure 12.4: ENTERING ORDER INFORMATION PRODUCES A "THANKS!"

A first attempt to hide the flash might involve adding the following line to line_items/create.js.rjs:

```
page[:notice].hide
# rest as before...
```

However, this doesn't work. If we come to the store for the first time, there's nothing in the flash, so the paragraph with an id of notice is not displayed. And, if there's no tag with the id of notice, the JavaScript generated by the RJS template that tries to hide it bombs out, and the rest of the template never gets run. As a result, you never see the cart update in the sidebar.

The solution is a little hack. We want to run the .hide only if the notice is present, but RJS doesn't give us the ability to generate JavaScript that tests for individual ids. It does, however, let us iterate over tags on the page that match a certain CSS selector pattern. So, let's iterate over all tags with an id of notice. The loop will find either one such tag, which we can hide, or none, in which case the hide won't get called.

depot_p/app/views/line_items/create.js.rjs

```
▶   page.select("#notice").each { |notice| notice.hide }

    page.replace_html('cart', render(@cart))
    page[:cart].visual_effect :blind_down if @cart.total_items == 1
    page[:current_item].visual_effect :highlight,
                                    :startcolor => "#88ff88",
                                    :endcolor => "#114411"
```

Now that we've captured the order, it is time to alert the ordering department. We will do that with feeds, specifically, an Atom-formatted feed of orders.

12.2 Iteration G2: Atom Feeds

Using a standard feed format, such as Atom, means you can immediately take advantage of a wide variety of preexisting clients. Because Rails already knows about ids, dates, and links, it can free you from having to worry about these pesky details and let you focus on producing a human-readable summary. We start by adding a new action to the resource and include Atom to the list of formats that we respond to:

depot_o/app/controllers/products_controller.rb

```
def who_bought
  @product = Product.find(params[:id])
  respond_to do |format|
    format.atom
    format.xml { render :xml => @product }
  end
end
```

> **Joe Asks...**
>
> **Why Atom?**
>
> There are a number of different feed formats, most notably RSS 1.0, RSS 2.0, and Atom, standardized in 2000, 2002, and 2005, respectively. These three are all widely supported. To aid with the transition, a number of sites provide multiple feeds for the same site, but this is no longer necessary, increases user confusion, and generally is not recommended.
>
> The Ruby language provides a low-level library, which can produce any of these formats, as well as a number of other less common versions of RSS. For best results, stick with one of the three main versions.
>
> The Rails framework is all about picking reasonable defaults and has chosen Atom as the default for feed formats. It is specified as an Internet standards track protocol for the Internet community by the IETF, and Rails provides a higher-level helper named atom_feed that takes care of a number of details based on knowledge of Rails naming conventions for things like ids and dates.

By adding format.atom, we cause Rails to look for a template named who_bought.atom.builder. Such a template can make use of the generic XML functionality that Builder provides as well as of the knowledge of the Atom feed format that the atom_feed helper provides:

`depot_o/app/views/products/who_bought.atom.builder`

```
atom_feed do |feed|
  feed.title "Who bought #{@product.title}"

  latest_order = @product.orders.sort_by(&:updated_at).last
  feed.updated( latest_order && latest_order.updated_at )

  @product.orders.each do |order|
    feed.entry(order) do |entry|
      entry.title "Order #{order.id}"
      entry.summary :type => 'xhtml' do |xhtml|
        xhtml.p "Shipped to #{order.address}"

        xhtml.table do
          xhtml.tr do
            xhtml.th 'Product'
            xhtml.th 'Quantity'
            xhtml.th 'Total Price'
          end
          order.line_items.each do |item|
            xhtml.tr do
              xhtml.td item.product.title
```

```
          xhtml.td item.quantity
          xhtml.td number_to_currency item.total_price
        end
      end
      xhtml.tr do
        xhtml.th 'total', :colspan => 2
        xhtml.th number_to_currency \
          order.line_items.map(&:total_price).sum
      end
    end

    xhtml.p "Paid by #{order.pay_type}"
  end
  entry.author do |author|
    entry.name order.name
    entry.email order.email
  end
    end
  end
 end
end
```

More information on Builder can be found in Section 25.1, *Generating XML with Builder*, on page 405.

At the overall feed level, we only need to provide two pieces of information: the title and the latest updated date. If there are no orders, the updated_at value will be null, and Rails will supply the current time instead.

Then we iterate over each order associated with this product. Note that there is no direct relationship between these two models. In fact, the relationship is indirect. Products have many line_items and line_items belong to a order. We could iterate and traverse, but by simply declaring that there is a relationship between products and orders *through* the line_items relationship, we can simplify our code:

depot_o/app/models/product.rb

```
class Product < ActiveRecord::Base
  default_scope :order => 'title'
  has_many :line_items
▶ has_many :orders, :through => :line_items
  #...
end
```

For each order, we provide a title, a summary, and an author. The summary can be full XHTML, and we use this to produce a table of product titles, quantity ordered, and total prices. We follow this table with a paragraph containing the pay_type.

To make this work, we need to define a route. This action will respond to HTTP GET requests and will operate on a member of the collection (in other words, on an individual product) as opposed to the entire collection itself (which in this case would mean all products):

`depot_o/config/routes.rb`

```ruby
Depot::Application.routes.draw do
  resources :orders

  resources :line_items

  resources :carts

  get "store/index"

▶ resources :products do
▶   get :who_bought, :on => :member
▶ end


  # ...

  # You can have the root of your site routed with "root"
  # just remember to delete public/index.html.
  # root :to => "welcome#index"
  root :to => 'store#index', :as => 'store'

  # ...
end
```

We can try it for ourselves:

```
depot> curl --silent http://localhost:3000/products/3/who_bought.atom
<?xml version="1.0" encoding="UTF-8"?>
<feed xml:lang="en-US" xmlns="http://www.w3.org/2005/Atom">
  <id>tag:localhost,2005:/products/3/who_bought</id>
  <link type="text/html" href="http://localhost:3000" rel="alternate"/>
  <link type="application/atom+xml"
        href="http://localhost:3000/info/who_bought/3.atom" rel="self"/>
  <title>Who bought Programming Ruby 1.9</title>
  <updated>2010-04-25T03:14:05Z</updated>
  <entry>
    <id>tag:localhost,2005:Order/1</id>
    <published>2010-04-25T03:14:05Z</published>
    <updated>2010-04-25T03:14:05Z</updated>
    <link rel="alternate" type="text/html"
          href="http://localhost:3000/orders/1"/>
    <title>Order 1</title>
    <summary type="xhtml">
      <div xmlns="http://www.w3.org/1999/xhtml">
        <p>Shipped to 123 Main St</p>
        <table>
          ...
        </table>
        <p>Paid by check</p>
      </div>
    </summary>
```

```
    <author>
      <name>Dave Thomas</name>
      <email>customer@pragprog.com</email>
    </author>
  </entry>
</feed>
```

Looks good. Now we can subscribe to this in our favorite feed reader.

12.3 Iteration G3: Pagination

At the moment, we have a few products, a few carts at any one time, and a few line items per cart or order, but we can have essentially an unlimited number of orders, and we hope to have many—enough so that displaying all of them on an orders page will quickly become unwieldy. Enter the will_paginate plugin. This plugin extends Rails to provide this much-needed function.

Why a plugin? Back in Rails 1.0, this functionality was part of Rails itself. But there were competing ideas on how this could be implemented and improved, and the function was broken out in order to enable innovation to thrive.

The first thing we need to do is to inform Rails of our intent to use the plugin. We do that by modifying the Gemfile file. We need to specify that we want a version that is greater than or equal to 3.0.pre because previous versions don't work with Rails 3.0.

depot_q/Gemfile

```
source 'http://rubygems.org'

gem 'rails', '3.0.5'

# Bundle edge Rails instead:
# gem 'rails', :git => 'git://github.com/rails/rails.git'

gem 'sqlite3'

# Use unicorn as the web server
# gem 'unicorn'

# Deploy with Capistrano
# gem 'capistrano'

# To use debugger (ruby-debug for Ruby 1.8.7+, ruby-debug19 for Ruby 1.9.2+)
# gem 'ruby-debug'
# gem 'ruby-debug19', :require => 'ruby-debug'

# Bundle the extra gems:
# gem 'bj'
# gem 'nokogiri'
# gem 'sqlite3-ruby', :require => 'sqlite3'
# gem 'aws-s3', :require => 'aws/s3'
```

▶
▶ `gem 'will_paginate', '>= 3.0.pre'`

```
# Bundle gems for the local environment. Make sure to
# put test-only gems in this group so their generators
# and rake tasks are available in development mode:
# group :development, :test do
#   gem 'webrat'
# end
```

With this in place, we can use the bundle command to install our dependencies:

depot> **bundle install**

Depending on your operating system and your setup, you may need to run this command as root.

The bundle command will actually do much more. It will cross-check gem dependencies, find a configuration that works, and download and install whatever components are necessary. But this needn't concern us now; we added only one component, and we can rest assured that this one is included in the gems that the bundler installed.

We must do one last thing after updating or installing a new gem: restart the server. Although Rails does a good job of detecting and keeping up with your latest changes to your application, it is impossible to predict what needs to be done when an entire gem is added or replaced.

Now let's generate some test data. We could click repeatedly on the buttons we have, but computers are good at this. This isn't exactly seed data, simply something done once and thrown away. Let's create a file in the script directory.

> depot_q/script/load_orders.rb

```
Order.transaction do
  (1..100).each do |i|
    Order.create(:name => "Customer #{i}", :address => "#{i} Main Street",
      :email => "customer-#{i}@example.com", :pay_type => "Check")
  end
end
```

This will create 100 orders with no line items in them. Feel free to modify the script to create line items if you are so inclined. Note that this code does all this work in one transaction. This isn't precisely required for this activity but does speed up the processing.

Note that we don't have any require statements or initialization to open or close the database. We will allow Rails to take care of this for us:

```
rails runner script/load_orders.rb
```

Now that the setup is done, we are ready to make the changes necessary to our application. First, we will modify our controller to call paginate, passing it in the page and the order in which we want the results displayed:

depot_p/app/controllers/orders_controller.rb

```
def index
▶  @orders = Order.paginate .page=>params[:page], :order=>'created at desc',
▶    :per_page => 10

  respond_to do |format|
    format.html # index.html.erb
    format.xml  { render :xml => @orders }
  end
end
```

Next, we will add links to the bottom of our index view:

depot_q/app/views/orders/index.html.erb

```
<h1>Listing orders</h1>

<table>
  <tr>
    <th>Name</th>
    <th>Address</th>
    <th>Email</th>
    <th>Pay type</th>
    <th></th>
    <th></th>
    <th></th>
  </tr>

<% @orders.each do |order| %>
  <tr>
    <td><%= order.name %></td>
    <td><%= order.address %></td>
    <td><%= order.email %></td>
    <td><%= order.pay_type %></td>
    <td><%= link_to 'Show', order %></td>
    <td><%= link_to 'Edit', edit_order_path(order) %></td>
    <td><%= link_to 'Destroy', order, :confirm => 'Are you sure?',
            :method => :delete %></td>
  </tr>
<% end %>
</table>

<br />

<%= link_to 'New Order', new_order_path %>
▶ <p><%= will_paginate @orders %></p>
```

And that is all there is to it! The default is to show thirty entries per page, and the links will show up only if there are more than one page of orders.

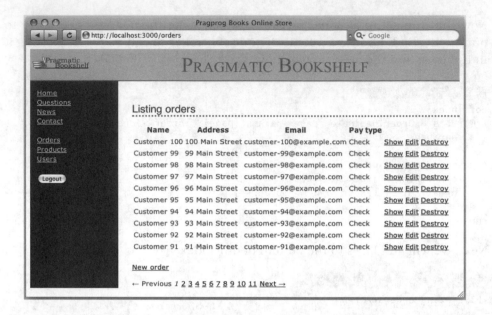

Figure 12.5: Showing ten orders out of more than a hundred

The controller specifies the number of orders to display on a page using the :per_page option. See Figure 12.5.

The customer likes it. We've implemented product maintenance, a basic catalog, and a shopping cart, and now we have a simple ordering system. Obviously we'll also have to write some kind of fulfillment application, but that can wait for a new iteration. (And that iteration is one that we'll skip in this book; it doesn't have much new to say about Rails.)

What We Just Did

In a fairly short amount of time, we did the following:

- We created a form to capture details for the order and linked it to a new order model.

- We added validation and used helper methods to display errors to the user.

- We installed and used a plugin to paginate the list of orders.

- We provided a feed so that the administrator can monitor orders as they come in.

Playtime

Here's some stuff to try on your own:

- Get HTML-, XML-, and JSON-formatted views working for who_bought requests. Experiment with including the order information in the XML view by rendering @product.to_xml(:include => :orders). Do the same thing for JSON.

- What happens if you click the [Checkout] button in the sidebar while the checkout screen is already displayed? Can you find a way to disable the button in this circumstance? (Hint: variables set in the controller are available in layouts and partials as well as in the directly rendered template.)

- The list of possible payment types is currently stored as a constant in the Order class. Can you move this list into a database table? Can you still make validation work for the field?

(You'll find hints at http://www.pragprog.com/wikis/wiki/RailsPlayTime.)

Chapter 13

Task H: Sending Mail

At this point, we have a website that will respond to requests and will provide feeds that allow sales of individual titles to be checked on periodically. At times it makes sense to have something more than that. For those times, what we need is the ability to actively target a message to somebody specific when an event occurs. It could be wanting to notify a system administrator when an exception occurs. It could be a user feedback form. In this chapter, we will opt to simply send confirmation emails to people who have placed orders. Once we complete that, we will create tests not only for the mail support that we just added but for the entire user scenario we have created so far.

13.1 Iteration H1: Sending Confirmation Emails

There are three basic parts to sending email in Rails: configuring how email is to be sent, determining when to send the email, and specifying what you want to say. We will cover each of these three in turn.

Email Configuration

Email configuration is part of a Rails application's environment and involves a Depot::Application.configure block. If you want to use the same configuration for development, testing, and production, add the configuration to environment.rb in the config directory; otherwise, add different configurations to the appropriate files in the config/environments directory.

Inside the block, you will need to have one or more statements. You first have to decide how you want mail delivered:

```
config.action_mailer.delivery_method = :smtp | :sendmail | :test
```

The :smtp and :sendmail options are used when you want Action Mailer to attempt to deliver email. You'll clearly want to use one of these methods in production.

The :test setting is great for unit and functional testing, which we will make use of in Section 13.1, *Function Testing Email*, on page 175. Email will not be delivered; instead, it will be appended to an array (accessible via the attribute ActionMailer::Base.deliveries). This is the default delivery method in the test environment. Interestingly, though, the default in development mode is :smtp. If you want Rails to deliver email during the development of your application, this is good. If you'd rather disable email delivery in development mode, edit the file development.rb in the directory config/environments, and add the following lines:

```
Depot::Application.configure do
  config.action_mailer.delivery_method = :test
end
```

The :sendmail setting delegates mail delivery to your local system's sendmail program, which is assumed to be in /usr/sbin. This delivery mechanism is not particularly portable, because sendmail is not always installed in this directory on different operating systems. It also relies on your local sendmail supporting the -i and -t command options.

You achieve more portability by leaving this option at its default value of :smtp. If you do so, you'll need also to specify some additional configuration to tell Action Mailer where to find an SMTP server to handle your outgoing email. This may be the machine running your web application, or it may be a separate box (perhaps at your ISP if you're running Rails in a noncorporate environment). Your system administrator will be able to give you the settings for these parameters. You may also be able to determine them from your own mail client's configuration.

The following are typical settings for Gmail. Adapt them as you need.

```
Depot::Application.configure do
  config.action_mailer.delivery_method = :smtp

  config.action_mailer.smtp_settings = {
    :address             => "smtp.gmail.com",
    :port                => 587,
    :domain              => "domain.of.sender.net",
    :authentication      => "plain",
    :user_name           => "dave",
    :password            => "secret",
    :enable_starttls_auto => true
  }
end
```

As with all configuration changes, you'll need to restart your application if you make changes to any of the environment files.

Sending Email

Now that we have everything configured, let's write some code to send emails.

By now you shouldn't be surprised that Rails has a generator script to create mailers. What might be surprising is where it creates them. In Rails, a mailer is a class that's stored in the app/mailers directory. It contains one or more methods, with each method corresponding to an email template. To create the body of the email, these methods in turn use views (in just the same way that controller actions use views to create HTML and XML). So, let's create a mailer for our store application. We'll use it to send two different types of email: one when an order is placed and a second when the order ships. The rails generate mailer command takes the name of the mailer class, along with the names of the email action methods:

```
depot> rails generate mailer Notifier order_received order_shipped
  create  app/mailers/notifier.rb
  invoke  erb
  create    app/views/notifier
  create    app/views/notifier/order_received.text.erb
  create    app/views/notifier/order_shipped.text.erb
  invoke  test_unit
  create    test/functional/notifier_test.rb
```

Notice that we've created a Notifier class in app/mailers and two template files, one for each email type, in app/views/notifier. (We also created a test file—we'll look into this later in Section 13.1, *Function Testing Email*, on page 175.)

Each method in the mailer class is responsible for setting up the environment for sending a particular email. Let's look at an example before going into the details. Here's the code that was generated for our Notifier class, with one default changed:

depot_p/app/mailers/notifier.rb

```
class Notifier < ActionMailer::Base
  default :from => 'Sam Ruby <depot@example.com>'

  # Subject can be set in your I18n file at config/locales/en.yml
  # with the following lookup:
  #
  #   en.notifier.order_received.subject
  #
  def order_received
    @greeting = "Hi"

    mail :to => "to@example.org"
  end
```

```
  # Subject can be set in your I18n file at config/locales/en.yml
  # with the following lookup:
  #
  #   en.notifier.order_shipped.subject
  #
  def order_shipped
    @greeting = "Hi"

    mail :to => "to@example.org"
  end
end
```

If you are thinking to yourself that this looks like a controller, it is because it very much does. One method per action. Instead of a call to render, there is a call to mail. Mail accepts a number of parameters including :to (as shown), :cc, :from, and :subject, each of which does pretty much what you would expect them to do. Values that are common to all mail calls in the mailer can be set as defaults by simply calling default, as is done for :from at the top of this class. Feel free to tailor this to your needs.

The comments in this class also indicate that subject lines are already enabled for translation, a subject we cover in Chapter 15, *Task J: Internationalization*, on page 205. For now, we will simply use the :subject parameter.

As with controllers, templates contain the text to be sent, and controllers and mailers can provide values to be inserted into those templates via instance variables.

Email Templates

The generate script created two email templates in app/views/notifier, one for each action in the Notifier class. These are regular .erb files. We'll use them to create plain-text emails (we'll see later how to create HTML email). As with the templates we use to create our application's web pages, the files contain a combination of static text and dynamic content. We can customize the template in order_received.text.erb; this is the email that is sent to confirm an order:

depot_r/app/views/notifier/order_received.text.erb

```
Dear <%= @order.name %>

Thank you for your recent order from The Pragmatic Store.

You ordered the following items:

<%= render @order.line_items %>

We'll send you a separate e-mail when your order ships.
```

The partial template that renders a line item formats a single line with the item quantity and the title. Because we're in a template, all the regular helper methods, such as truncate, are available:

```
<%= sprintf("%2d x %s",
            line_item.quantity,
            truncate(line_item.product.title, :length => 50)) %>
```

We now have to go back and fill in the order_received method in the Notifier class:

```
def order_received(order)
  @order = order

  mail :to => order.email, :subject => 'Pragmatic Store Order Confirmation'
end
```

What we did here is add order as an argument to the method-received call, add code to copy the parameter passed into an instance variable, and update the call to mail specifying where to send the email and what subject line to use.

Generating Emails

Now that we have our template set up and our mailer method defined, we can use them in our regular controllers to create and/or send emails.

```
def create
  @order = Order.new(params[:order])
  @order.add_line_items_from_cart(current_cart)

  respond_to do |format|
    if @order.save
      Cart.destroy(session[:cart_id])
      session[:cart_id] = nil
      Notifier.order_received(@order).deliver
      format.html { redirect_to(store_url, :notice =>
        'Thank you for your order.') }
      format.xml  { render :xml => @order, :status => :created,
        :location => @order }
    else
      format.html { render :action => "new" }
      format.xml  { render :xml => @order.errors,
        :status => :unprocessable_entity }
    end
  end
end
```

And we need to update the order_shipped just like we did for order_received:

depot_r/app/mailers/notifier.rb

```
def order_shipped(order)
  @order = order

  mail :to => order.email, :subject => 'Pragmatic Store Order Shipped'
end
```

At this point, we have enough of the basics in place that you can place an order and have a plain email sent to yourself, presuming that you didn't disable the sending of email in development mode. Now let's spice up the email with a bit of formatting.

Delivering Multiple Content Types

Some people prefer receiving email in plain-text format, while others like the look of an HTML email. Rails makes it easy to send email messages that contain alternative content formats, allowing the user (or their email client) to decide what they'd prefer to view.

In the preceding section, we created a plain-text email. The view file for our order_received action was called order_received.text.erb. This is the standard Rails naming convention. We can also create HTML-formatted emails.

Let's try this with the order shipped notification. We don't need to modify any code; we simply need to create a new template:

depot_r/app/views/notifier/order_shipped.html.erb

```
<h3>Pragmatic Order Shipped</h3>
<p>
  This is just to let you know that we've shipped your recent order:
</p>

<table>
  <tr><th colspan="2">Qty</th><th>Description</th></tr>
<%= render @order.line_items %>
</table>
```

We don't even need to modify the partial, because the existing one we already have will do just fine:

depot_r/app/views/line_items/_line_item.html.erb

```
<% if line_item == @current_item %>
<tr id="current_item">
<% else %>
<tr>
<% end %>
  <td><%= line_item.quantity %>&times;</td>
  <td><%= line_item.product.title %></td>
  <td class="item_price"><%= number_to_currency(line_item.total_price) %></td>
</tr>
```

Joe Asks...

Can I Also Receive Email?

Action Mailer makes it easy to write Rails applications that handle incoming email. Unfortunately, you need to find a way to retrieve appropriate emails from your server environment and inject them into the application; this requires a bit more work.

The easy part is handling an email within your application. In your Action Mailer class, write an instance method called receive that takes a single parameter. This parameter will be a Mail::Message object corresponding to the incoming email. You can extract fields, the body text, and/or attachments and use them in your application.

All the normal techniques for intercepting incoming email end up running a command, passing that command the content of the email as standard input. If we make the Rails runner script the command that's invoked whenever an email arrives, we can arrange to pass that email into our application's email-handling code. For example, using procmail-based interception, we could write a rule that looks something like the example that follows. Using the arcane syntax of procmail, this rule copies any incoming email whose subject line contains *Bug Report* through our runner script:

```
RUBY=/opt/local/bin/ruby
TICKET_APP_DIR=/Users/dave/Work/depot
HANDLER='IncomingTicketHandler.receive(STDIN.read)'

:0 c
* ^Subject:.*Bug Report.*
| cd $TICKET_APP_DIR && $RUBY runner $HANDLER
```

The receive class method is available to all Action Mailer classes. It takes the email text, parses it into a TMail object, creates a new instance of the receiver's class, and passes the Mail object to the receive instance method in that class.

But, for email templates, there's a little bit more naming magic. If you create multiple templates with the same name but with different content types embedded in their filenames, Rails will send all of them in one email, arranging the content so that the email client will be able to distinguish each.

This means you will want to either update or delete the plain-text template that Rails provided for the order_shipped notifier.

Function Testing Email

When we used the generate script to create our order mailer, it automatically constructed a corresponding notifier.rb file in the application's test/functional directory. It is pretty straightforward; it simply calls each action and verifies selected portions of the email produced. As we have tailored the email, let's update the test case to match:

`depot_r/test/functional/notifier_test.rb`

```ruby
require 'test_helper'

class NotifierTest < ActionMailer::TestCase
  test "order_received" do
▶   mail = Notifier.order_received(orders(:one))
▶   assert_equal "Pragmatic Store Order Confirmation", mail.subject
▶   assert_equal ["dave@example.org"], mail.to
▶   assert_equal ["depot@example.com"], mail.from
▶   assert_match /1 x Programming Ruby 1.9/, mail.body.encoded
  end

  test "order_shipped" do
▶   mail = Notifier.order_shipped(orders(:one))
▶   assert_equal "Pragmatic Store Order Shipped", mail.subject
▶   assert_equal ["dave@example.org"], mail.to
▶   assert_equal ["depot@example.com"], mail.from
▶   assert_match /<td>1&times;<\/td>\s*<td>Programming Ruby 1.9<\/td>/,
▶     mail.body.encoded
  end

end
```

The test method instructs the mail class to create (but not to send) an email, and we use assertions to verify that the dynamic content is what we expect. Note the use of assert_match to validate just part of the body content. Your results may differ depending on how you tailored the default :from line in your Notifier.

At this point, we have verified that the message we intend to create is formatted correctly, but we haven't verified that it is sent when the customer completes the ordering process. For that, we employ integration tests.

13.2 Iteration H2: Integration Testing of Applications

Rails organizes tests into unit, functional, and integration tests. Before explaining integration tests, let's have a brief recap of what we have covered so far:

Unit testing of models

> Model classes contain business logic. For example, when we add a product to a cart, the cart model class checks to see whether that product is already in the cart's list of items. If so, it increments the quantity of that item; if not, it adds a new item for that product.

Functional testing of controllers

> Controllers direct the show. They receive incoming web requests (typically user input), interact with models to gather application state, and then respond by causing the appropriate view to display something to the user. So when we're testing controllers, we're making sure that a given request is answered with an appropriate response. We still need models, but we already have them covered with unit tests.

The next level of testing is to exercise the flow through our application. In many ways, this is like testing one of the stories that our customer gave us when we first started to code the application. For example, we might have been told the following: *A user goes to the store index page. They select a product, adding it to their cart. They then check out, filling in their details on the checkout form. When they submit, an order is created in the database containing their information, along with a single line item corresponding to the product they added to their cart. Once the order has been received, an email is sent confirming their purchase.*

This is ideal material for an integration test. Integration tests simulate a continuous session between one or more virtual users and our application. You can use them to send in requests, monitor responses, follow redirects, and so on.

When you create a model or controller, Rails creates the corresponding unit or functional tests. Integration tests are not automatically created, however, but you can use a generator to create one.

```
depot> rails generate integration_test user_stories
      invoke  test_unit
      create    test/integration/user_stories_test.rb
```

Notice that Rails automatically adds _test to the name of the test.

Let's look at the generated file:

```
require 'test_helper'

class UserStoriesTest < ActionController::IntegrationTest
  fixtures :all

  # Replace this with your real tests.
  test "the truth" do
    assert true
  end
end
```

Let's launch straight in and implement the test of our story. Because we'll only be testing the purchase of a product, we'll need only our products fixture.

So instead of loading all the fixtures, let's load only this one:

```
fixtures :products
```

Now let's build a test named *buying a product*. By the end of the test, we know we'll want to have added an order to the orders table and a line item to the line_items table, so let's empty them out before we start. And, because we'll be using the Ruby book fixture data a lot, let's load it into a local variable:

depot_r/test/integration/user_stories_test.rb
```
LineItem.delete_all
Order.delete_all
ruby_book = products(:ruby)
```

Let's attack the first sentence in the user story: *A user goes to the store index page.*

depot_r/test/integration/user_stories_test.rb
```
get "/"
assert_response :success
assert_template "index"
```

This almost looks like a functional test. The main difference is the get method. In a functional test, we check just one controller, so we specify just an action when calling get. In an integration test, however, we can wander all over the application, so we need to pass in a full (relative) URL for the controller and action to be invoked.

The next sentence in the story goes *They select a product, adding it to their cart.* We know that our application uses an Ajax request to add things to the cart, so we'll use the xml_http_request method to invoke the action. When it returns, we'll check that the cart now contains the requested product:

depot_r/test/integration/user_stories_test.rb
```
xml_http_request :post, '/line_items', :product_id => ruby_book.id
assert_response :success

cart = Cart.find(session[:cart_id])
assert_equal 1, cart.line_items.size
assert_equal ruby_book, cart.line_items[0].product
```

In a thrilling plot twist, the user story continues: *They then check out....* That's easy in our test:

depot_r/test/integration/user_stories_test.rb
```
get "/orders/new"
assert_response :success
assert_template "new"
```

At this point, the user has to fill in their details on the checkout form. Once they do and they post the data, our application creates the order and redirects to the index page. Let's start with the HTTP side of the world by posting the form data to the save_order action and verifying we've been redirected to the index. We'll also check that the cart is now empty. The test helper method post_via_redirect generates the post request and then follows any redirects returned until a nonredirect response is returned.

depot_r/test/integration/user_stories_test.rb

```
post_via_redirect "/orders",
                  :order => { :name    => "Dave Thomas",
                              :address => "123 The Street",
                              :email   => "dave@example.com",
                              :pay_type => "Check" }
assert_response :success
assert_template "index"
cart = Cart.find(session[:cart_id])
assert_equal 0, cart.line_items.size
```

Next, we'll wander into the database and make sure we've created an order and corresponding line item and that the details they contain are correct. Because we cleared out the orders table at the start of the test, we'll simply verify that it now contains just our new order:

depot_r/test/integration/user_stories_test.rb

```
orders = Order.all
assert_equal 1, orders.size
order = orders[0]

assert_equal "Dave Thomas",       order.name
assert_equal "123 The Street",    order.address
assert_equal "dave@example.com",  order.email
assert_equal "Check",             order.pay_type

assert_equal 1, order.line_items.size
line_item = order.line_items[0]
assert_equal ruby_book, line_item.product
```

Finally, we'll verify that the mail itself is correctly addressed and has the expected subject line:

depot_r/test/integration/user_stories_test.rb

```
mail = ActionMailer::Base.deliveries.last
assert_equal ["dave@example.com"], mail.to
assert_equal 'Sam Ruby <depot@example.com>', mail[:from].value
assert_equal "Pragmatic Store Order Confirmation", mail.subject
```

And that's it. Here's the full source of the integration test:

`depot_r/test/integration/user_stories_test.rb`

```ruby
require 'test_helper'

class UserStoriesTest < ActionDispatch::IntegrationTest
  fixtures :products

  # A user goes to the index page. They select a product, adding it to their
  # cart, and check out, filling in their details on the checkout form. When
  # they submit, an order is created containing their information, along with a
  # single line item corresponding to the product they added to their cart.

  test "buying a product" do
    LineItem.delete_all
    Order.delete_all
    ruby_book = products(:ruby)

    get "/"
    assert_response :success
    assert_template "index"

    xml_http_request :post, '/line_items', :product_id => ruby_book.id
    assert_response :success

    cart = Cart.find(session[:cart_id])
    assert_equal 1, cart.line_items.size
    assert_equal ruby_book, cart.line_items[0].product

    get "/orders/new"
    assert_response :success
    assert_template "new"

    post_via_redirect "/orders",
                      :order => { :name     => "Dave Thomas",
                                  :address  => "123 The Street",
                                  :email    => "dave@example.com",
                                  :pay_type => "Check" }
    assert_response :success
    assert_template "index"
    cart = Cart.find(session[:cart_id])
    assert_equal 0, cart.line_items.size

    orders = Order.all
    assert_equal 1, orders.size
    order = orders[0]

    assert_equal "Dave Thomas",      order.name
    assert_equal "123 The Street",   order.address
    assert_equal "dave@example.com", order.email
    assert_equal "Check",            order.pay_type

    assert_equal 1, order.line_items.size
    line_item = order.line_items[0]
    assert_equal ruby_book, line_item.product
```

```
      mail = ActionMailer::Base.deliveries.last
      assert_equal ["dave@example.com"], mail.to
      assert_equal 'Sam Ruby <depot@example.com>', mail[:from].value
      assert_equal "Pragmatic Store Order Confirmation", mail.subject
   end
end
```

Taken together, unit, functional, and integration tests give you the flexibility to test aspects of your application either in isolation or in combination with each other. In Section 26.5, *Finding More at RailsPlugins.org*, on page 430, we will tell you where you can find add-ons that take this to the next level and allow you to write plain-text descriptions of behaviors that can be read by your customer and be verified automatically.

Speaking of our customer, it is time to wrap this iteration up and see what functionality is next in store for Depot.

What We Just Did

Without much code and with just a few templates, we have managed to pull off the following:

- We configured our development, test, and production environments for our Rails application to enable the sending of outbound emails.

- We created and tailored a mailer that will send confirmation emails in both plain-text and HTML formats to people who order our products.

- We created both a functional test for the emails produced, as well as an integration test that covers the entire order scenario.

Playtime

- Add a ship_date column to the orders table, and send a notification when this value is updated by the OrdersController.

- Update the application to send an email to the system administrator, namely, yourself, when there is an application failure such as the one we handled in Section 10.2, *Iteration E2: Handling Errors*, on page 116.

- Add integration tests for both of the previous items.

In this chapter, we'll see

- adding virtual attributes to models,
- using more validations,
- coding forms without underlying models,
- adding authentication to a session,
- using rails console,
- using database transactions, and
- writing an Active Record hook.

Chapter 14

Task I: Logging In

We have a happy customer—in a very short time we've jointly put together a basic shopping cart that she can start showing to her users. There's just one more change that she'd like to see. Right now, anyone can access the administrative functions. She'd like us to add a basic user administration system that would force you to log in to get into the administration parts of the site.

We're happy to do that, because it gives us a chance to look at virtual attributes and filters, and it lets us tidy up the application somewhat.

Chatting with our customer, it seems as if we don't need a particularly sophisticated security system for our application. We just need to recognize a number of people based on usernames and passwords. Once recognized, these folks can use all of the administration functions.

14.1 Iteration I1: Adding Users

Let's start by creating a model and database table to hold our administrators' usernames and passwords. Rather than store passwords in plain text, we will store a 256-bit SHA2 digest hash value of the password and a second value, called a *salt* in cryptographic circles.

This serves a number of purposes: even if our database is compromised, the hash won't reveal the original password, so it can't be used to log in as this user using the forms, nor can it be used elsewhere in the all-too-common case where a single user uses a password in multiple places.

```
depot> rails generate scaffold user \
  name:string hashed_password:string salt:string
```

Now run the migration as usual:

```
depot> rake db:migrate
```

Now we have to flesh out the user model. This turns out to be fairly complex because it has to work with the plain-text version of the password from the application's perspective but maintain a salt value and a hashed password in the database. Let's look at the model in sections. First, here's the validation:

depot_r/app/models/user.rb

```ruby
class User < ActiveRecord::Base
  validates :name, :presence => true, :uniqueness => true

  validates :password, :confirmation => true
  attr_accessor :password_confirmation
  attr_reader   :password

  validate   :password_must_be_present

  private

    def password_must_be_present
      errors.add(:password, "Missing password") unless hashed_password.present?
    end
end
```

That's a fair amount of validation for such a simple model. We check that the name is present and unique (that is, no two users can have the same name in the database). Then there's the mysterious :confirmation => true parameter.

You know those forms that prompt you to enter a password and then make you reenter it in a separate field so they can validate that you typed what you thought you typed? Well, Rails can automatically validate that the two passwords match. We'll see how that works in a minute. For now, we just have to know that we need two password fields, one for the actual password and the other for its confirmation.

Finally, we check that the password has been set. But we don't check the password attribute itself. Why? Because it doesn't really exist—at least not in the database. Instead, we check for the presence of its proxy, the hashed password. But to understand that, we have to look at how we handle password storage.

Now we need to create a hashed password, and we do so in three steps. First, we create a unique salt value (we talk about salts in a few paragraphs). Then we combine this salt value with the plain-text password and produce a single string. Then we run an SHA2 digest on the result, returning a 40-character string of hex digits. We'll write this as a public class method. (We'll also need to remember to require the digest/sha2 library in our file. See the listing starting on page 186 to see where it goes.)

`depot_r/app/models/user.rb`

```
def User.encrypt_password(password, salt)
  Digest::SHA2.hexdigest(password + "wibble" + salt)
end
```

In cryptography, salt strings[1] are random bits used to make it harder to crack the password. We'll create a salt string by concatenating a random number and the object id of the user object. It doesn't much matter what the salt is as long as it's unpredictable (using the time as a salt, for example, has lower entropy than a random string). We store this new salt into the model object's salt attribute. As this should be a private method, place it after the private keyword in the source:

`depot_r/app/models/user.rb`

```
def generate_salt
  self.salt = self.object_id.to_s + rand.to_s
end
```

There's a subtlety in this code we haven't seen before. Note that we wrote self.salt =.... This forces the assignment to use the salt= accessor method—we're saying "call the method salt= in the current object." Without the self., Ruby would have thought we were assigning to a local variable, and our code would have no effect.

Although using the instance variable directly would achieve the correct results, it would also tie you to a representation that may not always be the same. The attribute salt/salt= is the "official" interface to the underlying model attributes, so it is better to use them rather than instance variables.

Another way of looking at it is that because the attributes form part of the public interface of the class, then the class should eat its own dog food and use that interface too. If you use @xxx internally and .xxx externally, the door is wide open for some kind of mismatch down the road.

Now we need to write some code so that whenever a new plain-text password is stored into a user object we automatically create a hashed version (which will get stored in the database). We'll do that by making the plain-text password a *virtual attribute* of the model—it looks like an attribute to our application, but it isn't persisted into the database.

If it weren't for the need to create the hashed version, we could do this simply using Ruby's attr_accessor declaration:

```
attr_accessor :password
```

---

1. http://en.wikipedia.org/wiki/Salt_(cryptography)

Behind the scenes, attr_accessor generates two accessor methods: a reader called password and a writer called password=. The fact that the writer method name ends in an equals sign means that it can be assigned to. So, rather than using standard accessors, we'll simply implement our own public methods and have the writer also create a new salt and set the hashed password:

depot_r/app/models/user.rb

```
def password=(password)
  @password = password

  if password.present?
    generate_salt
    self.hashed_password = self.class.encrypt_password(password, salt)
  end
end
```

Again, we make use of the self to access hashed_password, but we do *not* use self to access the password assignment function because that would simply recurse.

There's one last change. Let's write a public class method that returns a user object if the caller supplies the correct name and password. Because the incoming password is in plain text, we have to read the user record using the name as a key and then use the salt value in that record to construct the hashed password again. We then return the user object if the hashed password matches. We can use this method to authenticate a user.

depot_r/app/models/user.rb

```
def User.authenticate(name, password)
  if user = find_by_name(name)
    if user.hashed_password == encrypt_password(password, user.salt)
      user
    end
  end
end
```

The user model contains a fair amount of code, but it shows how models can carry a fair amount of business logic. Let's review the entire model before moving on to the controller:

depot_r/app/models/user.rb

```
require 'digest/sha2'

class User < ActiveRecord::Base
  validates :name, :presence => true, :uniqueness => true

  validates :password, :confirmation => true
  attr_accessor :password_confirmation
  attr_reader   :password
```

```
    validate  :password_must_be_present

  def User.authenticate(name, password)
    if user = find_by_name(name)
      if user.hashed_password == encrypt_password(password, user.salt)
        user
      end
    end
  end

  def User.encrypt_password(password, salt)
    Digest::SHA2.hexdigest(password + "wibble" + salt)
  end

  # 'password' is a virtual attribute
  def password=(password)
    @password = password

    if password.present?
      generate_salt
      self.hashed_password = self.class.encrypt_password(password, salt)
    end
  end

  private

    def password_must_be_present
      errors.add(:password, "Missing password") unless hashed_password.present?
    end

    def generate_salt
      self.salt = self.object_id.to_s + rand.to_s
    end
end
```

With this code in place, we have the ability to present both a password and a password confirmation field in a form, as well as the ability to authenticate a user given a name and a password.

Administering Our Users

In addition to the model and table we set up, we already have some scaffolding generated to administer the model. However, this scaffolding needs some tweaks to make use of the new password fields we just defined.

Let's start with the controller. It defines the standard methods: index, show, new, edit, update, and delete. But in the case of users, there isn't really much to show, except a name and an unintelligible password hash. So, let's avoid the redirect to showing the user after a create operation. Instead, let's redirect to the user's index and add the username to the flash notice.

String interpolation ↪ page 40

depot_r/app/controllers/users_controller.rb

```
def create
  @user = User.new(params[:user])

  respond_to do |format|
    if @user.save
▶     format.html { redirect_to(users_url,
▶       :notice => "User #{@user.name} was successfully created.") }
      format.xml  { render :xml => @user,
        :status => :created, :location => @user }
    else
      format.html { render :action => "new" }
      format.xml  { render :xml => @user.errors,
        :status => :unprocessable_entity }
    end
  end
end
```

Let's do the same for an update operation:

depot_r/app/controllers/users_controller.rb

```
def update
  @user = User.find(params[:id])

  respond_to do |format|
    if @user.update_attributes(params[:user])
▶     format.html { redirect_to(users_url,
▶       :notice => "User #{@user.name} was successfully updated.") }
      format.xml  { head :ok }
    else
      format.html { render :action => "edit" }
      format.xml  { render :xml => @user.errors,
        :status => :unprocessable_entity }
    end
  end
end
```

While we are here, let's also order the users returned in the index by name:

depot_r/app/controllers/users_controller.rb

```
def index
▶ @users = User.order(:name)

  respond_to do |format|
    format.html # index.html.erb
    format.xml  { render :xml => @users }
  end
end
```

Now that the controller changes are done, let's attend to the view. As it stands now, the view doesn't display notice information, and the table contains too much information. Specifically, the table shows the hashed password and salt.

We will proceed to add the notice and delete both the th and td lines for these fields:

depot_r/app/views/users/index.html.erb

```
<h1>Listing users</h1>
► <% if notice %>
► <p id="notice"><%= notice %></p>
► <% end %>

<table>
  <tr>
    <th>Name</th>
    <th></th>
    <th></th>
    <th></th>
  </tr>

<% @users.each do |user| %>
  <tr>
    <td><%= user.name %></td>
    <td><%= link_to 'Show', user %></td>
    <td><%= link_to 'Edit', edit_user_path(user) %></td>
    <td><%= link_to 'Destroy', user, :confirm => 'Are you sure?',
        :method => :delete %></td>
  </tr>
<% end %>
</table>

<br />

<%= link_to 'New User', new_user_path %>
```

Finally, we need to update the form used both to create a new user and to update an existing user. First, we replace the hashed password and salt text fields with password and password confirmation fields. Then we add legend and fieldset tags. And finally we wrap the output in a *<div>* tag with a class that we previously defined in our stylesheet.

depot_r/app/views/users/_form.html.erb

```
<div class="depot_form">

<%= form_for @user do |f| %>
  <% if @user.errors.any? %>
    <div id="error_explanation">
      <h2><%= pluralize(@user.errors.count, "error") %>
        prohibited this user from being saved:</h2>
      <ul>
      <% @user.errors.full_messages.each do |msg| %>
        <li><%= msg %></li>
      <% end %>
      </ul>
    </div>
  <% end %>
```

```
<fieldset>
<legend>Enter User Details</legend>

  <div>
    <%= f.label :name %>:
    <%= f.text_field :name, :size => 40 %>
  </div>

  <div>
    <%= f.label :password, 'Password' %>:
    <%= f.password_field :password, :size => 40 %>
  </div>

  <div>
    <%= f.label :password_confirmation, 'Confirm' %>:
    <%= f.password_field :password_confirmation, :size => 40 %>
  </div>

  <div>
    <%= f.submit %>
  </div>

  </fieldset>
<% end %>

</div>
```

Let's try it. Navigate to http://localhost:3000/users/new. For a stunning example of page design, see Figure 14.1, on the facing page.

After clicking Create User , the index is redisplayed with a cheery flash notice. If we look in our database, you'll see that we've stored the user details. (Of course, the values in your row will be different, because the salt value is effectively random.)

```
depot> sqlite3 -line db/development.sqlite3 "select * from users"
            id = 1
          name = dave
hashed_password = a12b1dbb97d3843ee27626b2bb96447941887ded
          salt = 203333500.653238054564258
    created_at = 2011-02-11 21:40:19
    updated_at = 2011-02-11 21:40:19
```

Like we have done before, we need to update our tests to reflect the validation and redirection changes we have made:

depot_s/test/functional/users_controller_test.rb

```
require 'test_helper'

class UsersControllerTest < ActionController::TestCase
  setup do
▶    @input_attributes = {
```

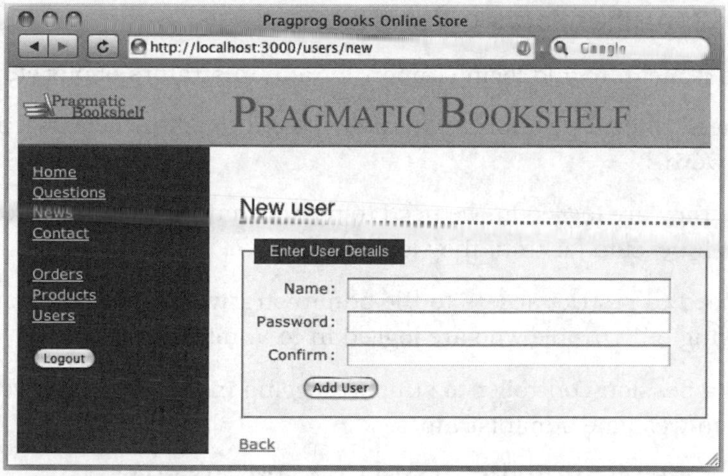

Figure 14.1: ENTERING USER DETAILS

```
►      :name                 => "sam",
►      :password             => "private",
►      :password_confirmation => "private"
►    }

    @user = users(:one)
  end
  #...
  test "should create user" do
    assert_difference('User.count') do
►     post :create, :user => @input_attributes
    end

►   assert_redirected_to users_path
  end
  #...
  test "should update user" do
►   put :update, :id => @user.to_param, :user => @input_attributes
►   assert_redirected_to users_path
  end
end
```

At this point, we can administer our users; we need to first authenticate users, then restrict administrative functions to be accessible only by administrators.

14.2 Iteration I2: Authenticating Users

What does it mean to add login support for administrators of our store?

- We need to provide a form that allows them to enter their username and password.

- Once they are logged in, we need to record that fact somehow for the rest of their session (or until they log out).

- We need to restrict access to the administrative parts of the application, allowing only people who are logged in to administer the store.

We'll need a session controller to support logging in and out, and we'll need a controller to welcome administrators.

```
depot> rails generate controller sessions new create destroy
depot> rails generate controller admin index
```

The SessionsController#create action will need to record something in session to say that an administrator is logged in. Let's have it store the id of their User object using the key :user_id. The login code looks like this:

depot_r/app/controllers/sessions_controller.rb

```
def create
►   if user = User.authenticate(params[:name], params[:password])
►     session[:user_id] = user.id
►     redirect_to admin_url
►   else
►     redirect_to login_url, :alert => "Invalid user/password combination"
►   end
end
```

We are also doing something new here: using a form that isn't directly associated with a model object. To see how that works, let's look at the template for the sessions#new action:

depot_r/app/views/sessions/new.html.erb

```
<div class="depot_form">
  <% if flash[:alert] %>
    <p id="notice"><%= flash[:alert] %></p>
  <% end %>

  <%= form_tag do %>
    <fieldset>
      <legend>Please Log In</legend>

      <div>
        <label for="name">Name:</label>
        <%= text_field_tag :name, params[:name] %>
      </div>
```

```
    <div>
      <label for="password">Password:</label>
      <%= password_field_tag :password, params[:password] %>
    </div>

    <div>
      <%= submit_tag "Login" %>
    </div>
  </fieldset>
<% end %>
</div>
```

This form is different from ones we saw earlier. Rather than using form_for, it uses form_tag, which simply builds a regular HTML <*form*>. Inside that form, it uses text_field_tag and password_field_tag, two helpers that create HTML <*input*> tags. Each helper takes two parameters. The first is the name to give to the field, and the second is the value with which to populate the field. This style of form allows us to associate values in the params structure directly with form fields—no model object is required. In our case, we chose to use the params object directly in the form. An alternative would be to have the controller set instance variables.

See Figure 14.2, on the next page. Note how the value of the form field is communicated between the controller and the view using the params hash: the view gets the value to display in the field from params[:name], and when the user submits the form, the new field value is made available to the controller the same way.

If the user successfully logs in, we store the id of the user record in the session data. We'll use the presence of that value in the session as a flag to indicate that an admin user is logged in.

As you might expect, the controller actions for logging out are considerably simpler:

`depot_r/app/controllers/sessions_controller.rb`

```
def destroy
▶   session[:user_id] = nil
▶   redirect_to store_url, :notice => "Logged out"
end
```

Finally, it's about time to add the index page, the first screen that administrators see when they log in. Let's make it useful—we'll have it display the total number of orders in our store. Create the template in the file index.html.erb in the directory app/views/admin. (This template uses the pluralize helper, which in this case generates the string order or orders depending on the cardinality of its first parameter.)

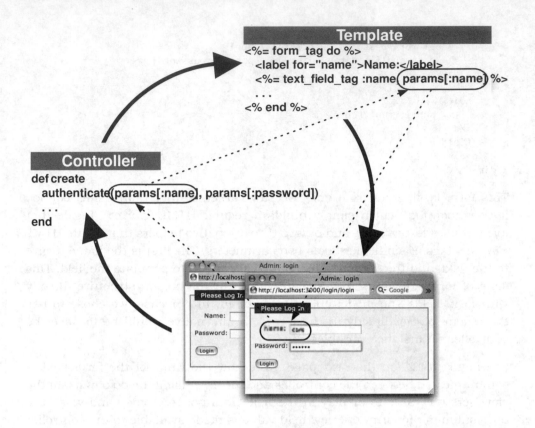

Figure 14.2: Parameters flow between controllers, templates, and browsers

depot_r/app/views/admin/index.html.erb

```
<h1>Welcome</h1>

It's <%= Time.now %>
We have <%= pluralize(@total_orders, "order") %>.
```

The index action sets up the count:

depot_r/app/controllers/admin_controller.rb

```
class AdminController < ApplicationController
  def index
►   @total_orders = Order.count
  end

end
```

We have one more task to do before we can use this. Whereas previously we relied on the scaffolding generator to create our model and routes for us, this time we simply generated a controller because there is no database-backed model for this controller. Unfortunately, without the scaffolding conventions to guide it, Rails has no way of knowing which actions are to respond to GET requests, which are to respond to POST requests, and so on, for this controller. We need to provide this information by editing our config/routes.rb file:

depot_r/config/routes.rb
```ruby
Depot::Application.routes.draw do
►  get 'admin' => 'admin#index'

►  controller :sessions do
►    get    'login'  => :new
►    post   'login'  => :create
►    delete 'logout' => :destroy
►  end


  resources :users

  resources :orders

  resources :line_items

  resources :carts

  get "store/index"
  resources :products do
    get :who_bought, :on => :member
  end


  # ...

  # You can have the root of your site routed with "root"
  # just remember to delete public/index.html.
  # root :to => "welcome#index"
  root :to => 'store#index', :as => 'store'

  # ...
end
```

We've touched this before, when we added a root statement in Section 8.1, *Iteration C1: Creating the Catalog Listing*, on page 89. What the generate command will add to this file are fairly generic get statements for each of the actions specified. You can (and should) delete the routes provided for sessions/new, sessions/create, and sessions/destroy.

Figure 14.3: ADMINISTRATIVE INTERFACE

In the case of admin, we will shorten the URL that the user has to enter (by removing the /index part) and map it to the full action. In the case of session actions, we will completely change the URL (replacing things like session/create with simply login) as well as tailoring the HTTP action that we will match. Note that login is mapped to both the new and create actions, the difference being whether the request was an HTTP GET or HTTP POST.

We also make use of a shortcut: wrapping the session route declarations in a block and passing it to a controller class method. This saves us a bit of typing as well as making the routes easier to read. We will describe all that you can do in this file in Section 20.1, *Dispatching Requests to Controllers*, on page 301.

With these routes in place, we can experience the joy of logging in as an administrator. See Figure 14.3.

We need to replace the functional tests in the session controller to match what we just implemented:

`depot_s/test/functional/sessions_controller_test.rb`

```ruby
require 'test_helper'

class SessionsControllerTest < ActionController::TestCase
  test "should get new" do
    get :new
    assert_response :success
  end

  test "should login" do
    dave = users(:one)
    post :create, :name => dave.name, :password => 'secret'
    assert_redirected_to admin_url
    assert_equal dave.id, session[:user_id]
  end
```

```
►    test "should fail login" do
►      dave = users(.one)
►      post :create, :name => dave.name, :password => 'wrong'
►      assert_redirected_to login_url
►    end

►    test "should logout" do
►      delete :destroy
►      assert_redirected_to store_url
►    end

  end
```

And we need to update the test fixtures to match:

depot_s/test/fixtures/users.yml

```
<% SALT = "NaCl" unless defined?(SALT) %>

one:
  name: dave
  hashed_password: <%= User.encrypt_password('secret', SALT) %>
  salt: <%= SALT %>

two:
  name: MyString
  hashed_password: MyString
  salt: MyString
```

Note the use of dynamically computed values in the fixture, specifically for the value of hashed_password. While salt values need to be random, for testing purposes, we are using a simple value.

We show our customer where we are, but she points out that we still haven't controlled access to the administrative pages (which was, after all, the point of this exercise).

14.3 Iteration I3: Limiting Access

We want to prevent people without an administrative login from accessing our site's admin pages. It turns out that it's easy to implement using the Rails *filter* facility.

Rails filters allow you to intercept calls to action methods, adding your own processing before they are invoked, after they return, or both. In our case, we'll use a *before filter* to intercept all calls to the actions in our admin controller. The interceptor can check session[:user_id]. If it's set and if it corresponds to a user in the database, the application knows an administrator is logged in, and the call can proceed. If it's not set, the interceptor can issue a redirect, in this case to our login page.

Where should we put this method? It could sit directly in the admin controller, but, for reasons that will become apparent shortly, let's put it instead in ApplicationController, the parent class of all our controllers. This is in the file application_controller.rb in the directory app/controllers. Note too that we chose to restrict access to this method. This prevents it from ever being exposed to end users as an action.

depot_r/app/controllers/application_controller.rb

```ruby
class ApplicationController < ActionController::Base
▶   before_filter :authorize
    protect_from_forgery

    private

      def current_cart
        Cart.find(session[:cart_id])
      rescue ActiveRecord::RecordNotFound
        cart = Cart.create
        session[:cart_id] = cart.id
        cart
      end

      # ...
▶
▶     protected
▶
▶       def authorize
▶         unless User.find_by_id(session[:user_id])
▶           redirect_to login_url, :notice => "Please log in"
▶         end
▶       end
    end
```

The before_filter line causes the authorization to be invoked before every action in our application.

This is going too far. We have just limited access to the store itself to administrators. That's not good.

We could go back and change things so that we mark only those methods that specifically need authorization. Such an approach is called *blacklisting* and is prone to errors of omission. A much better approach is to "whitelist" or list methods or controllers for which authorization is *not* required. We do this simply by inserting a skip_before_filter call within the StoreController:

depot_r/app/controllers/store_controller.rb

```ruby
class StoreController < ApplicationController
▶   skip_before_filter :authorize
```

And again for the SessionsController class:

depot_r/app/controllers/sessions_controller.rb

```
class SessionsController < ApplicationController
►   skip_before_filter :authorize
```

We're not done yet; now we need to allow people to create, update, and delete carts:

depot_r/app/controllers/carts_controller.rb

```
class CartsController < ApplicationController
►     skip_before_filter :authorize, :only => [:create, :update, :destroy]
►
```

Create line items:

depot_r/app/controllers/line_items_controller.rb

```
class LineItemsController < ApplicationController
►     skip_before_filter :authorize, :only => :create
►
```

And create orders (which includes access to the new form):

depot_r/app/controllers/orders_controller.rb

```
class OrdersController < ApplicationController
►     skip_before_filter :authorize, :only => [:new, :create]
►
```

With the authorization logic in place, we can now navigate to http://localhost: 3000/products. The filter method intercepts us on the way to the product listing and shows us the login screen instead.

Unfortunately, this change pretty much invalidates most of our functional tests because most operations will now redirect to the login screen instead of doing the function desired. Fortunately, we can address this globally by creating a setup method in the test_helper. While we are there, we also define some helper methods to login_as and logout a user.

depot_s/test/test_helper.rb

```
class ActiveSupport::TestCase
  # ...

  # Add more helper methods to be used by all tests here...
  def login_as(user)
    session[:user_id] = users(user).id
  end

  def logout
    session.delete :user_id
  end
```

```
    def setup
      login_as :one if defined? session
    end
  end
```

Note that the setup method will call login_as only if session is defined. This prevents the login from being executed in tests that do not involve a controller.

We show our customer and are rewarded with a big smile and a request: could we add a sidebar and put links to the user and product administration stuff in it? And while we're there, could we add the ability to list and delete administrative users? You betcha!

14.4 Iteration I4: Adding a Sidebar, More Administration

Let's start with adding links to various administration functions to the sidebar in the layout and have them show up only if there is :user_id in the session:

`depot_r/app/views/layouts/application.html.erb`

```erb
<!DOCTYPE html>
<html>
<head>
  <title>Pragprog Books Online Store</title>
  <%= stylesheet_link_tag "scaffold" %>
  <%= stylesheet_link_tag "depot", :media => "all" %>
  <%= javascript_include_tag :defaults %>
  <%= csrf_meta_tag %>
</head>
<body id="store">
  <div id="banner">
    <%= image_tag("logo.png") %>
    <%= @page_title || "Pragmatic Bookshelf" %>
  </div>
  <div id="columns">
    <div id="side">
      <% if @cart %>
        <%= hidden_div_if(@cart.line_items.empty?, :id => "cart") do %>
          <%= render @cart %>
        <% end %>
      <% end %>

      <a href="http://www....">Home</a><br />
      <a href="http://www..../faq">Questions</a><br />
      <a href="http://www..../news">News</a><br />
      <a href="http://www..../contact">Contact</a><br />
►
►         <% if session[:user_id] %>
►           <br />
►           <%= link_to 'Orders',   orders_path   %><br />
►           <%= link_to 'Products', products_path %><br />
►           <%= link_to 'Users',    users_path    %><br />
►           <br />
```

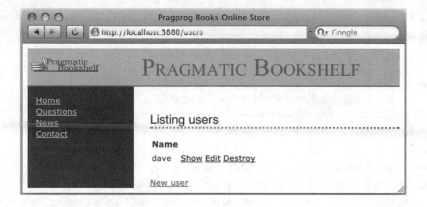

Figure 14.4: LISTING OUR USERS

```
►        <%= button_to 'Logout', logout_path, :method => :delete   %>
►      <% end %>
     </div>
     <div id="main">
       <%= yield %>
     </div>
   </div>
 </body>
 </html>
```

Now it is all starting to come together. We can log in, and by clicking a link on the sidebar, we can see a list of users. Let's see whether we can break something.

Would the Last Admin to Leave...

We bring up the user list screen that looks something like Figure 14.4; then we click the Destroy link next to *dave* to delete that user. Sure enough, our user is removed. But to our surprise, we're then presented with the login screen instead. We just deleted the only administrative user from the system. When the next request came in, the authentication failed, so the application refused to let us in. We have to log in again before using any administrative functions.

But now we have an embarrassing problem: there are no administrative users in the database, so we can't log in.

Fortunately, we can quickly add a user to the database from the command line. If you invoke the command rails console, Rails invokes Ruby's irb utility, but it does so in the context of your Rails application. That means you can interact with your application's code by typing Ruby statements and looking at the values they return.

We can use this to invoke our user model directly, having it add a user into the database for us:

```
depot> rails console
Loading development environment.
>> User.create(:name => 'dave', :password => 'secret',
               :password_confirmation => 'secret')
=> #<User:0x2933060 @attributes={...} ... >
>> User.count
=> 1
```

The >> sequences are prompts. After the first, we call the User class to create a new user, and after the second, we call it again to show that we do indeed have a single user in our database. After each command we enter, rails console displays the value returned by the code (in the first case, it's the model object, and in the second case, it's the count).

Panic over. We can now log back in to the application. But how can we stop this from happening again? There are several ways. For example, we could write code that prevents you from deleting your own user. That doesn't quite work—in theory, A could delete B at just the same time that B deletes A. Instead, let's try a different approach. We'll delete the user inside a database transaction. If after we've deleted the user there are then no users left in the database, we'll roll the transaction back, restoring the user we just deleted.

To do this, we'll use an Active Record hook method. We've already seen one of these: the validate hook is called by Active Record to validate an object's state. It turns out that Active Record defines twenty or so hook methods, each called at a particular point in an object's life cycle. We'll use the after_destroy hook, which is called after the SQL delete is executed. If a method by this name is publicly visible, it will conveniently be called in the same transaction as the delete, so if it raises an exception, the transaction will be rolled back. The hook method looks like this:

depot_s/app/models/user.rb

```
after_destroy :ensure_an_admin_remains

def ensure_an_admin_remains
  if User.count.zero?
    raise "Can't delete last user"
  end
end
```

The key concept here is the use of an exception to indicate an error when deleting the user. This exception serves two purposes. First, because it is raised inside a transaction, it causes an automatic rollback. By raising the exception if the users table is empty after the deletion, we undo the delete and restore that last user.

Second, the exception signals the error back to the controller, where we use a begin/end block to handle it and report the error to the user in the flash. If you want only to abort the transaction but not otherwise signal an exception, raise an ActiveRecord::Rollback exception instead, because this is the only exception that won't be passed on by ActiveRecord::Base.transaction.

`depot_s/app/controllers/users_controller.rb`

```
def destroy
  @user = User.find(params[:id])
  begin
    @user.destroy
    flash[:notice] = "User #{@user.name} deleted"
  rescue Exception => e
    flash[:notice] = e.message
  end

  respond_to do |format|
    format.html { redirect_to(users_url) }
    format.xml  { head :ok }
  end
```

This code still has a potential timing issue—it is still possible for two administrators each to delete the last two users if their timing is right. Fixing this would require more database wizardry than we have space for here.

In fact, the login system described in this chapter is rather rudimentary. Most applications these days use a plugin to do this. A number of plugins are available that provide ready-made solutions that not only are more comprehensive than the authentication logic shown here but generally require less code and effort on your part to use. See Section 26.5, *Finding More at RailsPlugins.org*, on page 430 for a couple of examples.

What We Just Did

By the end of this iteration, we've done the following:

- We created a virtual attribute representing the plain-text password and coded it to create the hashed version whenever the plain-text version is updated.

- We controlled access to the administration functions using before filters to invoke an authorize method.

- We saw how to use rails console to interact directly with a model (and dig us out of a hole after we deleted the last user).

- We saw how a transaction can help prevent deleting the last user.

Playtime

Here's some stuff to try on your own:

- When the system is freshly installed on a new machine, there are no administrators defined in the database, and hence no administrator can log on. But, if no administrator can log on, then no one can create an administrative user. Change the code so that if no administrator is defined in the database, any username works to log on (allowing you to quickly create a real administrator).

- Experiment with rails console. Try creating products, orders, and line items. Watch for the return value when you save a model object—when validation fails, you'll see false returned. Find out why by examining the errors:

```
>> prd = Product.new
=> #<Product id: nil, title: nil, description: nil, image_url:
nil, created_at: nil, updated_at: nil, price:
#<BigDecimal:246aa1c,'0.0',4(8)>>
>> prd.save
=> false
>> prd.errors.full_messages
=> ["Image url must be a URL for a GIF, JPG, or PNG image",
    "Image url can't be blank", "Price should be at least 0.01",
    "Title can't be blank", "Description can't be blank"]
```

(You'll find hints at http://www.pragprog.com/wikis/wiki/RailsPlayTime.)

In this chapter, we'll see

- localizing templates, and
- database design considerations for I18n.

Chapter 15

Task J: Internationalization

Now we have a basic cart working, and our customer starts to inquire about languages other than English, noting that her company has a big push on for expansion in emerging markets. Unless we can present something in a language that visitors to our customer's website will understand, our customer will be leaving money on the table. We can't have that.

The first problem is that none of us is a professional translator. The customer reassures us that this is not something that we need to concern ourselves with because that part of the effort will be outsourced. All we need to worry about is *enabling* translation. Furthermore, we don't have to worry about the administration pages just yet, because all the administrators speak English. What we have to focus on is the store.

That's a relief—but is still a tall order. We are going to need to define a way to enable the user to select a language, we are going to have to provide the translations themselves, and we are going to have to change the views to use these translations. But we are up to the task, and armed with a bit of memory of high-school Spanish, we set off to work.

 **Joe Asks. . .**

If I Stick to One Language, Do I Need to Read This Chapter?

The short answer is no. In fact, many Rails applications are for a small or homogeneous group and never need translating. That being said, pretty much everybody that does find that they need translation agrees that it is best if this is done early. So, unless you are sure that translation will not ever be needed, it is our recommendation that you at least understand what would be involved so that you can make an informed decision.

◀ 205 ▶

15.1 Iteration J1: Selecting the Locale

We start by creating a new configuration file that encapsulates our knowledge of what locales are available and which one is to be used as the default.

`depot_s/config/initializers/i18n.rb`

```
#encoding: utf-8
I18n.default_locale = :en

LANGUAGES = [
  ['English',                    'en'],
  ["Espa&ntilde;ol".html_safe, 'es']
]
```

This code is doing two things.

The first thing it does is use the I18n module to set the default locale. I18n is a funny name, but it sure beats typing out *internationalization* all the time. Internationalization, after all, starts with an *i*, ends with an *n*, and has eighteen letters in between.

Then it defines a list of associations between display names and locale names. Unfortunately, all we have available at the moment is a U.S. keyboard, and español has a character that can't be directly entered via our keyboard. Different operating systems have different ways of dealing with this, and often the easiest way is to simply copy and paste the correct text from a website. If you do this, just make sure your editor is configured for UTF-8. Meanwhile, we've opted to use the HTML equivalent of "n con tilde" character in Spanish. If we didn't do anything else, the markup itself would be shown. But by calling html_safe, we inform Rails that the string is safe to be interpreted as containing HTML.

To get Rails to pick up this configuration change, the server needs to be restarted.

Since each page that is translated will have an en and es version (for now, more will be added later), it makes sense to include this in the URL. Let's plan to put the locale up front, make it optional, and have it default to the current locale, which in turn will default to English.

To implement this cunning plan, let's start with modifying config/routes.rb:

`depot_s/config/routes.rb`

```
Depot::Application.routes.draw do
  get 'admin' => 'admin#index'
  controller :sessions do
    get    'login'  => :new
    post   'login'  => :create
    delete 'logout' => :destroy
  end
```

```
    scope '(:locale)' do
      resources :users
      resources :orders
      resources :line_items
      resources :carts
      resources :products do
        get :who_bought, :on => :member
      end
      root :to => 'store#index', :as => 'store'
    end
  end
```

What we have done is nested our resources and root declarations inside a scope declaration for :locale. Furthermore, :locale is in parentheses, which is the way to say that it is optional. Note that we did not choose to put the administrative and session functions inside this scope, because it is not our intent to translate them at this time.

What this means is that both http://localhost:3000/ will use the default locale, namely, English, and therefore be routed exactly the same as http://localhost:3000/en. http://localhost:3000/es will route to the same controller and action, but we will want this to cause the locale to be set differently.

To do this, we need to create a before_filter and to set the default_url_options. The logical place to do both is in the common base class for all of our controllers, which is ApplicationController:

depot_s/app/controllers/application_controller.rb

```
class ApplicationController < ActionController::Base
  before_filter :set_i18n_locale_from_params
  # ...
  protected
    def set_i18n_locale_from_params
      if params[:locale]
        if I18n.available_locales.include?(params[:locale].to_sym)
          I18n.locale = params[:locale]
        else
          flash.now[:notice] =
            "#{params[:locale]} translation not available"
          logger.error flash.now[:notice]
        end
      end
    end

    def default_url_options
      { :locale => I18n.locale }
    end
end
```

This set_i18n_locale_from_params does pretty much what it says: it sets the locale in the session from the params, but only if there is a locale in the params;

Figure 15.1: ENGLISH VERSION OF THE FRONT PAGE

otherwise, it leaves the locale alone. Care is taken to provide a message for both the user and the administrator when there is a failure.

And default_url_options also does pretty much what it says, in that it provides a hash of URL options that are to be considered as present whenever they aren't otherwise provided. In this case, we are providing a value for the :locale parameter. This is needed when a view on a page that does not have the locale specified attempts to construct a link to a page that does. We will see that in use soon.

With this in place, we can see the results in Figure 15.1.

At this point, the English version of the page is available both at the root of the website and at pages that start with /en. Additionally, a message on the screen says that the translation is not available (as we can see in Figure 15.2, on the facing page), which will also leave a message in the log indicating that the file wasn't found. It might not look like it, but that's progress.

15.2 Iteration J2: Translating the Storefront

Now it is time to begin providing the translated text. Let's start with the layout, because it is pretty visible. We replace any text that needs to be translated with calls to I18n.translate . Not only is this method conveniently aliased as I18n.t, but there also is a helper provided named t.

Figure 15.2: TRANSLATION NOT AVAILABLE

The parameter to the translate function is a unique dot-qualified name. We can choose any name we like, but if we use the † helper function provided, names that start with a dot will first be expanded using the name of the template. So, let's do that.

`depot_s/app/views/layouts/application.html.erb`

```erb
<!DOCTYPE html>
<html>
<head>
  <title>Pragprog Books Online Store</title>
  <%= stylesheet_link_tag "scaffold" %>
  <%= stylesheet_link_tag "depot", :media => "all" %>
  <%= javascript_include_tag :defaults %>
  <%= csrf_meta_tag %>
</head>
<body id="store">
  <div id="banner">
    <%= image_tag("logo.png") %>
    <%= @page_title || t('.title') %>
  </div>
  <div id="columns">
    <div id="side">
      <% if @cart %>
        <%= hidden_div_if(@cart.line_items.empty?, :id => "cart") do %>
          <%= render @cart %>
        <% end %>
      <% end %>
```

```
▶              <a href="http://www...."><%= t('.home') %></a><br />
▶              <a href="http://www..../faq"><%= t('.questions') %></a><br />
▶              <a href="http://www..../news"><%= t('.news') %></a><br />
▶              <a href="http://www..../contact"><%= t('.contact') %></a><br />

            <% if session[:user_id] %>
              <br />
              <%= link_to 'Orders',   orders_path   %><br />
              <%= link_to 'Products', products_path %><br />
              <%= link_to 'Users',    users_path    %><br />
              <br />
              <%= button_to 'Logout', logout_path, :method => :delete   %>
            <% end %>
          </div>
          <div id="main">
            <%= yield %>
          </div>
        </div>
      </body>
    </html>
```

Since this view is named layouts/application.html.erb, the English mappings will
expand to en.layouts.application. Here's the corresponding locale file:

depot_s/config/locales/en.yml

```
en:

  layouts:
    application:
      title:        "Pragmatic Bookshelf"
      home:         "Home"
      questions:    "Questions"
      news:         "News"
      contact:      "Contact"
```

and next in Spanish:

depot_s/config/locales/es.yml

```
es:

  layouts:
    application:
      title:        "Publicaciones de Pragmatic"
      home:         "Inicio"
      questions:    "Preguntas"
      news:         "Noticias"
      contact:      "Contacto"
```

YAML
↪ page 47

The format is YAML, the same as the one used to configure the databases.
YAML simply consists of indented names and values, where the indentation in
this case matches the structure that we created in our names.

Figure 15.3: BABY STEPS: TRANSLATED TITLES AND SIDEBAR

To get Rails to recognize that there are new YAML files, the server needs to be restarted.

At this point, we can see in Figure 15.3 the actual translated text appearing in our browser window.

Next to be updated is the main title as well as the Add to Cart button. Both can be found in the store index template:

depot_s/app/views/store/index.html.erb

```
<% if notice %>
<p id="notice"><%= notice %></p>
<% end %>

<h1><%= t('.title_html') %></h1>

<% @products.each do |product| %>
  <div class="entry">
    <%= image_tag(product.image_url) %>
    <h3><%= product.title %></h3>
    <%= sanitize(product.description) %>
    <div class="price_line">
      <span class="price"><%= number_to_currency(product.price) %></span>
      <%= button_to t('.add_html'), line_items_path(:product_id => product),
        :remote => true %>
    </div>
  </div>
<% end %>
```

And here's the corresponding updates to the locales files, first in English:

`depot_s/config/locales/en.yml`

```
en:

  store:
    index:
      title_html:  "Your Pragmatic Catalog"
      add_html:    "Add to Cart"
```

and then in Spanish:

`depot_s/config/locales/es.yml`

```
es:

  store:
    index:
      title_html:  "Su Cat&aacute;logo de Pragmatic"
      add_html:    "A&ntilde;adir al Carrito"
```

Note that since title_html and add_html end in the characters _html, we are free to use HTML entity names for characters that do not appear on our keyboard. If we did not name the translation key this way, what you would end up seeing on the page is the markup itself. This is yet another convention that Rails has adopted to make your coding life easier. Rails will also treat names that contain html as a component (in other words, the string .html.) as HTML key names.

By refreshing the page in the browser window, we see the results shown in Figure 15.4, on the facing page.

Feeling confident, we move onto the cart partial:

`depot_s/app/views/carts/_cart.html.erb`

```
▶ <div class="cart_title"><%= t('.title') %></div>
  <table>
    <%= render(cart.line_items) %>

    <tr class="total_line">
      <td colspan="2">Total</td>
      <td class="total_cell"><%= number_to_currency(cart.total_price) %></td>
    </tr>

  </table>
▶ <%= button_to t('.checkout'), new_order_path, :method => :get %>
▶ <%= button_to t('.empty'), cart, :method => :delete,
      :confirm => 'Are you sure?' %>
```

Figure 15.4: TRANSLATED HEADING AND BUTTON

And again, the translations:

`depot_s/config/locales/en.yml`

```
en:

  carts:
    cart:
      title:        "Your Cart"
      empty:        "Empty cart"
      checkout:     "Checkout"
```

`depot_s/config/locales/es.yml`

```
es:

  carts:
    cart:
      title:        "Carrito de la Compra"
      empty:        "Vaciar Carrito"
      checkout:     "Comprar"
```

At this point, we notice our first problem. Languages are not the only thing that varies from locale to locale; currencies do too. And the customary way that numbers are presented varies too.

So, first we check with our customer, and we verify that we are not worrying about exchange rates at the moment (whew!), because that will be taken care of by the credit card and/or wire companies, but we do need to display the string "USD" or "$US" after the value when we are showing the result in Spanish.

Another variation is the way that numbers themselves are displayed. Decimal values are delimited by a comma, and separators for the thousands place are indicated by a dot.

Currency is a lot more complicated than it first appears, and that's a lot of decisions to be made. Fortunately, Rails knows to look in your translations file for this information; all we need to do is supply it. First for en:

depot_s/config/locales/en.yml

```
en:

  number:
    currency:
      format:
        unit:       "$"
        precision:  2
        separator:  "."
        delimiter:  ","
        format:     "%u%n"
```

And then for es:

depot_s/config/locales/es.yml

```
es:

  number:
    currency:
      format:
        unit:       "$US"
        precision:  2
        separator:  ","
        delimiter:  "."
        format:     "%n %u"
```

We've specified the unit, precision, separator, and delimiter for number.currency.
format. That much is pretty self-explanatory. The format is a bit more involved:
%n is a placeholder for the number itself;   is a nonbreaking space character, preventing this value from being split across multiple lines; and %u is a
placeholder for the unit.

15.3 Iteration J3: Translating Checkout

Now we feel that we are in the home stretch. The new order page is next:

`depot_s/app/views/orders/new.html.erb`

```
<div class="depot_form">
  <fieldset>
    <legend><%= t('.legend') %></legend>
    <%= render 'form' %>
  </fieldset>
</div>
```

Then the form that is used by this page:

`depot_s/app/views/orders/_form.html.erb`

```
<%= form_for(@order) do |f| %>
  <% if @order.errors.any? %>
    <div id="error_explanation">
      <h2><%= pluralize(@order.errors.count, "error") %>
      prohibited this order from being saved:</h2>

      <ul>
      <% @order.errors.full_messages.each do |msg| %>
        <li><%= msg %></li>
      <% end %>
      </ul>
    </div>
  <% end %>
```

```erb
<div class="field">
  <%= f.label :name %><br />
  <%= f.text_field :name, :size => 40 %>
</div>
<div class="field">
▶ <%= f.label :address, t('.address_html') %><br />
  <%= f.text_area :address, :rows => 3, :cols => 40 %>
</div>
<div class="field">
  <%= f.label :email %><br />
  <%= f.email_field :email, :size => 40 %>
</div>
<div class="field">
  <%= f.label :pay_type %><br />
  <%= f.select :pay_type, Order::PAYMENT_TYPES,
▶               :prompt => t('.pay_prompt_html') %>
</div>
<div class="actions">
▶ <%= f.submit t('.submit') %>
</div>
<% end %>
```

Note that we do not normally have to explicitly call I18n functions on labels, unless we want to do something special like allowing HTML entities. Here are the corresponding locale definitions:

depot_s/config/locales/en.yml

```yaml
en:

  orders:
    new:
      legend:          "Please Enter Your Details"
      form:
        name:          "Name"
        address_html:  "Address"
        email:         "E-mail"
        pay_type:      "Pay with"
        pay_prompt_html: "Select a payment method"
        submit:        "Place Order"
```

depot_s/config/locales/es.yml

```yaml
es:

  orders:
    new:
      legend:          "Por favor, introduzca sus datos"
      form:
        name:          "Nombre"
        address_html:  "Direcci&oacute;n"
        email:         "E-mail"
        pay_type:      "Pagar con"
        pay_prompt_html: "Seleccione un m&eacute;todo de pago"
        submit:        "Realizar Pedido"
```

Figure 15.5: READY TO TAKE YOUR MONEY—IN SPANISH

See Figure 15.5 for the completed form.

All looks good until we hit the `Realizar Pedido` button prematurely and see Figure 15.6, on the following page. The error messages that Active Record produces can also be translated; what we need to do is supply the translations:

depot_s/config/locales/es.yml

```
es:

  activerecord:
    errors:
      messages:
        inclusion: "no est&aacute; incluido en la lista"
        blank:     "no puede quedar en blanco"
    errors:
      template:
        body:      "Hay problemas con los siguientes campos:"
        header:
          one:     "1 error ha impedido que este %{model} se guarde"
          other:   "%{count} errores han impedido que este %{model} se guarde"
```

Note that messages with counts typically have two forms: errors.template.header. one is the message that is produced when there is one error, and errors.template. header.other is produced otherwise. This gives the translators the opportunity

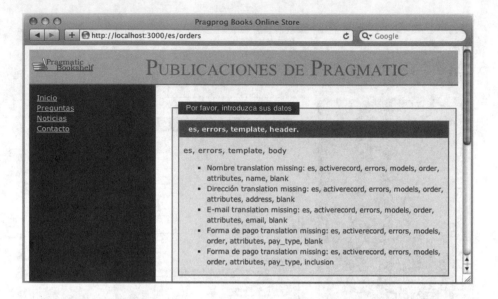

Figure 15.6: TRANSLATION MISSING

to provide the correct pluralization of nouns and to match the verbs with the nouns.

Since we once again made use of HTML entities, we will want these error messages to be displayed as is (or in Rails parlance, *raw*):

> depot_t/app/views/orders/_form.html.erb

```
<li><%= raw msg %></li>
```

We will also need to adjust the translation for the error messages:

> depot_t/app/views/orders/_form.html.erb

```
<%= form_for(@order) do |f| %>
  <% if @order.errors.any? %>
    <div id="error_explanation">
      <h2><%= t('errors.template.header', :count=>@order.errors.size,
        :model=>t('activerecord.models.order')) %>.</h2>
      <p><%= t('errors.template.body') %></p>

      <ul>
      <% @order.errors.full_messages.each do |msg| %>
        <li><%= raw msg %></li>
      <% end %>
      </ul>
    </div>
  <% end %>
<!-- ... -->
```

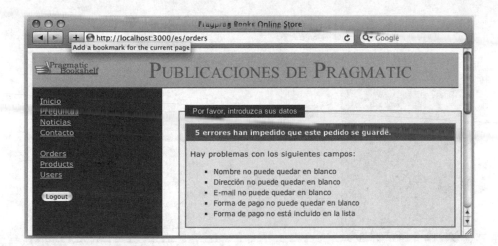

Figure 15.7: ENGLISH NOUNS IN SPANISH SENTENCES

Note that we are passing the count and model name (which is, itself, enabled for translation) on the translate call for the error template header.

With these changes in place, we try again and see improvement in Figure 15.7.

Better, but the names of the model and attributes bleed through the interface. This is OK in English, because the names we picked work for English. We need to provide translations for each.

This, too, goes into the YAML file:

depot_t/config/locales/es.yml

```
es:

  activerecord:
    models:
      order:        "pedido"
    attributes:
      order:
        address:    "Direcci&oacute;n"
        name:       "Nombre"
        email:      "E-mail"
        pay_type:   "Forma de pago"
```

Note that there is no need to provide English equivalents for this, because those messages are built in to Rails.

We are pleased to see the model and attribute names translated in Figure 15.8, on the following page; we fill out the form, we submit the order, and we get a "Thank you for your order" message.

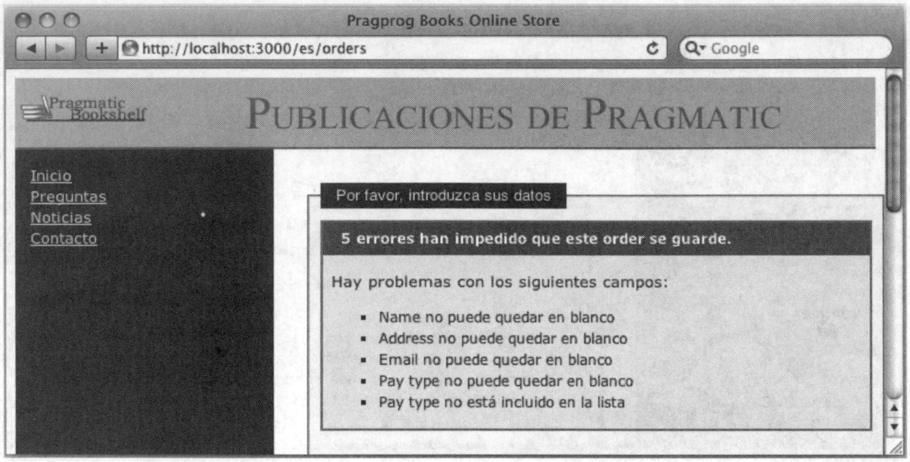

Figure 15.8: MODEL NAMES ARE NOW TRANSLATED TOO.

We need to update the flash messages:

`depot_t/app/controllers/orders_controller.rb`

```ruby
def create
  @order = Order.new(params[:order])
  @order.add_line_items_from_cart(current_cart)

  respond_to do |format|
    if @order.save
      Cart.destroy(session[:cart_id])
      session[:cart_id] = nil
      Notifier.order_received(@order).deliver
      format.html { redirect_to(store_url, :notice =>
        I18n.t('.thanks')) }
      format.xml  { render :xml => @order, :status => :created,
        :location => @order }
    else
      format.html { render :action => "new" }
      format.xml  { render :xml => @order.errors,
        :status => :unprocessable_entity }
    end
  end
end
```

Finally, we provide the translations:

`depot_t/config/locales/en.yml`

```yaml
en:

  thanks:         "Thank you for your order"
```

Figure 15.9: THANKING THE CUSTOMER IN SPANISH

depot_t/config/locales/es.yml

```
es:

    thanks:          "Gracias por su pedido"
```

See the cheery message in Figure 15.9.

15.4 Iteration J4: Add a Locale Switcher

We've completed the task, but we really need to advertise its availability more. We spy some unused area in the top-right side of the layout, so we add a form immediately before the image_tag:

depot_t/app/views/layouts/application.html.erb

```
►  <%= form_tag store_path, :class => 'locale' do %>
     <%= select_tag 'set_locale',
       options_for_select(LANGUAGES, I18n.locale.to_s),
       :onchange => 'this.form.submit()' %>
     <%= submit_tag 'submit' %>
     <%= javascript_tag "$$('.locale input').each(Element.hide)" %>
►  <% end %>
```

The form_tag specifies the path to the store as the page to be redisplayed when the form is submitted. A class attribute lets us associate the form with some CSS.

The select_tag is used to define the one input field for this form, namely, locale. It is an options list based on the LANGUAGES array that we set up in the configuration file, with the default being the current locale (also made available via the I18n module). We also set up an onchange event handler, which will submit this form whenever the value changes. This works only if JavaScript is enabled, but it is handy.

Then we add a submit_tag for the cases when JavaScript is not available. To handle the case where JavaScript is available and the submit button is unnecessary, we add a tiny bit of JavaScript that will hide each of the input tags in the locale form, even though we know that there is only one.

Next, we modify the store controller to redirect to the store path for a given locale if the :set_locale form is used:

`depot_t/app/controllers/store_controller.rb`

```
def index
►   if params[:set_locale]
►     redirect_to store_path(:locale => params[:set_locale])
►   else
      @products = Product.all
►     @cart = current_cart
►   end
end
```

Finally, we add a bit of CSS:

`depot_t/public/stylesheets/depot.css`

```
.locale {
  float: right;
  margin: -0.25em 0.1em;
}
```

For the actual selector, see Figure 15.10, on the facing page. We can now switch back and forth between languages with a single mouse click.

At this point, we can now place orders in two languages, and our thoughts turn to actual deployment. But because it has been a busy day, it is time to put down our tools and relax. We will start on deployment in the morning.

What We Just Did

By the end of this iteration, we've done the following:

- We set the default locale for our application and provided a means for the user to select an alternate locale.

- We created translation files for text fields, currency amounts, errors, and model names.

Figure 15.10: LOCALE SELECTOR IN TOP RIGHT

- We altered layouts and views to call out to the I18n module by way of the t helper in order to translate textual portions of the interface.

Playtime

Here's some stuff to try on your own:

- Add a locale column to the products database, and adjust the index view to select only the products that match the locale. Adjust the products view so that you can view, enter, and alter this new column. Enter a few products in each locale, and test the resulting application.

- Determine the current exchange rate between U.S. dollars and euros, and localize the currency display to display euros when ES_es is selected.

- Translate the Order::PAYMENT_TYPES shown in the drop-down. You will need to keep the option value (which is sent to the server) the same. Only change what is displayed.

(You'll find hints at http://www.pragprog.com/wikis/wiki/RailsPlayTime.)

In this chapter, we'll see

- running our application in a production web server,
- configuring the database for MySQL,
- using Bundler and Git for version control, and
- deploying our application using Capistrano.

Chapter 16

Task K: Deployment and Production

Deployment is supposed to mark a happy point in the lifetime of our application. It's when we take the code that we've so carefully crafted and upload it to a server so that other people can use it. It's when the beer, champagne, and hors d'oeuvres are supposed to flow. Shortly thereafter, our application will be written about in *Wired* magazine, and we'll be overnight names in the geek community.

The reality, however, is that it often takes quite a bit of up-front planning in order to pull off a smooth and repeatable deployment of your application.

By the time we are through with this chapter, our setup will look like Figure 16.1, on the next page.

 **Joe Asks. . .**

Can I Deploy to Microsoft Windows?

Although you can deploy applications to Windows environments, the overwhelming amount of Rails tools and shared knowledge assumes a Unix-based operating system such as Linux or Mac OS X. One such tool, Phusion Passenger, is highly recommended by the Ruby on Rails development team and covered in this chapter.

The techniques described in this chapter can be used by those developing on Windows and deploying to Linux or Mac OS X.

If deploying on Windows is a requirement for your installation, then you can find good advice in Chapter 6 of *Deploying Rails Applications: A Step-by-Step Guide* (ZT08).

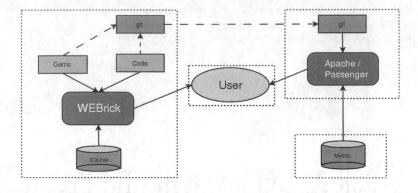

Figure 16.1: APPLICATION DEPLOYMENT ROAD MAP

At the moment, we've been doing all of our work on one machine, though user interaction with our web server *could* be done on a separate machine. In the figure, the user's machine is in the center, and the WEBRick web server is on the left. This server makes use of SQLite3, various gems you have installed, and your application code. Your code may or may not have also been placed in Git by this point; either way, it will be by the end of the chapter, as will be the gems you are using.

This Git repository will be replicated on the production server, which again could be another machine but need not be. This server will be running a combination of Apache httpd and Phusion Passenger. This code will access a MySQL database on what may yet be a *fourth* machine.

Capistrano will be the tool we use to update the deployment server(s) remotely, safely, and repeatably from the comfort of our development machine.

That's a lot of moving parts!

Instead of doing it all at once, we will do it in three iterations. Iteration K1 will get the Depot application up and running with Apache, MySQL, and Passenger—a truly production-quality web server environment.

We will leave Git, Bundler, and Capistrano to a second iteration. These tools will enable us to separate our development activities from our deployment environment. This means that by the time we are done, we will be deploying twice; but that's only this first time and only to ensure that each of the parts are working independently. It also allows us to focus on a smaller set of variables at any one time, which will simplify the process of untangling any problems that we might encounter.

In a third iteration, we will cover various administrative and cleanup tasks. Let's get started!

16.1 Iteration K1: Deploying with Phusion Passenger and MySQL

So far, as we've been developing a Rails application on our local machine, we've probably been using WEBrick or Mongrel when we run our server. For the most part, it doesn't matter. The rails server command will sort out the most appropriate way to get our application running in development mode on port 3000. However, a deployed Rails application works a bit differently. We can't just fire up a single Rails server process and let it do all the work. Well, we *could*, but it's far from ideal. The reason for this is that Rails is single-threaded. It can work on only one request at a time.

The Web, however, is an extremely concurrent environment. Production web servers, such as Apache, Lighttpd, and Zeus, can work on several requests—even tens or hundreds of requests—at the same time. A single-process, single-threaded Ruby-based web server can't possibly keep up. Luckily, it doesn't have to keep up. Instead, the way that we deploy a Rails application into production is to use a front-end server, such as Apache, to handle requests from the client. Then, you use the HTTP proxying of Passenger to send requests that should be handled by Rails to one of any number of back-end application processes.

Installing Passenger

The first step is to ensure that the Apache web server is installed. For Mac OS X users, and many Linux users, it is already installed with the operating system. Windows users can find instructions on installing this product on the Apache website.[1]

The next step is to install Passenger:

```
$ sudo gem install passenger
$ sudo passenger-install-apache2-module
```

If the necessary dependencies are not met, the latter command will tell you what you need to do. For example, on a Ubuntu 10.04 (Lucid Lynx) Linux, you will find that you need to install build-essential, apache2-prefork-dev, libapr1-dev, and libaprutil1-dev. If this happens, follow the provided instructions, and try the passenger install command again.

Once the dependencies are satisfied, this command causes a number of sources to be compiled and the configuration files to be updated. During the process, it will ask us to update our Apache configuration. The first will be to enable your freshly built module and will involve adding lines such as the

---

1. http://httpd.apache.org/docs/2.2/platform/windows.html#inst

following to our Apache configuration. (Note: Passenger will tell you the exact lines to copy and paste into this file, so use those, not these. Also, we've had to wrap the LoadModule line to make it fit the page. When you type it, it all goes on one line.)

```
LoadModule passenger_module /opt/local/lib/ruby/gems/1.8/gems/passenger-2.2.11↩
    /ext/apache2/mod_passenger.so
PassengerRoot /opt/local/lib/ruby/gems/1.8/gems/passenger-2.2.11
PassengerRuby /opt/local/bin/ruby
```

To find out where your Apache configuration file is, try issuing the following command:

```
$ apachectl -V | grep SERVER_CONFIG_FILE
```

On some systems, the command name is apache2ctl; on others, it's httpd. Experiment until you find the correct command.

If we want to serve multiple applications with the same Apache web server, we will first need to verify that the following line is present in the configuration files already:

```
NameVirtualHost *:80
```

If this line is not present, add it before a line that contains the text Listen 80.

Deploying our Application Locally

The next step is to deploy our application. Whereas the previous step needs to be done only once per server, this step is actually once per application. Substitute your host's name in the following ServerName line:

```
<VirtualHost *:80>
   ServerName depot.yourhost.com
   DocumentRoot /home/rubys/work/depot/public/
</VirtualHost>
```

Note here that the DocumentRoot is set to our public directory in our Rails application.

Once this is in place, repeat this VirtualHost block once per application, adjusting the ServerName and DocumentRoot in each block. We will also need to mark the public directory as readable. The final version will look something like the following:

```
<VirtualHost *:80>
   ServerName depot.yourhost.com
   DocumentRoot /home/rubys/work/depot/public/

  <Directory /home/rubys/work/depot/public>
    Order allow,deny
    Allow from all
  </Directory>
</VirtualHost>
```

The final step is to restart our Apache web server:

```
$ sudo apachectl restart
```

You will now need to configure your client so that it maps the host name you chose to the correct machine. This is done in a file named /etc/hosts. On Windows machines, this file can be found in C:\windows\system32\drivers\etc\. To edit this file, you will need to open the file as an administrator.

A typical /etc/hosts line will look like the following:

```
127.0.0.1 depot.yourhost.com
```

That's it! We can now access our application using the host (or virtual host) we specified. Unless we used a port number other than 80, there is no longer any need for us to specify a port number on our URL.

There are a few things to be aware of:

- If, when restarting your server you see a message that The address or port is invalid, this means the NameVirtualHost line is already present, perhaps in another configuration file in the same directory. If so, remove the line you added because this directive needs to be present only once.
- If we want to run in an environment other than production, we can include a RailsEnv directive in each VirtualHost in our Apache configuration:
  ```
  RailsEnv development
  ```
- We can restart our application without restarting Apache at any time by creating a file named restart.txt in the tmp of our application:
  ```
  $ touch tmp/restart.txt
  ```
  Once the server restarts, this file will be deleted.
- The output of the passenger-install-apache2-module command will tell us where we can find additional documentation.

Using MySQL for the Database

The SQLite website[2] is refreshingly honest when it comes to describing what this database is good at and what it is not good at. In particular, SQLite is not recommended for high-volume, high-concurrency websites with large datasets. And, of course, we want our website to be such a website.

There are plenty of alternatives to SQLite, both free and commercial. We will go with MySQL. It already is included in OS X, it is available via your native packaging tool in Linux, and an installer is provided for Microsoft Windows on the MySQL website.[3]

---

2. http://www.sqlite.org/whentouse.html
3. http://www.mysql.com/downloads/mysql/#downloads

In addition to installing the MySQL database, you will also need to add the mysql gem to the Gemfile:

```
depot_t/Gemfile
```

```
group :production do
  gem 'mysql'
end
```

By putting this gem in group production, it will not be loaded when running in development or test. If you like, you can put sqlite3 gem into (separate) development and test groups.

Install the gem using bundle install. You may need to locate and install the MySQL database development files for your operating system first. On Ubuntu, for example, you will need to install libmysqlclient-dev.

You can use the mysql command-line client to create your database, or if you're more comfortable with tools such as phpmyadmin or CocoaMySQL, go for it:

```
depot> mysql -u root
mysql> CREATE DATABASE depot_production;
mysql> GRANT ALL PRIVILEGES ON depot_production.*
    ->    TO 'username'@'localhost' IDENTIFIED BY 'password';
mysql> EXIT;
```

If you picked a different database name, remember it, because you will need to adjust the configuration file to match the name you picked. Let's look at that configuration file now.

The database.yml contains information on database connections. It contains three sections, one each for the development, test, and production databases. The current production section contains the following:

```
production:
  adapter: sqlite3
  database: db/production.sqlite3
  pool: 5
  timeout: 5000
```

We replace that section with something like the following:

```
production:
  adapter: mysql
  encoding: utf8
  reconnect: false
  database: depot_production
  pool: 5
  username: username
  password: password
  host: localhost
```

Change the username, password, and database fields as necessary.

Loading the Database

Next, we apply our migrations:

```
depot> rake db:setup RAILS_ENV="production"
```

One of two things will happen. If all is set up correctly, you will see output like the following:

```
-- create_table("carts", {:force=>true})
   -> 0.1722s
-- create_table("line_items", {:force=>true})
   -> 0.1255s
-- create_table("orders", {:force=>true})
   -> 0.1171s
-- create_table("products", {:force=>true})
   -> 0.1172s
-- create_table("users", {:force=>true})
   -> 0.1255s
-- initialize_schema_migrations_table()
   -> 0.0006s
-- assume_migrated_upto_version(20110211000008, "db/migrate")
   -> 0.0008s
```

If, instead, you see an error of some sort, don't panic! It's probably a simple configuration issue. Here are some things to try:

- Check the name you gave for the database in the production: section of database.yml. It should be the same as the name of the database you created (using mysqladmin or some other database administration tool).
- Check that the username and password in database.yml match what you created on the facing page.
- Check that your database server is running.
- Check that you can connect to it from the command line. If using MySQL, run the following command:
  ```
  depot> mysql depot_production
  mysql>
  ```
- If you can connect from the command line, can you create a dummy table? (This tests that the database user has sufficient access rights to the database.)
  ```
  mysql> create table dummy(i int);
  mysql> drop table dummy;
  ```
- If you can create tables from the command line but rake db:migrate fails, double-check the database.yml file. If there are socket: directives in the file, try commenting them out by putting a hash character (#) in front of each.
- If you see an error saying No such file or directory... and the filename in the error is mysql.sock, your Ruby MySQL libraries can't find your MySQL database. This might happen if you installed the libraries before you

installed the database or if you installed the libraries using a binary distribution and that distribution made the wrong assumption about the location of the MySQL socket file. To fix this, the best idea is to reinstall your Ruby MySQL libraries. If this isn't an option, double-check that the socket: line in your database.yml file contains the correct path to the MySQL socket on your system.

- If you get the error Mysql not loaded, it means you're running an old version of the Ruby MySQL library. Rails needs at least version 2.5.

- Some readers also report getting the error message Client does not support authentication protocol requested by server; consider upgrading MySQL client. To resolve this incompatibility between the installed version of MySQL and the libraries used to access it, follow the instructions at http://dev.mysql.com/doc/mysql/en/old-client.html and issue a MySQL command such as set password for 'some_user'@'some_host' = OLD_PASSWORD('newpwd');.

- If you're using MySQL under Cygwin on Windows, you may have problems if you specify a host of localhost. Try using 127.0.0.1 instead.

- Finally, you might have problems in the format of the database.yml file. The YAML library that reads this file is strangely sensitive to tab characters. If your file contains tab characters, you'll have problems. (And you thought you'd chosen Ruby over Python because you didn't like Python's significant whitespace, eh?)

Rerun the rake db:setup as many times as you need to in order to correct any configuration issues you may have.

If all this sounds scary, don't worry. In reality, database connections work like a charm most of the time. And once you have Rails talking to the database, you don't have to worry about it again.

At this point, you are up and running. Nothing looks any different when you are running as a single user. The differences become apparent only when you have a large number of concurrent users or a large database.

The next step is to split our development from our production machine.

16.2   Iteration K2: Deploying Remotely with Capistrano

If you are a large shop, having a pool of dedicated servers that you administer so that you can ensure that they are running the same version of the necessary software is the way to go. For more modest needs, a shared server will do, but we will have to take additional care to deal with the fact that the versions of software installed may not always match the version that we have installed on our development machine.

Don't worry, we'll talk you through it.

Prepping Your Deployment Server

Although putting our software under version control is a really, really, really good idea during development, not putting our software under version control when it comes to deployment is downright foolhardy—enough so that the software that we have selected to manage your deployment, namely, Capistrano, all but requires it.

Plenty of software configuration management (SCM) systems are available. Subversion, for example, is a particularly good one. But if you haven't yet chosen one, go with Git, which is easy to set up and doesn't require a separate server process. The examples that follow will be based on Git, but if you picked a different SCM system, don't worry. Capistrano doesn't much care which one you pick, just so long as you pick one.

The first step is to create an empty repository on a machine accessible by your deployment servers. In fact, if we have only one deployment server, there is no reason that it can't do double duty as your Git server. So, log onto that server, and issue the following commands:

```
$ mkdir -p ~/git/depot.git
$ cd ~/git/depot.git
$ git --bare init
```

The next thing to be aware of is that even if the SCM server and our web server are the same physical machine, Capistrano will be accessing our SCM software as if it were remote. We can make this smoother by generating a public key (if you don't already have one) and then using it to give ourselves permission to access our own server:

```
$ test -e ~/.ssh/id_dsa.pub || ssh-keygen -t dsa
$ cat ~/.ssh/id_dsa.pub >> ~/.ssh/authorized_keys2
```

Test this by ssh'ing into your own server. Among other things, this will ensure that your known_hosts file is updated.

While we are here, we should attend to two other things. The first is quite trivial: Capistrano will insert a directory named current between our application directory name and the Rails subdirectories, including the public subdirectory. This means you will have to adjust your DocumentRoot in your httpd.conf if you control your own server or in a control panel for your shared host:

```
DocumentRoot /home/rubys/work/depot/current/public/
```

That's it for the server! From here on out, we will be doing everything from your development machine.

Getting an Application Under Control

The first thing we are going to do is update our Gemfile to indicate that we are using Capistrano.

```
depot_t/Gemfile
```
```ruby
source 'http://rubygems.org'

gem 'rails', '3.0.5'

# Bundle edge Rails instead:
# gem 'rails', :git => 'git://github.com/rails/rails.git'

gem 'sqlite3'
group :production do
  gem 'mysql'
end

# Use unicorn as the web server
# gem 'unicorn'

# Deploy with Capistrano
gem 'capistrano'

# To use debugger (ruby-debug for Ruby 1.8.7+, ruby-debug19 for Ruby 1.9.2+)
# gem 'ruby-debug'
# gem 'ruby-debug19', :require => 'ruby-debug'

# Bundle the extra gems:
# gem 'bj'
# gem 'nokogiri'
# gem 'sqlite3-ruby', :require => 'sqlite3'
# gem 'aws-s3', :require => 'aws/s3'

gem 'will_paginate', '>= 3.0.pre'

# Bundle gems for the local environment. Make sure to
# put test-only gems in this group so their generators
# and rake tasks are available in development mode:
# group :development, :test do
#   gem 'webrat'
# end
```

We can now install Capistrano using bundle install. We used this command previously on page 164 to install the will_paginate gem.

If you haven't already put your application under configuration control, do so now:

```
$ cd your_application_directory
$ git init
$ git add .
$ git commit -m "initial commit"
```

This next step is optional but might be a good idea if either you don't have full control of the deployment server or you have many deployment servers to manage. We are going to use a second feature of Bundler, namely, the pack command. What it does is put the version of the software that you are dependent on into the repository:

```
$ bundle pack
$ git add Gemfile.lock vendor/cache
$ git commit -m "bundle gems"
```

We will explain more of the features of Bundler in Section 25.3, *Managing Dependencies with Bundler*, on page 409.

From here, it is a simple matter to push all your code out to the server:

```
$ git remote add origin ssh://user@host/~/git/depot.git
$ git push origin master
```

With these few steps, you have gained control over what is being deployed. You control *what* is being committed to your local repository. You control *when* this is being pushed out to your server. Next up, you will control putting this code into production.

Deploying the Application Remotely

We previously deployed the application locally on a server. Now we are going to do a second deployment, this time remotely.

The prep work is now done. Our code is now on the SCM server where it can be accessed by the app server. Again, it matters not whether these two servers are the same; what is important here is the *roles* that are being performed.

To add the necessary files to the project for Capistrano to do its magic, execute the following command:

```
$ capify .
[add] writing './Capfile'
[add] writing './config/deploy.rb'
[done] capified!
```

From the output, we can see that Capistrano set up two files. The first, Capfile, is Capistrano's analog to a Rakefile. We won't need to touch this file further. The second, config/deploy.rb, contains the recipes needed to deploy our application. Capistrano will provide us with a minimal version of this file, but the following is a somewhat more complete version that you can download and use as a starting point:

depot_t/config/deploy.rb

```
# be sure to change these
set :user, 'rubys'
set :domain, 'depot.pragprog.com'
set :application, 'depot'

# file paths
set :repository,  "#{user}@#{domain}:git/#{application}.git"
set :deploy_to, "/home/#{user}/#{domain}"
```

```
# distribute your applications across servers (the instructions below put them
# all on the same server, defined above as 'domain', adjust as necessary)
role :app, domain
role :web, domain
role :db, domain, :primary => true

# you might need to set this if you aren't seeing password prompts
# default_run_options[:pty] = true

# As Capistrano executes in a non-interactive mode and therefore doesn't cause
# any of your shell profile scripts to be run, the following might be needed
# if (for example) you have locally installed gems or applications.  Note:
# this needs to contain the full values for the variables set, not simply
# the deltas.
# default_environment['PATH']='<your paths>:/usr/local/bin:/usr/bin:/bin'
# default_environment['GEM_PATH']='<your paths>:/usr/lib/ruby/gems/1.8'

# miscellaneous options
set :deploy_via, :remote_cache
set :scm, 'git'
set :branch, 'master'
set :scm_verbose, true
set :use_sudo, false

namespace :deploy do
  desc "cause Passenger to initiate a restart"
  task :restart do
    run "touch #{current_path}/tmp/restart.txt"
  end

  desc "reload the database with seed data"
  task :seed do
    run "cd #{current_path}; rake db:seed RAILS_ENV=production"
  end
end

after "deploy:update_code", :bundle_install
desc "install the necessary prerequisites"
task :bundle_install, :roles => :app do
  run "cd #{release_path} && bundle install"
end
```

We will need to edit several properties to match our application. We certainly will need to change the :user, :domain, and :application. The :repository matches where we put our Git file earlier. The :deploy_to may need to be tweaked to match where we told Apache it could find the config/public directory for the application.

The default_run_options and default_environment are to be used only if you have specific problems. The "miscellaneous options" provided are based on Git.

Two tasks are defined. One tells Capistrano how to restart Passenger. The other installs the gems from the copy that we previously placed on the Git repository. Feel free to adjust these tasks as you see fit.

The first time we deploy our application, we have to perform an additional step to set up the basic directory structure to deploy into on the server:

```
$ cap deploy:setup
```

When we execute this command, Capistrano will prompt us for our server's password. If it fails to do so and fails to log in, we might need to uncomment out the default_run_options line in our deploy.rb file and try again. Once it can connect successfully, it will make the necessary directories. After this command is done, we can check out the configuration for any other problems:

```
$ cap deploy:check
```

As before, we might need to uncomment out and adjust the default_environment lines in our deploy.rb. We can repeat this command until it completes successfully, addressing any issues it may identify.

Now we're ready to do the deployment. Since we have done all of the necessary prep work and checked the results, it should go smoothly:

```
$ cap deploy:migrations
```

At this point, we should be off to the races.

Rinse, Wash, Repeat

Once we've gotten this far, our server is ready to have new versions of our application deployed to it any time we want. All we need to do is check our changes into the repository and then redeploy. At this point, we have two Capistrano files that haven't been checked in. Although they aren't needed by the app server, we can still use them to test the deployment process:

```
$ git add .
$ git commit -m "add cap files"
$ git push
$ cap deploy
```

The first three commands will update the SCM server. Once you become more familiar with Git, you may want to have finer control over when and which files are added, you may want to incrementally commit multiple changes before deployment, and so on. It is only the final command that will update our app, web, and database servers.

If for some reason we need to step back in time and go back to a previous version of our application, we can use this:

```
$ cap deploy:rollback
```

We now have a fully deployed application and can deploy as needed to update the code running on the server. Each time we deploy our application, a new version of it is checked out onto the server, some symlinks are updated, and the Passenger processes are restarted.

16.3 Iteration K3: Checking Up on a Deployed Application

Once we have our application deployed, we'll no doubt need to check up on how it's running from time to time. We can do this in two primary ways. The first is to monitor the various log files output by both our front-end web server and the Apache server running our application. The second is to connect to our application using rails console.

Looking at Log Files

To get a quick look at what's happening in our application, we can use the tail command to examine log files as requests are made against our application. The most interesting data will usually be in the log files from the application itself. Even if Apache is running multiple applications, the logged output for each application is placed in the production.log file for that application.

Assuming that our application is deployed into the location we showed earlier, here's how we look at our running log file:

```
# On your server
$ cd /home/rubys/work/depot/
$ tail -f log/production.log
```

Sometimes, we need lower-level information—what's going on with the data in our application? When this is the case, it's time to break out the most useful live server debugging tool.

Using Console to Look at a Live Application

We've already created a large amount of functionality in our application's model classes. Of course, we created these to be used by our application's controllers. But we can also interact with them directly. The gateway to this world is the rails console script. We can launch it on our server with this:

```
# On your server
$ cd /home/rubys/work/depot/
$ rails console production
Loading production environment.
irb(main):001:0> p = Product.find_by_title("Pragmatic Version Control")
=> #<Product:0x24797b4 @attributes={. . .}
irb(main):002:0> p.price = 32.95
=> 32.95
irb(main):003:0> p.save
=> true
```

Once we have a console session open, we can poke and prod all the various methods on our models. We can create, inspect, and delete records. In a way, it's like having a root console to your application.

Once you put an application into production, we need to take care of a few chores to keep your application running smoothly. These chores aren't automatically taken care of for us, but, luckily, we can automate them.

Dealing with Log Files

As an application runs, it will constantly add data to its log file. Eventually, the log files can grow extremely large. To overcome this, most logging solutions can *roll over* log files to create a progressive set of log files of increasing age. This will break up our log files into manageable chunks that can be archived or even deleted after a certain amount of time has passed.

The Logger class supports rollover. We need to specify how many (or how often) log files we want and the size of each, using a line like one of the following in the file config/environments/production.rb:

```
config.logger = Logger.new(config.paths.log.first, 'daily')
```

Or perhaps this:

```
require 'active_support/core_ext/numeric/bytes'
config.logger = Logger.new(config.paths.log.first, 10, 10.megabytes)
```

Note that in this case an explicit require of active_support is needed because this statement is processed early in the initialization of your application—before the Active Support libraries have been included. In fact, one of the configuration options that Rails provides is to not include Active Support libraries at all:

```
config.active_support.bare = true
```

Alternately, we can direct our logs to the system logs for our machine:

```
config.logger = SyslogLogger.new
```

Find more options at http://rubyonrails.org/deploy.

Moving On to Launch and Beyond

Once we've set up our initial deployment, we're ready to finish the development of our application and launch it into production. We'll likely set up additional deployment servers, and the lessons we learn from our first deployment will tell us a lot about how we should structure later deployments. For example, we'll likely find that Rails is one of the slower components of our system—more of the request time will be spent in Rails than in waiting on the database or filesystem. This indicates that the way to scale up is to add machines to split up the Rails load across.

However, we might find that the bulk of the time a request takes is in the database. If this is the case, we'll want to look at how to optimize our database activity. Maybe we'll want to change how we access data. Or maybe we'll need to custom craft some SQL to replace the default Active Record behaviors.

One thing is for sure: every application will require a different set of tweaks over its lifetime. The most important activity to do is to listen to it over time and discover what needs to be done. Our job isn't done when we launch our application. It's actually just starting.

While our job is just starting when we first deploy our application to production, we have completed our tour of the Depot application. After we recap what we did in this chapter, let's look back at what we have accomplished in remarkably few lines of code.

What We Just Did

We covered a lot of ground in this chapter. We took our code that ran locally on our development machine for a single user and placed it on a different machine, running a different web server, accessing a different database, and possibly even running a different operating system.

To accomplish this, we used a number of different products:

- We installed and configured Phusion Passenger and Apache httpd, a production-quality web server.

- We installed and configured MySQL, a production-quality database server.

- We got our application's dependencies under control using Bundler and Git.

- We installed and configured Capistrano, which enables us to confidently and repeatably deploy our application.

Playtime

Here's some stuff to try on your own:

- If we have multiple developers collaborating on development, we might feel uncomfortable putting the details of the configuration of our database (potentially including passwords!) into our configuration management system. To address this, copy the completed database.yml into the shared directory, and write a task instructing Capistrano to copy this file into your current directory each time you deploy.

• Introduce a change to the schema to add a price to a line item. Make sure that the migration fills in this value. Modify the add_product method in the Cart model to capture this information from the product. Modify the total_price method in the LineItem model to compute the sum using this value. Modify the _line_item partial to display this value.

Once you have this change working, deploy this change.

In this chapter, we'll see

- reviewing Rails concepts: model, view, controller, configuration, testing, and deployment; and
- documenting what we have done.

Chapter 17

Depot Retrospective

Congratulations! By making it this far, you have obtained a solid understanding of the basics of every Rails application. There is much more to learn, which we will pick back up again in Part III. For now, relax, and let's recap what we've seen in Part II.

17.1 Rails Concepts

InChapter 3, *The Architecture of Rails Applications*, on page 29 we introduced models, views, and controllers. Now let's see how we applied each of these concepts in the Depot application. Then let's explore how we used configuration, testing, and deployment.

Model

Models are where all of the persistent data retained by your application is managed. In developing the Depot application, we created five models: Cart, LineItem, Order, Product, and User.

By default, all models have id, created_at, and updated_at attributes. To our models, we added attributes of type string (examples: title, name), integer (quantity), text (description, address), decimal (price), and foreign keys (product_id, cart_id). We even created a virtual attribute that is never stored in the database, namely, a password.

We created has_many and belongs_to relationships that we can use to navigate between our model objects, such as from Carts to LineItems to Products.

We employed migrations to update the databases, not only to introduce new schema information but also to modify existing data. We demonstrated that they can be applied in a fully reversible manner.

The models we created were not merely passive receptacles for our data. For starters, they actively validate the data, preventing errors from propagating.

We created validations for presence, inclusion, numericality, range, uniqueness, format, and confirmation. (And length too, if you completed the exercises). We created custom validations for ensuring that deleted products are not referenced by any line item. We used an Active Record hook to ensure that an administrator always remains and a transaction to roll back incomplete updates on failure.

We also created logic to add a product to a cart, add all line items from a cart to an order, encrypt and authenticate a password, and compute various totals.

Finally, we created a default sort order for products for display purposes.

View

Views control the way our application presents itself to the external world. By default, Rails scaffolding provides edit, index, new, and show, as well as a partial named form that is shared between edit and new. We modified a number of these, as well as creating new partials for carts and line items.

In addition to the model backed resource views, we created entirely new views for admin, sessions, and the store itself.

We updated an overall layout to establish a common look and feel for the entire site. We linked in a stylesheet. We made use of RJS templates to generate JavaScript that takes advantage of Web 2.0 technologies to make our website more interactive.

We made use of a helper to determine when to hide the cart from the main view.

We localized the customer views for display both in English and in Spanish.

While we focused primarily on HTML views, we also created plain-text views and Atom views. Not all of the views were designed for browsers: we created views for email too, and those views were able to share partials for displaying line items.

Controller

By the time we were done, we created eight controllers: one each for the five models and the three additional ones in order to support the views for admin, sessions, and the store itself.

These controllers interacted with the models in a number of ways: from finding and fetching data and putting it into instance variables to updating models and saving data entered via forms. When done, we either redirected to another action or rendered a view. We rendered views in HTML, JSON, and Atom.

We created filters that were run before selected actions to authorize requests. We placed logic common to a number of controllers into the common base class for all controllers, namely, ApplicationController.

We managed sessions, keeping track of the logged-in user (for administrators) and carts (for customers). We kept track of the current locale used for internationalization of our output. We captured errors, logged them, and informed the user via notices. We paginated orders through the use of the will_paginate plugin.

We also sent confirmation emails on receipt of an order.

Configuration

While conventions keep to a minimum the amount of configuration required for a Rails application, we did do a bit of customization.

We modified our database configuration in order to use MySQL in production.

We defined routes for our resources, our admin and session controllers, and the *root* of our website, namely, our storefront. We defined a who_bought member of our products resource in order to access Atom feeds that contain this information.

We created an initializer for i18n purposes and updated the locales information for both English (en) and Spanish (es).

We created seed data for our database.

We created a Capistrano script for deployment, including the definition of a few custom tasks.

Testing

We maintained and enhanced tests throughout.

We employed unit tests to validation methods. We also tested increasing the quantity on a given line item.

Rails provided basic tests for all our scaffolded controllers, which we maintained as we made changes. We added tests along the way for things such as Ajax and ensuring that a cart has items before we create an order.

We used fixtures to provide test data to fuel our tests.

Finally, we created an integration test to test an end-to-end scenario involving a user adding a product to a cart, entering an order, and receiving a confirmation email.

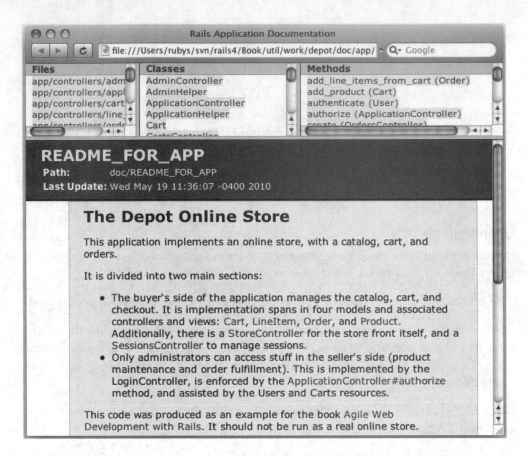

Figure 17.1: OUR APPLICATION'S INTERNAL DOCUMENTATION

Deployment

We deployed our application to a production-quality web server (Apache httpd) using a production-quality database server (MySQL). Along the way, we installed and configured Phusion Passenger to run our application, Bundler to track dependencies, and Git to configuration manage our code. Capistrano was employed to orchestrate updating the deployed web server in production from our development machine.

We made use of test and production environments to prevent our experimentation during development from affecting production. Our development environment made use of the lightweight SQLite database server and a lightweight web server, most likely WEBrick. Our tests were run in a controlled environment with test data provided by fixtures.

17.2 Documenting What We Have Done

To complete our retrospective, let's take a look at the code from two new perspectives.

Rails makes it easy to run Ruby's RDoc[1] utility on all the source files in an application to create good-looking programmer documentation. But before we generate that documentation, we should probably create a nice introductory page so that future generations of developers will know what our application does.

To do this, edit the file doc/README_FOR_APP, and enter anything you think might be useful. This file will be processed using RDoc, so you have a fair amount of formatting flexibility.

You can generate the documentation in HTML format using the rake command:

```
depot> rake doc:app
```

This generates documentation into the directory doc/app. See Figure 17.1, on the facing page.

Finally, we might be interested to see how much code we've written. There's a Rake task for that, too.

```
depot> rake stats
(in /Users/dave/Work/depot)
```

Name	Lines	LOC	Classes	Methods	M/C	LOC/M
Controllers	636	409	9	45	5	7
Helpers	24	24	0	1	0	22
Models	192	101	5	12	2	6
Libraries	0	0	0	0	0	0
Integration tests	201	138	2	9	4	13
Functional tests	424	285	9	0	0	0
Unit tests	163	123	13	2	0	59
Total	1640	1080	38	69	1	13

```
  Code LOC: 534     Test LOC: 546     Code to Test Ratio: 1:1.0
```

If you think about it, you have accomplished a lot and not with all that much code. Furthermore, much of that code was generated for you. This is the magic of Rails.

---

1. http://rdoc.sourceforge.net/

Part III

Rails in Depth

In this chapter, we'll see

- the directory structure of a Rails application,
- naming conventions,
- generating documentation for Rails itself,
- adding Rake tasks, and
- configuration.

Chapter 18

Finding Your Way Around Rails

Having survived our Depot project, you are now prepared to dig deeper into Rails. For the rest of the book, we'll go through Rails topic by topic (which pretty much means module by module). You have seen most of these modules in action before. We will cover not only what each module does but also how to extend or even replace the module and why you might want to do so.

The chapters in Part III cover all the major subsystems of Rails: Active Record, Active Resource, Action Pack (including both Action Controller and Action View), and Active Support. This is followed by an in-depth look at migrations.

Then we are going to delve into the interior of Rails and show how the components are put together, how they start up, and how they can be replaced. Having shown how the parts of Rails can be put together, we'll complete this book with a survey of a number of popular replacement parts, many of which can be used outside of Rails.

But first, we need to set the scene. This chapter covers all the high-level stuff you need to know to understand the rest: directory structures, configuration, and environments.

18.1 Where Things Go

Rails assumes a certain runtime directory layout and provides application and scaffold generators, which will create this layout for you. For example, if we generate *my_app* using the command rails new my_app, the top-level directory for our new application appears as shown in Figure 18.1, on page 253. Let's start with the text files in the top of the application directory:

- config.ru configures the Rack Webserver Interface, either to create Rails Metal applications or to use Rack Middlewares in your Rails application. These are discussed further in the Rails Guides.[1]

---

1. http://guides.rubyonrails.org/rails_on_rack.html

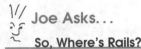

Joe Asks...

So, Where's Rails?

One of the interesting aspects of Rails is how componentized it is. From a developer's perspective, you spend all your time dealing with high-level modules such as Active Record and Action View. There is a component called Rails, but it sits below the other components, silently orchestrating what they do and making them all work together seamlessly. Without the Rails component, not much would happen. But at the same time, only a small part of this underlying infrastructure is relevant to developers in their day-to-day work. We'll cover the parts that *are* relevant in the rest of this chapter.

- Gemfile specifies the dependencies of your Rails application. You have already seen this in use when the will_paginate plugin was added to the Depot application. Application dependencies also include the database, web server, and even scripts used for deployment.

  Technically, this file is not used by Rails itself but rather by your application. You can find calls to the Bundler[2] in the config/boot.rb and config/application.rb files.

- Rakefile defines tasks to run tests, create documentation, extract the current structure of your schema, and more. Type rake --tasks at a prompt for the full list. Type rake --describe *task* to see a more complete description of a specific task.

- README contains general information about the Rails framework itself.

Now let's look at what goes into each directory (although not necessarily in order).

A Place for Our Application

Most of our work takes place in the app directory. The main code for the application lives below the app directory, as shown in Figure 18.2, on page 254. We'll talk more about the structure of the app directory as we look at the various Rails modules such as Active Record, Action Controller, and Action View in more detail later in the book.

A Place for our Tests

As we have seen in Section 7.2, *Iteration B2: Unit Testing of Models*, on page 80, Section 8.4, *Iteration C4: Functional Testing of Controllers*, on page 97, and

---

2. https://github.com/carlhuda/bundler

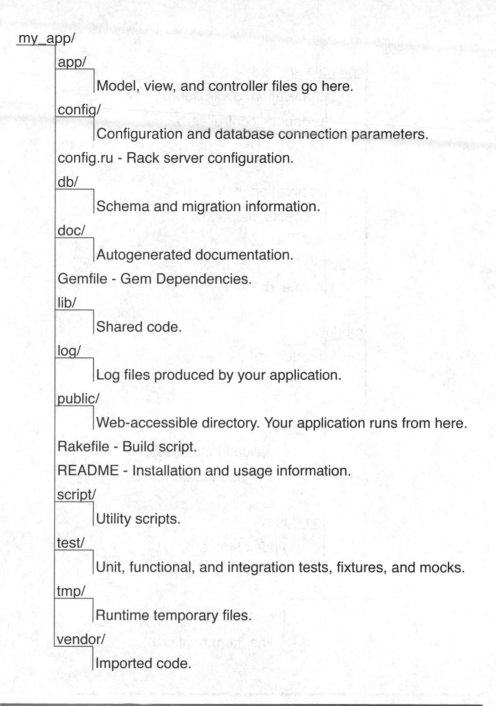

```
my_app/
    app/
        Model, view, and controller files go here.
    config/
        Configuration and database connection parameters.
    config.ru - Rack server configuration.
    db/
        Schema and migration information.
    doc/
        Autogenerated documentation.
    Gemfile - Gem Dependencies.
    lib/
        Shared code.
    log/
        Log files produced by your application.
    public/
        Web-accessible directory. Your application runs from here.
    Rakefile - Build script.
    README - Installation and usage information.
    script/
        Utility scripts.
    test/
        Unit, functional, and integration tests, fixtures, and mocks.
    tmp/
        Runtime temporary files.
    vendor/
        Imported code.
```

Figure 18.1: ALL RAILS APPLICATIONS HAVE THIS TOP-LEVEL DIRECTORY STRUCTURE.

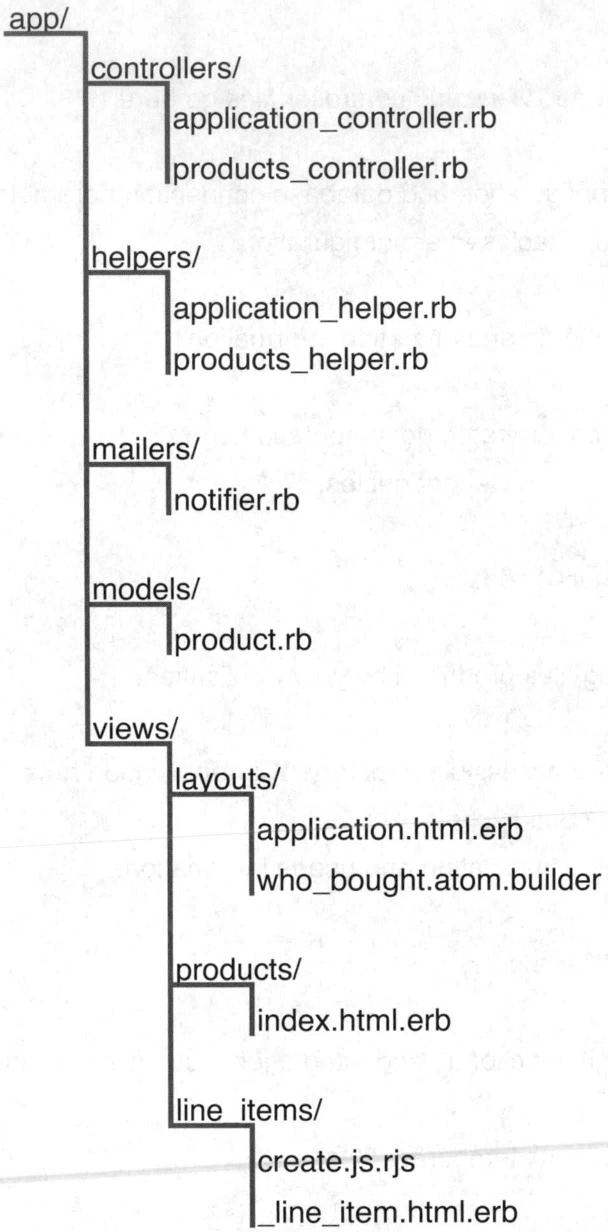

```
app/
    controllers/
        application_controller.rb
        products_controller.rb

    helpers/
        application_helper.rb
        products_helper.rb

    mailers/
        notifier.rb

    models/
        product.rb

    views/
        layouts/
            application.html.erb
            who_bought.atom.builder

        products/
            index.html.erb

        line_items/
            create.js.rjs
            _line_item.html.erb
```

Figure 18.2: THE MAIN CODE FOR OUR APPLICATION LIVES IN THE APP DIRECTORY.

Section 13.2, *Iteration H2: Integration Testing of Applications*, on page 176, Rails has ample provisions for testing your application, and the test directory is the home for all testing-related activities, including fixtures that define data used by our tests.

A Place for Documentation

As we saw in Section 17.2, *Documenting What We Have Done*, on page 247, Rails provides the doc:app Rake task to generate documentation, which it places in the doc/ directory. In addition to this command, Rails provides other tasks that generate documentation: doc:rails will provide documentation for the version of Rails you are running, and doc:guides will provide usage guides. Before you build the guides, you will need to add the gem RedCloth (note: case *is* significant) to your Gemfile and run bundle install.

Rails also provides other document-related tasks. To see them all, enter the command rake -T doc.

A Place for Supporting Libraries

The lib directory holds application code that doesn't fit neatly into a model, view, or controller. For example, you may have written a library that creates PDF receipts that your store's customers can download.[3] These receipts are sent directly from the controller to the browser (using the send_data method). The code that creates these PDF receipts will sit naturally in the lib directory.

The lib directory is also a good place to put code that's shared among models, views, or controllers. Maybe you need a library that validates a credit card number's checksum, that performs some financial calculation, or that works out the date of Easter. Anything that isn't directly a model, view, or controller should be slotted into lib.

Don't feel that you have to stick a bunch of files directly into the lib directory. Feel free to create subdirectories in which you group related functionality under lib. For example, on the Pragmatic Programmer site, the code that generates receipts, customs documentation for shipping, and other PDF-formatted documentation is in the directory lib/pdf_stuff.

In previous versions of Rails, the files in the lib directory were automatically included in the search. This is now an option that you need to explicitly enable. To do so, place the following in config/application.rb:

```
config.autoload_paths += %W(#{Rails.root}/lib)
```

Once you have files in the lib directory and the lib added to your autoload paths, you can use them in the rest of your application. If the files contain classes or modules and the files are named using the lowercase form of the class

---

3. ...which we did in the Pragmatic Programmer store.

or module name, then Rails will load the file automatically. For example, we might have a PDF receipt writer in the file receipt.rb in the directory lib/pdf_stuff. As long as our class is named PdfStuff::Receipt, Rails will be able to find and load it automatically.

↪ page 50

For those times where a library cannot meet these automatic loading conditions, you can use Ruby's require mechanism. If the file is in the lib directory, you can require it directly by name. For example, if our Easter calculation library is in the file lib/easter.rb, we can include it in any model, view, or controller using this:

```
require "easter"
```

If the library is in a subdirectory of lib, remember to include that directory's name in the require statement. For example, to include a shipping calculation for airmail, we might add the following line:

```
require "shipping/airmail"
```

A Place for Our Rake Tasks

You'll also find an empty tasks directory under lib. This is where you can write your own Rake tasks, allowing you to add automation to your project. This isn't a book about Rake, so we won't go into it deeply here, but here's a simple example. Rails provides a Rake task to tell you the latest migration that has been performed.

But it may be helpful to see a list of *all* the migrations that have been performed. We'll write a Rake task that prints out the versions listed in the schema_migration table. These tasks are Ruby code, but they need to be placed into files with the extension .rake. We'll call ours db_schema_migrations.rake:

depot_t/lib/tasks/db_schema_migrations.rake

```
namespace :db do
  desc "Prints the migrated versions"
  task :schema_migrations => :environment do
    puts ActiveRecord::Base.connection.select_values(
      'select version from schema_migrations order by version' )
  end
end
```

We can run this from the command line just like any other Rake task:

```
depot> rake db:schema_migrations
(in /Users/rubys/Work/...)
20110211000001
20110211000002
20110211000003
20110211000004
20110211000005
20110211000006
20110211000007
```

Consult the Rake documentation at http://rubyrake.org/ for more information on writing Rake tasks.

A Place for Our Logs

As Rails runs, it produces a bunch of useful logging information. This is stored (by default) in the log directory. Here you'll find three main log files, called development.log, test.log, and production.log. The logs contain more than just simple trace lines; they also contain timing statistics, cache information, and expansions of the database statements executed.

Which file is used depends on the environment in which your application is running (and we'll have more to say about environments when we talk about the config directory in Section 18.1, *A Place for Configuration*, on page 259).

A Place for Static Web Pages

Thepublic directory is the external face of your application. The web server takes this directory as the base of the application. In here you place *static* (in other words, unchanging) files, such as stylesheets, JavaScript, and perhaps even some web pages.

A Place for Scripts

If you find it helpful to write scripts that are run from the command line and perform various maintenance tasks for your application, the script directory is the place to put them.

This directory also holds the Rails script. This is the script that is run when you run the rails command from the command line. The first argument you pass to that script determines the function Rails will perform:

benchmarker
> Generates performance numbers on one or more methods in your application.

console
> Allows you to interact with your Rails application methods.

dbconsole
> Allows you to directly interact with your database via the command line.

destroy
> Removes autogenerated files created by generate.

generate
> A code generator. Out of the box, it will create controllers, mailers, models, scaffolds, and web services. You can also download additional

generator modules from the Rails website.[4] Run generate with no arguments for usage information on a particular generator, for example: rails
generate migration.

new
> Generates Rails application code.

plugin
> Helps you install and administer plugins—pieces of functionality that
> extend the capabilities of Rails.

profiler
> Creates a runtime-profile summary of a URI request processed by your
> application.

runner
> Executes a method in your application outside the context of the Web.
> This is the noninteractive equivalent of rails console. You could use this to
> invoke cache expiry methods from a cron job or handle incoming email.

server
> Runs your Rails application in a self-contained web server, using Mongrel
> (if it is available on your box) or WEBrick. We've been using this in our
> Depot application during development.

A Place for Temporary Files

It probably isn't a surprise that Rails keeps its temporary files tucked in the
tmp directory. You'll find subdirectories for cache contents, sessions, and sockets in here. Generally these files are cleaned up automatically by Rails, but
occasionally if things go wrong, you might need to look in here and delete old
files.

A Place for Third-Party Code

Thevendor directory is where third-party code lives. Nowadays, this code will
typically come from two sources.

First, Rails installs plugins into the directories below vendor/plugins. Plugins
are ways of extending Rails functionality, both during development and at
runtime.

Second, you can install Rails and all of its dependencies into the vendor directory, as we saw in Section 16.2, *Getting an Application Under Control*, on
page 233

If you want to go back to using the system-wide version of gems, you can delete
the vendor/cache directory.

---

4. http://wiki.rubyonrails.org/rails/pages/AvailableGenerators

A Place for Configuration

The config directory contains files that configure Rails. In the process of developing Depot, we configured a few routes, configured the database, created an initializer, modified some locales, and defined deployment instructions. The rest of the configuration was done via Rails conventions.

Before running your application, Rails loads and executes config/environment.rb and config/application.rb. The standard environment that these files set up automatically includes the following directories (relative to your application's base directory) in your application's load path:

- The app/controllers directory and its subdirectories
- The app/models directory and all of its subdirectories whose names start with an underscore or a lowercase letter
- The vendor directory and the lib contained in each plugin subdirectory
- The directories app, app/helpers, app/mailers, app/services, config, and lib

Each of these directories is added to the load path only if it exists.

In addition, Rails will load a per environment configuration file. This file lives in the environments directory and is where you place configuration options that vary depending on the environment.

This is done because Rails recognizes that your needs, as a developer, are very different when writing code, testing code, and running that code in production. When writing code, you want lots of logging, convenient reloading of changed source files, in-your-face notification of errors, and so on. In testing, you want a system that exists in isolation so you can have repeatable results. In production, your system should be tuned for performance, and users should be kept away from errors.

The switch that dictates the runtime environment is external to your application. This means that no application code needs to be changed as you move from development through testing to production. In Chapter 16, *Task K: Deployment and Production*, on page 225, you specified the environment on the rake command using a RAILS_ENV parameter and to Phusion Passenger using a RailsEnv line in your Apache configuration file. When starting WEBrick with the rails server command, you use the -e option:

```
depot> rails server -e development
depot> rails server -e test
depot> rails server -e production
```

If you have special requirements, for example, if you favor having a *staging* environment, you can create your own environments. You'll need to add a new section to the database configuration file and a new file to the config/environments directory.

What you put into these configuration file is entirely up to you. You can find a list of configuration parameters you can set in the Configuring Rails Applications guide you generated with the rake doc:guides command on page 255. This information is also available online.[5]

18.2 Naming Conventions

Newcomers to Rails are sometimes puzzled by the way it automatically handles the naming of things. They're surprised that they call a model class Person and Rails somehow knows to go looking for a database table called people. In this section, you'll learn how this implicit naming works.

The rules here are the default conventions used by Rails. You can override all of these conventions using configuration options.

Mixed Case, Underscores, and Plurals

We often name variables and classes using short phrases. In Ruby, the convention is to have variable names where the letters are all lowercase and words are separated by underscores. Classes and modules are named differently: there are no underscores, and each word in the phrase (including the first) is capitalized. (We'll call this *mixed case*, for fairly obvious reasons.) These conventions lead to variable names such as order_status and class names such as LineItem.

Rails takes this convention and extends it in two ways. First, it assumes that database table names, such as variable names, have lowercase letters and underscores between the words. Rails also assumes that table names are always plural. This leads to table names such as orders and third_parties.

On another axis, Rails assumes that files are named in lowercase with underscores.

Rails uses this knowledge of naming conventions to convert names automatically. For example, your application might contain a model class that handles line items. You'd define the class using the Ruby naming convention, calling it LineItem. From this name, Rails would automatically deduce the following:

- That the corresponding database table will be called line_items. That's the class name, converted to lowercase, with underscores between the words and pluralized.

- Rails would also know to look for the class definition in a file called line_item.rb (in the app/models directory).

---

5. http://guides.rubyonrails.org/configuring.html

Model Naming	
Table	`line_items`
File	`app/models/line_item.rb`
Class	`LineItem`

Controller Naming	
URL	`http://../store/list`
File	`app/controllers/store_controller.rb`
Class	`StoreController`
Method	`list`
Layout	`app/views/layouts/store.html.erb`

View Naming	
URL	`http://../store/list`
File	`app/views/store/list.html.erb (or .builder or .rjs)`
Helper	`module StoreHelper`
File	`app/helpers/store_helper.rb`

Figure 18.3: HOW NAMING CONVENTIONS WORK ACROSS A RAILS APPLICATION

Rails controllers have additional naming conventions. If our application has a store controller, then the following happens:

- Rails assumes the class is called StoreController and that it's in a file named store_controller.rb in the app/controllers directory.
- It also assumes there's a helper module named StoreHelper in the file store_helper.rb located in the app/helpers directory.
- It will look for view templates for this controller in the app/views/store directory.
- It will by default take the output of these views and wrap them in the layout template contained in the file store.html.erb or store.xml.erb in the directory app/views/layouts.

All these conventions are shown in Figure 18.3.

There's one extra twist. In normal Ruby code you have to use the require keyword to include Ruby source files before you reference the classes and modules in those files. Because Rails knows the relationship between filenames and class names, require is normally not necessary in a Rails application. Instead, the first time you reference a class or module that isn't known, Rails uses the naming conventions to convert the class name to a filename and tries to load that file behind the scenes. The net effect is that you can typically reference (say) the name of a model class, and that model will be automatically loaded into your application.

Grouping Controllers into Modules

So far, all our controllers have lived in the app/controllers directory. It is sometimes convenient to add more structure to this arrangement. For example, our store might end up with a number of controllers performing related but disjoint administration functions. Rather than pollute the top-level namespace, we might choose to group them into a single admin namespace.

Rails does this using a simple naming convention. If an incoming request has a controller named (say) admin/book, Rails will look for the controller called book_controller in the directory app/controllers/admin. That is, the final part of the controller name will always resolve to a file called *name*_controller.rb, and any leading path information will be used to navigate through subdirectories, starting in the app/controllers directory.

Imagine that our program has two such groups of controllers (say, admin/*xxx* and content/*xxx*) and that both groups define a book controller. There'd be a file called book_controller.rb in both the admin and content subdirectories of app/controllers. Both of these controller files would define a class named Book-Controller. If Rails took no further steps, these two classes would clash.

To deal with this, Rails assumes that controllers in subdirectories of the directory app/controllers are in Ruby modules named after the subdirectory. Thus, the book controller in the admin subdirectory would be declared like this:

```
class Admin::BookController < ActionController::Base
  # ...
end
```

The book controller in the content subdirectory would be in the Content module:

```
class Content::BookController < ActionController::Base
  # ...
end
```

The two controllers are therefore kept separate inside your application.

The templates for these controllers appear in subdirectories of app/views. Thus, the view template corresponding to this request:

```
http://my.app/admin/book/edit/1234
```

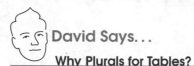

David Says...

Why Plurals for Tables?

Because it sounds good in conversation. Really. "Select a Product from products." And "Order has_many :line_items."

The intent is to bridge programming and conversation by creating a domain language that can be shared by both. Having such a language means cutting down on the mental translation that otherwise confuses the discussion of a *product description* with the client when it's really implemented as *merchandise body*. These communications gaps are bound to lead to errors.

Rails sweetens the deal by giving you most of the configuration for free if you follow the standard conventions. Developers are thus rewarded for doing the right thing, so it's less about giving up "your ways" and more about getting productivity for free.

will be in this file:

```
app/views/admin/book/edit.html.erb
```

You'll be pleased to know that the controller generator understands the concept of controllers in modules and lets you create them with commands such as this:

```
myapp> rails generate controller Admin::Book action1 action2 ...
```

What We Just Did

Everything in Rails has a place, and we systematically explored each of those nooks and crannies. In each place, files and the data contained in them follow naming conventions, and we covered that too. Along the way, we filled in a few missing pieces:

- We generated both API and user guide documentation for Rails itself.
- We added a Rake task to print the migrated versions.
- We showed how to separately configure each of the Rails execution environments.

Next up is the major subsystems of Rails, starting with the largest, Active Record.

In this chapter, we'll see

- the establish connection method;
- tables, classes, columns, and attributes,
- ids and relationships;
- create, read, update and delete operations; and
- callbacks and transactions.

Chapter 19

Active Record

Active Record is the object-relational mapping (ORM) layer supplied with Rails. It is the part of Rails that implements your application's model.

In this chapter, we'll build on the mapping data to rows and columns that we did in Depot. Then we'll look at using Active Record to manage table relationships and in the process cover create, read, update, and delete operations (commonly referred to in the industry as CRUD methods). Finally, we will dig into the Active Record object life cycle (including callbacks and transactions).

19.1 Defining Your Data

In Depot, we defined a number of models, including one for an Order. This particular model has a number of attributes, such as an email address of type String. In addition to the attributes that we defined, Rails provided an attribute named id that contains the primary key for the record. Rails also provides several additional attributes, including attributes that track when each row was last updated. Finally, Rails supports relationships between models, such as the relationship between orders and line items.

When you think about it, Rails provides a lot of support for models. Let's examine each in turn.

Organizing Using Tables and Columns

Each subclass of ActiveRecord::Base, such as our Order class, wraps a separate database table. By default, Active Record assumes that the name of the table associated with a given class is the plural form of the name of that class. If the class name contains multiple capitalized words, the table name is assumed to have underscores between these words.

Class Name	Table Name	Class Name	Table Name
Order	orders	LineItem	line_items
TaxAgency	tax_agencies	Person	people
Batch	batches	Datum	data
Diagnosis	diagnoses	Quantity	quantities

These rules reflect DHH's philosophy that class names should be singular while the names of tables should be plural.

Although Rails handles most irregular plurals correctly, occasionally you may stumble across one that is not handled correctly. If you encounter such a case, you can add to Rails' understanding of the idiosyncrasies and inconsistencies of the English language by modifying the inflection file provided:

`depot_t/config/initializers/inflections.rb`

```
# Be sure to restart your server when you modify this file.

# Add new inflection rules using the following format
# (all these examples are active by default):
# ActiveSupport::Inflector.inflections do |inflect|
#   inflect.plural /^(ox)$/i, '\1en'
#   inflect.singular /^(ox)en/i, '\1'
#   inflect.irregular 'person', 'people'
#   inflect.uncountable %w( fish sheep )
# end

ActiveSupport::Inflector.inflections do |inflect|
  inflect.irregular 'tax', 'taxes'
end
```

If you have legacy tables you have to deal with or don't like this behavior, you can control the table name associated with a given model by setting the table_name for a given class:

```
class Sheep < ActiveRecord::Base
  self.table_name = "sheep"
end
```

Instances of Active Record classes correspond to rows in a database table. These objects have attributes corresponding to the columns in the table. You probably noticed that our definition of class Order didn't mention any of the columns in the orders table. That's because Active Record determines them dynamically at runtime. Active Record reflects on the schema inside the database to configure the classes that wrap tables.

In the Depot application, our orders table is defined by the following migration:

```
def self.up
  create_table :orders do |t|
    t.string :name
    t.text :address
    t.string :email
    t.string :pay_type, :limit => 10

    t.timestamps
  end
end
```

Let's use the handy-dandy rails console command to play with this model. First, we'll ask for a list of column names:

```
depot> rails console
Loading development environment (Rails 3.0.5)
>> Order.column_names
=> ["id", "name", "address", "email", "pay_type", "created_at", "updated_at"]
```

Then we'll ask for the details of the pay_type column:

```
>> Order.columns_hash["pay_type"]
=> #<ActiveRecord::ConnectionAdapters::SQLiteColumn:0x7fe673f7da80
  @name="pay_type", @null=true, @default=nil, @sql_type="varchar(10)",
  @type=:string, @scale=nil, @precision=nil, @primary=false,
  @limit=10>
```

Notice that Active Record has gleaned a fair amount of information about the pay_type column. It knows that it's a string of at most ten characters, it has no default value, it isn't the primary key, and it may contain a null value. Rails obtained this information by asking the underlying database the first time we tried to use the Order class.

The attributes of an Active Record instance generally correspond to the data in the corresponding row of the database table. For example, our orders table might contain the following data:

```
depot> sqlite3 -line db/development.sqlite3 "select * from orders limit 1"
        id = 1
      name = Dave Thomas
   address = 123 Main St
     email = customer@example.com
  pay_type = Check
created_at = 2010-06-18 00:36:57.355069
updated_at = 2010-06-18 00:36:57.355069
```

If we fetched this row into an Active Record object, that object would have seven attributes. The id attribute would be 1 (a Fixnum), the name attribute would be the string "Dave Thomas", and so on.

David Says...

Where Are Our Attributes?

The notion of a database administrator (DBA) as a separate role from programmer has led some developers to see strict boundaries between code and schema. Active Record blurs that distinction, and no other place is that more apparent than in the lack of explicit attribute definitions in the model.

But fear not. Practice has shown that it makes little difference whether we're looking at a database schema, a separate XML mapping file, or inline attributes in the model. The composite view is similar to the separations already happening in the Model-View-Control pattern—just on a smaller scale.

Once the discomfort of treating the table schema as part of the model definition has dissipated, you'll start to realize the benefits of keeping DRY. When you need to add an attribute to the model, you simply create a new migration and reload the application.

Taking the "build" step out of schema evolution makes it just as agile as the rest of the code. It becomes much easier to start with a small schema and extend and change it as needed.

We access these attributes using accessor methods. Rails automatically constructs both attribute readers and attribute writers when it reflects on the schema:

```
o = Order.find(1)
puts o.name                 #=> "Dave Thomas"
o.name = "Fred Smith"       # set the name
```

Setting the value of an attribute does not change anything in the database—we must save the object for this change to become permanent.

The value returned by the attribute readers is cast by Active Record to an appropriate Ruby type if possible (so, for example, if the database column is a timestamp, a Time object will be returned). If we want to get the raw value of an attribute, we append _before_type_cast to its name, as shown in the following code:

```
product.price_before_type_cast      #=> "29.95", a string
product.updated_at_before_type_cast #=> "2008-05-13 10:13:14"
```

Inside the code of the model, we can use the read_attribute and write_attribute private methods. These take the attribute name as a string parameter.

SQL Type	Ruby Class	SQL Type	Ruby Class
int, integer	Fixnum	float, double	Float
decimal, numeric	BigDecimal[1]	char, varchar, string	String
interval, date	Date	datetime, time	Time
clob, blob, text	String	boolean	see text

[1] Decimal and numeric columns are mapped to integers when their scale is 0

Figure 19.1: MAPPING SQL TYPES TO RUBY TYPES

We can see the mapping between SQL types and their Ruby representation in Figure 19.1. Decimal and Boolean columns are slightly tricky.

Rails maps columns with Decimals with no decimal places to Fixnum objects; otherwise, it maps them to BigDecimal objects, ensuring that no precision is lost.

In the case of Boolean, it turns out that not all databases have a native boolean type. In the case of MySQL, a value of 0 is used for false, and a value of 1 is used for true. Unfortunately, Ruby treats everything that is not false or nil as true, so direct usage of these values is problematic. Instead, append a question mark to the column name:

```
user = User.find_by_name("Dave")
if user.superuser?
  grant_privileges
end
```

In addition to the attributes we define, there are a number of attributes that Rails either provides automatically or have special meaning.

Additional Columns Provided by Active Record

A number of column names have special significance to Active Record. Here's a summary:

created_at, created_on, updated_at, updated_on
> This is automatically updated with the timestamp of a row's creation or last update. Make sure the underlying database column is capable of receiving a date, datetime, or string. Rails applications conventionally use the _on suffix for date columns and the _at suffix for columns that include a time.

lock_version

> Rails will track row version numbers and perform optimistic locking if a table contains lock_version.

type

> Active Record can be subclassed. When you do so, all of the attributes for all of the subclasses are kept in the same table. The type attribute is used to name the column that will be used to track the type of a row.

id

> This is the default name of a table's primary key column (page 270).

xxx_id

> This is the default name of a foreign key reference to a table named with the plural form of xxx.

xxx_count

> This maintains a counter cache for the child table xxx.

Additional plugins, such as act_as_list,[1] may define additional columns.

Both primary keys and foreign keys play a vital role in database operations and merit additional discussion.

19.2 Locating and Traversing Records

In the Depot application, LineItems have direct relationships to three other models: Cart, Order, and Product. Additionally, models can have indirect relationships mediated by resource objects. The relationship between Orders and Products through LineItems is an example of such a relationship.

All of this is made possible through ids.

Identifying Individual Rows

Active Record classes correspond to tables in a database. Instances of a class correspond to the individual rows in a database table. Calling Order.find(1), for instance, returns an instance of an Order class containing the data in the row with the primary key of 1.

If you're creating a new schema for a Rails application, you'll probably want to go with the flow and let it add the id primary key column to all your tables. However, if you need to work with an existing schema, Active Record gives you a simple way of overriding the default name of the primary key for a table.

For example, we may be working with an existing legacy schema that uses the ISBN as the primary key for the books table.

---

1. https://github.com/rails/acts_as_list

We specify this in our Active Record model using something like the following:

```
class LegacyBook < ActiveRecord::Base
  self.primary_key = "isbn"
end
```

Normally, Active Record takes care of creating new primary key values for records that we create and add to the database—they'll be ascending integers (possibly with some gaps in the sequence). However, if we override the primary key column's name, we also take on the responsibility of setting the primary key to a unique value before we save a new row. Perhaps surprisingly, we still set an attribute called id to do this. As far as Active Record is concerned, the primary key attribute is always set using an attribute called id. The primary_key= declaration sets the name of the column to use in the table. In the following code, we use an attribute called id even though the primary key in the database is isbn:

```
book = LegacyBook.new
book.id = "0-12345-6789"
book.title = "My Great American Novel"
book.save

# ...

book = LegacyBook.find("0-12345-6789")
puts book.title      # => "My Great American Novel"
p book.attributes   #=> {"isbn" =>"0-12345-6789",
                          "title"=>"My Great American Novel"}
```

Just to make life more confusing, the attributes of the model object have the column names isbn and title—id doesn't appear. When you need to set the primary key, use id. At all other times, use the actual column name.

Model objects also redefine the Ruby id and hash methods to reference the model's primary key. This means that model objects with valid ids may be used as hash keys. It also means that unsaved model objects cannot reliably be used as hash keys (because they won't yet have a valid id).

One final note: Rails considers two model objects as equal (using ==) if they are instances of the same class and have the same primary key. This means that unsaved model objects may compare as equal even if they have different attribute data. If you find yourself comparing unsaved model objects (which is not a particularly frequent operation), you might need to override the == method.

As we will see, ids also play an important role in relationships.

Specifying Relationships in Models

Active Record supports three types of relationship between tables: one-to-one, one-to-many, and many-to-many. You indicate these relationships by adding declarations to your models: has_one, has_many, belongs_to, and the wonderfully named has_and_belongs_to_many.

One-to-One Relationships

A one-to-one association (or, more accurately, a one-to-zero-or-one relationship) is implemented using a foreign key in one row in one table to reference at most a single row in another table. A *one-to-one* relationship might exist between orders and invoices: for each order there's at most one invoice.

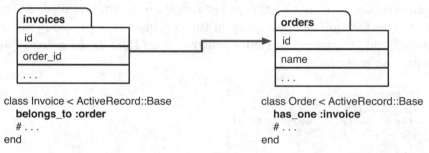

As the example shows, we declare this in Rails by adding a has_one declaration to the Order model and by adding a belongs_to declaration to the Invoice model.

There's an important rule illustrated here: the model for the table that contains the foreign key *always* has the belongs_to declaration.

One-to-Many Relationships

A one-to-many association allows you to represent a collection of objects. For example, an order might have any number of associated line items. In the database, all the line item rows for a particular order contain a foreign key column referring to that order.

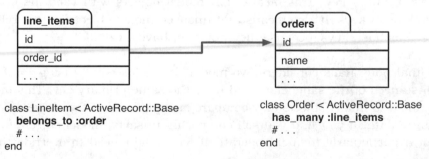

In Active Record, the parent object (the one that logically contains a collection of child objects) uses has_many to declare its relationship to the child table, and the child table uses belongs_to to indicate its parent. In our example, class LineItem belongs_to :order, and the orders table has_many :line_items.

Note that again, because the line item contains the foreign key, it has the belongs_to declaration.

Many-to-Many Relationships

Finally, we might categorize our products. A product can belong to many categories, and each category may contain multiple products. This is an example of a *many-to-many* relationship. It's as if each side of the relationship contains a collection of items on the other side.

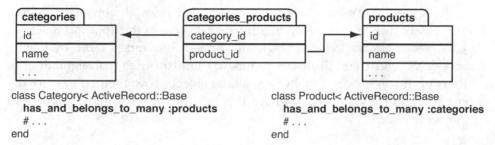

```
class Category< ActiveRecord::Base
  has_and_belongs_to_many :products
  # . . .
end
```

```
class Product< ActiveRecord::Base
  has_and_belongs_to_many :categories
  # . . .
end
```

In Rails we can express this by adding the has_and_belongs_to_many declaration to both models.

Many-to-many associations are symmetrical—both of the joined tables declare their association with each other using "habtm."

Rails implements many-to-many associations using an intermediate join table. This contains foreign key pairs linking the two target tables. Active Record assumes that this join table's name is the concatenation of the two target table names in alphabetical order. In our example, we joined the table categories to the table products, so Active Record will look for a join table named categories_products.

We can also define join tables directly. In the Depot application, we defined a LineItems join, which joined Products to either Carts or Orders. Defining it ourselves also gave us a place to store an additional attribute, namely, a quantity.

Now that we have covered data definitions, the next thing you would naturally want to do is access the data contained within the database, so let's do that.

19.3 Creating, Reading, Updating, and Deleting (CRUD)

Names such as SQLite and MySQL emphasize that all access to a database is via the Structured Query Language (SQL). In most cases, Rails will take care of this for you, but that is completely up to you. As you will see, you can provide clauses or even entire SQL statements for the database to execute.

If you are familiar with SQL already, as you read this section take note of how Rails provides places for familiar clauses such as select, from, where, group by, and so on. If you are not already familiar with SQL, one of the strengths of Rails is that you can defer knowing more about such things until you actually need to access the database at this level.

In this section, we'll continue to work with the Order model from the Depot application for an example. We will be using ActiveRecord methods to apply the four basic database operations: create, read, update, and delete.

Creating New Rows

Given that Rails represents tables as classes and rows as objects, it follows that we create rows in a table by creating new objects of the appropriate class. We can create new objects representing rows in our orders table by calling Order.new. We can then fill in the values of the attributes (corresponding to columns in the database). Finally, we call the object's save method to store the order back into the database. Without this call, the order would exist only in our local memory.

```
e1/ar/new_examples.rb
```

```
an_order = Order.new
an_order.name     = "Dave Thomas"
an_order.email    = "dave@example.com"
an_order.address  = "123 Main St"
an_order.pay_type = "check"
an_order.save
```

Active Record constructors take an optional block. If present, the block is invoked with the newly created order as a parameter. This might be useful if you wanted to create and save away an order without creating a new local variable.

```
e1/ar/new_examples.rb
```

```
Order.new do |o|
  o.name    = "Dave Thomas"
  # . . .
  o.save
end
```

Finally, Active Record constructors accept a hash of attribute values as an optional parameter. Each entry in this hash corresponds to the name and value of an attribute to be set. This is useful for doing things like storing values from HTML forms into database rows.

```
e1/ar/new_examples.rb
```

```
an_order = Order.new(
  :name    => "Dave Thomas",
  :email   => "dave@example.com",
```

```
  :address  => "123 Main St",
  :pay_type => "check")
an_order.save
```

Note that in all of these examples we did not set the id attribute of the new row. Because we used the Active Record default of an integer column for the primary key, Active Record automatically creates a unique value and sets the id attribute as the row is saved. We can subsequently find this value by querying the attribute.

e1/ar/new_examples.rb

```
an_order = Order.new
an_order.name = "Dave Thomas"
# ...
an_order.save
puts "The ID of this order is #{an_order.id}"
```

The new constructor creates a new Order object in memory; we have to remember to save it to the database at some point. Active Record has a convenience method, create, that both instantiates the model object and stores it into the database.

e1/ar/new_examples.rb

```
an_order = Order.create(
  :name     => "Dave Thomas",
  :email    => "dave@example.com",
  :address  => "123 Main St",
  :pay_type => "check")
```

You can pass create an array of attribute hashes; it'll create multiple rows in the database and return an array of the corresponding model objects:

e1/ar/new_examples.rb

```
orders = Order.create(
  [ { :name     => "Dave Thomas",
      :email    => "dave@example.com",
      :address  => "123 Main St",
      :pay_type => "check"
    },
    { :name     => "Andy Hunt",
      :email    => "andy@example.com",
      :address  => "456 Gentle Drive",
      :pay_type => "po"
    } ] )
```

The *real* reason that new and create take a hash of values is that you can construct model objects directly from form parameters:

```
@order = Order.new(params[:order])
```

If you think this line looks familiar, it is because you have seen it before. It appears in orders_controller.rb in the Depot application.

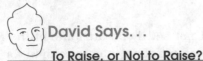

David Says...

To Raise, or Not to Raise?

When you use a finder driven by primary keys, you're looking for a particular record. You expect it to exist. A call to Person.find(5) is based on our knowledge of the people table. We want the row with an id of 5. If this call is unsuccessful—if the record with the id of 5 has been destroyed—we're in an exceptional situation. This mandates the raising of an exception, so Rails raises RecordNotFound.

On the other hand, finders that use criteria to search are looking for a *match*. So, Person.where(:name => 'Dave').first is the equivalent of telling the database (as a black box) "Give me the first person row that has the name Dave." This exhibits a distinctly different approach to retrieval; we're not certain up front that we'll get a result. It's entirely possible the result set may be empty. Thus, returning nil in the case of finders that search for one row and an empty array for finders that search for many rows is the natural, nonexceptional response.

Reading Existing Rows

Reading from a database involves first specifying which particular rows of data you are interested in—you'll give Active Record some kind of criteria, and it will return objects containing data from the row(s) matching the criteria.

The simplest way of finding a row in a table is by specifying its primary key. Every model class supports the find method, which takes one or more primary key values. If given just one primary key, it returns an object containing data for the corresponding row (or throws a RecordNotFound exception). If given multiple primary key values, find returns an array of the corresponding objects. Note that in this case a RecordNotFound exception is raised if *any* of the ids cannot be found (so if the method returns without raising an error, the length of the resulting array will be equal to the number of ids passed as parameters):

```
an_order = Order.find(27)    # find the order with id == 27
```

```
# Get a list of product ids from a form, then
# sum the total price
product_list = params[:product_ids]
total =  Product.find(product_list).sum(&:price)
```

Often, though, you need to read in rows based on criteria other than their primary key value. Active Record provides a range of options for performing these queries. We'll start by looking at an alternate way to express simple where clauses and then look at additional ways to modify the queries Rails generates for you.

Dynamic Finders

Probably the most common search performed on databases is to return the row or rows where a column matches a given value. A query might be *return all the orders for Dave* or *get all the blog postings with a subject of "Rails Rocks."* In many other languages and frameworks, you'd construct SQL queries to perform these searches. Active Record uses Ruby's dynamic power to do this for you.

For example, our Order model has attributes such as name, email, and address. We can use these names in finder methods to return rows where the corresponding columns match some value:

e1/ar/find_examples.rb
```
order  = Order.find_by_name("Dave Thomas")
orders = Order.find_all_by_name("Dave Thomas")
orders = Order.find_all_by_email(params['email'])
```

If you invoke a model's class method where the method name starts find_by_, find_last_by_, or find_all_by_, Active Record converts it to a finder, using the rest of the method's name to determine the column to be checked. Thus, the call to this:

```
order = Order.find_by_name("Dave Thomas")
```

is (effectively) converted by Active Record into this:

```
order = Order.where(:name => "Dave Thomas").first
```

Similarly, calls to find_all_by_*xxx* and to find_last_by_*xxx* substitute calls to all and last, respectively, for the implicit call to first.

Appending a bang (!) character to the find_by_ call will cause a ActiveRecord::RecordNotFound exception to be raised instead of returning nil if it can't find a matching record:

```
order = Order.find_by_name!("Dave Thomas")
```

The magic doesn't stop there. Active Record will also create finders that search on multiple columns. For example, you could write this:

```
user = User.find_by_name_and_password(name, pw)
```

This is equivalent to the following:

```
user = User.where(:name => name, :password => pw).first
```

To determine the names of the columns to check, Active Record simply splits the name that follows the find_by_ or find_all_by_ around the string and_. This is good enough most of the time but breaks down if you ever have a column name such as tax_and_shipping. In these cases, you'll have to use other methods to construct the where clause.

There are times when you want to ensure you always have a model object to work with. If there isn't one in the database, you want to create one. Dynamic finders can handle this. Calling a method whose name starts find_or_initialize_by_ or find_or_create_by_ will call either new or create on the model class if the finder would otherwise return nil. The new model object will be initialized so that its attributes corresponding to the finder criteria have the values passed to the finder method, and it will have been saved to the database if the create variant is used.

```
cart = Cart.find_or_initialize_by_user_id(user.id)
cart.items << new_item
cart.save
```

And, no, there isn't a find_by_ form that lets you use _or_ rather than _and_ between column names.

SQL and Active Record

To illustrate how Active Record works with SQL, let's pass a simple string to the where method call corresponding to a SQL where clause. For example, to return a list of all orders for Dave with a payment type of "po," we could use this:

```
pos = Order.where("name = 'Dave' and pay_type = 'po'")
```

The result will be an ActiveRecord::Relation object containing all the matching rows, each neatly wrapped in an Order object.

That's fine if our condition is predefined, but how do we handle the situation where the name of the customer is set externally (perhaps coming from a web form)? One way is to substitute the value of that variable into the condition string:

```
# get the name from the form
name = params[:name]
# DON'T DO THIS!!!
pos = Order.where("name = '#{name}' and pay_type = 'po'")
```

As the comment suggests, this really isn't a good idea. Why? It leaves the database wide open to something called a *SQL injection* attack, which we describe in more detail in the Rails Guides that you generated on page 255. For now, take it as a given that substituting a string from an external source into a SQL statement is effectively the same as publishing your entire database to the whole online world.

Instead, the safe way to generate dynamic SQL is to let Active Record handle it. Doing this allows Active Record to create properly escaped SQL, which is immune from SQL injection attacks. Let's see how this works.

If we pass multiple parameters to a where call, Rails treats the first parameter as a template for the SQL to generate. Within this SQL, we can embed placeholders, which will be replaced at runtime by the values in the rest of the array.

One way of specifying placeholders is to insert one or more question marks in the SQL. The first question mark is replaced by the second element of the array, the next question mark by the third, and so on. For example, we could rewrite the previous query as this:

```
name = params[:name]
pos = Order.where(["name = ? and pay_type = 'po'", name])
```

We can also use named placeholders. We do that by placing placeholders of the form :name into the string and by providing corresponding values in a hash, where the keys correspond to the names in the query:

```
name     = params[:name]
pay_type = params[:pay_type]
pos = Order.where("name = :name and pay_type = :pay_type",
                  {:pay_type => pay_type, :name => name})
```

We can take this a step further. Because params is effectively a hash, we can simply pass it all to the condition. If we have a form that can be used to enter search criteria, we can use the hash of values returned from that form directly:

```
pos = Order.where("name = :name and pay_type = :pay_type",
                  params[:order])
```

We can take this even further. If we pass just a hash as the condition, Rails generates a where clause using the hash keys as column names and the hash values as the values to match. Thus, we could have written the previous code even more succinctly:

```
pos = Order.where(params[:order])
```

Be careful with this latter form of condition: it takes *all* the key/value pairs in the hash you pass in when constructing the condition. An alternative would be to specify which parameters to use explicitly:

```
pos = Order.where(:name => params[:name],
                  :pay_type => params[:pay_type])
```

Regardless of which form of placeholder you use, Active Record takes great care to quote and escape the values being substituted into the SQL. Use these forms of dynamic SQL, and Active Record will keep you safe from injection attacks.

Using Like Clauses

We might be tempted to do something like the code on the next page to use parameterized like clauses in conditions.

```
# Doesn't work
User.where("name like '?%'", params[:name])
```

Rails doesn't parse the SQL inside a condition and so doesn't know that the name is being substituted into a string. As a result, it will go ahead and add extra quotes around the value of the name parameter. The correct way to do this is to construct the full parameter to the like clause and pass that parameter into the condition:

```
# Works
User.where("name like ?", params[:name]+"%")
```

Of course, if we do this, we need to consider that characters such as percent signs, should they happen to appear in the value of the name parameter, will be treated as wildcards.

Subsetting the Records Returned

Now that we know how to specify conditions, let's turn our attention to the various methods supported by ActiveRecord::Relation, starting with first and all.

As you may have guessed, first returns the first row in the relation. It returns nil if the relation is empty. Similarly, all returns all the rows as an array. ActiveRecord::Relation also supports many of the methods of Array objects, such as each and map. It does so by implicitly calling the all first.

It's important to understand that the query is not evaluated until one of these methods is used. This enables us to modify the query in a number of ways, namely, by calling additional methods, prior to making this call. Let's look at these methods now.

order

SQL that rows will be returned in any particular order unless we explicitly add an order by clause to the query. The order method lets us specify the criteria we'd normally add after the order by keywords. For example, the following query would return all of Dave's orders, sorted first by payment type and then by shipping date (the latter in descending order):

```
orders = Order.where(:name => 'Dave').
  order("pay_type, shipped_at DESC")
```

limit

We can limit the number of rows returned by calling the limit method. Generally when we use the limit method, we'll probably also want to specify the sort order to ensure consistent results. For example, the following returns the first ten matching orders:

```
orders = Order.where(:name => 'Dave').
  order("pay_type, shipped_at DESC").
  limit(10)
```

offset

The offset method goes hand in hand with the limit method. It allows us to specify the offset of the first row in the result set that will be returned.

```
# The view wants to display orders grouped into pages,
# where each page shows page_size orders at a time.
# This method returns the orders on page page_num (starting
# at zero).
def Order.find_on_page(page_num, page_size)
  order(:id).limit(page_size).offset(page_num*page_size)
end
```

We can use offset in conjunction with limit to step through the results of a query *n* rows at a time.

select

By default, ActiveRecord::Relation fetches all the columns from the underlying database table—it issues a select * from... to the database. Override this with the select method, which takes a string that will appear in place of the * in the select statement.

This method allows us to limit the values returned in cases where we need only a subset of the data in a table. For example, our table of podcasts might contain information on the title, speaker, and date and might also contain a large BLOB containing the MP3 of the talk. If you just wanted to create a list of talks, it would be inefficient to also load up the sound data for each row. The select method lets us choose which columns to load.

```
list = Talk.select("title, speaker, recorded_on")
```

joins

The joins method lets us specify a list of additional tables to be joined to the default table. This parameter is inserted into the SQL immediately after the name of the model's table and before any conditions specified by the first parameter. The join syntax is database-specific. The following code returns a list of all line items for the book called *Programming Ruby*:

```
LineItem.select('li.quantity').
  where("pr.title = 'Programming Ruby 1.9'").
  joins("as li inner join products as pr on li.product_id = pr.id")
```

readonly

The readonly method causes ActiveRecord::Resource to return Active Record objects that cannot be stored back into the database.

If we use the joins or select methods, objects will automatically be marked read-only.

group

The group method adds a group by clause to the SQL generated by find:

```
summary = LineItem.select("sku, sum(amount) as amount").
                   group("sku")
```

lock

The lock method takes an optional string as a parameter. If we pass it a string, it should be a SQL fragment in our database's syntax that specifies a kind of lock. With MySQL, for example, a *share mode* lock gives us the latest data in a row and guarantees that no one else can alter that row while we hold the lock. We could write code that debits an account only if there are sufficient funds using something like the following:

```
Account.transaction do
  ac = Account.where(:id=>id).lock("LOCK IN SHARE MODE").first
  ac.balance -= amount if ac.balance > amount
  ac.save
end
```

If we don't specify a string value or we give lock a value of true, the database's default exclusive lock is obtained (normally this will be "for update"). We can often eliminate the need for this kind of locking using transactions (discussed starting on page 296).

Databases can do more than simply find and reliably retrieve data, they can also do a bit of data reduction analysis. Rails provides access to these methods too.

Getting Column Statistics

Rails has the ability to perform statistics on the values in a column. For example, given a table of orders, we can calculate the following:

```
average = Order.average(:amount)  # average amount of orders
max     = Order.maximum(:amount)
min     = Order.minimum(:amount)
total   = Order.sum(:amount)
number  = Order.count
```

These all correspond to aggregate functions in the underlying database, but they work in a database-independent manner.

As before, methods can be combined:

```
Order.where("amount > 20").minimum(:amount)
```

These functions aggregate values. By default, they return a single result, producing, for example, the minimum order amount for orders meeting some condition. However, if you include the group method, the functions instead produce a series of results, one result for each set of records where the grouping expression has the same value. For example, the following calculates the maximum sale amount for each state:

```
result = Order.maximum(:amount).group(:state)
puts result  #=> [["TX", 12345], ["NC", 3456], ...]
```

This code returns an ordered hash. You index it using the grouping element ("TX", "NC", ... in our example). You can also iterate over the entries in order using each. The value of each entry is the value of the aggregation function.

The order and limit methods come into their own when using groups.

For example, the following returns the three states with the highest orders, sorted by the order amount:

```
result = Order.group(:state).
              order("max(amount) desc").
              limit(3)
```

This code is no longer database independent—in order to sort on the aggregated column, we had to use the SQLite syntax for the aggregation function (max, in this case).

Scopes

As these chains of method calls grow longer, making the chains themselves available for reuse becomes a concern. Once again, Rails delivers. An Active Record *scope* can be associated with a Proc and therefore may have arguments:

lambda
↪ page 50

```
class Order < ActiveRecord::Base
  scope :last_n_days, lambda { |days| where('updated < ?' , days) }
end
```

Such a named scope would make finding the last week's worth of orders a snap:

```
orders = Order.last_n_days(7)
```

Simpler scopes can simply be a set of method calls:

```
class Order < ActiveRecord::Base
  scope :checks, where(:pay_type => :check)
end
```

Scopes can also be combined. Finding the last week's worth of orders that were paid by check is just as easy:

```
orders = Order.checks.last_n_days(7)
```

In addition to making your application code easier to write and easier to read, scopes can make your code more efficient. The previous statement, for example, is implemented as a single SQL query.

ActiveRecord::Relation objects are equivalent to an anonymous scope:

```
in_house = Order.where('email LIKE "%@pragprog.com"')
```

Of course, relations can also be combined:

```
in_house.checks.last_n_days(7)
```

Scopes aren't limited to where conditions; we can do pretty much anything we can do in a method call: limit, order, join, and so on. Just be aware that Rails doesn't know how to handle multiple order or limit clauses, so be sure to use these only once per call chain.

In nearly every case, these methods that we have been describing are sufficient. But Rails is not satisfied with only being able to handle nearly every case, so for the cases that require a human-crafted query, there is an API for that too.

Writing Our Own SQL

Each of the methods we have been looking at contributes to the construction of a full SQL query string. The method find_by_sql lets our application take full control. It accepts a single parameter containing a SQL select statement (or an array containing SQL and placeholder values, as for find) and returns a (potentially empty) array of model objects from the result set. The attributes in these models will be set from the columns returned by the query. We'd normally use the select * form to return all columns for a table, but this isn't required.

e1/ar/find_examples.rb

```
orders = LineItem.find_by_sql("select line_items.* from line_items, orders " +
                  " where order_id = orders.id              " +
                  "   and orders.name = 'Dave Thomas'       ")
```

Only those attributes returned by a query will be available in the resulting model objects. We can determine the attributes available in a model object using the attributes, attribute_names, and attribute_present? methods. The first returns a hash of attribute name/value pairs, the second returns an array of names, and the third returns true if a named attribute is available in this model object.

e1/ar/find_examples.rb

```
orders = Order.find_by_sql("select name, pay_type from orders")

first = orders[0]
p first.attributes
p first.attribute_names
p first.attribute_present?("address")
```

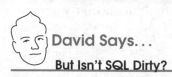

David Says...

But Isn't SQL Dirty?

Ever since developers first wrapped relational databases with an object-oriented layer, they've debated the question of how deep to run the abstraction. Some object-relational mappers seek to eliminate the use of SQL entirely, hoping for object-oriented purity by forcing all queries through an OO layer.

Active Record does not. It was built on the notion that SQL is neither dirty nor bad, just verbose in the trivial cases. The focus is on removing the need to deal with the verbosity in those trivial cases (writing a ten-attribute insert by hand will leave any programmer tired) but keeping the expressiveness around for the hard queries—the type SQL was created to deal with elegantly.

Therefore, you shouldn't feel guilty when you use find_by_sql to handle either performance bottlenecks or hard queries. Start out using the object-oriented interface for productivity and pleasure, and then dip beneath the surface for a close-to-the-metal experience when you need to do so.

This code produces the following:

```
{"name"=>"Dave Thomas", "pay_type"=>"check"}
["name", "pay_type"]
false
```

find_by_sql can also be used to create model objects containing derived column data. If we use the as xxx SQL syntax to give derived columns a name in the result set, this name will be used as the name of the attribute.

`e1/ar/find_examples.rb`

```
items = LineItem.find_by_sql("select *,                           " +
                             " products.price as unit_price,       " +
                             " quantity*products.price as total_price,  " +
                             " products.title as title            " +
                             " from line_items, products           " +
                             " where line_items.product_id = products.id ")
li = items[0]
puts "#{li.title}: #{li.quantity}x#{li.unit_price} => #{li.total_price}"
```

As with conditions, we can also pass an array to find_by_sql, where the first element is a string containing placeholders. The rest of the array can be either a hash or a list of values to be substituted.

```
Order.find_by_sql(["select * from orders where amount > ?",
                  params[:amount]])
```

In the old days of Rails, people frequently resorted to using find_by_sql. Since then, all the options added to the basic find method mean that you can avoid resorting to this low-level method.

Reloading Data

In an application where the database is potentially being accessed by multiple processes (or by multiple applications), there's always the possibility that a fetched model object has become stale—someone may have written a more recent copy to the database.

To some extent, this issue is addressed by transactional support (which we describe on page 296). However, there'll still be times where you need to refresh a model object manually. Active Record makes this easy—simply call its reload method, and the object's attributes will be refreshed from the database:

```
stock = Market.find_by_ticker("RUBY")
loop do
  puts "Price = #{stock.price}"
  sleep 60
  stock.reload
end
```

In practice, reload is rarely used outside the context of unit tests.

Updating Existing Rows

After such a long discussion of finder methods, you'll be pleased to know that there's not much to say about updating records with Active Record.

If you have an Active Record object (perhaps representing a row from our orders table), you can write it to the database by calling its save method. If this object had previously been read from the database, this save will update the existing row; otherwise, the save will insert a new row.

If an existing row is updated, Active Record will use its primary key column to match it with the in-memory object. The attributes contained in the Active Record object determine the columns that will be updated—a column will be updated in the database only if its value has been changed. In the following example, all the values in the row for order 123 can be updated in the database table:

```
order = Order.find(123)
order.name = "Fred"
order.save
```

However, in the following example, the Active Record object contains just the attributes id, name, and paytype—only these columns can be updated when the object is saved. (Note that you have to include the id column if you intend to save a row fetched using find_by_sql.)

```
orders = Order.find_by_sql("select id, name, pay_type from orders where id=123")
first = orders[0]
first.name = "Wilma"
first.save
```

In addition to the save method, Active Record lets us change the values of attributes and save a model object in a single call to update_attribute:

```
order = Order.find(123)
order.update_attribute(:name, "Barney")

order = Order.find(321)
order.update_attributes(:name => "Barney",
                        :email => "barney@bedrock.com")
```

The update_attributes method is most commonly used in controller actions where it merges data from a form into an existing database row:

```
def save_after_edit
  order = Order.find(params[:id])
  if order.update_attributes(params[:order])
    redirect_to :action => :index
  else
    render :action => :edit
  end
end
```

We can combine the functions of reading a row and updating it using the class methods update and update_all. The update method takes an id parameter and a set of attributes. It fetches the corresponding row, updates the given attributes, saves the result to the database, and returns the model object.

```
order = Order.update(12, :name => "Barney", :email => "barney@bedrock.com")
```

We can pass update an array of ids and an array of attribute value hashes, and it will update all the corresponding rows in the database, returning an array of model objects.

Finally, the update_all class method allows us to specify the set and where clauses of the SQL update statement. For example, the following increases the prices of all products with *Java* in their title by 10 percent:

```
result = Product.update_all("price = 1.1*price", "title like '%Java%'")
```

The return value of update_all depends on the database adapter; most (but not Oracle) return the number of rows that were changed in the database.

save, save!, create, and create!

It turns out that there are two versions of the save and create methods. The variants differ in the way they report errors:

- save returns true if the record was saved; it returns nil otherwise.

- save! returns true if the save was successful; it raises an exception otherwise.
- create returns the Active Record object regardless of whether it was successfully saved. You'll need to check the object for validation errors if you want to determine whether the data was written.
- create! returns the Active Record object on success; it raises an exception otherwise.

Let's look at this in a bit more detail.

Plain old save returns true if the model object is valid and can be saved:

```
if order.save
  # all OK
else
  # validation failed
end
```

It's up to us to check on each call to save to see that it did what we expected. The reason Active Record is so lenient is that it assumes save is called in the context of a controller's action method and that the view code will be presenting any errors back to the end user. And for many applications, that's the case.

However, if we need to save a model object in a context where we want to make sure to handle all errors programmatically, we should use save!. This method raises a RecordInvalid exception if the object could not be saved:

```
begin
  order.save!
rescue RecordInvalid => error
  # validation failed
end
```

Deleting Rows

Active Record supports two styles of row deletion. First, it has two class-level methods, delete and delete_all, that operate at the database level. The delete method takes a single id or an array of ids and deletes the corresponding row(s) in the underlying table. delete_all deletes rows matching a given condition (or all rows if no condition is specified). The return values from both calls depend on the adapter but are typically the number of rows affected. An exception is not thrown if the row doesn't exist prior to the call.

```
Order.delete(123)
User.delete([2,3,4,5])
Product.delete_all(["price > ?", @expensive_price])
```

The various destroy methods are the second form of row deletion provided by Active Record. These methods all work via Active Record model objects.

The destroy instance method deletes from the database the row corresponding to a particular model object. It then freezes the contents of that object, preventing future changes to the attributes.

```
order = Order.find_by_name("Dave")
order.destroy
# ... order is now frozen
```

There are two class-level destruction methods, destroy (which takes an id or an array of ids) and destroy_all (which takes a condition). Both read the corresponding rows in the database table into model objects and call the instance-level destroy method of those objects. Neither method returns anything meaningful.

```
Order.destroy_all(["shipped_at < ?", 30.days.ago])
```

Why do we need both the delete and destroy class methods? The delete methods bypass the various Active Record callback and validation functions, while the destroy methods ensure that they are all invoked. In general, it is better to use the destroy methods if you want to ensure that your database is consistent according to the business rules defined in your model classes.

We covered validation in Chapter 7, *Task B: Validation and Unit Testing*, on page 75. We cover callbacks next.

19.4 Participating in the Monitoring Process

Active Record controls the life cycle of model objects—it creates them, monitors them as they are modified, saves and updates them, and watches sadly as they are destroyed. Using callbacks, Active Record lets our code participate in this monitoring process. We can write code that gets invoked at any significant event in the life of an object. With these callbacks we can perform complex validation, map column values as they pass in and out of the database, and even prevent certain operations from completing.

Active Record defines twenty callbacks. Eighteen of these form before/after pairs and bracket some operation on an Active Record object. For example, the before_destroy callback will be invoked just before the destroy method is called, and after_destroy will be invoked after. The two exceptions are after_find and after_initialize, which have no corresponding before_xxx callback. (These two callbacks are different in other ways, too, as we'll see later.)

In Figure 19.2, on the next page, we can see how Rails wraps the eighteen paired callbacks around the basic create, update, and destroy operations on model objects. Perhaps surprisingly, the before and after validation calls are not strictly nested.

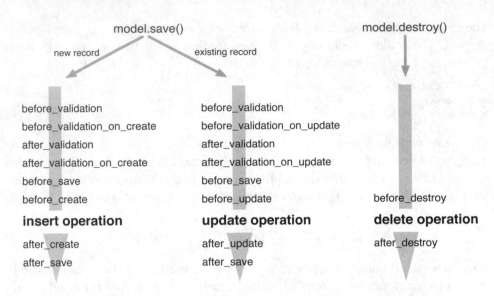

Figure 19.2: SEQUENCE OF ACTIVE RECORD CALLBACKS

In addition to these eighteen calls, the after_find callback is invoked after any find operation, and after_initialize is invoked after an Active Record model object is created.

To have your code execute during a callback, you need to write a handler and associate it with the appropriate callback.

There are two basic ways of implementing callbacks.

First, you can define the callback instance method directly. If you want to handle the *before save* event, for example, you could write this:

```
class Order < ActiveRecord::Base
  # ..
  def before_save
    self.payment_due ||= Time.now + 30.days
  end
end
```

The second basic way to define a callback is to declare handlers. A handler can be either a method or a block. You associate a handler with a particular event using class methods named after the event. To associate a method, declare it as private or protected, and specify its name as a symbol to the handler declaration. To specify a block, simply add it after the declaration. This block receives the model object as a parameter.

```
class Order < ActiveRecord..Base

  before_validation :normalize_credit_card_number

  after_create do |order|
    logger.info "Order #{order.id} created"
  end

  protected

  def normalize_credit_card_number
    self.cc_number.gsub!(/[-\s]/, '')
  end
end
```

You can specify multiple handlers for the same callback. They will generally be invoked in the order they are specified unless a handler returns false (and it must be the actual value false), in which case the callback chain is broken early.

Because of a performance optimization, the only way to define callbacks for the after_find and after_initialize events is to define them as methods. If you try declaring them as handlers using the second technique, they'll be silently ignored. (Sometimes folks ask why this was done. Rails has to use reflection to determine whether there are callbacks to be invoked. When doing real database operations, the cost of doing this is normally not significant compared to the database overhead. However, a single database select statement could return hundreds of rows, and both callbacks would have to be invoked for each. This slows the query down significantly. The Rails team decided that performance trumps consistency in this case.)

Grouping Related Callbacks Together

If you have a group of related callbacks, it may be convenient to group them into a separate handler class. These handlers can be shared between multiple models. A handler class is simply a class that defines callback methods (before_save, after_create, and so on). Create the source files for these handler classes in app/models.

In the model object that uses the handler, you create an instance of this handler class and pass that instance to the various callback declarations. A couple of examples will make this clearer.

If our application uses credit cards in multiple places, we might want to share our normalize_credit_card_number method across multiple models. To do that, we'd extract the method into its own class and name it after the event we want it to handle. This method will receive a single parameter, the model object that generated the callback.

```ruby
class CreditCardCallbacks

  # Normalize the credit card number
  def before_validation(model)
    model.cc_number.gsub!(/[-\s]/, '')
  end
end
```

Now, in our model classes, we can arrange for this shared callback to be invoked:

```ruby
class Order < ActiveRecord::Base
  before_validation CreditCardCallbacks.new
  # ...
end

class Subscription < ActiveRecord::Base
  before_validation CreditCardCallbacks.new
  # ...
end
```

In this example, the handler class assumes that the credit card number is held in a model attribute named cc_number; both Order and Subscription would have an attribute with that name. But we can generalize the idea, making the handler class less dependent on the implementation details of the classes that use it.

For example, we could create a generalized encryption and decryption handler. This could be used to encrypt named fields before they are stored in the database and to decrypt them when the row is read back. You could include it as a callback handler in any model that needed the facility.

The handler needs to encrypt a given set of attributes in a model just before that model's data is written to the database. Because our application needs to deal with the plain-text versions of these attributes, it arranges to decrypt them again after the save is complete. It also needs to decrypt the data when a row is read from the database into a model object. These requirements mean we have to handle the before_save, after_save, and after_find events. Because we need to decrypt the database row both after saving and when we find a new row, we can save code by aliasing the after_find method to after_save—the same method will have two names.

`e1/ar/encrypt.rb`

```ruby
class Encrypter

  # We're passed a list of attributes that should
  # be stored encrypted in the database
  def initialize(attrs_to_manage)
    @attrs_to_manage = attrs_to_manage
  end
```

```ruby
# Before saving or updating, encrypt the fields using the NSA and
# DHS approved Shift Cipher
def before_save(model)
  @attrs_to_manage.each do |field|
    model[field].tr!("a-z", "b-za")
  end
end

# After saving, decrypt them back
def after_save(model)
  @attrs_to_manage.each do |field|
    model[field].tr!("b-za", "a-z")
  end
end

# Do the same after finding an existing record
alias_method :after_find, :after_save
end
```

This example uses trivial encryption—you might want to beef it up before using this class for real.

We can now arrange for the Encrypter class to be invoked from inside our orders model:

```ruby
require "encrypter"

class Order < ActiveRecord::Base
  encrypter = Encrypter.new([:name, :email])

  before_save encrypter
  after_save  encrypter
  after_find  encrypter

protected
  def after_find
  end
end
```

We create a new Encrypter object and hook it up to the events before_save, after_save, and after_find. This way, just before an order is saved, the method before_save in the encrypter will be invoked, and so on.

So, why do we define an empty after_find method? Remember that we said that for performance reasons after_find and after_initialize are treated specially. One of the consequences of this special treatment is that Active Record won't know to call an after_find handler unless it sees an actual after_find method in the model class. We have to define an empty placeholder to get after_find processing to take place.

This is all very well, but every model class that wants to use our encryption handler would need to include some eight lines of code, just as we did with our Order class. We can do better than that. We'll define a helper method that does all the work and make that helper available to all Active Record models. To do that, we'll add it to the ActiveRecord::Base class:

e1/ar/encrypt.rb
```ruby
class ActiveRecord::Base
  def self.encrypt(*attr_names)
    encrypter = Encrypter.new(attr_names)

    before_save encrypter
    after_save  encrypter
    after_find  encrypter

    define_method(:after_find) { }
  end
end
```

Given this, we can now add encryption to any model class's attributes using a single call.

e1/ar/encrypt.rb
```ruby
class Order < ActiveRecord::Base
  encrypt(:name, :email)
end
```

A simple driver program lets us experiment with this:

e1/ar/encrypt.rb
```ruby
o = Order.new
o.name = "Dave Thomas"
o.address = "123 The Street"
o.email    = "dave@example.com"
o.save
puts o.name

o = Order.find(o.id)
puts o.name
```

On the console, we see our customer's name (in plain text) in the model object:

```
ar> ruby encrypt.rb
Dave Thomas
Dave Thomas
```

In the database, however, the name and email address are obscured by our industrial-strength encryption:

```
depot> sqlite3 -line db/development.sqlite3 "select * from orders"
     id = 1
user_id =
   name = Dbwf Tipnbt
address = 123 The Street
  email = ebwf@qsbhqsph.dpn
```

Callbacks are a fine technique, but they can sometimes result in a model class taking on responsibilities that aren't really related to the nature of the model. For example, on page 290 we created a callback that generated a log message when an order was created. That functionality isn't really part of the basic Order class—we put it there because that's where the callback executed.

Active Record *observers* overcome that limitation.

Observers

An Active Record observer is an object that transparently links itself into a model class, registering itself for callbacks as if it were part of the model but without requiring any changes in the model itself. Here's our previous logging example written using an observer:

e1/ar/observer.rb
```
class OrderObserver < ActiveRecord::Observer
  def after_save(an_order)
    an_order.logger.info("Order #{an_order.id} created")
  end
end
```

When ActiveRecord::Observer is subclassed, it looks at the name of the new class, strips the word Observer from the end, and assumes that what is left is the name of the model class to be observed. In our example, we called our observer class OrderObserver, so it automatically hooked itself into the model Order.

Sometimes this convention breaks down. When it does, the observer class can explicitly list the model or models it wants to observe using the observe method:

e1/ar/observer.rb
```
class AuditObserver < ActiveRecord::Observer

  observe Order, Payment, Refund

  def after_save(model)
    model.logger.info("[Audit] #{model.class.name} #{model.id} created")
  end
end
```

By convention, observer source files live in app/models.

Instantiating Observers

So far we've defined our observers. However, we also need to instantiate them—if we don't, they simply won't fire. How we instantiate observers depends on whether we're using them inside or outside the context of a Rails application.

If you're using observers within a Rails application, you need to list them in your application's application.rb file (in the config directory):

```
config.active_record.observers = :order_observer, :audit_observer
```

If instead you're using your Active Record objects in a stand-alone application (that is, you're not running Active Record within a Rails application), you need to create instances of the observers manually using instance:

```
OrderObserver.instance
AuditObserver.instance
```

In a way, observers bring to Rails much of the benefits of first-generation aspect-oriented programming in languages such as Java. They allow you to inject behavior into model classes without changing any of the code in those classes.

19.5 Transactions

A database transaction groups a series of changes together in such a way that either the database applies all of the changes or it applies none of the changes. The classic example of the need for transactions (and one used in Active Record's own documentation) is transferring money between two bank accounts. The basic logic is simple:

```
account1.deposit(100)
account2.withdraw(100)
```

However, we have to be careful. What happens if the deposit succeeds but for some reason the withdrawal fails (perhaps the customer is overdrawn)? We'll have added $100 to the balance in account1 without a corresponding deduction from account2. In effect, we'll have created $100 out of thin air.

Transactions to the rescue. A transaction is something like the Three Musketeers with their motto "All for one and one for all." Within the scope of a transaction, either every SQL statement succeeds or they all have no effect. Putting that another way, if any statement fails, the entire transaction has no effect on the database.

In Active Record we use the transaction method to execute a block in the context of a particular database transaction. At the end of the block, the transaction is committed, updating the database, *unless* an exception is raised within the block, in which case the database rolls back all of the changes. Because transactions exist in the context of a database connection, we have to invoke them with an Active Record class as a receiver.

Thus, we could write this:

```
Account.transaction do
  account1.deposit(100)
  account2.withdraw(100)
end
```

Let's experiment with transactions. We'll start by creating a new database table. (Make sure your database supports transactions, or this code won't work for you.)

e1/ar/transactions.rb

```
create_table :accounts, :force => true do |t|
  t.string   :number
  t.decimal :balance, :precision => 10, :scale => 2, :default => 0
end
```

Next, we'll define a simple bank account class. This class defines instance methods to deposit money to and withdraw money from the account. It also provides some basic validation—for this particular type of account, the balance can never be negative.

e1/ar/transactions.rb

```
class Account < ActiveRecord::Base
  validate :price_must_be_at_least_a_cent

  def withdraw(amount)
    adjust_balance_and_save(-amount)
  end

  def deposit(amount)
    adjust_balance_and_save(amount)
  end

  private

  def adjust_balance_and_save(amount)
    self.balance += amount
    save!
  end

  def price_must_be_at_least_a_cent
    errors.add(:balance, "is negative") if balance < 0
  end
end
```

Let's look at the helper method, adjust_balance_and_save. The first line simply updates the balance field. The method then calls save! to save the model data. (Remember that save! raises an exception if the object cannot be saved—we use the exception to signal to the transaction that something has gone wrong.)

So, now let's write the code to transfer money between two accounts. It's pretty straightforward:

`e1/ar/transactions.rb`

```
peter = Account.create(:balance => 100, :number => "12345")
paul  = Account.create(:balance => 200, :number => "54321")

Account.transaction do
  paul.deposit(10)
  peter.withdraw(10)
end
```

We check the database, and, sure enough, the money got transferred:

```
depot> sqlite3 -line db/development.sqlite3 "select * from accounts"
     id = 1
 number = 12345
balance = 90

     id = 2
 number = 54321
balance = 210
```

Now let's get radical. If we start again but this time try to transfer $350, we'll run Peter into the red, which isn't allowed by the validation rule. Let's try it:

`e1/ar/transactions.rb`

```
peter = Account.create(:balance => 100, :number => "12345")
paul  = Account.create(:balance => 200, :number => "54321")
```

`e1/ar/transactions.rb`

```
Account.transaction do
  paul.deposit(350)
  peter.withdraw(350)
end
```

When we run this, we get an exception reported on the console:

```
.../validations.rb:736:in 'save!': Validation failed: Balance is negative
from transactions.rb:46:in 'adjust_balance_and_save'
    :         :         :
from transactions.rb:80
```

Looking in the database, we can see that the data remains unchanged:

```
depot> sqlite3 -line db/development.sqlite3 "select * from accounts"
     id = 1
 number = 12345
balance = 100

     id = 2
 number = 54321
balance = 200
```

However, there's a trap waiting for you here. The transaction protected the database from becoming inconsistent, but what about our model objects? To see what happened to them, we have to arrange to intercept the exception to allow the program to continue running:

e1/ar/transactions.rb

```
peter = Account.create(:balance => 100, :number => "12345")
paul  = Account.create(:balance => 200, :number => "54321")
```

e1/ar/transactions.rb

```
begin
  Account.transaction do
    paul.deposit(350)
    peter.withdraw(350)
  end
rescue
  puts "Transfer aborted"
end

puts "Paul has #{paul.balance}"
puts "Peter has #{peter.balance}"
```

What we see is a little surprising:

```
Transfer aborted
Paul has 550.0
Peter has -250.0
```

Although the database was left unscathed, our model objects were updated anyway. This is because Active Record wasn't keeping track of the before and after states of the various objects—in fact it couldn't, because it had no easy way of knowing just which models were involved in the transactions.

Built-in Transactions

When we discussed parent and child tables in Section 19.2, *Specifying Relationships in Models*, on page 272, we said that Active Record takes care of saving all the dependent child rows when you save a parent row. This takes multiple SQL statement executions (one for the parent and one each for any changed or new children). Clearly, this change should be atomic, but until now we haven't been using transactions when saving these interrelated objects. Have we been negligent?

Fortunately, no. Active Record is smart enough to wrap all the updates and inserts related to a particular save (and also the deletes related to a destroy) in a transaction; either they all succeed or no data is written permanently to the database. You need explicit transactions only when you manage multiple SQL statements yourself.

While we have covered the basics, transactions are actually very subtle. They exhibit the so-called ACID properties: they're Atomic, they ensure Consistency, they work in Isolation, and their effects are Durable (they are made permanent when the transaction is committed). It's worth finding a good database book and reading up on transactions if you plan to take a database application live.

What We Just Did

We learned the relevant data structures and naming conventions for tables, classes, columns, attributes, ids, and relationships. We saw how to create, read, update, and delete this data. Finally, we now understand how transactions and callbacks can be used to prevent inconsistent changes.

This, coupled with validation as described in Chapter 7, *Task B: Validation and Unit Testing*, on page 75, covers all the essentials of Active Record that every Rails programmer needs to know. If you have specific needs beyond what is covered here, look to the Rails Guides that you generated on page 255 for more information.

The next major subsystem to cover is Action Pack, which covers both the view and controller portions of Rails.

In this chapter, we'll see

- Representational State Transfer (REST);
- defining how requests are routed to controllers;
- selecting a data representation;
- testing routes;
- the controller environment;
- rendering and redirecting; and
- sessions, flash, and filters.

Chapter 20

Action Dispatch and Action Controller

Action Pack lies at the heart of Rails applications. It consists of three Ruby modules: ActionDispatch, ActionController, and ActionView. Action Dispatch routes requests to controllers. Action Controller converts requests into responses. Action View is used by Action Controller to format those responses.

As a concrete example, in the Depot application, we routed the root of the site (/) to the index method of the StoreController. At the completion of that method, the template in app/views/store/index.html.erb was rendered. Each of these activities was orchestrated by modules in the ActionPack component.

Working together, these three submodules provide support for processing incoming requests and generating outgoing responses. In this chapter, we'll look at both Action Dispatch and Action Controller. In the next chapter, we will cover Action View.

When we looked at Active Record, we saw it could be used as a freestanding library; you can use Active Record as part of a nonweb Ruby application. Action Pack is different. Although it is possible to use it directly as a framework, you probably won't. Instead, you'll take advantage of the tight integration offered by Rails. Components such as Action Controller, Action View, and Active Record handle the processing of requests, and the Rails environment knits them together into a coherent (and easy-to-use) whole. For that reason, we'll describe Action Controller in the context of Rails. Let's start by looking at how Rails applications handle requests. We'll then dive down into the details of routing and URL handling. We'll continue by looking at how you write code in a controller. Finally, we will cover sessions, flash, and filters.

20.1 Dispatching Requests to Controllers

At its simplest, a web application accepts an incoming request from a browser, processes it, and sends a response.

The first question that springs to mind is, how does the application know what to do with the incoming request? A shopping cart application will receive requests to display a catalog, add items to a cart, create an order, and so on. How does it route these requests to the appropriate code?

It turns out that Rails provides two ways to define how to route a request: a comprehensive way that you will use when you need to and a convenient way that you will generally use whenever you can.

The comprehensive way lets you define a direct mapping of URLs to actions based on pattern matching, requirements, and conditions. The convenient way lets you define routes based on resources, such as the models that you define. And because the convenient way is built on the comprehensive way, you can freely mix and match the two approaches.

In both cases, Rails encodes information in the request URL and uses a subsystem called *Action Dispatch* to determine what should be done with that request. The actual process is very flexible, but at the end of it Rails has determined the name of the *controller* that handles this particular request, along with a list of any other request parameters. In the process, either one of these additional parameters or the HTTP method itself is used to identify the *action* to be invoked in the target controller.

Rails routes support the mapping between URLs and actions based on the contents of the URL and on the HTTP method used to invoke the request. We've seen how to do this on a URL-by-URL basis using anonymous or named routes. Rails also supports a higher-level way of creating groups of related routes. To understand the motivation for this, we need to take a little diversion into the world of Representational State Transfer.

REST: Representational State Transfer

The ideas behind REST were formalized in Chapter 5 of Roy Fielding's 2000 PhD dissertation.[1] In a REST approach, servers communicate with clients using stateless connections. All the information about the state of the interaction between the two is encoded into the requests and responses between them. Long-term state is kept on the server as a set of identifiable *resources*. Clients access these resources using a well-defined (and severely constrained) set of resource identifiers (URLs in our context). REST distinguishes the content of resources from the presentation of that content. REST is designed to support highly scalable computing while constraining application architectures to be decoupled by nature.

There's a lot of abstract stuff in this description. What does REST mean in practice?

---

1. http://www.ics.uci.edu/~fielding/pubs/dissertation/rest_arch_style.htm

First, the formalities of a RESTful approach mean that network designers know when and where they can cache responses to requests. This enables load to be pushed out through the network, increasing performance and resilience while reducing latency.

Second, the constraints imposed by REST can lead to easier-to-write (and maintain) applications. RESTful applications don't worry about implementing remotely accessible services. Instead, they provide a regular (and simple) interface to a set of resources. Your application implements a way of listing, creating, editing, and deleting each resource, and your clients do the rest.

Let's make this more concrete. In REST, we use a simple set of verbs to operate on a rich set of nouns. If we're using HTTP, the verbs correspond to HTTP methods (GET, PUT, POST, and DELETE, typically). The nouns are the resources in our application. We name those resources using URLs.

The Depot application that we produced contained a set of products. There are implicitly two resources here. First, there are the individual products. Each constitutes a resource. There's also a second resource: the collection of products.

To fetch a list of all the products, we could issue an HTTP GET request against this collection, say on the path /products. To fetch the contents of an individual resource, we have to identify it. The Rails way would be to give its primary key value (that is, its id). Again we'd issue a GET request, this time against the URL /products/1.

To create a new product in our collection we use an HTTP POST request directed at the /products path, with the post data containing the product to add. Yes, that's the same path we used to get a list of products. If you issue a GET to it, it responds with a list, and if you do a POST to it, it adds a new product to the collection.

Take this a step further. We've already seen you can retrieve the content of a product—you just issue a GET request against the path /products/1. To update that product, you'd issue an HTTP PUT request against the same URL. And, to delete it, you could issue an HTTP DELETE request, again using the same URL.

Take this further. Maybe our system also tracks users. Again, we have a set of resources to deal with. REST tells us to use the same set of verbs (GET, POST, PUT, and DELETE) against a similar-looking set of URLs (/users, /users/1, ...).

Now we see some of the power of the constraints imposed by REST. We're already familiar with the way Rails constrains us to structure our applications a certain way. Now the REST philosophy tells us to structure the interface to our applications too. Suddenly our world gets a lot simpler.

Rails has direct support for this type of interface; it adds a kind of macro route facility, called *resources*. Let's take a look at how the config/routes.rb might have looked back in Section 6.1, *Creating a Rails Application*, on page 61.

```
Depot::Application.routes.draw do |map|
▶   resources :products
end
```

The resources line caused seven new routes to be added to our application. Along the way, it assumed that the application will have a controller named ProductsController, containing seven actions with given names.

You can take a look at the routes that were generated for us. We do this by making use of the handy rake routes command:

```
    products GET    /products(.:format)
                    {:action=>"index", :controller=>"products"}
             POST   /products(.:format)
                    {:action=>"create", :controller=>"products"}
 new_product GET    /products/new(.:format)
                    {:action=>"new", :controller=>"products"}
edit_product GET    /products/:id/edit(.:format)
                    {:action=>"edit", :controller=>"products"}
     product GET    /products/:id(.:format)
                    {:action=>"show", :controller=>"products"}
             PUT    /products/:id(.:format)
                    {:action=>"update", :controller=>"products"}
             DELETE /products/:id(.:format)
                    {:action=>"destroy", :controller=>"products"}
```

All the routes defined are spelled out in a columnar format. The lines will generally wrap on your screen; in fact, they had to be broken into two lines per route to fit on this page. The columns are (optional) route name, HTTP method, route path, and (on a separate line on this page) route requirements.

Fields in parentheses are optional parts of the path. Field names preceded by a colon name variables into which this part of the path is placed for later processing by the controller.

Now let's look at the seven controller actions that these routes reference. Although we created our routes to manage the products in our application, let's broaden this out in these descriptions and talk about resources—after all, the same seven methods will be required for all resource-based routes:

index

> Returns a list of the resources.

create

> Creates a new resource from the data in the POST request, adding it to the collection.

now

> Constructs a new resource and passes it to the client. This resource will not have been saved on the server. You can think of the new action as creating an empty form for the client to fill in.

show

> Returns the contents of the resource identified by params[:id].

update

> Updates the contents of the resource identified by params[:id] with the data associated with the request.

edit

> Returns the contents of the resource identified by params[:id] in a form suitable for editing.

destroy

> Destroys the resource identified by params[:id].

You can see that these seven actions contain the four basic CRUD operations (create, read, update, and delete). They also contain an action to list resources and two auxiliary actions that return new and existing resources in a form suitable for editing on the client.

If for some reason you don't need or want all seven actions, you can limit the actions produced using :only or :except options on your resources:

```
resources :comments, :except => [:update, :destroy]
```

Several of the routes are named routes enabling you to use helper functions such as products_url and edit_product_url(:id=>1).

Note that each route is defined with an optional format specifier. We will cover formats in more detail in Section 20.1, *Selecting a Data Representation*, on page 309.

Let's take a look at the controller code:

depot_a/app/controllers/products_controller.rb

```
class ProductsController < ApplicationController
  # GET /products
  # GET /products.xml
  def index
    @products = Product.all

    respond_to do |format|
      format.html # index.html.erb
      format.xml  { render :xml => @products }
    end
  end
```

```
# GET /products/1
# GET /products/1.xml
def show
  @product = Product.find(params[:id])

  respond_to do |format|
    format.html # show.html.erb
    format.xml  { render :xml => @product }
  end
end

# GET /products/new
# GET /products/new.xml
def new
  @product = Product.new

  respond_to do |format|
    format.html # new.html.erb
    format.xml  { render :xml => @product }
  end
end

# GET /products/1/edit
def edit
  @product = Product.find(params[:id])
end

# POST /products
# POST /products.xml
def create
  @product = Product.new(params[:product])

  respond_to do |format|
    if @product.save
      format.html { redirect_to(@product,
        :notice => 'Product was successfully created.') }
      format.xml  { render :xml => @product, :status => :created,
        :location => @product }
    else
      format.html { render :action => "new" }
      format.xml  { render :xml => @product.errors,
        :status => :unprocessable_entity }
    end
  end
end

# PUT /products/1
# PUT /products/1.xml
def update
  @product = Product.find(params[:id])

  respond_to do |format|
    if @product.update_attributes(params[:product])
      format.html { redirect_to(@product,
```

```
            :notice => 'Product was successfully updated.') }
          format.xml  { head :ok }
      else
          format.html { render :action => "edit" }
          format.xml  { render :xml => @product.errors,
            :status => :unprocessable_entity }
      end
    end
  end

  # DELETE /products/1
  # DELETE /products/1.xml
  def destroy
    @product = Product.find(params[:id])
    @product.destroy

    respond_to do |format|
      format.html { redirect_to(products_url) }
      format.xml  { head :ok }
    end
  end
end
```

Notice how we have one action for each of the RESTful actions. The comment before each shows the format of the URL that invokes it.

Notice also that many of the actions contain a respond_to block. As we saw on page 125, Rails uses this to determine the type of content to send in a response. The scaffold generator automatically creates code that will respond appropriately to requests for HTML or XML content. We'll play with that in a little while.

The views created by the generator are fairly straightforward. The only tricky thing is the need to use the correct HTTP method to send requests to the server. For example, the view for the index action looks like this:

depot_a/app/views/products/index.html.erb

```
<h1>Listing products</h1>

<table>
  <tr>
    <th>Title</th>
    <th>Description</th>
    <th>Image url</th>
    <th>Price</th>
    <th></th>
    <th></th>
    <th></th>
  </tr>
```

```
<% @products.each do |product| %>
  <tr>
    <td><%= product.title %></td>
    <td><%= product.description %></td>
    <td><%= product.image_url %></td>
    <td><%= product.price %></td>
    <td><%= link_to 'Show', product %></td>
    <td><%= link_to 'Edit', edit_product_path(product) %></td>
    <td><%= link_to 'Destroy', product, :confirm => 'Are you sure?',
            :method => :delete %></td>
  </tr>
<% end %>
</table>

<br />

<%= link_to 'New Product', new_product_path %>
```

The links to the actions that edit a product and add a new product should both use regular GET methods, so a standard link_to works fine. However, the request to destroy a product must issue an HTTP DELETE, so the call includes the :method => :delete option to link_to.

Adding Additional Actions

Rails resources provide you with an initial set of actions, but you don't need to stop there. In Section 12.2, *Iteration G2: Atom Feeds*, on page 159, we added an interface to allow people to fetch a list of people who bought any given product. To do that with Rails, we use an extension to the resources call:

```
Depot::Application.routes.draw do
  resources :products do
    get :who_bought, :on => :member
  end
end
```

That syntax is straightforward. It says "We want to add a new action named who_bought, invoked via an HTTP GET. It applies to each member of the collection of products."

Instead of specifying :member, if we instead specified :collection, then the route would apply to the collection as a whole. This is often used for scoping; for example, you may have collections of products on clearance or products that have been discontinued.

Nested Resources

Often our resources themselves contain additional collections of resources. For example, we may want to allow folks to review our products. Each review would be a resource, and collections of review would be associated with each product resource.

Rails provides a convenient and intuitive way of declaring the routes for this type of situation:

```
resources :products do
  resources :reviews
end
```

This defines the top-level set of products routes and additionally creates a set of subroutes for reviews. Because the review resources appear inside the products block, a review resource *must* be qualified by a product resource. This means that the path to a review must always be prefixed by the path to a particular product. To fetch the review with id 4 for the product with an id of 99, you'd use a path of /products/99/reviews/4.

The named route for /products/:product_id/reviews/:id is product_review, not simply review. This naming simply reflects the nesting of these resources.

As always, you can see the full set of routes generated by our configuration by using the rake routes command.

Shallow Route Nesting

At times, nested resources can produce cumbersome URLs. A solution to this is to use shallow route nesting:

```
resources :products, :shallow => true do
  resources :reviews
end
```

This will enable the recognition of the following routes:

```
/products/1         => product_path(1)
/products/1/reviews => product_reviews_index_path(1)
/reviews/2          => reviews_path(2)
```

Try the rake routes command to see the full mapping.

Selecting a Data Representation

One of the goals of a REST architecture is to decouple data from its representation. If a human uses the URL path /products to fetch some products, they should see nicely formatted HTML. If an application asks for the same URL, it could elect to receive the results in a code-friendly format (YAML, JSON, or XML, perhaps).

We've already seen how Rails can use the HTTP Accept header in a respond_to block in the controller. However, it isn't always easy (and sometimes it's plain impossible) to set the Accept header. To deal with this, Rails allows you to pass the format of response you'd like as part of the URL. To do this, set a :format parameter in your routes to the file extension of the MIME type you'd like returned. As you have seen, Rails accomplishes this by including a field called :format in your route definitions:

```
GET     /products(.:format)
        {:action=>"index", :controller=>"products"}
```

Because a full stop (period) is a separator character in route definitions, :format is treated as just another field. Because we give it a nil default value, it's an optional field.

Having done this, we can use a respond_to block in our controllers to select our response type depending on the requested format:

```
def show
  respond_to do |format|
    format.html
    format.xml  { render :xml => @product.to_xml }
    format.yaml { render :text => @product.to_yaml }
  end
end
```

Given this, a request to /store/show/1 or /store/show/1.html will return HTML content, while /store/show/1.xml will return XML and /store/show/1.yaml will return YAML. You can also pass the format in as an HTTP request parameter:

```
GET HTTP://pragprog.com/store/show/123?format=xml
```

The routes defined by resources have this facility enabled by default.

Although the idea of having a single controller that responds with different content types seems appealing, the reality is tricky. In particular, it turns out that error handling can be tough. Although it's acceptable on error to redirect a user to a form, showing them a nice flash message, you have to adopt a different strategy when you serve XML. Consider your application architecture carefully before deciding to bundle all your processing into single controllers.

Rails makes it simple to develop an application that is based on resource-based routing. Many claim it greatly simplifies the coding of their applications. However, it isn't always appropriate. Don't feel compelled to use it if you can't find a way of making it work. And you can always mix and match. Some controllers can be resource based, and others can be based on actions. Some controllers can even be resource based with a few extra actions.

Testing Routes

So far we've been exploring routes by viewing them using rake routes. When it comes time to roll out an application, though, we might want to be a little more formal and include unit tests that verify our routes work as expected. Rails includes a number of test helpers that make this easy:

assert_generates(path, options, defaults={}, extras={}, message=nil)

> Verifies that the given set of options generates the specified path.

depot_t/test/unit/routing_test.rb

```ruby
def test_generates
  assert_generates("/", :controller => "store", :action => "index")
  assert_generates("/products",
                    { :controller => "products", :action => "index"})
  assert_generates("/line_items",
                    { :controller => "line_items", :action => "create",
                      :product_id => "1"},
                    {:method => :post}, { :product_id => "1"})
end
```

The extras parameter is used to tell the request the names and values of additional request parameters (in the third assertion in the previous code, this would be product_id=1). The test framework does not add these as strings to the generated URL; instead, it tests that the values it would have added appears in the extras hash.

The defaults parameter can be used to specify the HTTP method.

assert_recognizes(options, path, extras={}, message=nil)

> Verifies that routing returns a specific set of options given a path.

depot_t/test/unit/routing_test.rb

```ruby
def test_recognizes
  # Check the default index action gets generated
  assert_recognizes({"controller" => "store", "action" => "index"}, "/")

  # Check routing to an action
  assert_recognizes({"controller" => "products", "action" => "index"},
                     "/products")

  # And routing with a parameter
  assert_recognizes({ "controller" => "line_items",
                      "action" => "create",
                      "product_id" => "1" },
                    {:path => "/line_items", :method => :post},
                    {"product_id" => "1"})
end
```

The path parameter lets you specify routes that are conditional on the HTTP verb of the request. You can test these by passing a hash, rather than a string, as the second parameter to assert_recognizes. The hash should contain two elements: :path will contain the incoming request path, and :method will contain the HTTP verb to be used.

The extras parameter again contains the additional URL parameters. In the third assertion in the preceding code example, we use the extras parameter to verify that had the URL ended ?product_id=1, the resulting params hash would contain the appropriate values.

assert_routing(path, options, defaults={}, extras={}, message=nil)

Combines the previous two assertions, verifying that the path generates the options and then that the options generate the path.

```
depot_t/test/unit/routing_test.rb
```

```ruby
def test_routing
  assert_routing("/", :controller => "store", :action => "index")
  assert_routing("/products", :controller => "products", :action => "index")
  assert_routing({:path => "/line_items", :method => :post},
                 { :controller => "line_items", :action => "create",
                   :product_id => "1"},
                 {}, { :product_id => "1"})
end
```

It's important to use symbols as the keys and use strings as the values in the options hash. If you don't, asserts that compare your options with those returned by routing will fail.

20.2 Processing of Requests

In the previous section, we worked out how Action Dispatch routes an incoming request to the appropriate code in your application. Now let's see what happens inside that code.

Action Methods

When a controller object processes a request, it looks for a public instance method with the same name as the incoming action. If it finds one, that method is invoked. If it doesn't find one and the controller implements method_missing, that method is called, passing in the action name as the first parameter and an empty argument list as the second. If no method can be called, the controller looks for a template named after the current controller and action. If found, this template is rendered directly. If none of these things happens, an Unknown Action error is generated.

Controller Environment

The controller sets up the environment for actions (and, by extension, for the views that they invoke). Many of these methods provide direct access to information contained in the URL or request.

action_name

The name of the action currently being processed.

cookies

The cookies associated with the request. Setting values into this object stores cookies on the browser when the response is sent. Rails support for sessions is based on cookies. We discuss sessions on page 323.

headers

A hash of HTTP headers that will be used in the response. By default, Cache-Control is set to no-cache. You might want to set Content-Type headers for special-purpose applications. Note that you shouldn't set cookie values in the header directly—use the cookie API to do this.

params

A hash-like object containing request parameters (along with pseudo-parameters generated during routing). It's hash-like because you can index entries using either a symbol or a string—params[:id] and params['id'] return the same value. Idiomatic Rails applications use the symbol form.

request

The incoming request object. It includes these attributes:

- request_method returns the request method, one of :delete, :get, :head, :post, or :put.

- method returns the same value as request_method except for :head, which it returns as :get because these two are functionally equivalent from an application point of view.

- delete?, get?, head?, post?, and put? return true or false based on the request method.

- xml_http_request? and xhr? return true if this request was issued by one of the Ajax helpers. Note that this parameter is independent of the method parameter.

- url, which returns the full URL used for the request.

- protocol, host, port, path, and query_string, which returns components of the URL used for the request, based on the following pattern: protocol://host:port/path?query_string.

- domain, which returns the last two components of the domain name of the request.

- host_with_port, which is a host:port string for the request.

- port_string, which is a :port string for the request if the port is not the default port (80 for HTTP, 443 for HTTPS).

- ssl?, which is true if this is an SSL request; in other words, the request was made with the HTTPS protocol.

- remote_ip, which returns the remote IP address as a string. The string may have more than one address in it if the client is behind a proxy.

- path_without_extension, path_without_format_and_extension, format_and_extension, and relative_path return portions of the full path.

- env, the environment of the request. You can use this to access values set by the browser, such as this:

  ```
  request.env['HTTP_ACCEPT_LANGUAGE']
  ```

- accepts, which is the value of the accepts MIME type for the request.

- format, which is the value of the content-type for the request. If no format is available, the first of the accept types will be used.

- mime_type, which is the MIME type associated with the extension.

- content_type, which is the MIME type for the request. This is useful for put and post requests.

- headers, which is the complete set of HTTP headers.

- body, which is the request body as an I/O stream.

- content_length, which is the number of bytes purported to be in the body.

Rails leverages a gem named Rack to provide much of this functionality. See the documentation of Rack::Request for full details.

response

> The response object, filled in during the handling of the request. Normally, this object is managed for you by Rails. As we'll see when we look at filters on page 330, we sometimes access the internals for specialized processing.

session

> A hash-like object representing the current session data. We describe this on page 323.

In addition, a logger is available throughout Action Pack.

Responding to the User

Part of the controller's job is to respond to the user. There are basically four ways of doing this:

- The most common way is to render a template. In terms of the MVC paradigm, the template is the view, taking information provided by the controller and using it to generate a response to the browser.

- The controller can return a string directly to the browser without invoking a view. This is fairly rare but can be used to send error notifications.

- The controller can return nothing to the browser. This is sometimes used when responding to an Ajax request. In all cases, however, the controller returns a set of HTTP headers, because some kind of response is expected.

- The controller can send other data to the client (something other than HTML). This is typically a download of some kind (perhaps a PDF document or a file's contents).

A controller always responds to the user exactly one time per request. This means that you should have just one call to a render, redirect_to, or send_*xxx* method in the processing of any request. (A DoubleRenderError exception is thrown on the second render.)

Because the controller must respond exactly once, it checks to see whether a response has been generated just before it finishes handling a request. If not, the controller looks for a template named after the controller and action and automatically renders it. This is the most common way that rendering takes place. You may have noticed that in most of the actions in our shopping cart tutorial we never explicitly rendered anything. Instead, our action methods set up the context for the view and return. The controller notices that no rendering has taken place and automatically invokes the appropriate template.

You can have multiple templates with the same name but with different extensions (for example, .html.erb, .xml.builder, and .js.rjs). If you don't specify an extension in a render request, Rails assumes html.erb.

Rendering Templates

A *template* is a file that defines the content of a response for our application. Rails supports three template formats out of the box: *erb*, which is embedded Ruby code (typically with HTML); *builder*, a more programmatic way of constructing XML content; and *RJS*, which generates JavaScript. We'll talk about the contents of these files starting on page 333.

By convention, the template for action *action* of controller *controller* will be in the file app/views/*controller*/*action.type.xxx* (where *type* is the file type, such as html, atom, or js; and *xxx* is one of erb, builder, or rjs). The app/views part of the name is the default. You can override this for an entire application by setting this:

```
ActionController.prepend_view_path dir_path
```

The render method is the heart of all rendering in Rails. It takes a hash of options that tell it what to render and how to render it.

It is tempting to write code in our controllers that looks like this:

```
# DO NOT DO THIS
def update
  @user = User.find(params[:id])
  if @user.update_attributes(params[:user])
    render :action => show
  end
  render :template => "fix_user_errors"
end
```

It seems somehow natural that the act of calling render (and redirect_to) should somehow terminate the processing of an action. This is not the case. The previous code will generate an error (because render is called twice) in the case where update_attributes succeeds.

Let's look at the render options used in the controller here (we'll look separately at rendering in the view starting on page 354):

render()

> With no overriding parameter, the render method renders the default template for the current controller and action. The following code will render the template app/views/blog/index.html.erb:
>
> ```
> class BlogController < ApplicationController
>   def index
>     render
>   end
> end
> ```
>
> So will the following (as the default behavior of a controller is to call render if the action doesn't):
>
> ```
> class BlogController < ApplicationController
>   def index
>   end
> end
> ```
>
> And so will this (because the controller will call a template directly if no action method is defined):
>
> ```
> class BlogController < ApplicationController
> end
> ```

render(:text => *string*)

> Sends the given string to the client. No template interpretation or HTML escaping is performed.
>
> ```
> class HappyController < ApplicationController
>   def index
>     render(:text => "Hello there!")
>   end
> end
> ```

render(:inline => *string*, [:type => *"erb"|"builder"|"rjs"*], [:locals => *hash*])

Interprets *string* as the source to a template of the given type, rendering the results back to the client. You can use the :locals hash to set the values of local variables in the template.

The following code adds method_missing to a controller if the application is running in development mode. If the controller is called with an invalid action, this renders an inline template to display the action's name and a formatted version of the request parameters.

```
class SomeController < ApplicationController

  if RAILS_ENV == "development"
    def method_missing(name, *args)
      render(:inline => %{
        <h2>Unknown action: #{name}</h2>
        Here are the request parameters:<br/>
        <%= debug(params) %> })
    end
  end
end
```

render(:action => *action_name*)

Renders the template for a given action in this controller. Sometimes folks use the :action form of render when they should use redirects. See the discussion starting on page 320 for why this is a bad idea.

```
def display_cart
  if @cart.empty?
    render(:action => :index)
  else
    # ...
  end
end
```

Note that calling render(:action...) does not call the action method; it simply displays the template. If the template needs instance variables, these must be set up by the method that calls the render method.

Let's repeat this, because this is a mistake that beginners often make: calling render(:action...) does not invoke the action method. It simply renders that action's default template.

render(:file => *path*, [:use_full_path => *true|false*], [:locals => *hash*])

Renders the template in the given path (which must include a file extension). By default this should be an absolute path to the template, but if the :use_full_path option is true, the view will prepend the value of the template base path to the path you pass in. The template base path is set in the configuration for your application. If specified, the values in the :locals hash are used to set local variables in the template.

render(:template => *name*, [:locals => *hash*])

> Renders a template and arranges for the resulting text to be sent back to the client. The :template value must contain both the controller and action parts of the new name, separated by a forward slash. The following code will render the template app/views/blog/short_list:

```ruby
class BlogController < ApplicationController
  def index
    render(:template => "blog/short_list")
  end
end
```

render(:partial => *name*, ...)

> Renders a partial template. We talk about partial templates in depth on page 354.

render(:nothing => true)

> Returns nothing—sends an empty body to the browser.

render(:xml => *stuff*)

> Renders *stuff* as text, forcing the content type to be application/xml.

render(:json => *stuff*, [:callback => *hash*])

> Renders *stuff* as JSON, forcing the content type to be application/json. Specifying :callback will cause the result to be wrapped in a call to the named callback function.

render(:update) do |page| ... end

> Renders the block as an RJS template, passing in the page object.

```ruby
render(:update) do |page|
  page[:cart].replace_html :partial => 'cart', :object => @cart
  page[:cart].visual_effect :blind_down if @cart.total_items == 1
end
```

All forms of render take optional :status, :layout, and :content_type parameters. The :status parameter provides the value used in the status header in the HTTP response. It defaults to "200 OK". Do not use render with a 3xx status to do redirects; Rails has a redirect method for this purpose.

The :layout parameter determines whether the result of the rendering will be wrapped by a layout (we first came across layouts on page 92, and we'll look at them in depth starting on page 349). If the parameter is false, no layout will be applied. If set to nil or true, a layout will be applied only if there is one associated with the current action. If the :layout parameter has a string as a value, it will be taken as the name of the layout to use when rendering. A layout is never applied when the :nothing option is in effect.

The :content_type parameter lets you specify a value that will be passed to the browser in the Content-Type HTTP header.

Sometimes it is useful to be able to capture what would otherwise be sent to the browser in a string. The render_to_string method takes the same parameters as render but returns the result of rendering as a string—the rendering is not stored in the response object and so will not be sent to the user unless you take some additional steps. Calling render_to_string does not count as a real render. You can invoke the real render method later without getting a DoubleRender error.

Sending Files and Other Data

We've looked at rendering templates and sending strings in the controller. The third type of response is to send data (typically, but not necessarily, file contents) to the client.

send_data

Sends a string containing binary data to the client.

```
send_data(data, options...)
```

Sends a data stream to the client. Typically the browser will use a combination of the content type and the disposition, both set in the options, to determine what to do with this data.

```
def sales_graph
  png_data = Sales.plot_for(Date.today.month)
  send_data(png_data, :type => "image/png", :disposition => "inline")
end
```

Options:

:disposition	string	Suggests to the browser that the file should be displayed inline (option inline) or downloaded and saved (option attachment, the default).
:filename	string	A suggestion to the browser of the default filename to use when saving this data.
:status	string	The status code (defaults to "200 OK").
:type	string	The content type, defaulting to application/octet-stream.
:url_based_filename	boolean	If true and :filename is not set, prevents Rails from providing the basename of the file in the Content-Disposition header. Specifying this is necessary in order to make some browsers handle i18n filenames correctly.

send_file

Sends the contents of a file to the client.

```
send_file(path, options...)
```

Sends the given file to the client. The method sets the Content-Length, Content-Type, Content-Disposition, and Content-Transfer-Encoding headers.

Options:

:buffer_size	*number*	The amount sent to the browser in each write if streaming is enabled (:stream is true).
:disposition	*string*	Suggests to the browser that the file should be displayed inline (option inline) or downloaded and saved (option attachment, the default).
:filename	*string*	A suggestion to the browser of the default filename to use when saving the file. If not set, defaults to the filename part of *path*.
:status	*string*	The status code (defaults to "200 OK").
:stream	*true or false*	If false, the entire file is read into server memory and sent to the client. Otherwise, the file is read and written to the client in :buffer_size chunks.
:type	*string*	The content type, defaulting to application/octet-stream.

You can set additional headers for either send_ method using the headers attribute in the controller.

```
def send_secret_file
  send_file("/files/secret_list")
  headers["Content-Description"] = "Top secret"
end
```

We show how to upload files starting on page 339.

Redirects

An HTTP redirect is sent from a server to a client in response to a request. In effect, it says, "I can't handle this request, but here's some URL that can." The redirect response includes a URL that the client should try next along with some status information saying whether this redirection is permanent (status code 301) or temporary (307). Redirects are sometimes used when web pages are reorganized; clients accessing pages in the old locations will get referred to the page's new home. More commonly, Rails applications use redirects to pass the processing of a request off to some other action.

Redirects are handled behind the scenes by web browsers. Normally, the only way you'll know that you've been redirected is a slight delay and the fact that the URL of the page you're viewing will have changed from the one you requested. This last point is important—as far as the browser is concerned, a redirect from a server acts pretty much the same as having an end user enter the new destination URL manually.

Redirects turn out to be important when writing well-behaved web applications. Let's look at a simple blogging application that supports comment posting. After a user has posted a comment, our application should redisplay the article, presumably with the new comment at the end.

It's tempting to code this using logic such as the following:

```ruby
class BlogController
  def display
    @article = Article.find(params[:id])
  end

  def add_comment
    @article = Article.find(params[:id])
    comment  = Comment.new(params[:comment])
    @article.comments << comment
    if @article.save
      flash[:note] = "Thank you for your valuable comment"
    else
      flash[:note] = "We threw your worthless comment away"
    end
    # DON'T DO THIS
    render(:action => 'display')
  end
end
```

The intent here was clearly to display the article after a comment has been posted. To do this, the developer ended the add_comment method with a call to render(:action=>'display'). This renders the display view, showing the updated article to the end user. But think of this from the browser's point of view. It sends a URL ending in blog/add_comment and gets back an index listing. As far as the browser is concerned, the current URL is still the one that ends in blog/add_comment. This means that if the user hits Refresh or Reload (perhaps to see whether anyone else has posted a comment), the add_comment URL will be sent again to the application. The user intended to refresh the display, but the application sees a request to add another comment. In a blog application, this kind of unintentional double entry is inconvenient. In an online store, it can get expensive.

In these circumstances, the correct way to show the added comment in the index listing is to redirect the browser to the display action. We do this using the Rails redirect_to method. If the user subsequently hits Refresh, it will simply reinvoke the display action and not add another comment:

```ruby
def add_comment
  @article = Article.find(params[:id])
  comment = Comment.new(params[:comment])
  @article.comments << comment
  if @article.save
    flash[:note] = "Thank you for your valuable comment"
  else
    flash[:note] = "We threw your worthless comment away"
  end
  redirect_to(:action => 'display')
end
```

Rails has a simple yet powerful redirection mechanism. It can redirect to an action in a given controller (passing parameters), to a URL (on or off the current server), or to the previous page. Let's look at these three forms in turn.

redirect_to

Redirects to an action.

```
redirect_to(:action => ..., options...)
```

Sends a temporary redirection to the browser based on the values in the options hash. The target URL is generated using url_for, so this form of redirect_to has all the smarts of Rails routing code behind it.

redirect_to

Redirects to a URL.

```
redirect_to(path)
```

Redirects to the given path. If the path does not start with a protocol (such as http://), the protocol and port of the current request will be prepended. This method does not perform any rewriting on the URL, so it should not be used to create paths that are intended to link to actions in the application (unless you generate the path using url_for or a named route URL generator).

```ruby
def save
  order = Order.new(params[:order])
  if order.save
    redirect_to :action => "display"
  else
    session[:error_count] ||= 0
    session[:error_count] += 1
    if session[:error_count] < 4
      self.notice = "Please try again"
    else
      # Give up -- user is clearly struggling
      redirect_to("/help/order_entry.html")
    end
  end
end
```

redirect_to

Redirects to the referrer.

```
redirect_to(:back)
```

Redirects to the URL given by the HTTP_REFERER header in the current request.

```ruby
def save_details
  unless params[:are_you_sure] == 'Y'
    redirect_to(:back)
  else
    ...
  end
end
```

By default all redirections are flagged as temporary (they will affect only the current request). When redirecting to a URL, it's possible you might want to make the redirection permanent. In that case, set the status in the response header accordingly:

```
headers["Status"] = "301 Moved Permanently"
redirect_to("http://my.new.home")
```

Because redirect methods send responses to the browser, the same rules apply as for the rendering methods—you can issue only one per request.

So far, we have been looking at requests and responses in isolation. Rails also provides a number of mechanisms that span requests.

20.3 Objects and Operations That Span Requests

While the bulk of the state that persists across requests belongs in the database and is accessed via Active Record, some other bits of state have different life spans and need to be managed differently. In the Depot application, while the Cart itself was stored in the database, knowledge of which cart is the current cart was managed by sessions. Flash notices were used to communicate simple messages such as "Can't delete the last user" to the next request after a redirect. And filters were used to extract locale data from the URLs themselves.

In this section, we will explore each of these mechanisms in turn.

Rails Sessions

A Rails session is a hash-like structure that persists across requests. Unlike raw cookies, sessions can hold any objects (as long as those objects can be marshaled), which makes them ideal for holding state information in web applications. For example, in our store application, we used a session to hold the shopping cart object between requests. The Cart object could be used in our application just like any other object. But Rails arranged things such that the cart was saved at the end of handling each request and, more important, that the correct cart for an incoming request was restored when Rails started to handle that request. Using sessions, we can pretend that our application stays around between requests.

marshal
↪ page 48

And that leads to an interesting question: exactly where does this data stay around between requests? One choice is for the server to send it down to the client as a cookie. This is the default for Rails 3.0. It places limitations on the size and increases the bandwidth but means that there is less for the server to manage and clean up. Note that the contents are cryptographically signed but (by default) unencrypted, which means that users can see but not tamper with the contents.

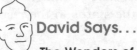

David Says...

The Wonders of a Cookie-Based Session

The default Rails session store sounds like a crazy idea when you hear it at first. You're going to actually store the values on the client?! But what if I want to store the nuclear launch codes in the session and I can't have the client actually knowing those?

Yoo, the default store is not suitable for storing secrets you need to keep from the client. But that's actually a valuable constraint that'll lead you to avoid the perils of keeping complex objects that can go out of date in the session. And the paper dragon of the nuclear launch codes is just about never a real, relevant concern.

Neither is the size constraint. Cookies can be only about 4KB big, so you can't stuff them with all sorts of malarkey. That again fits the best practices of storing only references, like a cart_id, not the actual cart itself.

The key security concern you should be worried about is whether the client is actually able to change the session. You want to ensure the integrity of the values that you put. It'd be no good if the client could change his cart_id from a 5 to 8 and get someone else's cart. Thankfully, Rails protects you against exactly this case by signing the session and raising an exception that warns of the tampering if it doesn't match.

The benefits you get back is that there is no load on the database from fetching and saving the session on every request, and there are no cleanup duties either. If you keep your session on the filesystem or in the database, you'll have to deal with how to clean up stale sessions, which is a real hassle. No one likes to be on cleanup duty. The cookie-based sessions know how to clean up after themselves. What's not to love about that?

The other option is to store the data on the server. There are two parts to this. First, Rails has to keep track of sessions. It does this by creating (by default) a 32-hex character key (which means there are 16^{32} possible combinations). This key is called the *session id*, and it's effectively random. Rails arranges to store this session id as a cookie (with the key _session_id) on the user's browser. Because subsequent requests come into the application from this browser, Rails can recover the session id.

Second, Rails keeps a persistent store of session data on the server, indexed by the session id. When a request comes in, Rails looks up the data store using the session id. The data that it finds there is a serialized Ruby object. It deserializes this and stores the result in the controller's session attribute, where the data is available to our application code. The application can add to and modify this data to its heart's content. When it finishes processing each request, Rails writes the session data back into the data store. There it sits until the next request from this browser comes along.

What should you store in a session? You can store anything you want, subject to a few restrictions and caveats:

- There are some restrictions on what kinds of object you can store in a session. The details depend on the storage mechanism you choose (which we'll look at shortly). In the general case, objects in a session must be serializable (using Ruby's Marshal functions). This means, for example, that you cannot store an I/O object in a session. serialize ↪ page 48

- You probably don't want to store massive objects in session data—put them in the database, and reference them from the session. This is particularly true for cookie-based sessions, where the overall limit is 4KB.

- You probably don't want to store volatile objects in session data. For example, you might want to keep a tally of the number of articles in a blog and store that in the session for performance reasons. But, if you do that, the count won't get updated if some other user adds an article.

  It is tempting to store objects representing the currently logged-in user in session data. This might not be wise if your application needs to be able to invalidate users. Even if a user is disabled in the database, their session data will still reflect a valid status.

  Store volatile data in the database, and reference it from the session instead.

- You probably don't want to store critical information solely in session data. For example, if your application generates an order confirmation number in one request and stores it in session data so that it can be saved to the database when the next request is handled, you risk losing that number if the user deletes the cookie from their browser. Critical information needs to be in the database.

There's one more caveat, and it's a big one. If you store an object in session data, then the next time you come back to that browser, your application will end up retrieving that object. However, if in the meantime you've updated your application, the object in session data may not agree with the definition of that object's class in your application, and the application will fail while processing the request. There are three options here. One is to store the object in the database using conventional models and keep just the id of the row in the session. Model objects are far more forgiving of schema changes than the Ruby marshaling library. The second option is to manually delete all the session data stored on your server whenever you change the definition of a class stored in that data.

The third option is slightly more complex. If you add a version number to your session keys and change that number whenever you update the stored data, you'll only ever load data that corresponds with the current version of the application. You can potentially version the classes whose objects are stored in the session and use the appropriate classes depending on the session keys associated with each request. This last idea can be a lot of work, so you'll need to decide whether it's worth the effort.

Because the session store is hash-like, you can save multiple objects in it, each with its own key.

There is no need to also disable sessions for particular actions. Because sessions are lazily loaded, simply don't reference a session in any action in which you don't need a session.

Session Storage

Rails has a number of options when it comes to storing your session data. Each has good and bad points. We'll start by listing the options and then compare them at the end.

The session_store attribute of ActionController::Base determines the session storage mechanism—set this attribute to a class that implements the storage strategy. This class must be defined in the CGI::Session module. You use symbols to name the session storage strategy; the symbol is converted into a CamelCase class name.

session_store = :cookie_store

> This is the default session storage mechanism used by Rails, starting with version 2.0. This format represents objects in their marshaled form, which allows any serializable data to be stored in sessions but is limited to 4KB total. This is the option we used in the Depot application.

session_store = :p_store

> Data for each session is stored in a flat file in PStore format. This format keeps objects in their marshaled form, which allows any serializable data to be stored in sessions. This mechanism supports the additional configuration options :prefix and :tmpdir. The following code in the file environment.rb in the config directory might be used to configure PStore sessions:

```
Rails::Initializer.run do |config|
  config.action_controller.session_store = CGI::Session::PStore
  config.action_controller.session_options[:tmpdir] = "/Users/dave/tmp"
  config.action_controller.session_options[:prefix] = "myapp_session_"
  # ...
```

session_store = :active_record_store

> You can store your session data in your application's database using ActiveRecordStore. You can generate a migration that creates the sessions table using Rake:

```
depot> rake db:sessions:create
```

> Run rake db:migrate to create the actual table.

> If you look at the migration file, you'll see that Rails creates an index on the session_id column, because it is used to look up session data. Rails also defines a column called updated_at, so Active Record will automatically timestamp the rows in the session table—we'll see later why this is a good idea.

session_store = :drb_store

> DRb is a protocol that allows Ruby processes to share objects over a network connection. Using the DRbStore database manager, Rails stores session data on a DRb server (which you manage outside the web application). Multiple instances of your application, potentially running on distributed servers, can access the same DRb store. DRb uses Marshal to serialize objects.

session_store = :mem_cache_store

> memcached is a freely available, distributed object caching system maintained by Dormando.[2] The Rails MemCacheStore uses Michael Granger's Ruby interface[3] to memcached to store sessions. memcached is more complex to use than the other alternatives and is probably interesting only if you are already using it for other reasons at your site.

session_store = :memory_store

> This option stores the session data locally in the application's memory. Because no serialization is involved, any object can be stored in an in-memory session. As we'll see in a minute, this generally is not a good idea for Rails applications.

session_store = :file_store

> Session data is stored in flat files. It's pretty much useless for Rails applications, because the contents must be strings. This mechanism supports the additional configuration options :prefix, :suffix, and :tmpdir.

Comparing Session Storage Options

With all these session options to choose from, which should you use in your application? As always, the answer is "It depends."

---

2. http://memcached.org/
3. Available from http://deveiate.org/projects/RMemCache

There are few absolutes when it comes to performance, and everyone's context is different. Your hardware, network latencies, database choices, and possibly even the weather will impact how all the components of session storage interact. Our best advice is to start with the simplest workable solution and then monitor it. If it starts to slow you down, find out why before jumping out of the frying pan.

If you're a high-volume site, keeping the size of the session data small and going with cookie_store is the way to go.

If we rule out memory store as being too simplistic, file store as too restrictive, and memcached as overkill, the server-side choices boil down to PStore, Active Record store, and DRb-based storage. Should you need to store more in a session than you can with cookies, we recommend you start with an Active Record solution. If, as your application grows, you find this becoming a bottleneck, you can migrate to a DRb-based solution.

Session Expiry and Cleanup

One problem with all the server-side session storage solutions is that each new session adds something to the session store. This means you'll eventually need to do some housekeeping or you'll run out of server resources.

There's another reason to tidy up sessions. Many applications don't want a session to last forever. Once a user has logged in from a particular browser, the application might want to enforce a rule that the user stays logged in only as long as they are active; when they log out or some fixed time after they last use the application, their session should be terminated.

You can sometimes achieve this effect by expiring the cookie holding the session id. However, this is open to end-user abuse. Worse, it is hard to synchronize the expiry of a cookie on the browser with the tidying up of the session data on the server.

We therefore suggest that you expire sessions by simply removing their server-side session data. Should a browser request subsequently arrive containing a session id for data that has been deleted, the application will receive no session data; the session will effectively not be there.

Implementing this expiration depends on the storage mechanism being used.

For PStore-based sessions, the easiest approach is to run a sweeper task periodically (for example using cron(1) under Unix-like systems). This task should inspect the last modification times of the files in the session data directory, deleting those older than a given time.

For Active Record–based session storage, use the updated_at columns in the sessions table. You can delete all sessions that have not been modified in the last hour (ignoring daylight saving time changes) by having your sweeper task issue SQL such as this:

```
delete from sessions
 where now() - updated_at > 3600;
```

For DRb-based solutions, expiry takes place within the DRb server process. You'll probably want to record timestamps alongside the entries in the session data hash. You can run a separate thread (or even a separate process) that periodically deletes the entries in this hash.

In all cases, your application can help this process by calling reset_session to delete sessions when they are no longer needed (for example, when a user logs out).

Flash: Communicating Between Actions

When we use redirect_to to transfer control to another action, the browser generates a separate request to invoke that action. That request will be handled by our application in a fresh instance of a controller object—instance variables that were set in the original action are not available to the code handling the redirected action. But sometimes we need to communicate between these two instances. We can do this using a facility called the *flash*.

The flash is a temporary scratchpad for values. It is organized like a hash and stored in the session data, so you can store values associated with keys and later retrieve them. It has one special property. By default, values stored into the flash during the processing of a request will be available during the processing of the immediately following request. Once that second request has been processed, those values are removed from the flash.

Probably the most common use of the flash is to pass error and informational strings from one action to the next. The intent here is that the first action notices some condition, creates a message describing that condition, and redirects to a separate action. By storing the message in the flash, the second action is able to access the message text and use it in a view.

It is sometimes convenient to use the flash as a way of passing messages into a template in the current action. For example, our display method might want to output a cheery banner if there isn't another, more pressing note. It doesn't need that message to be passed to the next action—it's for use in the current request only. To do this, it could use flash.now, which updates the flash but does not add to the session data.

While flash.now creates a transient flash entry, flash.keep does the opposite, making entries that are currently in the flash stick around for another request cycle. If you pass no parameters to flash.keep, then all the flash contents are preserved.

Flashes can store more than just text messages—you can use them to pass all kinds of information between actions. Obviously, for longer-term information you'd want to use the session (probably in conjunction with your database) to store the data, but the flash is great if you want to pass parameters from one request to the next.

Because the flash data is stored in the session, all the usual rules apply. In particular, every object must be serializable. We strongly recommend passing only simple objects in the flash.

Filters

Filters enable you to write code in your controllers that wrap the processing performed by actions—you can write a chunk of code once and have it be called before or after any number of actions in your controller (or your controller's subclasses). This turns out to be a powerful facility. Using filters, we can implement authentication schemes, logging, response compression, and even response customization.

Rails supports three types of filter: before, after, and around. Filters are called just prior to and/or just after the execution of actions. Depending on how you define them, they either run as methods inside the controller or are passed the controller object when they are run. Either way, they get access to details of the request and response objects, along with the other controller attributes.

Before and After Filters

As their names suggest, before and after filters are invoked before or after an action. Rails maintains two chains of filters for each controller. When a controller is about to run an action, it executes all the filters on the before chain. It executes the action before running the filters on the after chain.

Filters can be passive, monitoring activity performed by a controller. They can also take a more active part in request handling. If a before filter returns false, processing of the filter chain terminates, and the action is not run. A filter may also render output or redirect requests, in which case the original action never gets invoked.

We saw an example of using filters for authorization in the administration part of our store example on page 197. We defined an authorization method that redirected to a login screen if the current session didn't have a logged-in user. We then made this method a before filter for all the actions in the administration controller.

Filter declarations also accept blocks and the names of classes. If a block is specified, it will be called with the current controller as a parameter. If a class is given, its filter class method will be called with the controller as a parameter.

By default, filters apply to all actions in a controller (and any subclasses of that controller). You can modify this with the :only option, which takes one or more actions to be filtered, and the :except option, which lists actions to be excluded from filtering.

The before_filter and after_filter declarations append to the controller's chain of filters. Use the variants prepend_before_filter and prepend_after_filter to put filters at the front of the chain.

After filters can be used to modify the outbound response, changing the headers and content if required. Some applications use this technique to perform global replacements in the content generated by the controller's templates (for example, substituting a customer's name for the string *<customer/>* in the response body). Another use might be compressing the response if the user's browser supports it.

Around filters wrap the execution of actions. You can write an around filter in two different styles. In the first, the filter is a single chunk of code. That code is called before the action is executed. If the filter code invokes yield, the action is executed. When the action completes, the filter code continues executing.

Thus, the code before the yield is like a before filter, and the code after the yield is the after filter. If the filter code never invokes yield, the action is not run—this is the same as having a before filter return false.

The benefit of around filters is that they can retain context across the invocation of the action.

As well as passing around_filter the name of a method, you can pass it a block or a filter class.

If you use a block as a filter, it will be passed two parameters: the controller object and a proxy for the action. Use call on this second parameter to invoke the original action.

A second form allows you to pass an object as a filter. This object should implement a method called filter. This method will be passed the controller object. It yields to invoke the action.

Like before and after filters, around filters take :only and :except parameters.

Around filters are (by default) added to the filter chain differently: the first around filter added executes first. Subsequently added around filters will be nested within existing around filters.

Filter Inheritance

If you subclass a controller containing filters, the filters will be run on the child objects as well as in the parent. However, filters defined in the children will not run in the parent.

If you don't want a particular filter to run in a child controller, you can override the default processing with the skip_before_filter and skip_after_filter declarations. These accept the :only and :except parameters.

You can use skip_filter to skip any filter (before, after, and around). However, it works only for filters that were specified as the (symbol) name of a method.

We made use of skip_before_filter in Section 14.3, *Iteration I3: Limiting Access*, on page 197.

What We Just Did

We learned how Action Dispatch and Action Controller cooperate to enable our server to respond to requests. The importance of this can't be emphasized enough. In nearly every application, this is the primary place where the creativity of your application is expressed. While Active Record and Action View are hardly passive, our routes and our controllers are the place where the action is.

We started this chapter by covering the concept of REST, which was the inspiration for the way in which Rails approaches routing of requests. We saw how this provided seven basic actions as a starting point and how to add more actions. We also saw how to select a data representation (for example, JSON or XML). And we covered how to test routes.

We then covered the environment that Action Controller provides for your actions, as well as the methods it provides for rendering and redirecting. Finally, we covered sessions, flash, and filters, each of which is available for use in your application's controllers.

Along the way, we showed how each of these concepts were used in the Depot application. Now that you have seen each in use and have been exposed to the theory behind each, how you combine and use these concepts is limited only by your own creativity.

In the next chapter, we will cover the remaining component of Action Pack, namely, Action View, which handles the rendering of results.

In this chapter, we'll see

- templates,
- forms; fields and uploading files,
- helpers, and
- layouts and partials.

Chapter 21

Action View

We've seen how the routing component determines which controller to use and how the controller chooses an action. We've also seen how the controller and action between them decide what to render to the user. Normally that rendering takes place at the end of the action, and typically it involves a template. That's what this chapter is all about. The ActionView module encapsulates all the functionality needed to render templates, most commonly generating HTML, XML, or JavaScript back to the user. As its name suggests, ActionView is the view part of our MVC trilogy.

In this chapter, we will start with templates, for which Rails provides a range of options. We will then cover a number of different ways in which users provide input: forms, file uploads, and links. We will complete this chapter by looking at a number of ways to reduce maintenance using helpers, layouts, and partials.

21.1 Using Templates

When you write a view, you're writing a template: something that will get expanded to generate the final result. To understand how these templates work, we need to look at three areas:

- Where the templates go
- The environment they run in
- What goes inside them

Where Templates Go

The render method expects to find templates in the app/views directory of the current application. Within this directory, the convention is to have a separate subdirectory for the views of each controller. Our Depot application, for instance, includes products and store controllers. As a result, we have templates in app/views/products and app/views/store. Each directory typically contains templates named after the actions in the corresponding controller.

You can also have templates that aren't named after actions. You render such templates from the controller using calls such as these:

```
render(:action   => 'fake_action_name')
render(:template => 'controller/name')
render(:file     => 'dir/template')
```

The last of these allows you to store templates anywhere on your filesystem. This is useful if you want to share templates across applications.

The Template Environment

Templates contain a mixture of fixed text and code. The code in the template adds dynamic content to the response. That code runs in an environment that gives it access to the information set up by the controller.

- All instance variables of the controller are also available in the template. This is how actions communicate data to the templates.

- The controller object's flash, headers, logger, params, request, response, and session are available as accessor methods in the view. Apart from the flash, view code probably should not use these directly, because the responsibility for handling them should rest with the controller. However, we do find this useful when debugging. For example, the following html.erb template uses the debug method to display the contents of the session, the details of the parameters, and the current response:

```
<h4>Session</h4>  <%= debug(session) %>
<h4>Params</h4>   <%= debug(params) %>
<h4>Response</h4> <%= debug(response) %>
```

- The current controller object is accessible using the attribute named controller. This allows the template to call any public method in the controller (including the methods in ActionController).

- The path to the base directory of the templates is stored in the attribute base_path.

What Goes in a Template

Out of the box, Rails supports three types of template:

- Builder templates use the Builder library to construct XML responses. We talk more about Builder in Section 25.1, *Generating XML with Builder*, on page 405.

- ERb templates are a mixture of content and embedded Ruby. They are typically used to generate HTML pages. We talk more about Erb in Section 25.2, *Generating HTML with ERb*, on page 407.

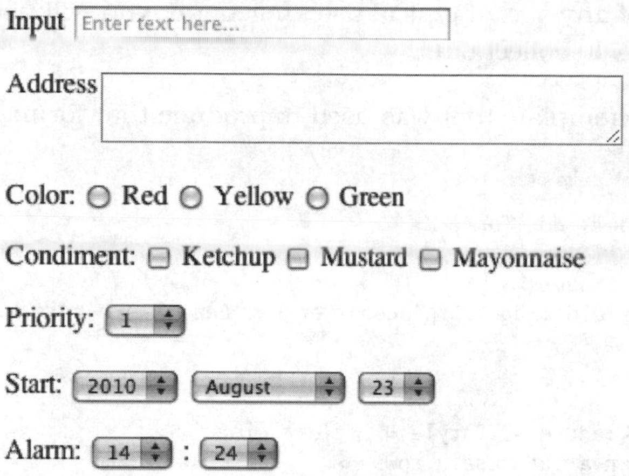

Input [Enter text here...]

Address [   ]

Color: ⦿ Red ⦿ Yellow ⦿ Green

Condiment: ☐ Ketchup ☐ Mustard ☐ Mayonnaise

Priority: [1 ▲▼]

Start: [2010 ▲▼] [August ▲▼] [23 ▲▼]

Alarm: [14 ▲▼] : [24 ▲▼]

Figure 21.1: SOME OF THE COMMON WAYS TO ENTER DATA INTO FORMS

- RJS templates create JavaScript to be executed in the browser and are typically used to interact with Ajaxified web pages. We already have seen and made use of RJS templates in Section 11.2, *Iteration F2: Creating an Ajax-Based Cart*, on page 131.

By far, the one that you will be using the most will be ERb. In fact, you made extensive use of ERb templates in developing the Depot application.

So far in this chapter, we have focused on producing output. In Chapter 20, *Action Dispatch and Action Controller*, on page 301, we focused on processing input. In a well-designed application, these two are not unrelated: the output we produce contains forms, links, and buttons that guide the end user to producing the next set of inputs. As you might expect by now, Rails provides considerable amount of help in this area too.

21.2 Generating Forms

HTML provides a number of elements, attributes, and attribute values that control how input is gathered. You certainly could hand-code your form directly into the template, but there really is no need to do that.

In this section, we will cover a number of *helpers* that Rails provides that assist with this process. In Section 21.5, *Using Helpers*, on page 343, we will show you how you can create your own helpers.

HTML provides a number of ways to collect data in forms. A few of the more common means are shown in Figure 21.1. Note that the form itself is not representative of any sort of typical use; in general, you will use only a subset of these methods to collect data.

Let's look at the template that was used to produce that form:

`views/app/views/form/input.html.erb`

```
Line 1  <%= form_for(:model) do |form| %>
   -      <p>
   -        <%= form.label :input %>
   -        <%= form.text_field :input, :placeholder => 'Enter text here...' %>
   5      </p>
   -
   -      <p>
   -        <%= form.label :address, :style => 'float: left' %>
   -        <%= form.text_area :address, :rows => 3, :cols => 40 %>
  10      </p>
   -
   -      <p>
   -        <%= form.label :color %>:
   -        <%= form.radio_button :color, 'red' %>
  15        <%= form.label :red %>
   -        <%= form.radio_button :color, 'yellow' %>
   -        <%= form.label :yellow %>
   -        <%= form.radio_button :color, 'green' %>
   -        <%= form.label :green %>
  20      </p>
   -
   -      <p>
   -        <%= form.label 'condiment' %>:
   -        <%= form.check_box :ketchup %>
  25        <%= form.label :ketchup %>
   -        <%= form.check_box :mustard %>
   -        <%= form.label :mustard %>
   -        <%= form.check_box :mayonnaise %>
   -        <%= form.label :mayonnaise %>
  30      </p>
   -
   -      <p>
   -        <%= form.label :priority %>:
   -        <%= form.select :priority, (1..10) %>
  35      </p>
   -
   -      <p>
   -        <%= form.label :start %>:
   -        <%= form.date_select :start %>
  40      </p>
   -
   -      <p>
   -        <%= form.label :alarm %>:
   -        <%= form.time_select :alarm %>
  45      </p>
   -    <% end %>
```

In that template, you will see a number of labels, such as the one on line 3. You use labels to associate text with an input field for a specified attribute. The text of the label will default to the attribute name unless you specify it explicitly.

You use the text and text_area helpers (on lines 4 and 9, respectively) to gather single-line and multiline input fields. You may specify a placeholder, which will be displayed inside the field until the user provides a value. Not every browser supports this function, but those that don't simply will display an empty box. Since this will degrade gracefully, there is no need for you to design to the least common denominator—make use of this feature, because those who can see it will benefit from it immediately.

Placeholders are one of the many small "fit and finish" features provided with HTML5, and once again, Rails is ready even if the browser your users have installed is not. You can use the search_field, telephone_field, url_field, email_field, number_field, and range_field helpers to prompt for a specific type of input. How the browser will make use of this information varies. Some may display the field slightly differently in order to more clearly identify its function. Safari on Mac, for example, will display search fields with rounded corners and will insert a little x for clearing the field once data entry begins. Some may provide added validation. For example, Opera will validate URL fields prior to submission. The iPad will even adjust the virtual on-screen keyboard to provide ready access to characters such as the @ sign when entering an email address.

Although the support for these functions varies by browser, those that don't provide extra support for these functions simply display a plain, unadorned input box. Once again, nothing is gained by waiting. If you have an input field that's expected to contain an email address, don't simply use text_field—go ahead and start using email_field now.

Lines 14, 24, and 34 demonstrate three different ways to provide a constrained set of options. Although the display may vary a bit from browser to browser, these are all well supported across all browsers. The select method is particularly flexible—it can be passed a simple Enumeration as shown here, an array of pairs of name/value pairs, or a Hash. A number of form options helpers[1] are available to produce such lists from various sources, including the database.

Finally, lines 39 and 44 show prompts for a date and time, respectively. As you might expect by now, Rails provides plenty of options here too.[2]

---

1. http://api.rubyonrails.org/classes/ActionView/Helpers/FormOptionsHelper.html
2. http://api.rubyonrails.org/classes/ActionView/Helpers/DateHelper.html

Not shown in this example are hidden_field and password_field. A hidden field is not displayed at all, but the value is passed back to the server. This may be useful as an alternative to storing transient data in sessions, enabling data from one request to be passed onto the next. Password fields are displayed, but the text entered in them is obscured.

This is more than an adequate starter set for most needs. Should you find that you have additional needs, you are quite likely to find a helper or plugin is already available for you. A good place to start is with the Rails Guides.[3]

Meanwhile, let's explore how the data forms submit is processed.

21.3 Processing Forms

In Figure 21.2, on the facing page, we can see how the various attributes in the model pass through the controller to the view, on to the HTML page, and back again into the model. The model object has attributes such as name, country, and password. The template uses helper methods to construct an HTML form to let the user edit the data in the model. Note how the form fields are named. The country attribute, for example, maps to an HTML input field with the name user[country].

When the user submits the form, the raw POST data is sent back to our application. Rails extracts the fields from the form and constructs the params hash. Simple values (such as the id field, extracted by routing from the form action) are stored directly in the hash. But, if a parameter name has brackets in it, Rails assumes that it is part of more structured data and constructs a hash to hold the values. Inside this hash, the string inside the brackets acts as the key. This process can repeat if a parameter name has multiple sets of brackets in it.

Form parameters	params
id=123	{ :id => "123" }
user[name]=Dave	{ :user => { :name => "Dave" }}
user[address][city]=Wien	{ :user => { :address => { :city => "Wien" }}}

In the final part of the integrated whole, model objects can accept new attribute values from hashes, which allows us to say this:

```
user.update_attributes(params[:user])
```

Rails integration goes deeper than this. Looking at the .html.erb file in Figure 21.2, we can see that the template uses a set of helper methods to create the form's HTML; these are methods such as form_for and text_field.

---

3. http://edgeguides.rubyonrails.org/form_helpers.html

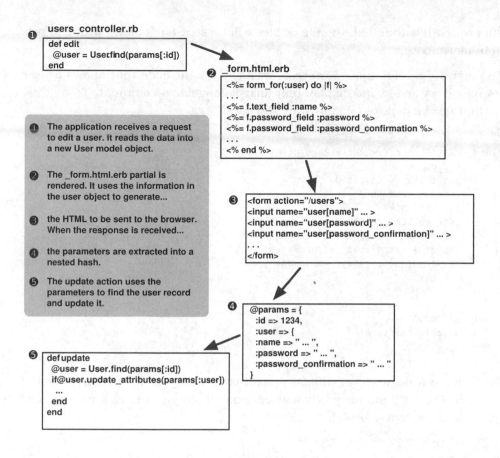

Figure 21.2: MODELS, CONTROLLERS, AND VIEWS WORK TOGETHER.

Before moving on, it is worth noting that params may be used for more than simple text. Entire files can be uploaded. We'll cover that next.

21.4 Uploading Files to Rails Applications

Your application may allow users to upload files. For example, a bug-reporting system might let users attach log files and code samples to a problem ticket, or a blogging application could let its users upload a small image to appear next to their articles.

In HTTP, files are uploaded as a *multipart/form-data* POST message. As the name suggests, forms are used to generate this type of message. Within that form, you'll use one or more *<input>* tags with type="file". When rendered by a browser, this tag allows the user to select a file by name. When the form is subsequently submitted, the file or files will be sent back along with the rest of the form data.

To illustrate the file upload process, we'll show some code that allows a user to upload an image and display that image alongside a comment. To do this, we first need a pictures table to store the data:

`e1/views/db/migrate/20110211000004_create_pictures.rb`

```ruby
class CreatePictures < ActiveRecord::Migration
  def self.up
    create_table :pictures do |t|
      t.string :comment
      t.string :name
      t.string :content_type
      # If using MySQL, blobs default to 64k, so we have to give
      # an explicit size to extend them
      t.binary :data, :limit => 1.megabyte
    end
  end

  def self.down
    drop_table :pictures
  end
end
```

We'll create a somewhat artificial upload controller just to demonstrate the process. The get action is pretty conventional; it simply creates a new picture object and renders a form:

`e1/views/app/controllers/upload_controller.rb`

```ruby
class UploadController < ApplicationController
  def get
    @picture = Picture.new
  end
  # . . .
end
```

The get template contains the form that uploads the picture (along with a comment). Note how we override the encoding type to allow data to be sent back with the response:

`e1/views/app/views/upload/get.html.erb`

```erb
<%= error_messages_for("picture") %>

<% form_for(:picture,
            :url => {:action => 'save'},
            :html => { :multipart => true }) do |form| %>

    Comment:              <%= form.text_field("comment") %><br/>
    Upload your picture: <%= form.file_field("uploaded_picture") %><br/>

    <%= submit_tag("Upload file") %>
<% end %>
```

The form has one other subtlety. The picture uploads into an attribute called uploaded_picture. However, the database table doesn't contain a column of that name. That means that there must be some magic happening in the model.

```
e1/views/app/models/picture.rb
class Picture < ActiveRecord::Base

  validates_format_of :content_type,
                      :with => /^image/,
                      :message => "--- you can only upload pictures"

  def uploaded_picture=(picture_field)
    self.name         = base_part_of(picture_field.original_filename)
    self.content_type = picture_field.content_type.chomp
    self.data         = picture_field.read
  end

  def base_part_of(file_name)
    File.basename(file_name).gsub(/[^\w._-]/, '')
  end
end
```

We define an accessor called uploaded_picture= to receive the file uploaded by the form. The object returned by the form is an interesting hybrid. It is file-like, so we can read its contents with the read method; that's how we get the image data into the data column. It also has the attributes content_type and original_filename, which let us get at the uploaded file's metadata. Accessor methods pick all this apart, resulting in a single object stored as separate attributes in the database.

Note that we also add a simple validation to check that the content type is of the form image/*xxx*. We don't want someone uploading JavaScript.

The save action in the controller is totally conventional:

```
e1/views/app/controllers/upload_controller.rb
def save
  @picture = Picture.new(params[:picture])
  if @picture.save
    redirect_to(:action => 'show', :id => @picture.id)
  else
    render(:action => :get)
  end
end
```

So, now that we have an image in the database, how do we display it? One way is to give it its own URL and simply link to that URL from an image tag. For example, we could use a URL such as upload/picture/123 to return the image for picture 123. This would use send_data to return the image to the browser.

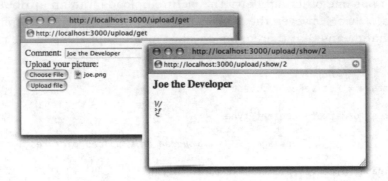

Figure 21.3: UPLOADING A FILE

Note how we set the content type and filename—this lets browsers interpret the data and supplies a default name should the user choose to save the image:

e1/views/app/controllers/upload_controller.rb

```ruby
def picture
  @picture = Picture.find(params[:id])
  send_data(@picture.data,
            :filename => @picture.name,
            :type => @picture.content_type,
            :disposition => "inline")
end
```

Finally, we can implement the show action, which displays the comment and the image. The action simply loads the picture model object:

e1/views/app/controllers/upload_controller.rb

```ruby
def show
  @picture = Picture.find(params[:id])
end
```

In the template, the image tag links back to the action that returns the picture content. In Figure 21.3, we can see the get and show actions in all their glory:

e1/views/app/views/upload/show.html.erb

```erb
<h3><%= @picture.comment %></h3>

<img src="<%= url_for(:action => 'picture', :id => @picture.id) %>"/>
```

You can optimize the performance of this technique by caching the picture action. (We discuss caching starting on page 359.)

If you'd like an easier way of dealing with uploading and storing images, take a look at thoughtbot's Paperclip[4] or Rick Olson's attachment_fu[5] plugins. Create a database table that includes a given set of columns (documented on Rick's site), and the plugin will automatically manage storing both the uploaded data and the upload's metadata. Unlike our previous approach, it handles storing the uploads in either your filesystem or a database table.

Forms and uploads are just two examples of helpers that Rails provides. Next we will show you how you can provide your own helpers and introduce you to a number of other helpers that code with Rails.

21.5 Using Helpers

Earlier we said that it's OK to put code in templates. Now we're going to modify that statement. It's perfectly acceptable to put *some* code in templates—that's what makes them dynamic. However, it's poor style to put too much code in templates.

There are three main reasons for this. First, the more code you put in the view side of your application, the easier it is to let discipline slip and start adding application-level functionality to the template code. This is definitely poor form; you want to put application stuff in the controller and model layers so that it is available everywhere. This will pay off when you add new ways of viewing the application.

The second reason is that html.erb is basically HTML. When you edit it, you're editing an HTML file. If you have the luxury of having professional designers create your layouts, they'll want to work with HTML. Putting a bunch of Ruby code in there just makes it hard to work with.

The final reason is that code embedded in views is hard to test, whereas code split out into helper modules can be isolated and tested as individual units.

Rails provides a nice compromise in the form of helpers. A *helper* is simply a module containing methods that assist a view. Helper methods are output-centric. They exist to generate HTML (or XML, or JavaScript)—a helper extends the behavior of a template.

Your Own Helpers

By default, each controller gets its own helper module. Additionally, there is an application-wide helper named application_helper.rb. It won't be surprising to learn that Rails makes certain assumptions to help link the helpers into the controller and its views. While all view helpers are available to all controllers, it

---

4. https://github.com/thoughtbot/paperclip#readme
5. https://github.com/technoweenie/attachment_fu

often is good practice to organize helpers. Helpers that are unique to the views associated with the ProductController tend to be placed in a helper module called ProductHelper in the file product_helper.rb in the app/helpers directory. You don't have to remember all these details—the rails generate controller script creates a stub helper module automatically.

In Section 11.4, *Iteration F4: Hiding an Empty Cart*, on page 136, we created such a helper method named hidden_div_if, which enabled us to hide the cart under specified conditions. We can use the same technique to clean up the application layout a bit. At the present time we have the following:

```
<h3><%= @page_title || "Pragmatic Store" %></h3>
```

Let's move the code that works out the page title into a helper method. Because we're in the store controller, we edit the file store_helper.rb in app/helpers.

```
module StoreHelper
  def page_title
    @page_title || "Pragmatic Store"
  end
end
```

Now the view code simply calls the helper method:

```
<h3><%= page_title %></h3>
```

(We might want to eliminate even more duplication by moving the rendering of the entire title into a separate partial template, shared by all the controller's views, but we don't talk about them until Section 21.6, *Partial-Page Templates*, on page 354.)

Helpers for Formatting and Linking

Rails comes with a bunch of built-in helper methods, available to all views. In this section, we'll touch on the highlights, but you'll probably want to look at the Action View RDoc for the specifics—there's a lot of functionality in there.

Formatting Helpers

One set of helper methods deals with dates, numbers, and text.

```
<%= distance_of_time_in_words(Time.now, Time.local(2010, 12, 25)) %>
```
   5 months

```
<%= distance_of_time_in_words(Time.now, Time.now + 33, false) %>
```
   1 minute

```
<%= distance_of_time_in_words(Time.now, Time.now + 33, true) %>
```
   Half a minute

```
<%= time_ago_in_words(Time.local(2010, 12, 25)) %>
```
   3 months

```
<%= number_to_currency(123.45) %>
```
$123.45

```
<%= number_to_currency(234.56, :unit => "CAN$", :precision => 0) %>
```
CAN$235

```
<%= number_to_human_size(123_456) %>
```
120.6 KB

```
<%= number_to_percentage(66.66666) %>
```
66.667%

```
<%= number_to_percentage(66.66666, :precision => 1) %>
```
66.7%

```
<%= number_to_phone(2125551212) %>
```
212-555-1212

```
<%= number_to_phone(2125551212, :area_code => true, :delimiter => " ") %>
```
(212) 555 1212

```
<%= number_with_delimiter(12345678) %>
```
12,345,678

```
<%= number_with_delimiter(12345678, :delimiter => "_") %>
```
12_345_678

```
<%= number_with_precision(50.0/3, :precision => 2) %>
```
16.67

The debug method dumps out its parameter using YAML and escapes the result so it can be displayed in an HTML page. This can help when trying to look at the values in model objects or request parameters.

```
<%= debug(params) %>
```

```
--- !ruby/hash:HashWithIndifferentAccess
name: Dave
language: Ruby
action: objects
controller: test
```

Yet another set of helpers deals with text. There are methods to truncate strings and highlight words in a string.

```
<%= simple_format(@trees) %>
```

Formats a string, honoring line and paragraph breaks. You could give it the plain text of the Joyce Kilmer poem *Trees*, and it would add the HTML to format it as follows.

```
<p> I think that I shall never see
<br />A poem lovely as a tree.</p>
```

```
<p>A tree whose hungry mouth is prest
<br />Against the sweet earth's flowing breast;
</p>
```

```
<%= excerpt(@trees, "lovely", 8) %>
```
...A poem lovely as a tre...

```
<%= highlight(@trees, "tree") %>
```
I think that I shall never see
A poem lovely as a <strong class="highlight">tree</strong>. A <strong class="highlight">tree</strong> whose hungry mouth is prest
Against the sweet earth's flowing breast;

```
<%= truncate(@trees, :length => 20) %>
```
I think that I sh...

There's a method to pluralize nouns.

```
<%= pluralize(1, "person") %> but <%= pluralize(2, "person") %>
```
1 person but 2 people

If you'd like to do what the fancy websites do and automatically hyperlink URLs and email addresses, there are helpers to do that. There's another that strips hyperlinks from text.

Back on page 70, we saw how the cycle helper can be used to return the successive values from a sequence each time it's called, repeating the sequence as necessary. This is often used to create alternating styles for the rows in a table or list. current_cycle and reset_cycle methods are also available.

Finally, if you're writing something like a blog site or you're allowing users to add comments to your store, you could offer them the ability to create their text in Markdown (BlueCloth)[6] or Textile (RedCloth)[7] format. These are simple formatters that take text with very simple, human-friendly markup and convert it into HTML.

Linking to Other Pages and Resources

TheActionView::Helpers::AssetTagHelper and ActionView::Helpers::UrlHelper modules contain a number of methods that let you reference resources external to the current template. Of these, the most commonly used is link_to, which creates a hyperlink to another action in your application:

```
<%= link_to "Add Comment", new_comments_path %>
```

The first parameter to link_to is the text displayed for the link. The next is a string or hash specifying the link's target.

6. https://github.com/rtomayko/rdiscount
7. http://redcloth.org/

An optional third parameter provides HTML attributes for the generated link:

```
<%= link_to "Delete", product_path(@product),
    { :class => "dangerous", :method => 'delete' }
%>
```

This third parameter also supports two additional options that modify the behavior of the link. Each requires JavaScript to be enabled in the browser.

The :method option is a hack—it allows you to make the link look to the application as if the request were created by a POST, PUT, or DELETE, rather than the normal GET method. This is done by creating a chunk of JavaScript that submits the request when the link is clicked—if JavaScript is disabled in the browser, a GET will be generated.

The :confirm option takes a short message. If present, JavaScript will be generated to display the message and get the user's confirmation before the link is followed:

```
<%= link_to "Delete", product_path(@product),
                    { :class => "dangerous",
                      :confirm => "Are you sure?",
                      :method => :delete}
%>
```

The button_to method works the same as link_to but generates a button in a self-contained form, rather than a straight hyperlink. This is the preferred method of linking to actions that have side effects. However, these buttons live in their own forms, which imposes a couple of restrictions: they cannot appear inline, and they cannot appear inside other forms.

Rails has conditional linking methods that generate hyperlinks if some condition is met and just return the link text otherwise. link_to_if and link_to_unless take a condition parameter, followed by the regular parameters to link_to. If the condition is true (for link_to_if) or false (for link_to_unless), a regular link will be created using the remaining parameters. If not, the name will be added as plain text (with no hyperlink).

The link_to_unless_current helper creates menus in sidebars where the current page name is shown as plain text and the other entries are hyperlinks:

```
<ul>
<% %w{ create list edit save logout }.each do |action| %>
   <li>
     <%= link_to_unless_current(action.capitalize, :action => action) %>
   </li>
<% end %>
</ul>
```

The link_to_unless_current helper may also be passed a block that is evaluated only if the current action is the action given, effectively providing an alternative to the link. There also is a current_page helper method that simply tests whether the current request URI was generated by the given options.

As with url_for, link_to and friends also support absolute URLs:

```
<%= link_to("Help", "http://my.site/help/index.html") %>
```

The image_tag helper creates <*img*> tags. Optional :size parameters (of the form *width*x*height*), or separate width and height parameters, define the size of the image:

```
<%= image_tag("/images/dave.png", :class => "bevel", :size => "80x120") %>
<%= image_tag("/images/andy.png", :class => "bevel",
            :width => "80", :height => "120") %>
```

If you don't give an :alt option, Rails synthesizes one for you using the image's filename. If the image path doesn't start with a / character, Rails assumes that it lives under the /images directory.

You can make images into links by combining link_to and image_tag:

```
<%= link_to(image_tag("delete.png", :size => "50x22"),
          product_path(@product),
          { :confirm    => "Are you sure?",
            :method     => :delete})
%>
```

The mail_to helper creates a mailto: hyperlink that, when clicked, normally loads the client's email application. It takes an email address, the name of the link, and a set of HTML options. Within these options, you can also use :bcc, :cc, :body, and :subject to initialize the corresponding email fields. Finally, the magic option :encode=>"javascript" uses client-side JavaScript to obscure the generated link, making it harder for spiders to harvest email addresses from your site. Unfortunately, it also means your users won't see the email link if they have JavaScript disabled in their browsers.

```
<%= mail_to("support@pragprog.com", "Contact Support",
          :subject => "Support question from #{@user.name}",
          :encode  => "javascript") %>
```

As a weaker form of obfuscation, you can use the :replace_at and :replace_dot options to replace the at sign and dots in the displayed name with other strings. This is unlikely to fool harvesters.

The AssetTagHelper module also includes helpers that make it easy to link to stylesheets and JavaScript code from your pages and to create autodiscovery Atom feed links. We created a stylesheet link in the layouts for the Depot application, where we used stylesheet_link_tag in the head:

`depot_r/app/views/layouts/application.html.erb`

```
<%= stylesheet_link_tag "scaffold" %>
<%= stylesheet_link_tag "depot", :media => "all" %>
```

The stylesheet_link_tag method can also take a parameter named :all, indicating that all styles in the stylesheet directory will be included. Adding :recursive => true will cause Rails to include all styles in all subdirectories too.

The javascript_include_tag method takes a list of JavaScript filenames (assumed to live in public/javascripts) and creates the HTML to load these into a page. In addition to :all, javascript_include_tag accepts as a parameter the value :defaults, which acts as a shortcut and causes Rails to load the files prototype.js, effects.js, dragdrop.js, and controls.js, along with application.js if it exists. Use the latter file to add your own JavaScript to your application's pages.

An RSS or Atom link is a header field that points to a URL in our application. When that URL is accessed, the application should return the appropriate RSS or Atom XML:

```
<html>
  <head>
    <%= auto_discovery_link_tag(:atom, products_url(:format => 'atom')) %>
  </head>
    . . .
```

Finally, the JavaScriptHelper module defines a number of helpers for working with JavaScript. These create JavaScript snippets that run in the browser to generate special effects and to have the page dynamically interact with our application.

By default, image and stylesheet assets are assumed to live in the images and stylesheets directories relative to the application's public directory. If the path given to an asset tag method includes a forward slash, then the path is assumed to be absolute, and no prefix is applied. Sometimes it makes sense to move this static content onto a separate box or to different locations on the current box. Do this by setting the configuration variable asset_host:

```
config.action_controller.asset_host = "http://media.my.url/assets"
```

Although this list of helpers may seem to be comprehensive, Rails provides many more, new helpers are introduced with each release, and a select few are retired or moved off into a plugin where they can be evolved at a different pace than Rails itself. Now would be a good time to review the online documentation that you produced on page 255 to see what other goodies Rails provides for you.

21.6 Reducing Maintenance with Layouts and Partials

So far in this chapter we've looked at templates as isolated chunks of code and HTML. But one of the driving ideas behind Rails is honoring the DRY principle and eliminating the need for duplication. The average website, though, has lots of duplication.

- Many pages share the same tops, tails, and sidebars.
- Multiple pages may contain the same snippets of rendered HTML (a blog site, for example, may display an article in multiple places).
- The same functionality may appear in multiple places. Many sites have a standard search component, or a polling component, that appears in most of the sites' sidebars.

Rails provides both layouts and partials that reduce the need for duplication in these three situations.

Layouts

Rails allows you to render pages that are nested inside other rendered pages. Typically this feature is used to put the content from an action within a standard site-wide page frame (title, footer, and sidebar). In fact, if you've been using the generate script to create scaffold-based applications, then you've been using these layouts all along.

When Rails honors a request to render a template from within a controller, it actually renders two templates. Obviously, it renders the one you ask for (or the default template named after the action if you don't explicitly render anything). But Rails also tries to find and render a layout template (we'll talk about how it finds the layout in a second). If it finds the layout, it inserts the action-specific output into the HTML produced by the layout.

Let's look at a layout template:

```
<html>
  <head>
    <title>Form: <%= controller.action_name %></title>
    <%= stylesheet_link_tag 'scaffold' %>
  </head>
  <body>

    <%= yield :layout %>

  </body>
</html>
```

The layout sets out a standard HTML page, with the head and body sections. It uses the current action name as the page title and includes a CSS file. In the body, there's a call to yield. This is where the magic takes place. When the template for the action was rendered, Rails stored its content, labeling it :layout. Inside the layout template, calling yield retrieves this text. In fact, :layout is the default content returned when rendering, so you can write yield instead of yield :layout. We personally prefer the slightly more explicit version.

If the my_action.html.erb template contained this:

```
<h1><%= @msg %></h1>
```

the browser would see the following HTML:

```html
<html>
  <head>
    <title>Form: my_action</title>
    <link href="/stylesheets/scaffold.css" media="screen"
          rel="Stylesheet" type="text/css" />
  </head>
  <body>

    <h1>Hello, World!</h1>

  </body>
</html>
```

Locating Layout Files

As you've probably come to expect, Rails does a good job of providing defaults for layout file locations, but you can override the defaults if you need something different.

Layouts are controller-specific. If the current request is being handled by a controller called *store*, Rails will by default look for a layout called store (with the usual .html.erb or .xml.builder extension) in the app/views/layouts directory. If you create a layout called application in the layouts directory, it will be applied to all controllers that don't otherwise have a layout defined for them.

You can override this using the layout declaration inside a controller. At its simplest, the declaration takes the name of a layout as a string. The following declaration will make the template in the file standard.html.erb or standard.xml.builder the layout for all actions in the store controller. The layout file will be looked for in the app/views/layouts directory.

```ruby
class StoreController < ApplicationController

  layout "standard"

  # ...
end
```

You can qualify which actions will have the layout applied to them using the :only and :except qualifiers:

```ruby
class StoreController < ApplicationController

  layout "standard", :except => [ :rss, :atom ]

  # ...
end
```

Specifying a layout of nil turns off layouts for a controller.

Sometimes you need to change the appearance of a set of pages at runtime. For example, a blogging site might offer a different-looking side menu if the user is logged in, or a store site might have different-looking pages if the site is down for maintenance. Rails supports this need with dynamic layouts. If the parameter to the layout declaration is a symbol, it's taken to be the name of a controller instance method that returns the name of the layout to be used:

```
class StoreController < ApplicationController

  layout :determine_layout

  # ...

  private

  def determine_layout
    if Store.is_closed?
      "store_down"
    else
      "standard"
    end
  end
end
```

Subclasses of a controller use the parent's layout unless they override it using the layout directive. Finally, individual actions can choose to render using a specific layout (or with no layout at all) by passing render the :layout option:

```
def rss
  render(:layout => false)   # never use a layout
end
```

```
def checkout
  render(:layout => "layouts/simple")
end
```

Passing Data to Layouts

Layouts have access to all the same data that's available to conventional templates. In addition, any instance variables set in the normal template will be available in the layout (because the regular template is rendered before the layout is invoked). This might be used to parameterize headings or menus in the layout. For example, the layout might contain this:

```
<html>
  <head>
    <title><%= @title %></title>
    <%= stylesheet_link_tag 'scaffold' %>
  </head>
  <body>
    <h1><%= @title %></h1>
    <%= yield :layout %>
  </body>
</html>
```

An individual template could set the title by assigning to the @title variable:

```
<% @title = "My Wonderful Life" %>
<p>
  Dear Diary:
</p>
<p>
  Yesterday I had pizza for dinner. It was nice.
</p>
```

In fact, we can take this further. The same mechanism that lets us use yield :layout to embed the rendering of a template into the layout also lets you generate arbitrary content in a template, which can then be embedded into any other template.

For example, different templates may need to add their own template-specific items to the standard page sidebar. We'll use the content_for mechanism in those templates to define content and then use yield in the layout to embed this content into the sidebar.

In each regular template, use a content_for to give a name to the content rendered inside a block. This content will be stored inside Rails and will not contribute to the output generated by the template.

```
<h1>Regular Template</h1>

<% content_for(:sidebar) do %>
  <ul>
    <li>this text will be rendered</li>
    <li>and saved for later</li>
    <li>it may contain <%= "dynamic" %> stuff</li>
  </ul>
<% end %>

<p>
  Here's the regular stuff that will appear on
  the page rendered by this template.
</p>
```

Then, in the layout, you use yield :sidebar to include this block into the page's sidebar:

```
<!DOCTYPE .... >
<html>
  <body>
    <div class="sidebar">
      <p>
        Regular sidebar stuff
      </p>
      <div class="page-specific-sidebar">
        <%= yield :sidebar %>
      </div>
    </div>
  </body>
</html>
```

This same technique can be used to add page-specific JavaScript functions into the <*head*> section of a layout, create specialized menu bars, and so on.

Partial-Page Templates

Web applications commonly display information about the same application object or objects on multiple pages. A shopping cart might display an order line item on the shopping cart page and again on the order summary page. A blog application might display the contents of an article on the main index page and again at the top of a page soliciting comments. Typically this would involve copying snippets of code between the different template pages.

Rails, however, eliminates this duplication with the *partial-page templates* (more frequently called *partials*). You can think of a partial as a kind of subroutine. You invoke it one or more times from within another template, potentially passing it objects to render as parameters. When the partial template finishes rendering, it returns control to the calling template.

Internally, a partial template looks like any other template. Externally, there's a slight difference. The name of the file containing the template code must start with an underscore character, differentiating the source of partial templates from their more complete brothers and sisters.

For example, the partial to render a blog entry might be stored in the file _article.html.erb in the normal views directory, app/views/blog:

```
<div class="article">
  <div class="articleheader">
    <h3><%= article.title %></h3>
  </div>
  <div class="articlebody">
    <%= article.body %>
  </div>
</div>
```

Other templates use the render(:partial=>) method to invoke this:

```
<%= render(:partial => "article", :object => @an_article) %>
<h3>Add Comment</h3>
. . .
```

The :partial parameter to render is the name of the template to render (but without the leading underscore). This name must be both a valid filename and a valid Ruby identifier (so a-b and 20042501 are not valid names for partials). The :object parameter identifies an object to be passed into the partial. This object will be available within the template via a local variable with the same name as the template. In this example, the @an_article object will be passed to the template, and the template can access it using the local variable article. That's why we could write things such as article.title in the partial.

Idiomatic Rails developers use a variable named after the template (article in this instance). In fact, it's normal to take this a step further. If the object to be passed to the partial is in a controller instance variable with the same name as the partial, you can omit the :object parameter. If, in the previous example, our controller had set up the article in the instance variable @article, the view could have rendered the partial using just this:

```
<%= render(:partial => "article") %>
<h3>Add Comment</h3>
. . .
```

You can set additional local variables in the template by passing render a :locals parameter. This takes a hash where the entries represent the names and values of the local variables to set.

```
render(:partial => 'article',
       :object  => @an_article,
       :locals  => { :authorized_by => session[:user_name],
                     :from_ip       => request.remote_ip })
```

Partials and Collections

Applications commonly need to display collections of formatted entries. A blog might show a series of articles, each with text, author, date, and so on. A store might display entries in a catalog, where each has an image, a description, and a price.

The :collection parameter to render works in conjunction with the :partial parameter. The :partial parameter lets us use a partial to define the format of an individual entry, and the :collection parameter applies this template to each member of the collection. To display a list of article model objects using our previously defined _article.html.erb partial, we could write this:

```
<%= render(:partial => "article", :collection => @article_list) %>
```

Inside the partial, the local variable article will be set to the current article from the collection—the variable is named after the template. In addition, the variable article_counter will be set to the index of the current article in the collection.

The optional :spacer_template parameter lets you specify a template that will be rendered between each of the elements in the collection. For example, a view might contain the following:

e1/views/app/views/partial/list.html.erb

```
<%= render(:partial       => "animal",
           :collection    => %w{ ant bee cat dog elk },
           :spacer_template => "spacer")
%>
```

This uses _animal.html.erb to render each animal in the given list, rendering the partial _spacer.html.erb between each. If _animal.html.erb contains this:

`e1/views/app/views/partial/_animal.html.erb`

```
<p>The animal is <%= animal %></p>
```

and _spacer.html.erb contains this:

`e1/views/app/views/partial/_spacer.html.erb`

```
<hr />
```

your users would see a list of animal names with a line between each.

Shared Templates

If the first option or :partial parameter to a render call is a simple name, Rails assumes that the target template is in the current controller's view directory. However, if the name contains one or more / characters, Rails assumes that the part up to the last slash is a directory name and the rest is the template name. The directory is assumed to be under app/views. This makes it easy to share partials and subtemplates across controllers.

The convention among Rails applications is to store these shared partials in a subdirectory of app/views called shared. Render shared partials using statements such as these:

```
<%= render("shared/header", :title => @article.title) %>
<%= render(:partial => "shared/post", :object => @article) %>
. . .
```

In this previous example, the @article object will be assigned to the local variable post within the template.

Partials with Layouts

Partials can be rendered with a layout, and you can apply a layout to a block within any template:

```
<%= render :partial => "user", :layout => "administrator" %>

<%= render :layout => "administrator" do %>
  # ...
<% end %>
```

Partial layouts are to be found directly in the app/views directory associated with the controller, along with the customary underbar prefix, for example, app/views/users/_administrator.html.erb.

Partials and Controllers

It isn't just view templates that use partials. Controllers also get in on the act. Partials give controllers the ability to generate fragments from a page using the same partial template as the view itself. This is particularly important when you use Ajax support to update just part of a page from the controller—use partials, and you know your formatting for the table row or line item that you're updating will be compatible with that used to generate its brethren initially.

Taken together, partials and layouts provide an effective way to make sure that the user interface portion of your application is maintainable. But being maintainable is only part of the story; doing so in a way that also performs well is also crucial.

What We Just Did

Views are the public face of Rails applications, and we have seen that Rails delivers extensive support for what you need to build robust and maintainable user and application programming interfaces.

We started with templates, of which Rails provides built-in support for three types: erb, builder, and rjs. Templates make it easy for us to provide HTML, XML, and JavaScript responses to any request. We will discuss adding another option in Section 26.3, *Beautifying Our Markup with Haml*, on page 425.

We dove into forms, which are the primary means by which users will interact with your application. Along the way, we covered uploading files.

We continued with helpers, which enable us to factor out complex application logic to allow our views to focus on presentation aspects. We explored a number of helpers that Rails provides, ranging from simple formatting to hypertext links, which are the final way in which users interact with HTML pages.

We completed our tour of Action View by covering two related ways of factoring out large chunks of content for reuse. We use layouts to factor out the outermost layers of a view and provide a common look and feel. We use partials to factor out common inner components, such as a single form or table.

That covers how a user with a browser will access our Rails application. Next up: covering how we can use caching techniques to reduce or even eliminate the computational overhead of rendering a view when the underlying data in the database has not changed between requests.

In this chapter, we'll see

- caching full pages statically,
- caching the results of an action,
- expiring pages from the cache, and
- caching a part of a page.

Chapter 22

Caching

Many applications seem to spend a lot of their time doing the same task over and over. A blog application renders the list of current articles for every visitor. A store application will display the same page of product information for everyone who requests it.

All this repetition costs us resources and time on the server. Rendering the front page of your site may require half a dozen database queries, and it may end up running through a number of Ruby methods and Rails templates. It isn't a big deal for an individual request, but multiply that by several thousand hits an hour, and suddenly your server is starting to glow a dull red. Your users will see this as slower response times.

In situations such as these, we can use caching to greatly reduce the load on our servers and increase the responsiveness of our applications. Rather than generate the same old content from scratch, time after time, we create it once and remember the result. The next time a request arrives for that same page, we deliver it from the cache rather than create it.

Rails offers three approaches to caching: *page caching*, *action caching*, and *fragment caching*.

22.1 Page Caching

Page caching is the simplest and most efficient form of Rails caching. The first time a user requests a particular URL, our application gets invoked and generates a page of HTML. The contents of this page are stored in the cache. The next time a request containing that URL is received, the HTML of the page will be delivered straight from the cache. Your application never sees the request. In fact, Rails is not involved at all. The web server itself handles the entire request, which makes page caching very, very efficient. Your application delivers these pages at the same speed that the server can deliver any other static content.

Sometimes, though, our application needs to be at least partially involved in handling these requests. For example, your store might display details of certain products only to a subset of users (perhaps premium customers get earlier access to new products). In this case, the page you display will have the same content, but you don't want to display it to just anyone—you need to filter access to the cached content. Rails provides *action caching* for this purpose. With action caching, your application controller is still invoked, and it's invoked before filters are run. However, the action itself is not called if there's an existing cached page.

Let's look at this in the context of a site that has public content and premium, members-only content. We have two controllers: an admin controller that verifies that someone is a member and a content controller with actions to show both public and premium content. The public content consists of a single page with links to premium articles. If someone requests premium content and they're not a member, we redirect them to an action in the admin controller that signs them up.

Ignoring caching for a minute, we can implement the content side of this application using a before filter to verify the user's status and a couple of action methods for the two kinds of content:

```
e1/cookies/app/controllers/content_controller.rb
class ContentController < ApplicationController
  before_filter :verify_premium_user, :except => :public_content

  def public_content
    @articles = Article.list_public
  end

  def premium_content
    @articles = Article.list_premium
  end

  private

  def verify_premium_user
    user = session[:user_id]
    user = User.find(user) if user
    unless user && user.active?
      redirect_to :controller => "login", :action => "signup_new"
    end
  end
end
```

Because the content pages are fixed, they can be cached. We can cache the public content at the page level, but we have to restrict access to the cached premium content to members, so we need to use action-level caching for it. To enable caching, we simply add two declarations to our class:

```ruby
class ContentController < ApplicationController
  before_filter :verify_premium_user, :except => :public_content

  caches_page    :public_content
  caches_action  :premium_content
```

The caches_page directive tells Rails to cache the output of public_content the first time it is produced. Thereafter, this page will be delivered directly from the web server.

The second directive, caches_action, tells Rails to cache the results of executing premium_content but still to execute the filters. This means that we'll still validate that the person requesting the page is allowed to do so, but we won't actually execute the action more than once.

Action caching is a good example of an *around filter*, described on page 330. The before part of the filter checks to see whether the cached item exists. If it does, it renders it directly to the user, preventing the real action from running. The after part of the filter saves the results of running the action in the cache.

caches_action can accept a number of options. A :cache_path option allows you to modify the action cache path. This can be useful for actions that handle a number of different conditions with different cache needs. :if and :unless allow you to pass a Proc that will control when an action should be passed. Finally, a :layout option, if false, will cause Rails to cache only your action content. This is useful when your layout has dynamic information.

Caching is, by default, enabled only in production environments. You can turn it on or off manually by setting this:

```ruby
ActionController::Base.perform_caching = true | false
```

You can make this change in your application's environment files (in config/environments), although the preferred syntax is slightly different there:

```ruby
config.action_controller.perform_caching = true
```

Note that both Rails action and page caching are strictly URL based. A page is cached according to the content of the URL that first generated it, and subsequent requests to that same URL will return the saved content.

This means that dynamic pages that depend on information not in the URL are poor candidates for caching. These include the following:

- Pages where the content is time based (although see Section 22.2, *Time-Based Expiry of Cached Pages*, on page 366).
- Pages whose content depends on session information. For example, if you customize pages for each of your users, you're unlikely to be able to cache them (although you might be able to take advantage of fragment caching, described starting on page 368).
- Pages generated from data that you don't control. For example, a page displaying information from our database might not be cachable if non-Rails applications can update that database too. Our cached page would become out-of-date without our application knowing.

However, caching *can* cope with pages generated from volatile content that's under your control. As we'll see in the next section, it's simply a question of removing the cached pages when they become outdated.

22.2 Expiring Pages

Creating cached pages is only one half of the equation. If the content initially used to create these pages changes, the cached versions will become out-of-date, and we'll need a way of expiring them.

The trick is to code the application to notice when the data used to create a dynamic page has changed and then to remove the cached version. The next time a request comes through for that URL, the cached page will be regenerated based on the new content.

Expiring Pages Explicitly

The low-level way to remove cached pages is with the methods expire_page and expire_action. These take the same parameters as url_for and expire the cached page that matches the generated URL.

For example, our content controller might have an action that allows us to create an article and another action that updates an existing article. When we create an article, the list of articles on the public page will become obsolete, so we call expire_page, passing in the action name that displays the public page. When we update an existing article, the public index page remains unchanged (at least, it does in our application), but any cached version of this particular article should be deleted. Because this cache was created using caches_action, we need to expire the page using expire_action, passing in the action name and the article id.

```
e1/cookies/app/controllers/content_controller.rb
def create_article
  article = Article.new(params[:article])
  if article.save
    expire_page   :action => "public_content"
  else
    # ...
  end
end

def update_article
  article = Article.find(params[:id])
  if article.update_attributes(params[:article])
    expire_action :action => "premium_content", :id => article
  else
    # ...
  end
end
```

The method that deletes an article does a bit more work—it has to both invalidate the public index page and remove the specific article page:

```
e1/cookies/app/controllers/content_controller.rb
def delete_article
  Article.destroy(params[:id])
  expire_page   :action => "public_content"
  expire_action :action => "premium_content", :id => params[:id]
end
```

Picking a Caching Store Strategy

Caching, like sessions, features a number of storage options. You can keep the fragments in files, in a database, in a DRb server, or in memcached servers. But whereas sessions usually contain small amounts of data and require only one row per user, fragment caching can easily create sizeable amounts of data, and you can have many per user. This makes database storage a poor fit.

For many setups, it's easiest to keep cache files on the filesystem. But you can't keep these cached files locally on each server, because expiring a cache on one server would not expire it on the rest. You therefore need to set up a network drive that all the servers can share for their caching.

As with session configuration, you can configure a file-based caching store globally in environment.rb or in a specific environment's file:

```
ActionController::Base.cache_store = :file_store, "#{RAILS_ROOT}/cache"
```

This configuration assumes that a directory named cache is available in the root of the application and that the web server has full read and write access to it. This directory can easily be symlinked to the path on the server that represents the network drive.

Regardless of which store you pick for caching fragments, you should be aware that network bottlenecks can quickly become a problem. If your site depends heavily on fragment caching, every request will need a lot of data transferring from the network drive to the specific server before it's again sent on to the user. To use this on a high-profile site, you really need to have a high-bandwidth internal network between your servers, or you will see slowdown.

The caching store system is available only for caching actions and fragments. Full-page caches need to be kept on the filesystem in the public directory. In this case, you will have to go the network drive route if you want to use page caching across multiple web servers. You can then symlink either the entire public directory (but that will also cause your images, stylesheets, and JavaScript to be passed over the network, which may be a problem) or just the individual directories that are needed for your page caches. In the latter case, you would, for example, symlink public/products to your network drive to keep page caches for your products controller.

Expiring Pages Implicitly

The expire_*xxx* methods work well, but they also couple the caching function to the code in your controllers. Every time you change something in the database, you also have to work out which cached pages this might affect. Although this is easy for smaller applications, this gets more difficult as the application grows. A change made in one controller might affect pages cached in another. Business logic in helper methods, which really shouldn't have to know about HTML pages, now needs to worry about expiring cached pages.

Fortunately, Rails *sweepers* can simplify some of this coupling. A sweeper is a special kind of observer on your model objects. When something significant happens in the model, the sweeper expires the cached pages that depend on that model's data.

Your application can have as many sweepers as it needs. You'll typically create a separate sweeper to manage the caching for each controller. Put your sweeper code in app/sweepers:

e1/cookies/app/sweepers/article_sweeper.rb

```
class ArticleSweeper < ActionController::Caching::Sweeper

  observe Article

  # If we create a new article, the public list of articles must be regenerated
  def after_create(article)
    expire_public_page
  end
```

```
# If we update an existing article, the cached version of that article is stale
def after_update(article)
  expire_article_page(article.id)
end

# Deleting a page means we update the public list and blow away the cached article
def after_destroy(article)
  expire_public_page
  expire_article_page(article.id)
end

private

def expire_public_page
  expire_page(:controller => "content", :action => 'public_content')
end

def expire_article_page(article_id)
  expire_action(:controller => "content",
                :action     => "premium_content",
                :id         => article_id)
end
end
```

The flow through the sweeper is somewhat convoluted:

- You first declare the sweeper as an observer on one or more Active Record classes. In our example case, it observes the Article model. (We first talked about observers back on page 295.) The sweeper uses hook methods (such as after_update) to expire cached pages if appropriate.

- The sweeper is also declared to be active in a controller using the directive cache_sweeper:

```
class ContentController < ApplicationController

  before_filter :verify_premium_user, :except => :public_content
  caches_page   :public_content
  caches_action :premium_content

  cache_sweeper :article_sweeper,
                :only => [ :create_article,
                           :update_article,
                           :delete_article ]
  # ...
```

- If a request comes in that invokes one of the actions that the sweeper is filtering, the sweeper is activated. If any of the Active Record observer methods fires, the page and action expiry methods will be called. If the Active Record observer gets invoked but the current action is not selected as a cache sweeper, the expire calls in the sweeper are ignored. Otherwise, the expiry takes place.

Time-Based Expiry of Cached Pages

Consider a site that shows fairly volatile information such as stock quotes or news headlines. If we did the style of caching where we expired a page whenever the underlying information changed, we'd be expiring pages constantly. The cache would rarely get used, and we'd lose the benefit of having it.

In these circumstances, you might want to consider switching to time-based caching, where you build the cached pages exactly as we did previously but don't expire them when their content becomes obsolete.

You run a separate background process that periodically goes into the cache directory and deletes the cache files. You choose how this deletion occurs—you could simply remove all files, the files created more than so many minutes ago, or the files whose names match some pattern. That part is application-specific.

The next time a request comes in for one of these pages, it won't be satisfied from the cache, and the application will handle it. In the process, it'll automatically repopulate that particular page in the cache, lightening the load for subsequent fetches of this page.

Where do you find the cache files to delete? Not surprisingly, this is configurable. Page cache files are by default stored in the public directory of your application. They'll be named after the URL they are caching, with an .html extension. For example, the page cache file for content/show/1 will be here:

```
app/public/content/show/1.html
```

This naming scheme is no coincidence; it allows the web server to find the cache files automatically. You can, however, override the defaults using this:

```
config.action_controller.page_cache_directory = "dir/name"
config.action_controller.page_cache_extension = ".html"
```

Action cache files are not by default stored in the regular filesystem directory structure and cannot be expired using this technique.

Playing Nice with Client Caches

When we said earlier that creating cached pages is only one half of the equation, we failed to mention that there are three halves. Oops.

Clients (generally, but not always, browsers) often have caches too. Intermediaries between your server and the client may also provide caching services. You can help optimize these caches (and therefore reduce load on your server) by providing HTTP headers. Doing so is entirely optional and won't always result in a bandwidth reduction, but on the other hand, sometimes the savings can be quite significant.

Expiration Headers

The most efficient request is the request that is never made. Many pages (particularly images, scripts, and stylesheets) change very rarely yet may be referenced fairly frequently. One way to ensure that re-retrievals are optimized out before they get to your server is to provide an Expires header.

Although an Expires header may provide a number of different options, the most common usage is to indicate how long the given response is to be considered "good for," suggesting that the client need not re-request this data in the interim. Calling the expires_in method in your controller achieves this result:

```
expires_in 20.minutes
expires_in 1.year
```

A server should not provide a date more than one year in the future on Expires headers.

An alternate use for the Expires header is to indicate that the response is not to be cached at all. This can be accomplished with the expires_now method, which understandably takes no parameters.

You can find additional information on more expiration options in the HTTP specification.[1]

Be aware that if you are using page-level caching, requests that are cached at the server won't get to your application, so this mechanism needs to also be implemented at the server level to be effective. Here's an example for the Apache web server:

```
ExpiresActive On
<FilesMatch "\.(ico|gif|jpe?g|png|js|css)$">
  ExpiresDefault "access plus 1 year"
</FilesMatch>
```

LastModified and ETag Support

The next best thing to eliminating requests entirely is to respond immediately with an HTTP 304 Not Modified response. This will instruct user agents and intermediaries to use the version of this page that they already have in their cache. At a minimum, such responses will save on bandwidth. Often this will enable you to eliminate the server load associated with producing a more complete response.

If you are already doing page-level caching with Apache, the web server will generally take care of this for you, based on the timestamp associated with the on-disk cache.

---

1. http://www.w3.org/Protocols/rfc2616/rfc2616-sec14.html#sec14.9.3

For all other requests, Rails will produce the necessary HTTP headers for you, if you call one of the stale? or fresh_when methods.

Both methods accept both a :last_modified timestamp (in UTC) and an :etag. The latter is either an object on which the response depends or an array of such objects. Such objects need to respond to either cache_key or to_param. ActiveRecord takes care of this for you.

stale? is typically used in if statements when custom rendering is involved:

```
def show
  @article = Article.find(params[:id])

  if stale?(:etag=>@article, :last_modified=>@article.created_at.utc)
    # ...
  end
end
```

fresh_when is often more convenient when you are making use of default rendering because it will produce a 304 Not Modified response for you:

```
def show
  fresh_when(:etag=>@article, :last_modified=>@article.created_at.utc)
end
```

In addition to the ability to cache a full page, Rails also provides support for caching *parts* of a page. We cover why that is useful and how to integrate it into your application next.

22.3 Fragment Caching

Caching parts of a page turns out to be remarkably useful in dynamic sites. Perhaps you customize the greeting and the sidebar on your blog application for each individual user. In this case, you can't use page caching, because the overall page is different for each user. But because the list of articles doesn't change between users, you can use fragment caching—you construct the HTML that displays the articles just once and include it in customized pages delivered to individual users.

Just to illustrate fragment caching, let's set up a pretend blog application. Here's the controller. It sets up @dynamic_content, representing content that should change each time the page is viewed. For our fake blog, we use the current time as this content.

e1/views/app/controllers/blog_controller.rb

```
class BlogController < ApplicationController
  def list
    @dynamic_content = Time.now.to_s
  end
end
```

Here's our mock Article class. It simulates a model class that in normal circumstances would fetch articles from the database. We've arranged for the first article in our list to display the time at which it was created.

`e1/views/app/models/article.rb`

```ruby
class Article
  attr_reader :body

  def initialize(body)
    @body = body
  end

  def self.find_recent
    [ new("It is now #{Time.now.to_s}"),
      new("Today I had pizza"),
      new("Yesterday I watched Spongebob"),
      new("Did nothing on Saturday") ]
  end
end
```

Now we'd like to set up a template that uses a cached version of the rendered articles but still updates the dynamic data. It turns out to be trivial.

`e1/views/app/views/blog/list.html.erb`

```erb
<%= @dynamic_content %>    <!-- Here's dynamic content. -->

<% cache do %>             <!-- Here's the content we cache -->
  <ul>
    <% for article in Article.find_recent %>
      <li><p><%= h(article.body) %></p></li>
    <% end %>
  </ul>
<% end %>                  <!-- End of cached content -->

<%= @dynamic_content %>    <!-- More dynamic content. -->
```

The magic is the cache method. All output generated in the block associated with this method will be cached. The next time this page is accessed, the dynamic content will still be rendered, but the stuff inside the block will come straight from the cache—it won't be regenerated. We can see this if we bring up our skeletal application and hit Refresh after a few seconds, as shown in Figure 22.1, on the following page. The times at the top and bottom of the page—the dynamic portion of our data—change on the refresh. However, the time in the center section remains the same, because it is being served from the cache. (If you're trying this at home and you see all three time strings change, chances are you're running your application in development mode. Caching is enabled by default only in production mode. If you're testing using WEBrick, the -e production option will do the trick.)

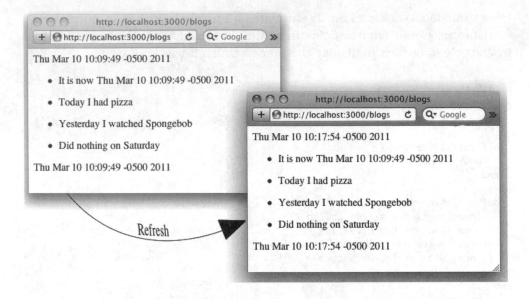

Figure 22.1: REFRESHING A PAGE WITH CACHED AND NONCACHED DATA

The key concept here is that the stuff that's cached is the fragment generated in the view. If we'd constructed the article list in the controller and then passed that list to the view, the future access to the page would not have to rerender the list, but the database would still be accessed on every request. Moving the database request into the view means it won't be called once the output is cached.

OK, you say, but that just broke the rule about putting application-level code into view templates. Can't we avoid that somehow? We can, but it means making caching just a little less transparent than it would otherwise be. The trick is to have the action test for the presence of a cached fragment. If one exists, the action bypasses the expensive database operation, knowing that the fragment will be used.

e1/views/app/controllers/blog1_controller.rb
```ruby
class Blog1Controller < ApplicationController

  def list
    @dynamic_content = Time.now.to_s
    unless read_fragment(:action => 'list')
      logger.info("Creating fragment")
      @articles = Article.find_recent
    end
  end

end
```

The action uses the read_fragment method to see whether a fragment exists for this action. If not, it loads the list of articles from the (fake) database. The view then uses this list to create the fragment.

e1/views/app/views/blog1/list.html.erb

```
<%= @dynamic_content %> <!-- Here's dynamic content. -->

<% cache do %>           <!-- Here's the content we cache -->
  <ul>
    <% for article in @articles %>
      <li><p><%= h(article.body) %></p></li>
    <% end %>
  </ul>
<% end %>               <!-- End of the cached content -->

<%= @dynamic_content %> <!-- More dynamic content. -->
```

Expiring Cached Fragments

Now that we have a cached version of the article list, our Rails application will be able to serve it whenever this page is referenced. If the articles are updated, however, the cached version will be out-of-date and should be expired. We do this with the expire_fragment method. By default, fragments are cached using the name of the controller and action that rendered the page (blog and list in our first case). To expire the fragment (for example, when the article list changes), the controller could call this:

e1/views/app/controllers/blog_controller.rb

```
expire_fragment(:controller => 'blog', :action => 'list')
```

Clearly, this naming scheme works only if there's just one fragment on the page. Fortunately, if you need more, you can override the names associated with fragments by adding parameters (using url_for conventions) to the cache method:

e1/views/app/views/blog2/list.html.erb

```
<% cache(:action => 'list', :part => 'articles') do %>
  <ul>
    <% for article in @articles %>
      <li><p><%= h(article.body) %></p></li>
    <% end %>
  </ul>
<% end %>

<% cache(:action => 'list', :part => 'counts') do %>
  <p>
    There are a total of <%= @article_count %> articles.
  </p>
<% end %>
```

In this example, two fragments are cached. The first has the additional :part parameter set to articles, and the second has it set to counts.

Within the controller, we can pass the same parameters to expire_fragment to delete particular fragments. For example, when we edit an article, we have to expire the article list, but the count is still valid. If instead we delete an article, we need to expire both fragments. The controller looks like this (we don't have any code that actually does anything to the articles in it—just look at the caching):

e1/views/app/controllers/blog2_controller.rb

```ruby
class Blog2Controller < ApplicationController

  def list
    @dynamic_content = Time.now.to_s
    @articles = Article.find_recent
    @article_count    = @articles.size
  end

  def edit
    # do the article editing
    expire_fragment(:action => 'list', :part => 'articles')
    redirect_to(:action => 'list')
  end

  def delete
    # do the deleting
    expire_fragment(:action => 'list', :part => 'articles')
    expire_fragment(:action => 'list', :part => 'counts')
    redirect_to(:action => 'list')
  end
end
```

The expire_fragment method can also take a single regular expression as a parameter, allowing us to expire all fragments whose names match:

```ruby
expire_fragment(%r{/blog2/list.*})
```

What We Just Did

We explored three techniques that can be used to make your site respond faster.

We learned how to cache entire pages and thereby avoid all Ruby, Rails, and database overhead when processing requests that can be served by the cache. This is useful for high-traffic pages that require database access to produce and yet rarely change. The product catalog listings from the Depot application is a prime example of such a page.

We learned how to cache the results of controller actions, avoiding rendering and database overhead. This is useful in cases where we want to continue to have filters run, generally for authentication purposes. Along the way we covered both explicit and implicit mechanisms to force expiration of pages in the cache.

Finally, we learned how to cache fragments of pages, which allows us full control over balancing optimization and the production of dynamic content.

This covers maintaining the cache in support of views. Next up: maintaining database schemas in support of models.

In this chapter, we'll see

- naming migration files,
- renaming and columns,
- creating and renaming tables,
- defining indices and keys,
- using native SQL.

Chapter 23

Migrations

Rails encourages an agile, iterative style of development. We don't expect to get everything right the first time. Instead, we write tests and interact with our customers to refine our understanding as we go.

For that to work, we need a supporting set of practices. We write tests to help us design our interfaces and to act as a safety net when we change things, and we use version control to store our application's source files, allowing us to undo mistakes and to monitor what changes day to day.

But there's another area of the application that changes, an area that we can't directly manage using version control. The database schema in a Rails application constantly evolves as we progress through the development: we add a table here, rename a column there, and so on. The database changes in step with the application's code.

With Rails, each of those steps is made possible through the use of a *migration*. You saw this in use throughout the development of the Depot application, starting when we created the first products table in Section 6.1, *Generating the Scaffold*, on page 62 and when we performed such tasks as adding a quantity to the line_items table in Section 10.1, *Iteration E1: Creating a Smarter Cart*, on page 111. Now it is time to dig deeper into how migrations work and what else you can do with them.

23.1 Creating and Running Migrations

A migration is simply a Ruby source file in your application's db/migrate directory. Each migration file's name starts with a number of digits (typically fourteen) and an underscore. Those digits are the key to migrations, because they define the sequence in which the migrations are applied—they are the individual migration's version number.

The version number itself is the Coordinated Universal Time (UTC) timestamp at the time the migration was created. These numbers contain the four-digit year, followed by two digits each for the month, day, hour, minute, and second, all based on the mean solar time at the Royal Observatory in Greenwich, London. Because migrations tend to be created relatively infrequently and the accuracy is recorded down to the second, the chances of any two people getting the same timestamp is vanishingly small. And the benefit of having timestamps that can be deterministically ordered far outweighs the miniscule risk of this occurring.

Here's what the db/migrate directory of our Depot application looks like:

```
depot> ls db/migrate
20110211000001_create_products.rb
20110211000002_create_carts.rb
20110211000003_create_line_items.rb
20110211000004_add_quantity_to_line_items.rb
20110211000005_combine_items_in_cart.rb
20110211000006_create_orders.rb
20110211000007_add_order_id_to_line_item.rb
20110211000008_create_users.rb
```

Although you could create these migration files by hand, it's easier (and less error prone) to use a generator. As we saw when we created the Depot application, there are actually two generators that create migration files:

- The *model* generator creates a migration to in turn create the table associated with the model (unless you specify the --skip-migration option). As the example that follows shows, creating a model called discount also creates a migration called *yyyyMMddhhmmss*_create_discounts.rb:

  ```
  depot> rails generate model discount
      exists  app/models/
      exists  test/unit/
      exists  test/fixtures/
      create  app/models/discount.rb
      create  test/unit/discount_test.rb
      create  test/fixtures/discounts.yml
      exists  db/migrate
  ▶   create  db/migrate/20110211000010_create_discounts.rb
  ```

- You can also generate a migration on its own:

  ```
  depot> rails generate migration add_price_column
      exists  db/migrate
  ▶   create  db/migrate/20110211000011_add_price_column.rb
  ```

Later, starting in *Anatomy of a Migration*, we'll see what goes in the migration files. But for now, let's jump ahead a little in the workflow and see how to run migrations.

Running Migrations

Migrations are run using the db:migrate Rake task:

```
depot> rake db:migrate
```

To see what happens next, let's dive down into the internals of Rails.

The migration code maintains a table called schema_migrations inside every Rails database. This table has just one column, called version, and it will have one row per successfully applied migration.

When you run rake db:migrate, the task first looks for the schema_migrations table. If it doesn't yet exist, it will be created.

The migration code then looks at all the migration files in db/migrate and skips from consideration any that have a version number (the leading digits in the filename) that is already in the database. It then proceeds to apply the remainder of the migrations, creating a row in the schema_migrations table for each.

If we were to run migrations again at this point, nothing much would happen. Each of the version numbers of the migration files would match with a row in the database, so there'd be no migrations to apply.

However, if we subsequently create a new migration file, it will have a version number not in the database. This is true even if the version number was *before* one or more of the already applied migrations. This can happen when multiple users are using a version control system to store the migration files. If we then run migrations, this new migration file—and only this migration file—will be executed. This may mean that migrations are run out of order, so you might want to take care and ensure that these migrations are independent. Or you might want to revert your database to a previous state and then apply the migrations in order.

You can force the database to a specific version by supplying the VERSION= parameter to the rake db:migrate command:

```
depot> rake db:migrate VERSION=20110211000009
```

If the version you give is greater than any of the migrations that have yet to be applied, these migrations will be applied.

If, however, the version number on the command line is less than one or more versions listed in the schema_migrations table, something different happens. In these circumstances, Rails looks for the migration file whose number matches the database version and *undoes* it. It repeats this process until there are no more versions listed in the schema_migrations table that exceed the number you specified on the command line. That is, the migrations are unapplied in reverse order to take the schema back to the version that you specify.

You can also redo one or more migrations:

```
depot> rake db:migrate:redo STEP=3
```

By default, redo will roll back one migration and rerun it. To roll back multiple migrations, pass the STEP= parameter.

23.2 Anatomy of a Migration

Migrations are subclasses of the Rails class ActiveRecord::Migration. The class you create should contain at least the two class methods up and down:

```
class SomeMeaningfulName < ActiveRecord::Migration
  def self.up
    # ...
  end

  def self.down
    # ...
  end
end
```

The name of the class, after all uppercase letters are downcased and preceded by an underscore, must match the portion of the filename after the version number. For example, the previous class could be found in a file named 20110211000017_some_meaningful_name.rb. No two migrations can contain classes with the same name.

The up method is responsible for applying the schema changes for this migration, while the down method undoes those changes. Let's make this more concrete. Here's a migration that adds an e_mail column to the orders table:

```
class AddEmailToOrders < ActiveRecord::Migration
  def self.up
    add_column :orders, :e_mail, :string
  end

  def self.down
    remove_column :orders, :e_mail
  end
end
```

See how the down method undoes the effect of the up method?

Column Types

The third parameter to add_column specifies the type of the database column. In the previous example, we specified that the e_mail column has a type of :string. But just what does this mean? Databases typically don't have column types of :string.

Remember that Rails tries to make your application independent of the underlying database; you could develop using SQLite 3 and deploy to Postgres if you wanted, for example. But different databases use different names for the types of columns. If you used a SQLite 3 column type in a migration, that migration might not work if applied to a Postgres database. So, Rails migrations insulate you from the underlying database type systems by using logical types. If we're migrating a SQLite 3 database, the :string type will create a column of type varchar(255). On Postgres, the same migration adds a column with the type char varying(255).

The types supported by migrations are :binary, :boolean, :date, :datetime, :decimal, :float, :integer, :string, :text, :time, and :timestamp. The default mappings of these types for the database adapters in Rails are shown in Figure 23.1, on the next page. Using this figure, you could work out that a column declared to be :integer in a migration would have the underlying type integer in SQLite 3 and number(38) in Oracle.

You can specify up to three options when defining most columns in a migration; decimal columns take an additional two options. Each of these options is given as a key => value pair. The common options are as follows:

:null => true or false
> If false, the underlying column has a not null constraint added (if the database supports it).

:limit => size
> This sets a limit on the size of the field. This basically appends the string (*size*) to the database column type definition.

:default => value
> This sets the default value for the column. Note that the default is calculated once, at the point the migration is run, so the following code will set the default column value to the date and time when the migration was run:

```
add_column :orders, :placed_at, :datetime, :default => Time.now
```

In addition, decimal columns take the options :precision and :scale. The :precision option specifies the number of significant digits that will be stored, and the :scale option determines where the decimal point will be located in these digits (think of the scale as the number of digits after the decimal point). A decimal number with a precision of 5 and a scale of 0 can store numbers from -99,999 to +99,999. A decimal number with a precision of 5 and a scale of 2 can store the range -999.99 to +999.99.

	db2	mysql	openbase	oracle
:binary	blob(32768)	blob	object	blob
:boolean	decimal(1)	tinyint(1)	boolean	number(1)
:date	date	date	date	date
:datetime	timestamp	datetime	datetime	date
:decimal	decimal	decimal	decimal	decimal
:float	float	float	float	number
:integer	int	int(11)	integer	number(38)
:string	varchar(255)	varchar(255)	char(4096)	varchar2(255)
:text	clob(32768)	text	text	clob
:time	time	time	time	date
:timestamp	timestamp	datetime	timestamp	date

	postgresql	sqlite	sqlserver	sybase
:binary	bytea	blob	image	image
:boolean	boolean	boolean	bit	bit
:date	date	date	date	datetime
:datetime	timestamp	datetime	datetime	datetime
:decimal	decimal	decimal	decimal	decimal
:float	float	float	float(8)	float(8)
:integer	integer	integer	int	int
:string	(note 1)	varchar(255)	varchar(255)	varchar(255)
:text	text	text	text	text
:time	time	datetime	time	time
:timestamp	timestamp	datetime	datetime	timestamp

Note 1: character varying(256)

Figure 23.1: MIGRATION AND DATABASE COLUMN TYPES

The :precision and :scale parameters are optional for decimal columns. However, incompatibilities between different databases lead us to strongly recommend that you include the options for each decimal column.

Here are some column definitions using the migration types and options:

```
add_column :orders, :attn, :string, :limit => 100
add_column :orders, :order_type,  :integer
add_column :orders, :ship_class, :string, :null => false, :default => 'priority'
add_column :orders, :amount, :decimal, :precision => 8, :scale => 2
```

Renaming Columns

When we refactor our code, we often change our variable names to make them more meaningful. Rails migrations allow us to do this to database column names, too. For example, a week after we first added it, we might decide that e_mail isn't the best name for the new column. We can create a migration to rename it using the rename_column method:

```
class RenameEmailColumn < ActiveRecord::Migration
  def self.up
    rename_column :orders, :e_mail, :customer_email
  end

  def self.down
    rename_column :orders, :customer_email, :e_mail
  end
end
```

Note that the rename doesn't destroy any existing data associated with the column. Also be aware that renaming is not supported by all the adapters.

Changing Columns

Use the change_column method to change the type of a column or to alter the options associated with a column. Use it the same way you'd use add_column, but specify the name of an existing column. Let's say that the order type column is currently an integer, but we need to change it to be a string. We want to keep the existing data, so an order type of 123 will become the string "123". Later, we'll use noninteger values such as "new" and "existing".

Changing from an integer column to a string is easy:

```
def self.up
 change_column :orders, :order_type, :string
end
```

However, the opposite transformation is problematic. We might be tempted to write the obvious down migration:

```
def self.down
 change_column :orders, :order_type, :integer
end
```

But if our application has taken to storing data like "new" in this column, the down method will lose it—"new" can't be converted to an integer. If that's acceptable, then the migration is acceptable as it stands. If, however, we want to create a one-way migration—one that cannot be reversed—we'll want to stop the down migration from being applied. In this case, Rails provides a special exception that we can throw:

```
class ChangeOrderTypeToString < ActiveRecord::Migration
  def self.up
    change_column :orders, :order_type, :string, :null => false
  end

  def self.down
    raise ActiveRecord::IrreversibleMigration
  end
end
```

23.3 Managing Tables

So far we've been using migrations to manipulate the columns in existing tables. Now let's look at creating and dropping tables:

```
class CreateOrderHistories < ActiveRecord::Migration
  def self.up
    create_table :order_histories do |t|
      t.integer :order_id, :null => false
      t.text :notes

      t.timestamps
    end
  end

  def self.down
    drop_table :order_histories
  end
end
```

create_table takes the name of a table (remember, table names are plural) and a block. (It also takes some optional parameters that we'll look at in a minute.) The block is passed a table definition object, which we use to define the columns in the table.

The calls to the various table definition methods should look familiar—they're similar to the add_column method we used previously except these methods don't take the name of the table as the first parameter, and the name of the method itself is the data type desired. This reduces repetition.

Note that we don't define the id column for our new table. Unless we say otherwise, Rails migrations automatically add a primary key called id to all tables they create. For a deeper discussion of this, see Section 23.3, *Primary Keys*, on page 386.

The timestamps method creates both the created_at and updated_at columns, with the correct timestamp data type. Although there is no requirement to add these columns to any particular table, this is yet another example of Rails making it easy for a common convention to be implemented easily and consistently.

Options for Creating Tables

You can pass a hash of options as a second parameter to create_table.

If you specify :force => true, the migration will drop an existing table of the same name before creating the new one. This is a useful option if you want to create a migration that forces a database into a known state, but there's clearly a potential for data loss.

The :temporary => true option creates a temporary table—one that goes away when the application disconnects from the database. This is clearly pointless in the context of a migration, but as we will see later, it does have its uses elsewhere.

The :options => "xxxx" parameter lets you specify options to your underlying database. These are added to the end of the CREATE TABLE statement, right after the closing parenthesis. Although this is rarely necessary with SQLite 3, it may at times be useful with other database servers. For example, some versions of MySQL allow you to specify the initial value of the autoincrementing id column. We can pass this in through a migration as follows:

```
create_table :tickets, :options => "auto_increment = 10000" do |t|
  t.text :description
  t.timestamps
end
```

Behind the scenes, migrations will generate the following DDL from this table description when configured for MySQL:

```
CREATE TABLE "tickets" (
  "id" int(11) default null auto_increment primary key,
  "description" text,
  "created_at" datetime,
  "updated_at" datetime
) auto_increment = 10000;
```

Be careful when using the :options parameter with MySQL. The Rails MySQL database adapter sets a default option of ENGINE=InnoDB. This overrides any local defaults you may have and forces migrations to use the InnoDB storage engine for new tables. However, if you override :options, you'll lose this setting; new tables will be created using whatever database engine is configured as the default for your site. You may want to add an explicit ENGINE=InnoDB to the options string to force the standard behavior in this case. You probably want to keep using InnoDB if you're using MySQL, because this engine gives you transaction support. You might need transaction support in your application, and you'll definitely need it in your tests if you're using the default of transactional test fixtures.

Renaming Tables

If refactoring leads us to rename variables and columns, then it's probably not a surprise that we sometimes find ourselves renaming tables, too. Migrations support the rename_table method:

```
class RenameOrderHistories < ActiveRecord::Migration
  def self.up
    rename_table :order_histories, :order_notes
  end

  def self.down
    rename_table :order_notes, :order_histories
  end
end
```

Note how the down method undoes the change by renaming the table back.

Problems with rename_table

There's a subtle problem when we rename tables in migrations.

For example, let's assume that in migration 4 we create the order_histories table and populate it with some data:

```
def self.up
  create_table :order_histories do |t|
    t.integer :order_id, :null => false
    t.text :notes

    t.timestamps
  end

  order = Order.find :first
  OrderHistory.create(:order_id => order, :notes => "test")
end
```

Later, in migration 7, we rename the table order_histories to order_notes. At this point we'll also have renamed the model OrderHistory to OrderNote.

Now we decide to drop our development database and reapply all migrations. When we do so, the migrations throw an exception in migration 4: our application no longer contains a class called OrderHistory, so the migration fails.

One solution, proposed by Tim Lucas, is to create local, dummy versions of the model classes needed by a migration within the migration itself. For example, the following version of the fourth migration will work even if the application no longer has an OrderHistory class:

```
class CreateOrderHistories < ActiveRecord::Migration
►   class Order < ActiveRecord::Base; end
►   class OrderHistory < ActiveRecord::Base; end

  def self.up
    create_table :order_histories do |t|
      t.integer :order_id, :null => false
      t.text :notes

      t.timestamps
    end

  order = Order.find :first
  OrderHistory.create(:order => order_id, :notes => "test")
  end

  def self.down
    drop_table :order_histories
  end
end
```

This works as long as our model classes do not contain any additional functionality that would have been used in the migration—all we're creating here is a bare-bones version.

Defining Indices

Migrations can (and probably should) define indices for tables. For example, we might notice that once your application has a large number of orders in the database, searching based on the customer's name takes longer than we'd like. It's time to add an index using the appropriately named add_index method:

```
class AddCustomerNameIndexToOrders < ActiveRecord::Migration
  def self.up
    add_index :orders, :name
  end

  def self.down
    remove_index :orders, :name
  end
end
```

If we give add_index the optional parameter :unique => true, a unique index will be created, forcing values in the indexed column to be unique.

By default the index will be given the name *index_table_on_column*. We can override this using the :name => "somename" option. If we use the :name option when adding an index, we'll also need to specify it when removing the index.

We can create a *composite index*—an index on multiple columns—by passing an array of column names to add_index. In this case, only the first column name will be used when naming the index.

Primary Keys

Rails assumes every table has a numeric primary key (normally called id) and ensures the value of this column is unique for each new row added to a table.

We'll rephrase that.

Rails really doesn't work too well unless each table has a numeric primary key. It is less fussy about the name of the column. So, for your average Rails application, our strong advice is to go with the flow and let Rails have its id column.

If you decide to be adventurous, you can start by using a different name for the primary key column (but keeping it as an incrementing integer). Do this by specifying a :primary_key option on the create_table call:

```
create_table :tickets, :primary_key => :number do |t|
  t.text :description

  t.timestamps
end
```

This adds the number column to the table and sets it up as the primary key:

```
$ sqlite3 db/development.sqlite3 ".schema tickets"
CREATE TABLE tickets ("number" INTEGER PRIMARY KEY AUTOINCREMENT
NOT NULL, "description" text DEFAULT NULL, "created_at" datetime
DEFAULT NULL, "updated_at" datetime DEFAULT NULL);
```

The next step in the adventure might be to create a primary key that isn't an integer. Here's a clue that the Rails developers don't think this is a good idea: migrations don't let you do this (at least not directly).

Tables with No Primary Key

Sometimes we may need to define a table that has no primary key. The most common case in Rails is for *join tables*—tables with just two columns where each column is a foreign key to another table. To create a join table using migrations, we have to tell Rails not to automatically add an id column:

```
create_table :authors_books, :id => false do |t|
  t.integer :author_id, :null => false
  t.integer :book_id,   :null => false
end
```

In this case, you might want to investigate creating one or more indices on this table to speed navigation between books and authors.

23.4 Advanced Migrations

Most Rails developers use the basic facilities of migrations to create and maintain their database schemas. However, every now and then it's useful to push migrations just a bit further. This section covers some more advanced migration usage.

Using Native SQL

Migrations give you a database-independent way of maintaining your application's schema. However, if migrations don't contain the methods you need to be able to do what you need to do, you'll need to drop down to database-specific code. Rails provides two ways to do this. One is with options arguments to methods like add_column. The second is the execute method.

A common example in our migrations is the addition of foreign key constraints to a child table.

When you use options or execute, you might well be tying your migration to a specific database engine, because any SQL you provide in these two locations uses your database's native syntax.

An optional second parameter to the execute method specifies a string that will be prepended to log messages produced during the execution of this SQL.

Extending Migrations

If you look at the line item migration in the preceding section, you might wonder about the duplication between the two option parameters. It would be nice to abstract the creation of foreign key constraints into a helper method.

We could do this by adding a method such as the following to our migration source file:

```
def self.foreign_key(from_table, from_column, to_table)
  constraint_name = "fk_#{from_table}_#{to_table}"

  execute %{
    CREATE TRIGGER #{constraint_name}_insert
    BEFORE INSERT ON #{from_table}
    FOR EACH ROW BEGIN
      SELECT
        RAISE(ABORT, "constraint violation: #{constraint_name}")
      WHERE
        (SELECT id FROM #{to_table} WHERE
          id = NEW.#{from_column}) IS NULL;
    END;
  }

  execute %{
    CREATE TRIGGER #{constraint_name}_update
    BEFORE UPDATE ON #{from_table}
    FOR EACH ROW BEGIN
      SELECT
        RAISE(ABORT, "constraint violation: #{constraint_name}")
      WHERE
        (SELECT id FROM #{to_table} WHERE
          id = NEW.#{from_column}) IS NULL;
    END;
  }
```

```
  execute %{
    CREATE TRIGGER #{constraint_name}_delete
    BEFORE DELETE ON #{to_table}
    FOR EACH ROW BEGIN
      SELECT
        RAISE(ABORT, "constraint violation: #{constraint_name}")
      WHERE
        (SELECT id FROM #{from_table} WHERE
          #{from_column} = OLD.id) IS NOT NULL;
    END;
  }

end
```

(The self. is necessary because migrations run as class methods, and we need to call foreign_key in this context.)

Within the up migration, we can call this new method using this:

```
def self.up
  create_table ... do
  end
  foreign_key(:line_items, :product_id, :products)
  foreign_key(:line_items, :order_id, :orders)
end
```

However, we may want to go a step further and make our foreign_key method available to all our migrations. To do this, create a module in the application's lib directory, and add the foreign_key method.

This time, however, make it a regular instance method, not a class method:

```
module MigrationHelpers

  def foreign_key(from_table, from_column, to_table)
    constraint_name = "fk_#{from_table}_#{to_table}"

    execute %{
      CREATE TRIGGER #{constraint_name}_insert
      BEFORE INSERT ON #{from_table}
      FOR EACH ROW BEGIN
        SELECT
          RAISE(ABORT, "constraint violation: #{constraint_name}")
        WHERE
          (SELECT id FROM #{to_table} WHERE id = NEW.#{from_column}) IS NULL;
      END;
    }

    execute %{
      CREATE TRIGGER #{constraint_name}_update
      BEFORE UPDATE ON #{from_table}
      FOR EACH ROW BEGIN
        SELECT
          RAISE(ABORT, "constraint violation: #{constraint_name}")
```

```
        WHERE
          (SELECT id FROM #{to_table} WHERE id = NEW.#{from_column}) IS NULL;
      END;
    }

    execute %{
      CREATE TRIGGER #{constraint_name}_delete
      BEFORE DELETE ON #{to_table}
      FOR EACH ROW BEGIN
        SELECT
          RAISE(ABORT, "constraint violation: #{constraint_name}")
        WHERE
          (SELECT id FROM #{from_table} WHERE #{from_column} = OLD.id) IS NOT NULL;
      END;
    }
  end
end
```

We can now add this to any migration by adding the following lines to the top of our migration file:

▶ `require "migration_helpers"`

`class CreateLineItems < ActiveRecord::Migration`

▶ `    extend MigrationHelpers`

The require line brings the module definition into the migration's code, and the extend line adds the methods in the MigrationHelpers module into the migration as class methods. We can use this technique to develop and share any number of migration helpers.

(And, if you'd like to make your life even easier, someone has written a plugin[1] that automatically handles adding foreign key constraints.)

Custom Messages and Benchmarks

Although not exactly an advanced migration, something that is useful to do within advanced migrations is to output our own messages and benchmarks. We can do this with the say_with_time method:

```
def self.up
  say_with_time "Updating prices..." do
    Person.all.each do |p|
      p.update_attribute :price, p.lookup_master_price
    end
  end
end
```

say_with_time prints the string passed before the block is executed and prints the benchmark after the block completes.

---

1. http://wiki.rubyonrails.org/rails/pages/AvailableGenerators

23.5 When Migrations Go Bad

Migrations suffer from one serious problem. The underlying DDL statements that update the database schema are not transactional. This isn't a failing in Rails—most databases just don't support the rolling back of create table, alter table, and other DDL statements.

Let's look at a migration that tries to add two tables to a database:

```
class ExampleMigration < ActiveRecord::Migration
  def self.up
    create_table :one do ...
    end
    create_table :two do ...
    end
  end

  def self.down
    drop_table :two
    drop_table :one
  end
end
```

In the normal course of events, the up method adds tables, one and two, and the down method removes them.

But what happens if there's a problem creating the second table? We'll end up with a database containing table one but not table two. We can fix whatever the problem is in the migration, but now we can't apply it—if we try, it will fail because table one already exists.

We could try to roll the migration back, but that won't work. Because the original migration failed, the schema version in the database wasn't updated, so Rails won't try to roll it back.

At this point, you could mess around and manually change the schema information and drop table one. But it probably isn't worth it. Our recommendation in these circumstances is simply to drop the entire database, re-create it, and apply migrations to bring it back up-to-date. You'll have lost nothing, and you'll know you have a consistent schema.

All this discussion suggests that migrations are dangerous to use on production databases. Should you run them? We really can't say. If you have database administrators in your organization, it'll be their call. If it's up to you, you'll have to weigh the risks. But, if you decide to go for it, you really must back up your database first. Then, you can apply the migrations by going to your application's directory on the machine with the database role on your production servers and executing this command:

```
depot> RAILS_ENV=production rake db:migrate
```

This is one of those times where the legal notice at the start of this book kicks in. We're not liable if this deletes your data.

23.6 Schema Manipulation Outside Migrations

All the migration methods described so far in this chapter are also available as methods on Active Record connection objects and so are accessible within the models, views, and controllers of a Rails application.

For example, you might have discovered that a particular long-running report runs a lot faster if the orders table has an index on the city column. However, that index isn't needed during the day-to-day running of the application, and tests have shown that maintaining it slows the application appreciably.

Let's write a method that creates the index, runs a block of code, and then drops the index. This could be a private method in the model or could be implemented in a library.

```
def run_with_index(column)
  connection.add_index(:orders, column)
  begin
    yield
  ensure
    connection.remove_index(:orders, column)
  end
end
```

The statistics-gathering method in the model can use this as follows:

```
def get_city_statistics
  run_with_index(:city) do
    # .. calculate stats
  end
end
```

What We Just Did

While we had been informally using migrations throughout the development of the Depot application and even into deployment, in this chapter we saw how migrations are the basis for a principled and disciplined approach to configuration management of the schema for your database.

You learned how to create, rename, and delete columns and tables; to manage indices and keys; to apply and back out entire sets of changes; and even to mix in your own custom SQL into the mix, all in a completely reproducible manner.

At this point we've covered the externals of Rails. The next few chapters are going to delve deeper. We are going to show you how to take Rails apart and put it back together. The first stop along the way is to show you how to use select Rails classes and methods outside the context of a web server.

In this chapter, we'll see

- invoking Rails methods,
- accessing Rails application data, and
- remote manipulation of databases.

Chapter 24

Nonbrowser Applications

Previous chapters focused primarily on server-to-human communications, mostly via HTML. But not all web interactions need to directly involve a person. This chapter focuses accessing your Rails application and data from within a stand-alone script.

There are a variety of reasons why you might want to access portions of your Rails application from outside a browser. For example, you may desire to have your database loaded or synchronized periodically using a background job kicked off by a utility like cron. You may have existing applications, perhaps even Rails applications, that want to directly access the data in (another) Rails application, possibly even on a different machine. You might just want a command-line interface, not because it is required but just because.

Whatever your reasons, Rails is there for you. As you will see, you will be able to pull in as little or as much of Rails as you need to get your job done.

We will start with the assumption that your application is on the same machine as your installation of Rails and your data, and then we will proceed to describing how you can do the same things on a remote machine.

24.1 A Stand-Alone Application Using Active Record

One of the first things you will want unfettered access to is your data. You will be pleased to know that you can make full use of Active Record from within a stand-alone application. First, we will show you the "hard" way to do so (the "scare quotes" is because it isn't all that hard—remember it is Rails we are talking about here, after all). Then we will show you the easy way.

We will start with a stand-alone program that uses Active Record to wrap a table of orders in a SQLite 3 database. After finding the order with a particular id, it modifies the purchaser's name and saves the result in the database, updating the original row.

```
require "rubygems"
require "active_record"

ActiveRecord::Base.establish_connection(:adapter => "sqlite3",
    :database => "db/development.sqlite3")

class Order < ActiveRecord::Base
end

order = Order.find(1)
order.name = "Dave Thomas"
order.save
```

That's all there is to it—in this case no configuration information (apart from
the database connection stuff) is required. Active Record figured out what we
needed based on the database schema itself and took care of all of the necessary details.

Now that you have seen the "hard" way, let's see the easy way—the one where
Rails will handle the connection for you and load all of your models.

```
require "config/environment.rb"
order = Order.find(1)
order.name = "Dave Thomas"
order.save
```

For this to work, Ruby will need to find the config/environment.rb for the application that you want to load. You can do this by specifying the full path to this
file on the require statement or by including path in the RUBYLIB environment
variable. Another environment variable to watch out for is RAILS_ENV, which is
used to select from the development, test, and production environments.

Once we have required this one file, we have access to roughly the same parts
of our applications as we did when we used rails console in Section 14.4, *Would
the Last Admin to Leave...*, on page 201.

That was done all with a single require. It couldn't be easier. But believe it or
not, at times you will want to access only a portion of the features that Rails
provides, outside the context of a Rails application. We cover that next.

24.2 A Library Function Using Active Support

Active Support is a set of libraries shared by all Rails components. Some of
what's in there is intended for Rails' internal use; however, all of it is available
for use by non-Rails applications.

This could be important if you develop a Rails application and in the course
of that development you produce a set of classes or even just a set of methods that you would like to make use of in a non-Rails application. You start
by copying and pasting this code into a separate file and then find out that

it doesn't run—not because this logic is dependent on your application in any way but because it makes use of other methods and classes that Rails provides.

We will start with a brief survey of some of the most important of these and along the way show how they can be made available to your application.

Core Extensions (core-ext)

Active Support extends some of Ruby's built-in classes in interesting, useful, and sometimes whimsical ways. In this section, we'll quickly list the most popular of these core extensions.

- *Array*: second, third, fourth, fifth and forty_two. These complement the first and last methods provided by Ruby itself.

- *CGI*: escape_skipping_slashes. As the name implies, it differs from escape in that it doesn't escape slashes.

- *Class*: Accessors for class attributes, delegating accessors, inheritable readers and writers, and descendants (aka subclasses). These methods are too numerous to enumerate; see the documentation for details.

- *Date*: yesterday, future?, next_month, and many, many more.

- *Enumerable*: group_by, sum, each_with_object, index_by, many?, and exclude?.

- *File*: atomic_write, and path.

- *Float*: Adds an optional precision argument to round.

- *Hash*: diff, deep_merge, except, stringify_keys, symbolize_keys, reverse_merge, and slice. Many of these methods also have variants ending in a exclamation point.

- *Integer*: ordinalize, multiple_of?. months, years. See also *Numeric*.

- *Kernel*: debugger, breakpoint. silence_warnings, enable_warnings.

- *Module*: Accessors for module attributes, aliasing support, delegation, deprecation, internal readers and writers, synchronization, and parentage.

- *Numeric*: bytes, kilobytes, megabytes, and so on; seconds, minutes, hours, and so on.

- *Object*: blank?, present?, duplicable?, instance_values, instance_variable_names, returning, and try.

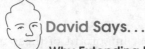

David Says...

Why Extending Base Classes Doesn't Lead to the Apocalypse

The awe that seeing 5.months + 30.minutes for the first time is usually replaced by a state of panic shortly thereafter. If everyone can just change how integers work, won't that lead to an utterly unmaintainable spaghetti land of hell? Yes, if everyone did that all the time, it would. But they don't, so it doesn't.

Don't think of Active Support as a collection of random extensions to the Ruby language that invites everyone and their brother to add their own pet feature to the string class. Think of it as a dialect of Ruby spoken universally by all Rails programmers. Because Active Support is a required part of Rails, you can always rely on that 5.months will work in any Rails application. That negates the problem of having a thousand personal dialects of Ruby.

Active Support gives us the best of both worlds when it comes to language extensions. It's contextual standardization.

- *String*: exclude?, pluralize, singularize, camelize, titleize, underscore, dasherize, demodulize, parameterize, tableize, classify, humanize, foreign_key, constantize, squish, mb_chars, at?, from, to, first, last, to_time, to_date, and try.

- *Time*: yesterday, future?, advance, and many, many more.

As you can see, this is a fairly long list. These methods tend to be fairly small; many are only a single line of code. Although you will probably only ever use a small percentage of these, all of them are available for use in your Rails application.

As you can also see, there is a lot there. Most of it you won't ever directly use. However, you'll quickly find yourself adopting a small portion of these additional methods as if they were part of the Ruby language itself. Although all of these methods are documented online,[1] the best way to learn is often to experiment directly by using rails console. Here are a few things to try:

- 2.years.ago
- [1,2,3,4].sum
- 5.gigabytes
- "man".pluralize
- String.methods.sort

---

1. http://as.rubyonrails.org/

Because there is no one best way to identify what subset works for you, simply be aware that these methods exist and check the documentation when you find yourself with what seems to be a common need because the Rails developers may have already added the method that you find missing.

Additional Active Support Classes

In addition to extending the base objects provided by Ruby, Active Support provides plenty of additional functionality. More so than with the core extensions, these classes tend to support specific needs of other Rails components, but you are welcome to make use of these functions directly.

- *BasicObject*: A backport of Ruby 1.9's class of the same name to Ruby 1.8.
- *Benchmarkable*: Measures the execution time of a block in a template and records the results to the log.
- *Cache::Store*: Various implementations of caches, based on files or memory; with synchronized or compressed as options.
- *Callbacks*: Provide hooks into the life cycle of an object.
- *Concern* and *Dependencies*: Helps manage dependencies in a modular way.
- *Configurable*: Provides a config Hash class variable.
- *Deprecation*: Provides behavior, reporting, and wrapping to support deprecation of methods.
- *Duration*: Additional methods such as ago and since.
- *Gzip*: Convenience methods to compress and decompress a String.
- *HashWithIndifferentAccess*: Allows both params[:key] and params['key'].
- *I18n*: Internationalization support.
- *Inflections*: Handles English's inconsistent rules for pluralization.
- *JSON*: JavaScript Object Notation encoding and decoding methods.
- *LazyLoadHooks*: Support for deferred initialization of modules.
- *Memoizable*: Caches the result of a method call.
- *MessageEncryptor*: Encrypts values that are to be stored someplace untrustworthy.
- *MessageVerifier*: Generates and verifies signed messages (prevents tampering).
- *MultiByte*: Encoding support (primarily for Ruby 1.8.7).
- *Notifications*: Instrumentation API.
- *OptionMerger*: Deep merge lambda expressions.
- *OrderedHash* and *OrderedOptions*: Provides ordered hash support (primarily for Ruby 1.8.7).

- *Railtie*: Defines core objects that the rest of the framework can depend on.
- *Rescueable*: Eases exception handling.
- *SecureRandom*: Generates random numbers suitable for generating session keys in HTTP cookies.
- *StringInquirer*: Provides a prettier way to test for equality.
- *TestCase*: Testing framework independent interface to test cases.
- *Time* and *TimeWithZone*: Even more support for time calculations and conversions.

So although this book will not go into the (currently) forty-nine methods and counting that, for example, TimeWithZone alone provides, the previous list will enable you to find the functions you need in the guides and API documentation. But what this book will do is show you how you can use these methods in your stand-alone application:

```
require "rubygems"
require "active_support/time"
Time.zone = 'Eastern Time (US & Canada)'
puts Time.zone.now
```

So if, like most people, you find yourself addicted to one or more of these extensions, you can simply require what you need (for example, require "active_support/basic_object" or require "active_support/core_ext") or pull in everything with require "active_support/all".

Using Action View Helpers

OK, so although this doesn't exactly fall under the category of Active Support, it is close enough. What applies to Active Support also applies to other parts of Rails, though most routing, controllers, and Action View methods tend to be relevant only to the processing of an active web request.

One notable exception is some of the Action View helpers. Here's an example of how you can access an Action View helper from a stand-alone application:

```
require "rubygems"
require "action_view"
require "action_view/helpers"
include ActionView::Helpers::DateHelper
puts distance_of_time_in_words_to_now(Time.parse("December 25"))
```

All in all, this is only slightly more work than getting access to the much more commonly needed Active Support methods, but it's still quite doable.

At this point, we've covered accessing some or all of Rails functionality from scripts running on the same machine as the server; now let's move on to accessing your Rails application remotely.

24.3 A Remote Application Using Active Resource

When writing an application, you may very well find yourself in a situation where not all of the data resides neatly tucked away and categorized in your database. It may not be in a database. It might not even be on your machine at all. That's what web services are about. And Active Resource is Rails' take on web services. Note that these are web services with a lowercase *w* and a lowercase *s*, not Web Services as in SOAP and WSDL and UDDI.

Accessing and Updating Simple Attributes

We will demonstrate Active Resource with live examples, picking up where we left off with the Depot application. The key difference is that this time we will be remotely accessing the Depot application via a client application. And for a client, we will use rails console. First, check to make sure the Depot server is running. Then let's create the client:

```
work> rails new depot_client
work> cd depot_client
```

Now, let's write a stub for the Product model:

depot_client/app/models/product.rb

```
class Product < ActiveResource::Base
  self.site = 'http://dave:secret@localhost:3000/'
end
```

There really isn't much to it. The Product class inherits from the ActiveResource::Base class. Inside, there is a single statement that identifies the username, password, host name, and port number. In a real-life application, the user and password would be obtained separately and not hard-coded into the model, but at this point, we are just exploring the concepts. Let's put that stub to use:

```
depot_client> rails console
Loading development environment (Rails 3.0.5)
>> Product.find(3).title
=> "Programming Ruby 1.9"
```

Success! Let's be a little bolder. How about we have a $5 off sale on this book?

```
depot_client> rails console
Loading development environment (Rails 3.0.5)
>> p = Product.find(3)
=> #<Product:0x282e7ac @prefix_options={}, ... >
>> puts p.price
49.5
=> nil
>> p.price-=5
=> #<BigDecimal:7f88f8ebfef0,'0.445E2',18(36)>
>> p.save
=> true
```

That simply seems too good to be true. But we can verify this very easily by simply visiting the store in our browser:

We don't know about you, but to us Active Resource seems to be so sufficiently advanced technology as to be indistinguishable from magic.

Relationships and Collections

Flush with success with Products, let's move on to Orders. We start by writing a stub:

`depot_client/app/models/order.rb`

```
class Order < ActiveResource::Base
  self.site = 'http://dave:secret@localhost:3000/'
end
```

Looks good. Let's try it:

```
depot_client> rails console
>> Order.find(1).name
=> "Dave Thomas"
>> Order.find(1).line_items
NoMethodError: undefined method 'line_items' for #<Order:0x2818970>
```

OK, at this point, we need to understand how things work under the covers. Back to theory, but not to worry, it's not much.

The way the magic works is that it exploits all the REST and XML interfaces that the scaffolding provides. To get a list of products, it goes to http://localhost:3000/products.xml. To fetch product #2, it will GET http://localhost:3000/products/2.xml. To save changes to product #2, it will PUT the updated product to http://localhost:3000/products/2.xml.

So, that's what the magic is—producing URLs, much like what was discussed in Chapter 20, *Action Dispatch and Action Controller*, on page 301. And producing (and consuming) XML, as we discussed in Section 20.1, *Selecting a Data Representation*, on page 309. Let's see that in action. First we make line_items a nested resource under orders. We do that by editing the config.routes file in the server application:

```
resources :orders do
  resources :line_items
end
```

Now change the line items controller to look for the :order_id in the params and treat it as part of the line item. The problem is that we changed what this method was expecting on page 106. So, we simply modify the code to handle both types of input:

depot_u/app/controllers/line_items_controller.rb

```
    def create
      @cart = current_cart
►     if params[:line_item]
►       # ActiveResource
►       params[:line_item][:order_id] = params[:order_id]
►       @line_item = LineItem.new(params[:line_item])
►     else
►       # HTML forms
        product = Product.find(params[:product_id])
        @line_item = @cart.add_product(product.id)
►     end

      respond_to do |format|
        if @line_item.save
          format.html { redirect_to(store_url) }
          format.js   { @current_item = @line_item }
          format.xml  { render :xml => @line_item,
            :status => :created, :location => @line_item }
        else
          format.html { render :action => "new" }
          format.xml  { render :xml => @line_item.errors,
            :status => :unprocessable_entity }
        end
      end
    end
```

Let's fetch the data, just to see what it looks like:

```
<?xml version="1.0" encoding="UTF-8"?>
<line-items type="array">
  <line-item>
    <price type="decimal">49.5</price>
    <created-at type="datetime">2010-02-11T03:11:44Z</created-at>
    <product-id type="integer">3</product-id>
    <quantity type="integer">1</quantity>
    <order-id type="integer">1</order-id>
    <updated-at type="datetime">2010-02-11T03:12:11Z</updated-at>
    <id type="integer">10</id>
    <cart-id type="integer" nil="true"></cart-id>
  </line-item>
  <line-item>
    <price type="decimal">42.95</price>
    <created-at type="datetime">2010-02-11T03:14:18Z</created-at>
    <product-id type="integer">2</product-id>
```

```
      <quantity type="integer">2</quantity>
      <order-id type="integer">102</order-id>
      <updated-at type="datetime">2010-02-11T03:14:25Z</updated-at>
      <id type="integer">11</id>
      <cart-id type="integer" nil="true"></cart-id>
    </line-item>
</line-items>
```

Now let's give Dave 20 percent off on his first purchase:

```
>> li = LineItem.find(:all, :params => {:order_id=>1}).first
=> #<LineItem:0x2823334 @prefix_options={:order_id=>1}, ... >
>> puts li.price
39.6
=> nil
>> li.price*=0.8
=> 31.68
>> li.save
=> true
```

So, everything here is working as it should. One thing to note is the use of :params. This is processed exactly as you would expect for URL generations. Parameters that match the site template provided for the ActiveResource class will be replaced. And parameters that remain will be tacked on as query parameters. The server uses the URL for routing and makes the parameters available as params array.

Finally, let's add a line item to an order:

```
>> li2 = LineItem.new(:order_id=>1, :product_id=>2, :quantity=>1,
>> :price=>0.0)
=> #<LineItem:0x7fd986812b00 @prefix_options={},
@attributes={"price"=>0, "product_id"=>2, "quantity"=>1, "order_id"=>1}>
>> li2.save
=> true
```

Pulling It All Together

Although ActiveResource at first seems like a bit of magic, it simply relies heavily on the concepts described earlier in this book. Here are a few pointers:

- Authentication uses the underlying authentication mechanism that your website already supports and doesn't go against the grain of the Web, like some other protocols tend to do. In any case, nobody can do anything with Active Resource that they couldn't already do.

  Be aware that if you are using basic authentication, you want to use Transport Layer Security (TLS), also known as Secure Sockets Layer (SSL) or HTTPS, to ensure that passwords can't be sniffed.

- Although Active Resource doesn't make effective use of sessions or cookies, this doesn't mean your server isn't continuing to produce them.

Either you want to turn off sessions for the interfaces used by Active Resource or you want to make sure you use cookie-based sessions. Otherwise, the server will end up managing a lot of sessions that are never needed. See Section 20.3, *Rails Sessions*, on page 323 for more details.

• In Section 20.1, *Adding Additional Actions*, on page 308, we described collections and members. ActiveResource defines four class methods for dealing with collections and four instance methods for dealing with members. The names of these methods are get, post, put, and delete. The method names determine the underlying HTTP method used.

The first parameter in each of these methods is the name of the collection or member. This information is simply used to construct the URL. You may specify additional :params, which either will match values in the self.site or will be added as query parameters.

You will likely end up using this a lot more than you would expect. Instead of fetching all orders, you might want to provide an interface that fetches only the orders that are recent or are overdue. What you can do in any of these methods is limited only by your imagination.

• Active Resource maps HTTP status codes into exceptions:

301, 302 ActiveResource::Redirection

400 ActiveResource::BadRequest

401 ActiveResource::UnauthorizedAccess

403 ActiveResource::ForbiddenAccess

404 ActiveResource::ResourceNotFound

405 ActiveResource::MethodNotAllowed

409 ActiveResource::ResourceConflict

422 ActiveResource::ResourceInvalid

401..499 ActiveResource::ClientError

• You can provide client-side validations by overriding validation methods in the ActiveResource base class. This behaves the same as validation does in ActiveRecord. Server-side validation failures result in a response code of 422, and you can access such failures in the same manner. We covered validation in Section 7.1, *Iteration B1: Validating!*, on page 75.

• Although the default format is XML, you can also use JSON as an alternative. Simply set self.format to :json in your client classes. Be aware that your client will see dates as ISO 8601/RFC 3339–formatted strings and will see decimals as instances of Float if you do so.

- In addition to self.site, you can separately set self.user and self.password.

- self.timeout enables you to specify how long a web service request should wait, in seconds, before giving up and raising a Timeout::Error.

What We Just Did

We broke free from the constraints of the browser and accessed Active Support, Action View, and Active Record methods directly from stand-alone script. This enables us to produce scripts that can be run from the command line, integrated into existing applications, or run periodically and automatically using facilities such as cron.

Finally, we used Active Resource to break free of the constraints of needing to run your script on the same machine as the application. Although this requires slightly more setup, it provides a workable, and secure, means to access the data you have inside a Rails application.

Next up: we will explore other separately installable components that are included in the bundle when you install Rails.

In this chapter, we'll see

- XML and HTML templates,
- managing application dependencies,
- scripting tasks, and
- interfacing with a web server.

Chapter 25

Rails' Dependencies

At this point, we have covered base Rails itself. But there is much more to the story. Much of what makes Rails great is functionality provided by components that Rails builds upon.

These components should be familiar, because you have used each one. Atom templates, HTML templates, rake db:migrate, bundle install, and rails server should all be familiar by now.

Although this chapter goes beyond your normal day-to-day activities and shows how each component can be used in isolation, it is not meant to be an exhaustive description of any of these components. Each component requires a small book in itself to do it justice. Instead, the intent of this chapter is to introduce you to a number of key components in order to provide the background necessary for you to begin self-directed explorations.

We start by introducing you to a number of such dependencies, beginning with the underlying templating engines that power views. Then we will explore *Bundler*, which is the component that is used to manage dependencies. Finally, we will show how these pieces are put together using Rack and Rake.

25.1 Generating XML with Builder

Builder is a freestanding library that lets you express structured text (such as XML) in code. A builder template (in a file with an .xml.builder extension) contains Ruby code that uses the Builder library to generate XML.

Here's a simple builder template that outputs a list of product names and prices in XML:

`depot_t/app/views/products/index.xml.builder`

```
xml.div(:class => "productlist") do

  xml.timestamp(Time.now)

  @products.each do |product|
    xml.product do
      xml.productname(product.title)
      xml.price(product.price, :currency => "USD")
    end
  end
end
```

If this reminds you of the template you created for use with the Atom helper in Section 12.2, *Iteration G2: Atom Feeds*, on page 159, that's because the Atom helper is built upon the functionality of Builder.

With an appropriate collection of products (passed in from the controller), the template might produce something such as this:

```
<div class="productlist">
  <timestamp>Wed Jul 21 07:01:41 -0400 2010</timestamp>
  <product>
    <productname>Debug It!</productname>
    <price currency="USD">34.95</price>
  </product>
  <product>
    <productname>Programming Ruby 1.9</productname>

    <price currency="USD">49.5</price>
  </product>
  <product>
    <productname>Web Design for Developers</productname>
    <price currency="USD">42.95</price>
  </product>
</div>
```

Notice how Builder has taken the names of methods and converted them to XML tags; when we said xml.price, it created a tag called *<price>* whose contents were the first parameter and whose attributes were set from the subsequent hash. If the name of the tag you want to use conflicts with an existing method name, you'll need to use the tag! method to generate the tag:

```
xml.tag!("id", product.id)
```

Builder can generate just about any XML you need. It supports namespaces, entities, processing instructions, and even XML comments. Take a look at the Builder documentation for details.

Although HTML looks superficially a lot like XML, it is enough of a different beast that a different templating engine is generally used to produce HTML. We cover that next.

25.2 Generating HTML with ERb

At its simplest, an ERb template is just a regular HTML file. If a template contains no dynamic content, it is simply sent as is to the user's browser. The following is a perfectly valid html.erb template:

```
<h1>Hello, Dave!</h1>
<p>
  How are you, today?
</p>
```

However, applications that just render static templates tend to be a bit boring to use. We can spice them up using dynamic content:

```
<h1>Hello, Dave!</h1>
<p>
  It's <%= Time.now %>
</p>
```

If you're a JSP programmer, you'll recognize this as an inline expression. Erb evaluates any code between <%= and %>, converts the results into a string using to_s, and finally substitutes that string into the resulting page. The expression inside the tags can be arbitrary code:

```
<h1>Hello, Dave!</h1>
<p>
  It's <%= require 'date'
          DAY_NAMES = %w{ Sunday Monday Tuesday Wednesday
                          Thursday Friday Saturday }
          today = Date.today
          DAY_NAMES[today.wday]
      %>
</p>
```

Putting lots of business logic into a template is generally considered to be a Very Bad Thing, and you'll risk incurring the wrath of the coding police should you get caught. We discussed a much better way of handling this with helpers on page 343.

Sometimes you need code in a template that doesn't directly generate any output. If you leave the equals sign off the opening tag, the contents are executed, but nothing is inserted into the template. We could have written the previous example as follows:

```
<% require 'date'
   DAY_NAMES = %w{ Sunday Monday Tuesday Wednesday
                   Thursday Friday Saturday }
   today = Date.today
%>
```

```
<h1>Hello, Dave!</h1>
<p>
  It's <%= DAY_NAMES[today.wday] %>.
  Tomorrow is <%= DAY_NAMES[(today + 1).wday] %>.
</p>
```

In the JSP world, this is called a *scriptlet*. Again, many folks will chastise you if they discover you adding code to templates. Ignore them—they're falling prey to dogma. There's nothing wrong with putting code in a template. Just don't put too much code in there (and especially don't put business logic in a template). As we have already seen, you can use helper methods to successfully resist this temptation.

You can think of the HTML text between code fragments as if each line were being written by a Ruby program. The <%...%> fragments are added to that same program. The HTML is interwoven with the explicit code that you write. As a result, code between <% and %> can affect the output of HTML in the rest of the template.

For example, consider this template:

```
<% 3.times do %>
Ho!<br/>
<% end %>
```

For safety reasons,[1] when you insert a value using <%=...%>, the results will be HTML escaped before being placed directly into the output stream. This is generally what you want.

If, however, the text you're substituting contains HTML that you *want* to be interpreted, this will cause the HTML tags to be escaped—if you create a string containing hello and then substitute it into a template, the user will see hello rather than *hello*. Rails provides two helpers to address this case.

The *raw* method will cause the string to pass right on through to the output without escaping. This provides the most amount of flexibility, as well as the least amount of security.

The *sanitize* method offers some protection. It takes a string containing HTML and cleans up dangerous elements: *<form>* and *<script>* tags are escaped, and *on=* attributes and links starting *javascript:* are removed.

The product descriptions in our Depot application were rendered as HTML (that is, they were marked as safe using the *raw* method). This allowed us to embed formatting information in them. If we allowed people outside our organization to enter these descriptions, it would be prudent to use the *sanitize* method to reduce the risk of our site being attacked successfully.

---

1. http://www.owasp.org/index.php/Cross-site_Scripting_%28XSS%29

These two templating engines are just two of the many gems that Rails depends on. At this point, it makes sense to talk about how such dependencies are managed.

25.3 Managing Dependencies with Bundler

Dependency management is a deceptively hard problem. During development, you may choose to install updated versions of gems that you depend on. Once you do this, you may find yourself not being able to reproduce problems that occur in production because your runs are picking up different versions of the gems your application depends on. Or perhaps you see problems that don't exist in production.

It turns out that dependencies are every bit as important to manage as your application source code or database schemas. If you are developing as part of a team, you want every member of the team to be using the same version of the dependencies. When you deploy, you want to ensure that the version of the dependencies that you tested with are installed on the target machine and are the ones actually used in production.

Bundler[2] takes care of this, based on a file named Gemfile that is placed in the top of your application directory. In this file, you list the dependencies of your application. Let's take a closer look at the Gemfile for the Depot application:

depot_u/Gemfile

```
source 'http://rubygems.org'

gem 'rails', '3.0.5'

# Bundle edge Rails instead:
# gem 'rails', :git => 'git://github.com/rails/rails.git'

gem 'sqlite3'
group :production do
  gem 'mysql'
end

# Use unicorn as the web server
# gem 'unicorn'

# Deploy with Capistrano
gem 'capistrano'

# To use debugger (ruby-debug for Ruby 1.8.7+, ruby-debug19 for Ruby 1.9.2+)
# gem 'ruby-debug'
# gem 'ruby-debug19', :require => 'ruby-debug'
```

---

2. http://gembundler.com/

```
# Bundle the extra gems:
# gem 'bj'
# gem 'nokogiri'
# gem 'sqlite3-ruby', :require => 'sqlite3'
# gem 'aws-s3', :require => 'aws/s3'

gem 'will_paginate', '>= 3.0.pre'

# Bundle gems for the local environment. Make sure to
# put test-only gems in this group so their generators
# and rake tasks are available in development mode:
# group :development, :test do
#   gem 'webrat'
# end
```

The first line specifies where to find new gems and new versions of existing gems. Feel free to repeat this line in order to list your own private gem repositories.

The next line lists what version of Rails to load. Note that it specifies a specific version. After this is a comment that you could use as an alternative in order to run the latest version of Rails.

The remaining lines list a few gems that you are using and a few gems that you might consider using. Some are placed in groups named :development, :test, or :production and will be made available only in those environments. Others include an optional :require parameter, which specifies the name to use on a require statement for the cases where it differs from the gem name.

On the line for will_paginate you see a version specifier that is preceded by a comparison operator. Although Gemfile files support a number of such operators, only two are commonly used. >= is for the unfortunately all too rare condition where the author of the Gemfile can be trusted to maintain strict backward compatibility so all that is needed to be specified is a minimum version number.

~> is more widely recommended. Essentially all of the parts of the version, with the exception of the last part, must be matched exactly, and the last part specifies a minimum. So, ~> 3.1.4 matches any version that starts with a 3.1 and is not less than 3.1.4. Similarly, ~> 3.0 means any version string that starts with a 3..

A Gemfile has a companion file, named Gemfile.lock. This second file is generally updated by one of two commands: bundle install and bundle update. The difference between the two is rather subtle.

Before proceeding, it is helpful to look at a Gemfile.lock file. Here is a small excerpt:

```
GEM
  specs:
    abstract (1.0.0)
    builder (2.1.2)
    capistrano (2.5.19)
      highline
      net-scp (>= 1.0.0)
      net-sftp (>= 2.0.0)
      net-ssh (>= 2.0.14)
      net-ssh-gateway (>= 1.0.0)
    erubis (2.6.6)
      abstract (>= 1.0.0)
```

bundle install will use the Gemfile.lock as a starting point and install only the versions of the various gems as specified in this file. For this reason, it is important that this file gets checked into your version control system, because this will ensure that your colleagues and deployment targets will all be using the exact same configuration.

bundle update will (unsurprisingly) update one or more named gems and will update the Gemfile.lock accordingly. If you want to use a specific version of a particular gem, the workflow would be to edit the Gemfile to express your constraints and then run bundle update listing the gems that you want to update. If you don't specify a list of gems, Bundler will attempt to update all gems—this is generally not recommended, particular when close to deployment.

Bundler also has a runtime component that is used to ensure that your application strictly loads only the versions of the gems listed in Gemfile.lock. We will explore that further by looking into how the server operates.

25.4 Interfacing with the Web Server with Rack

Rails runs your application in the context of a web server. So far, we have used two separate web servers: WEBRick, which comes built into the Ruby language itself, and Phusion Passenger, which integrates with the Apache HTTP web server. There are a number of other choices available, including Mongrel, Lighttpd, and Unicorn.

Based on this, you might come to the conclusion that Rails has code that allows it to plug into each of these web servers. In earlier releases of Rails, this was true; as of Rails 2.3, this integration was delegated to a gem named Rack.

So, Rails integrates with Rack, Rack integrates with (for example) Passenger, and Passenger integrates with Apache httpd.

Although generally this integration is invisible and taken care of for you when you run the command rails server, a file named config.ru is provided that allows you to directly start your application under Rack:

`depot_u/config.ru`

```
# This file is used by Rack-based servers to start the application.

require ::File.expand_path('../config/environment',  __FILE__)
run Depot::Application
```

You can use this file to start your Rails server with the following command:

```
rackup
```

Starting your server in this way is completely equivalent to running rails server. To demonstrate the power of what you can do with Rack alone, let's start over with a bare-bones Rack application:

`depot_u/app/store.rb`

```
require 'builder'
require 'active_record'

ActiveRecord::Base.establish_connection(
  :adapter => 'sqlite3',
  :database => 'db/development.sqlite3')

class Product < ActiveRecord::Base
end

class StoreApp
  def call(env)
    x = Builder::XmlMarkup.new :indent=>2

    x.declare! :DOCTYPE, :html
    x.html do
      x.head do
        x.title 'Pragmatic Bookshelf'
      end
      x.body do
        x.h1 'Pragmatic Bookshelf'

        Product.all.each do |product|
          x.h2 product.title
          x << "      #{product.description}\n"
          x.p product.price
        end
      end
    end

    response = Rack::Response.new(x.target!)
    response['Content-Type'] = 'text/html'
    response.finish
  end
end
```

In this application, we are taking advantage of a number of things we have learned so far. The first thing we do is to directly require active_record and builder. Then we establish a connection with our database and define a class for our Product. We won't need to do any of this once we integrate this application with our Rails application, but for now we are going totally bare-bones.

Then comes the application itself. It is a simple class that defines a single method named call. This method accepts a single parameter named env that contains information about the request and is not used by this application.

This application uses Builder to create a simple HTML rendering of a product list and then builds a response, sets the content type, and calls finish.

By creating a new rackup file, we can run this as a stand-alone application:

depot_u/store.ru
```
require 'rubygems'
require 'bundler/setup'

require './app/store'

use Rack::ShowExceptions

map '/store' do
  run StoreApp.new
end
```

The first thing this script does is to initialize Bundler, which will make available the right versions of all of the gems that will be required. Then it requires the store application.

Next, it pulls one of the standard *middleware* classes provided with Rack; this one formats a stack traceback when things go wrong. Middleware in Rack is like filters in Rails—both can inspect requests and adjust the responses produced.

You can see the list of middlewares that Rails provides for Rails applications using the command rake middleware.

Finally, we map the store URI to this application.

We can start this application using the rackup command:

```
rackup store.ru
```

By default, this rackup starts servers using port 9292 instead of port 3000. You can select the port using the -p option.

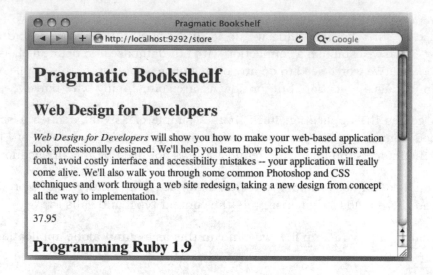

Figure 25.1: A MINIMAL, BUT WORKABLE, PRODUCT LISTING

Visiting this page using your browser results in the rather plain rendering of the product listings, as shown in Figure 25.1.

The disadvantage of a native Rack application as compared to a Rails application is that less is taken care of for it. The primary advantage is that it therefore it is possible to avoid some of the overhead of Rails and therefore process more requests per second.

In most cases, you won't want to create a completely stand-alone application but will want to have portions of your site bypass Rails' controller processing. You do this by defining a route:

depot_u/config/routes.rb

```
► require './app/store'
Depot::Application.routes.draw do
►   match 'store' => StoreApp.new
    get 'admin' => 'admin#index'
    controller :sessions do
      get    'login'  => :new
      post   'login'  => :create
      delete 'logout' => :destroy
    end
    scope '(:locale)' do
      resources :users
      resources :orders do
        resources :line_items
      end
```

```
      resources :line_items
      resources :carts
      resources :products do
        get :who_bought, :on => :member
      end
      root :to => 'store#index', :as => 'store'
    end
end
```

The server is not the only place where Rails components are used. We complete this chapter with a description of a tool you can use to orchestrate the execution of tasks.

25.5 Automating Tasks with Rake

Rake is a program that often is taken for granted. It is used to automate tasks, particularly tasks that may have a number of dependencies. The tasks are defined by the Rakefile that you will find in your application's root directory.

db:setup is an example of such a task. To see what subtasks are involved, run Rake with the --trace and --dry-run options:

```
$ rake --trace --dry-run db:setup
(in /home/rubys/work/depot)
** Invoke db:setup (first_time)
** Invoke db:create (first_time)
** Invoke db:load_config (first_time)
** Invoke rails_env (first_time)
** Execute (dry run) rails_env
** Execute (dry run) db:load_config
** Execute (dry run) db:create
** Invoke db:schema:load (first_time)
** Invoke environment (first_time)
** Execute (dry run) environment
** Execute (dry run) db:schema:load
** Invoke db:seed (first_time)
** Invoke db:abort_if_pending_migrations (first_time)
** Invoke environment
** Execute (dry run) db:abort_if_pending_migrations
** Execute (dry run) db:seed
** Execute (dry run) db:setup
```

Executing the right steps in the right order is vital for repeatable deployments; that's why this particular task was used in Section 16.1, *Loading the Database*, on page 231.

You can see a list of available tasks using rake --tasks. The tasks that Rails provides are just a starter set; you are welcome to create more tasks. You do so simply by creating new files in the lib/tasks directory containing Ruby code.

Here's an example that will back up the production database:

`depot_u/lib/tasks/db_backup.rake`

```
namespace :db do

  desc "Backup the production database"
  task :backup => :environment do
    backup_dir  = ENV['DIR'] || File.join(Rails.root, 'db', 'backup')

    source = File.join(Rails.root, 'db', "production.db")
    dest   = File.join(backup_dir, "production.backup")

    makedirs backup_dir
    sh "sqlite3 #{source} .dump > #{dest}"
  end

end
```

The first line contains a namespace. We put this backup task in the db namespace.

The second line contains a description. This description will show up when you list tasks. If you run the rails --tasks command again, you will see that your new task is included along with the ones that Rails provided.

The next line contains the task as well as any dependencies it might have. Depending on environment is roughly equivalent to loading everything that rails console provides.

The block passed to the task is standard Ruby code. In our example, we determine the source and destination directories (where the destination will default to db/backup but can be overridden by a DIR parameter on the command line), then proceed to make the backup directory (if necessary), and finally execute the sqlite3 dump command.

25.6 Survey of Rails' Dependencies

A good place to start is by looking back at the Gemfile.lock file. Some of the names you find in there will be obvious; others will not. To assist with this exploration, the following is a brief description of the names that you will find in there.

Of course, as Rails evolves, this list will inevitably change. But by knowing the name of the component, you have the starting point for further exploration. A good way to find out more given the name is to go to RubyGems.org,[3] enter the gem name in the search field, select the gem, and then click either the Documentation or Homepage link.

---

3. http://rubygems.org

arel
> A relational algebra; used by Active Record

actionmailer
> Part of Rails; see Chapter 13, *Task H: Sending Mail*, on page 169

actionpack
> Part of Rails; see Chapter 20, *Action Dispatch and Action Controller*, on page 301

activemodel
> Support for Active Record and Active Resource

activerecord
> Part of Rails; see Chapter 19, *Active Record*, on page 265

activeresource
> Part of Rails; see Section 24.3, *A Remote Application Using Active Resource*, on page 399

activesupport
> Part of Rails; see Section 24.2, *A Library Function Using Active Support*, on page 394

rails
> Container for the entire framework

railties
> Part of Rails; see the bottom of Section 26.5, *Finding More at RailsPlug-ins.org*, on page 430 for links to more information on the subject

abstract
> A library that enables you to define abstract methods in Ruby

builder
> A simple way to create XML markup; see Section 25.1, *Generating XML with Builder*, on page 405

capistrano
> Welcome to easy deployment; see Section 16.2, *Iteration K2: Deploying Remotely with Capistrano*, on page 232

erubis
> The implementation of ERb that Rails uses; see Section 25.2, *Generating HTML with ERb*, on page 407

highline
> IO library for command-line interfaces

i18n

Internationalization support; see Chapter 15, *Task J: Internationalization*, on page 205

mail

Mail support; see Chapter 13, *Task H: Sending Mail*, on page 169

mime-types

Determine file type based on extension, used by mail

mysql

Production database supported by Active Record; see Section 16.1, *Using MySQL for the Database*, on page 229

net-scp

Copy files securely

net-sftp

Transfer files securely

net-ssh

Connect to remote servers securely

net-ssh-gateway

Tunneling connections over SSH

polyglot

Custom language loaders

rack

Interface between Rails and web servers; see Section 25.4, *Interfacing with the Web Server with Rack*, on page 411

rack-cache

HTTP caching for rack

rack-cache-purge

Support for purging Rack-cache

rack-mount

Rack router; see Section 20.1, *Dispatching Requests to Controllers*, on page 301

rack-test

Testing API for routes; see Section 20.1, *Testing Routes*, on page 310

rake

Task automation; see Section 25.5, *Automating Tasks with Rake*, on page 415

sqlite3

> Development database supported by Active Record

thor

> Scripting framework used by the rails command

treetop

> Text parsing library, used by mail

tzinfo

> Time zone support

will_paginate

> Pagination of query results; see Section 12.3, *Iteration G3: Pagination*, on page 163

What We Just Did

We explored a small number of Rails' dependencies and then showed how dependencies themselves can be managed, integrated with a web server, and finally orchestrated from the command line. Along the way, we finally found out what the Rakefile, Gemfile, and Gemfile.lock files are that are in the top of our application directory.

Now that we have gone deeper into Rails, the next place to go is to branch out and to cover external plugins that can be used to extend the base Rails package that you get when you install Rails.

In this chapter, we'll see

- adding new classes to your application,
- adding Rake tasks and view helpers,
- adding a new templating language, and
- adding a generator and replacing the JavaScript libraries.

Chapter 26

Rails Plugins

Since the beginning of this book, we've talked incessantly about convention over configuration in that Rails has sensible defaults for just about everything. And more recently in the book, we've described Rails in terms of the underlying gems that you get when you install Rails. Now it is time to put those two thoughts together and reveal that the initial set of gems that Rails provides you is, itself, a sensible set of defaults—ones that you can both add to and change.

With Rails 3.0, gems are the primary way in which you *plug in* new functionality. Instead of describing this in the abstract, we will select a few plugins and use them to illustrate different aspects of how plugins are installed and what plugins can do. The fact that many of these plugins turn out to be immediately useful for your day-to-day work is simply a bonus!

Let's start with a simple plugin that can literally make you money.

26.1 Credit Card Processing with Active Merchant

Back on page 146 we mentioned that we were temporarily punting on the handling of credit cards. Being able to actually charge a customer is clearly an important part of taking an order. Although this functionality isn't built into the core of Rails, there is a gem that provides this functionality for us.

You've already seen how you control what gems get loaded by your application: you do this by editing your Gemfile. Since we are going to cover a number of such gems in this chapter, let's go ahead and add all of the ones that we will cover at once. You can actually add these any place you like; we've chosen to do so immediately under the line adding the dependency on will_paginate.

> depot_v/Gemfile

```
gem 'will_paginate', '>= 3.0.pre'
```
▶ `gem 'activemerchant', '~> 1.10.0'`
▶ `gem 'haml', '~> 3.0.18'`
▶ `gem 'jquery-rails', '~> 0.2.2'`

You will note that we follow best practices by specifying a minimum version and effectively specifying an upper bound on the version number so that this demo will pick a version that is unlikely to contain an incompatible change.

As for the gems we added, we will cover each in a separate section. This section will focus on Active Merchant.[1]

Once you have edited your Gemfile, you can go ahead install these gems, as well as any gems that they depend on, via bundle install. Additionally, if you have a Rails server up and running, restart it to pick up these changes. We won't be using the server in this section but will shortly. Make sure that the server is running the Depot application.

To demonstrate this functionality, we will create a small script, which we will place in the script directory:

> depot_v/script/creditcard.rb

```
credit_card = ActiveMerchant::Billing::CreditCard.new(
  :number       => '4111111111111111',
  :month        => '8',
  :year         => '2009',
  :first_name => 'Tobias',
  :last_name  => 'Luetke',
  :verification_value  => '123'
)

puts "Is #{credit_card.number} valid?  #{credit_card.valid?}"
```

There is not much to this script. It creates an instance of a ActiveMerchant::Billing::CreditCard class and then calls the valid? on this object. Let's run it.

```
$ rails runner script/creditcard.rb
Is 4111111111111111 valid?  false
```

There's not much to it; it just worked. Note that no require statements were necessary; simply listing the gem you want in your Gemfile makes the function available to your application.

At this point, you should be able to see how you could use this functionality in the Depot application. You know how to add a field to the Orders table via a migration. You know you how to add that field to the view. You know how to add validation logic to your model, which calls the valid? method that we used earlier. If you go to the merchant site, you can even find out how to authorize

---

1. http://www.activemerchant.org/

and capture a payment, though this does require you to have a login and a password with an existing commerce gateway. Once that is set up, you know how to call this logic from your controller.

Just think: all of that was made possible by the addition of a single line to your Gemfile.

As we stated at the beginning of this chapter, adding gems to your Gemfile is the preferred way to extend Rails 3.0. The advantages of doing so are numerous: all of your dependencies are tracked by Bundler, are all preloaded for immediate use by your application, and can be packed for easy deployment.

At the time of this writing, the instructions for installing ActiveMerchant have not been updated on their website: they describe three other ways to install this function, depending on the version of Rails you are using. What we have described is the method you should use whenever possible.

Next, we will cover an extension that is not made available as a gem.

26.2 Saving Bandwidth with Asset Packager

Inside your Depot application you now have multiple CSS files. These files are not as compact as they could possibly be; instead, they are written in a way that makes your development and maintenance easier. However, if your site gets significant traffic, it might make sense to deliver this same content in fewer requests and to have those requests serve fewer bytes.

This is the function that the Asset Packager plugin[2] provides. Unlike Active Merchant, Asset Packager is not currently made available as a gem. The primary disadvantages of nongem plugins vs. gem plugins is that you don't get any dependency tracking, a way to verify that the plugin is compatible with the version of other gems you have installed, or any convenient way to check for updates.

Because this function has no dependencies other than Rails itself, it has no need for dependency tracking. Also unlike Active Merchant, Asset Packager is not independent of Rails; it actually extends Rails functionality, which is why we are covering it now.

To install Asset Packager, use the rails plugin install command:

```
$ rails plugin install git://github.com/sbecker/asset_packager.git
```

This causes files to be placed into your vendor/plugins directory. These files can be checked into Git and deployed using Capistrano.

---

2. http://synthesis.sbecker.net/pages/asset_packager

What the Asset Packager plugin does is to add new Rake tasks that you can use. You already know how to list Rake tasks, and that is by using the -T option:

```
$ rake -T asset
(in /home/rubys/work/depot)
rake asset:packager:build_all    # Merge and compress assets
rake asset:packager:create_yml   # Generate asset_packages.yml from existing assets
rake asset:packager:delete_all   # Delete all asset builds
```

The very first thing you are going to want to do is to create a YAML file. You can build this on your own, but you might as well use the task that was provided to accomplish this:

```
$ rake asset:packager:create_yml
(in /home/rubys/work/depot)
config/asset_packages.yml example file created!
Please reorder files under 'base' so dependencies are loaded in correct order.
```

Let's take a look at the file produced:

```
depot_v/config/asset_packages.yml
---
javascripts:
- base:
  - jquery
  - jquery-ui
  - application
  - rails
stylesheets:
- base:
  - scaffold
  - depot
```

The basic idea here is simple: you list all of the stylesheets and scripts that you want packed and the order in which they are to be placed into the consolidated file. In many cases, the order doesn't matter, and the initial order that the asset packager provided for you will work just fine for us, so let's move onto the next task: building the bundles.

```
$ rake asset:packager:build_all
(in /home/rubys/work/depot)
Created /home/rubys/work/depot/public/javascripts/base_packaged.js
Created /home/rubys/work/depot/public/stylesheets/base_packaged.css
```

Now, if you take a look at the packaged stylesheet, you will see that the single combined base_packaged.css file is smaller than the depot.css file alone. The generated stylesheet (and script) can be checked into Git, or you can find instructions on how to create a Capistrano recipe for running this at deployment time on the asset_packager website mentioned earlier.

At this point, while you have a more efficient replacement for your CSS file, the original files continue to be used by your layout. This is easy to correct:

```
depot_v/app/views/layouts/application.html.erb
```

```
<!DOCTYPE html>
<html>
<head>
  <title>Pragprog Books Online Store</title>
►  <%= raw stylesheet_link_merged :base %>
►  <%= raw javascript_include_merged :base %>
  <%= csrf_meta_tag %>
</head>
<!-- ... -->
```

What we did here was to replace the two lines that used to call stylesheet_link_tag with a single line that calls stylesheet_link_merged and to replace the line that called javascript_include_tag with a line that calls javascript_include_merged.

Because this is a chapter that talks about what plugins in general can do instead of focusing on what any specific plugin happens to do, it is important to point out that stylesheet_link_merged and javascript_link_merged are two view helpers that were installed by the plugin.

So far, we have talked about simple additions: a new class, a few new tasks, and a couple of view helpers. Let's move onto something more significant: something that provides a clear alternative to one of the gems that Rails depends on.

26.3 Beautifying Our Markup with Haml

Let's take a look once again at a simple view that we use in the Depot application, in this case, one that presents our storefront:

```
depot_u/app/views/store/index.html.erb
```

```
<% if notice %>
<p id="notice"><%= notice %></p>
<% end %>
<h1><%= t('.title_html') %></h1>

<% @products.each do |product| %>
  <div class="entry">
    <%= image_tag(product.image_url) %>
    <h3><%= product.title %></h3>
    <%= sanitize(product.description) %>
    <div class="price_line">
      <span class="price"><%= number_to_currency(product.price) %></span>
      <%= button_to t('.add_html'), line_items_path(:product_id => product),
          :remote => true %>
    </div>
  </div>
<% end %>
```

This code gets the job done. It contains the basic HTML, with interspersed bits of Ruby code enclosed in <% and %> markup. Inside that markup, an equals sign is used to indicate that the value of the expression is to be converted to HTML and displayed.

This is not only an adequate solution to the problem at hand; it is also all that is really needed for a large number of Rails applications. Additionally, it is an ideal place to start for books—like this one—where some knowledge of HTML may be presumed, but many of the readers are new to Rails and often to Ruby itself. The last thing you would want to do in that situation is to introduce yet another new language.

But now that you are past that learning curve, let's go ahead and explore a new language—one that more closely integrates the production of markup with Ruby code, namely, HTML Abstraction Markup Language (Haml).

To start with, let's remove the file we just looked at:

```
$ rm app/views/store/index.html.erb
```

In its place, let's create a new file:

```
depot_v/app/views/store/index.html.haml
- if notice
  %p#notice= notice

%h1= t('.title_html')

- @products.each do |product|
  .entry
    = image_tag(product.image_url)
    %h3= product.title
    = sanitize(product.description)
    .price_line
      %span.price= number_to_currency(product.price)
      = button_to t('.add_html'), line_items_path(:product_id => product),
        :remote => true
```

Note the new extension: .html.haml. This indicates that the template is a Haml template instead of an ERB template.

The first thing you should notice is that the file is considerably smaller. Here's a quick overview of what is going on, based on what the first character is on each line:

- Dashes indicate a Ruby statement that does not produce any output
- Percent signs (%) indicate a HTML element.
- Equals signs (=) indicate a Ruby expression that does produce output to be displayed. This can be used on either lines by themselves or following HTML elements.

Figure 26.1: STOREFRONT USING HAML

- Dots (.) and hash (#) characters may be used to define class and id attributes, respectively. This can be combined with percent signs or used stand-alone. When used by itself, a div element is implied.
- A comma at the end of a line containing an expression implies a continuation. In the previous example, the button_to call is continued across two lines.

An important thing to note is that indentation is important in Haml. Returning to the same level of indentation closes the if statement, loop, or tag that is currently open. In this example, the paragraph is closed before the h1, the h1 is closed before the first div, but the div elements nest, with the first containing an h3 element and the second containing both a span and a button_to.

As you can also see, all of your familiar helpers are available, things like t, image_tag, and button_to. In every meaningful way, Haml is as integrated into your application as ERB is. You can mix and match: you can have some templates using ERB and others using Haml.

As you have already installed the Haml gem, there truly is nothing more you need to do. To see this in action, all you need to do is to visit your storefront. What you should see should match Figure 26.1.

If that looks unremarkable, that's because it should look *exactly* like it did before. And that, if you think about it, is all the more remarkable as the application layout continues to be implemented as a ERB template and the index itself is implemented using Haml. Despite this, everything integrates seamlessly and effortlessly.

Although this clearly is a deeper level of integration than simply adding a task or a helper, it still is an addition. Next, let's explore a true replacement.

26.4 Write Less and Do More with JQuery

The early days of Rails were also the early days of JavaScript libraries. Few people had a serious preference for one library over another, so Rails simply picked a good one and made it work. These days, many people do have a preference, and one of the more popular alternatives to Prototype is JQuery.

Let's look at the RJS file we created in Section 11.2, *Iteration F2: Creating an Ajax-Based Cart*, on page 131:

depot_u/app/views/line_items/create.js.rjs

```
page.select("#notice").each { |notice| notice.hide }

page.replace_html('cart', render(@cart))
page[:cart].visual_effect :blind_down if @cart.total_items == 1
page[:current_item].visual_effect :highlight,
                                  :startcolor => "#88ff88",
                                  :endcolor => "#114411"
```

Once again, like we did with the ERB file that we replaced with Haml, let's boldly remove the RJS file:

```
$ rm app/views/line_items/create.js.rjs
```

And now let's enter its replacement:

depot_v/app/views/line_items/create.js.erb

```
$("#notice").hide();

if ($('#cart tr').length == 1) { $('#cart').show('blind', 1000); }

$('#cart').html("<%= escape_javascript(render(@cart)) %>");

$('#current_item').css({'background-color':'#88ff88'}).
  animate({'background-color':'#114411'}, 1000);
```

If you look closely, you can see a lot of similarities between this file and the one it replaced. Each of the four statements has an equivalent: hide the #notice, replace the HTML for the cart, blind down[3] the current item by animating the background color from a start color to an end color.

There also are a number of key differences. For starters, the js.rjs file consists of Ruby statements, and the js.erb file is in JavaScript. More importantly, the

---

3. http://madrobby.github.com/scriptaculous/effect-blinddown/

RJS file is executed on the server and has access to the database models, and everything in the JQuery file with the exception of the code contained in the <% and %> markup is executed on the client and has access to the Document Object Model (DOM) of the browser. This difference was the reason for a small change in the order of these statements: the check for the length of the cart is done before the rendering. Note that a length of 1 is used because there is a row of table headers in the display, which is important if you are thinking in terms of the DOM.

There is one more change that is needed, because one line in the layout also uses another Prototype method:

`depot_v/app/views/layouts/application.html.erb`

```
<!-- ... -->
  <div id="banner">
    <%= form_tag store_path, :class => 'locale' do %>
      <%= select_tag 'set_locale',
        options_for_select(LANGUAGES, I18n.locale.to_s),
        :onchange => 'this.form.submit()' %>
      <%= submit_tag 'submit' %>
      <%= javascript_tag "$('.locale input').hide()" %>
    <% end %>
    <%= image_tag("logo.png") %>
    <%= @page_title || t('.title') %>
  </div>
<!-- ... -->
```

Unlike with Haml, which was a pure addition, there is an extra step we will need to perform, namely, to download the JQuery libraries and to remove the now unnecessary prototype libraries. To assist with this, jquery-rails installs a Rails generator that will take care of all the necessary steps. All we need to do is invoke it:

```
rails generate jquery:install --ui --force
      remove  public/javascripts/controls.js
      remove  public/javascripts/dragdrop.js
      remove  public/javascripts/effects.js
      remove  public/javascripts/prototype.js
    fetching  jQuery (1.4.3)
      create  public/javascripts/jquery.js
      create  public/javascripts/jquery.min.js
    fetching  jQuery UI (latest 1.x release)
      create  public/javascripts/jquery-ui.js
      create  public/javascripts/jquery-ui.min.js
    fetching  jQuery UJS adapter (github HEAD)
       force  public/javascripts/rails.js
```

The --ui parameter gets us the jquery-ui libraries. The --force option will replace the rails.js file.

With that, we are now ready. We can run our application, and we will see no differences. If you find that to be a bit underwhelming, try looking into the tablesorter library.[4] By downloading one script and adding a few lines of JavaScript, you can have tables where sorting by columns is as simple as clicking the headers.

Actually, though, there is one last difference, and you will see it when you run your functional tests:

```
Started
.........F...................................
Finished in 1.49875 seconds.
  1) Failure:
test_should_create_line_item_via_ajax(LineItemsControllerTest)
[/test/functional/line_items_controller_test.rb:65]:
No RJS statement that replaces or inserts HTML content.
46 tests, 76 assertions, 1 failures, 0 errors
```

The message that there are "No RJS statements" is clearly true, because we are not using RJS in our views anymore. The fix is a simple one; we switch from an assert_select_rjs to a assert_select_jquery call, adjusting the parameters to this call as appropriate:

depot_v/test/functional/line_items_controller_test.rb

```
test "should create line_item via ajax" do
  assert_difference('LineItem.count') do
    xhr :post, :create, :product_id => products(:ruby).id
  end
  assert_response :success
► assert_select_jquery :html, '#cart' do
    assert_select 'tr#current_item td', /Programming Ruby 1.9/
  end
end
```

For those who are interested in JQuery, there is much more to explore, but the point of this chapter is to introduce you to what can be done with a plugin, which is pretty much anything. In this case, the JQuery plugin completely replaces a component, which is part of the default installation of Rails.

26.5 Finding More at RailsPlugins.org

At this point, we have covered four plugins. You will find at least two orders of magnitude more at RailsPlugins.org,[5] which at the current time includes more than 500 plugins, most—but not all—of which work with Rails 3.

Here's a few more to explore, grouped by categories:

---

4. http://tablesorter.com/docs/
5. http://www.railsplugins.org/plugins

- Some plugins implement behavior that was previously in the core of Rails and has since been moved out. As an example, pagination was originally a core function of Rails and was subsequently moved to a plugin named classic_pagination.[6] It since has all but been replaced by the will_paginate plugin that we used in Section 12.3, *Iteration G3: Pagination*, on page 163. Others, like acts_as_tree,[7] have thrived as plugins. And still others, like rails_xss,[8] backport essential functionality from future versions of Rails in order to help with migration.

- Some plugins actually implement significant pieces of common application logic and even user interface. The devise[9] and authlogic[10] plugins implement user authentication and session management. We implemented these functions ourselves in Depot, but this is generally something we don't recommend. We've found that laziness pays: if somebody else has written a plugin for a function that you need to implement, that's all the more time that you can spend on your application.

- Some plugins replace large portions of rails. For example, datamapper[11] replaces ActiveRecord. The combination of cucumber,[12] rspec,[13] and webrat[14] can be used separately or together to replace test scripts with plain test stories, specifications, and browser simulation.

- hoptoad_notifier[15] and exception_notification[16] will help you monitor errors in your deployed servers.

Of course, this is but a small fraction of the set of plugins that are available. And this list is continually growing: there undoubtedly will be many more available by the time you read this.

Finally, you can obviously create your own plugins. Although doing so is beyond the scope of this book, you can find out more in the Rails Guides[17] and documentation.[18]

---

6. https://github.com/masterkain/classic_pagination#roadme
7. https://github.com/rails/acts_as_tree#readme
8. https://github.com/rails/rails_xss
9. https://github.com/plataformatec/devise#readme
10. https://github.com/binarylogic/authlogic#readme
11. http://datamapper.org/
12. http://cukes.info/
13. http://rspec.info/
14. https://github.com/brynary/webrat#readme
15. http://www.hoptoadapp.com/pages/home
16. https://github.com/rails/exception_notification#readme
17. http://guides.rubyonrails.org/plugins.html
18. http://api.rubyonrails.org/classes/Rails/Railtie.html

What We Just Did

Strictly speaking, this chapter exposed you to only one new Rails command: rails plugin install. In many cases the need for that command is being subsumed by bundler and Gemfile. Although this chapter did cover a few plugins, the purpose of this chapter wasn't to cover any particular plugin in depth but to introduce you to some of the capabilities that plugins can provide.

If we include the gems that we saw in previous chapters, we have seen plugins that simply add new features (Active Merchant and Capistrano), add some Rake tasks (Asset Packager), add some view helpers (again, Asset Packager), add some methods to model objects (will_paginate), add a new templating language (Haml), interface to a new database (mysql), and even replace the entire client-side scripting framework (jquery-rails).

If you think about it, there really isn't all that much that a plugin can't do.

In this chapter, we'll see

- reviewing Rails concepts: model, view, controller, configuration, testing, and deployment; and
- links to places for further exploration.

Chapter 27

Where to Go from Here

Congratulations! We've covered a lot of ground together.

In Part I, you installed Rails, verified the installation using a simple application, got exposed to the architecture of Rails, and got acquainted (or reacquainted) with the Ruby language.

In Part II, you iteratively built an application, built up test cases along the way, and ultimately deployed it using Capistrano. We designed this application to touch on all of the aspects of Rails that every developer needs to be aware of.

Whereas Parts I and II of this book each served a single purpose, Part III of this book served a dual role.

For some of you, Part III methodically filled in the gaps and covered enough for you to get real work done. For others, this will be the first steps of a much longer journey.

For most of you, the real value is a bit of both. A firm foundation is required in order for you to be able to explore further. And that's why we started this part with a chapter that not only covered the convention and configuration of Rails but also covered the generation of documentation.

Then we proceeded to devote a chapter each to the model, views, and controller, which are the backbone of the Rails architecture. We covered topics ranging from database relationships to the REST architecture to HTML forms and helpers.

We covered migration and caching as essential maintenance and tuning aspects of a deployed application.

Finally, we split Rails apart and explored the concept of gems from a number of different perspectives: from making use of individual Rails components separately to making full use of the foundation upon which Rails is built and finally to building and extending the framework to suit your needs.

At this point, you have the necessary context and background to explore deeper whatever areas suit your fancy or are needed to solve that vexing problem you face. We recommend you start by visiting the rubyonrails site[1] and exploring each of the links across the top of that page. Some of this will be quick refreshers of materials presented in this book, but you will also find plenty of links to current information on how report problems, learn more, and keep up-to-date.

Additionally, please continue to contribute to the wiki and forums mentioned in the book's introduction.

Pragmatic Bookshelf has more books on related Ruby and Rails subjects.[2] There also are plenty of related categories that go beyond Ruby and Rails, such as Agile Practices, Testing, Design, and Cloud Computing, and Tools, Frameworks, Languages. You can find these and other categories at http://www.pragprog.com/categories.

We hope you have enjoyed learning about Ruby on Rails as much as we have enjoyed writing this book!

---

1. http://rubyonrails.org/
2. http://www.pragprog.com/categories/ruby_and_rails

Appendix A

Bibliography

[TFH08]   David Thomas, Chad Fowler, and Andrew Hunt. *Programming Ruby: The Pragmatic Programmers' Guide.* The Pragmatic Programmers, LLC, Raleigh, NC, and Dallas, TX, third edition, 2008.

[ZT08]   Ezra Zygmuntowicz and Bruce Tate. *Deploying Rails Applications: A Step-by-Step Guide.* The Pragmatic Programmers, LLC, Raleigh, NC, and Dallas, TX, 2008.

Index

Going Further on Rails

Crafting Rails Applications

Rails 3 is a huge step forward. You can now easily extend the framework, change its behavior, and replace whole components to bend it to your will, all without messy hacks. This pioneering book is the first resource that deep dives into the new Rails 3 APIs and shows you how use them to write better web applications and make your day-to-day work with Rails more productive.

Crafting Rails Applications: Expert Practices for Everyday Rails
JosÃľ Valim
(180 pages) ISBN: 9781934356739. $33.00
http://pragprog.com/titles/jvrails

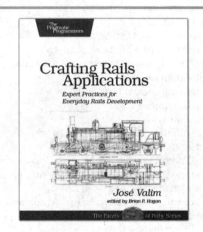

Rails Test Prescriptions

Your comprehensive guide to testing Rails applications, covering Test-Driven Development from both a theoretical perspective (why to test) and from a practical perspective (how to test effectively). It covers the core Rails testing tools and procedures for Rails 2 and Rails 3, and introduces popular add-ons, including RSpec, Shoulda, Cucumber, Factory Girl, and Rcov.

Rails Test Prescriptions: Keeping Your Application Healthy
Noel Rappin
(368 pages) ISBN: 9781934356647. $34.95
http://pragprog.com/titles/nrtest

More Ruby

Metaprogramming Ruby

This book describes metaprogramming as an essential component of Ruby. Once you understand the principles of Ruby, including the object model, scopes, and eigenclasses, you're on your way to applying metaprogramming both in your daily work and in your fun, after-hours projects. Whether you're a Ruby apprentice on the path to mastering the language or a Ruby wiz in search of new tips, this book is for you.

Metaprogramming Ruby
Paolo Perrotta
(240 pages) ISBN: 9781934356470. $32.95
http://pragprog.com/titles/ppmetr

Using JRuby

Ruby has the heart, and Java has the reach. With JRuby, you can bring the best of Ruby into the world of Java. Written in 100% Java, JRuby has Ruby's expressiveness and wide array of open-source libraries—it's an even better Ruby. With *Using JRuby*, the entire JRuby core team helps experienced Java developers and Rubyists exploit the interoperability of their respective languages. With JRuby, you'll be surprised at what's now possible.

Using JRuby: Bringing Ruby to Java
Charles O Nutter, Thomas Enebo, Nick Sieger, Ola Bini, and Ian Dees
(300 pages) ISBN: 978-1934356-65-4. $34.95
http://pragprog.com/titles/jruby

Getting Agile

Agile in a Flash

The best agile book isn't a book: Agile in a Flash is a unique deck of index cards that fit neatly in your pocket. You can tape them to the wall. Spread them out on your project table. Get stains on them over lunch. These cards are meant to be used, not just read.

Agile in a Flash: Speed-Learning Agile Software Development
Jeff Langr and Tim Ottinger
(110 pages) ISBN: 978-1-93435-671-5. $15.00
http://pragprog.com/titles/olag

The Agile Samurai

Faced with a software project of epic proportions? Tired of over-committing and under-delivering? Enter the dojo of the agile samurai, where agile expert Jonathan Rasmusson shows you how to kick-start, execute, and deliver your agile projects. You'll see how agile software delivery really works and how to help your team get agile fast, while having fun along the way.

The Agile Samurai: How Agile Masters Deliver Great Software
Jonathan Rasmusson
(275 pages) ISBN: 9781934356586. $34.95
http://pragprog.com/titles/jtrap

Think Better

Pomodoro Technique Illustrated

Do you ever look at the clock and wonder where the day went? You spent all this time at work and didn't come close to getting everything done. Tomorrow, try something new. In *Pomodoro Technique Illustrated*, Staffan Nöteberg shows you how to organize your work to accomplish more in less time. There's no need for expensive software or fancy planners. You can get started with nothing more than a piece of paper, a pencil, and a kitchen timer.

Pomodoro Technique Illustrated: The Easy Way to Do More in Less Time
Staffan Nöteberg
(144 pages) ISBN: 9781934356500. $24.95
http://pragprog.com/titles/snfocus

Pragmatic Thinking and Learning

Software development happens in your head. Not in an editor, IDE, or design tool. In this book by Pragmatic Programmer Andy Hunt, you'll learn how our brains are wired, and how to take advantage of your brain's architecture. You'll master new tricks and tips to learn more, faster, and retain more of what you learn.

• Use the Dreyfus Model of Skill Acquisition to become more expert • Leverage the architecture of the brain to strengthen different thinking modes • Avoid common "known bugs" in your mind • Learn more deliberately and more effectively • Manage knowledge more efficiently

Pragmatic Thinking and Learning:
Refactor your Wetware
Andy Hunt
(288 pages) ISBN: 978-1-9343560-5-0. $34.95
http://pragprog.com/titles/ahptl

The Pragmatic Bookshelf

The Pragmatic Bookshelf features books written by developers for developers. The titles continue the well-known Pragmatic Programmer style and continue to garner awards and rave reviews. As development gets more and more difficult, the Pragmatic Programmers will be there with more titles and products to help you stay on top of your game.

Visit Us Online

Home page for Agile Web Development with Rails, Fourth Edition
http://pragprog.com/titles/rails4
Source code from this book, errata, and other resources. Come give us feedback, too!

Register for Updates
http://pragprog.com/updates
Be notified when updates and new books become available.

Join the Community
http://pragprog.com/community
Read our weblogs, join our online discussions, participate in our mailing list, interact with our wiki, and benefit from the experience of other Pragmatic Programmers.

New and Noteworthy
http://pragprog.com/news
Check out the latest pragmatic developments, new titles and other offerings.

Save on the eBook

Save on the eBook versions of this title. Owning the paper version of this book entitles you to purchase the electronic versions at a terrific discount.

PDFs are great for carrying around on your laptop—they are hyperlinked, have color, and are fully searchable. Most titles are also available for the iPhone and iPod touch, Amazon Kindle, and other popular e-book readers.

Buy now at pragprog.com/coupon.

Contact Us

Online Orders: www.pragprog.com/catalog
Customer Service: support@pragprog.com
Non-English Versions: translations@pragprog.com
Pragmatic Teaching: academic@pragprog.com
Author Proposals: proposals@pragprog.com
Contact us: 1-800-699-PROG (+1 919 847 3884)